RECEIVED
APR 16 2013
BY:

THE INTERNATIONAL BANK OF BOB

BY THE SAME AUTHOR

Prisoner of Trebekistan: A Decade in Jeopardy!

Who Hates Whom: Well-Armed Fanatics, Intractable Conflicts, and Various Things Blowing Up—A Woefully Incomplete Guide™

THE INTERNATIONAL BANK OF BOB

Connecting Our Worlds One
$25 Kiva Loan at a Time

BOB HARRIS

WALKER & COMPANY
NEW YORK

ALEXANDRIA LIBRARY
ALEXANDRIA, VA 22304

Copyright © 2013 by Bob Harris

All rights reserved. No part of this book may be used or reproduced in any manner whatsoever without written permission from the publisher except in the case of brief quotations embodied in critical articles or reviews. For information address Walker & Company, 175 Fifth Avenue, New York, New York 10010.

Published by Walker Publishing Company, Inc., New York
A Division of Bloomsbury Publishing

All papers used by Walker & Company are natural, recyclable products made from wood grown in well-managed forests. The manufacturing processes conform to the environmental regulations of the country of origin.

LIBRARY OF CONGRESS CATALOGING-IN-PUBLICATION DATA

Harris, Bob, 1963–
The International Bank of Bob : connecting our worlds one $25 kiva loan at a time / Bob Harris. — 1st u.s. ed.
p. cm.
Includes bibliographical references and index.
ISBN 978-0-8027-7751-5
1. Microfinance.   2. Small business—Finance.   3. Harris, Bob, 1963–
I. Title.
HG178.3.H373 2013
332—dc23
2012036671

Visit Walker & Company's website at www.walkerbooks.com

First U.S. edition 2013

3 5 7 9 10 8 6 4 2

Typeset by Westchester Book Group
Printed in the U.S.A.

CONTENTS

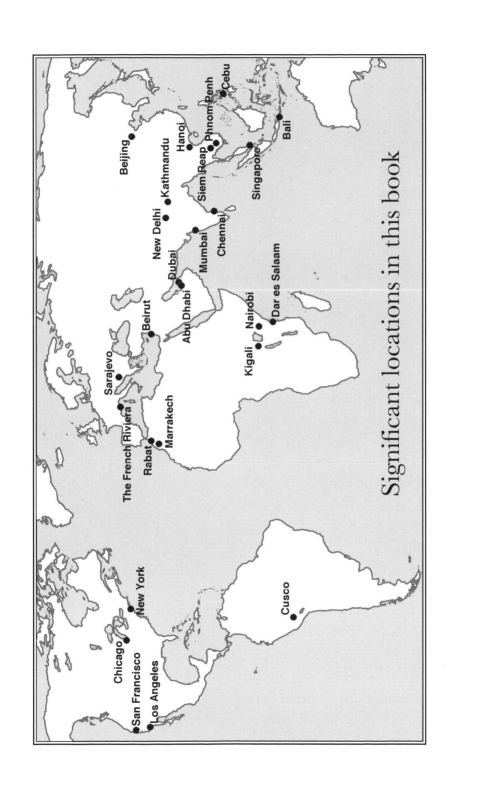

Significant locations in this book

AUTHOR'S NOTES

• Since "Bob" is coincidentally a name often given to ordinary, middle-class characters in American TV, film, and commercials, the phrase "Bank of Bob" is meant to playfully imply that lending a few bucks to support small enterprises in the developing world can be easy, fun, and something any ordinary person might enjoy. **I emphatically take zero credit for any aspect of the development of microfinance**, which belongs with Muhammad Yunus and Grameen Bank (who eventually shared a Nobel Peace Prize), FINCA, ACCION, BRAC, and many others at every level of the industry, for decades, worldwide. They're the fireworks display. I'm just a guy saying *ooh*.

• I don't speak or work for Kiva, Rang De, or anyone else. My goof-ups are mine, not theirs. That said, my relationships with a few people in this book have grown into enduring friendships, which could arguably compromise my objectivity. I don't think it did, but I'll just be honest about it, and you can judge for yourself. I did ask Kiva to fact-check their history and data at press time, trying to keep the book current. Other than that, rest assured: absolutely no one has had any editorial influence over the manuscript.

Sometimes this has included my actual editor, depending on my mood that day.

- The photos are my own personal shots, except for a few taken by Devra Berkowitz, a UN photographer who re-traced my travels in Cambodia and the Philippines a year later. Neither Kiva nor Rang De nor anyone else had any-thing to do with any of the photos, so if I've screwed some-thing up, holler at me, not them. In non-public settings or wherever any client's face might be visible, permission for use from the subject was always explicitly obtained, albeit often only in verbal form, since written releases in multi-ple languages with functional legalese operative in a dozen countries appeared to be prohibitively expensive to pre-pare and probably fallible anyway. Devra got permission as well, usually verbal but sometimes in writing, too. There is a difficult balance between (a) a desire to fully show the warmth and openness of the clients, sharing their strength and accomplishments, and (b) respect for their privacy and sometimes safety. These are judgment calls. Where I err, I hope it is on the side of caution.

- Except for the illustration on page 328, which is derived from a public domain NASA photo, I drew all the maps by hand with a free graphics program. These are based loosely on the CIA's online maps, which are in the public domain and fit my budget nicely. If a border is off by a smidge, no disrespect is intended. (I also reassure everyone in the de-veloping world that I have nothing to do with the CIA. I just used their free maps.)

- A few recent memoirs have played loosely with facts, so if anything here seems hard to believe, I don't blame you. Fortunately, I do nothing heroic, I overcome no difficult odds, and I don't pretend to have changed anybody's life all that much. They're doing the life-changing themselves. I'm just telling you about it. Plus, all of my 5,000+ Kiva loans are on view at www.kiva.org/lender/bobharris. I probably come off like enough of a goofball here for you to figure it's pretty accurate. As to Kiva, they have never received less than—and continue to hold—the highest four-star rating from CharityNavigator.org. At this writing, Kiva ranks in the 96th percentile among medium-sized charities, with a perfect score for accountability and transparency. (See Sources.) Every loan and its outcome remains on the site in perpetuity, and Kiva's financial statements and tax filings are open as can be at www.kiva.org/about/finances. This is all about as transparent as air.

- A few things I do hide: For the clients' safety and privacy, their last names are never used. I'm also a little fuzzy on exact locations, especially if somebody's neighbors might not smile on them hanging out with a guy from Ohio who gets free maps from the CIA. You'll also see a few pseudonyms, with the reason in a footnote on the name's first use. Speaking of which, to my friend in Beirut with surprisingly good beer, thanks, Kevin.*

- Unless otherwise noted, data is the most recent I could find while preparing the final draft in August and September 2012.

- More than 830,000 people have made Kiva loans as this book goes to press. Lenders tend to feel a strong sense of connection to the clients, so it's common to imagine ar-

---

* "Kevin" has a substantially less Western name. Some of Kevin's neighbors might not feel so excited about our beverage choices.

ranging field visits like the ones described here. Let this book be your vicarious pleasure instead. It took years of my life to make this project work in a way that was good for all concerned. As you'll see, most clients are working massive hours, and MFIs aren't set up to receive visitors without a darn good reason. I'd traveled to more than fifty countries before this project, and even so, the cultural, health, economic, political, and other challenges were often considerable. In short: kids, please don't try this at home.

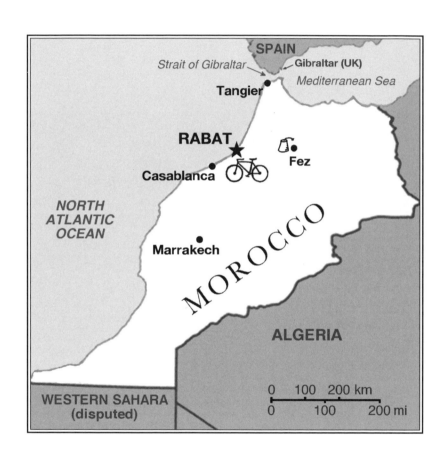

The Road to Morocco

Mohammed is a bicycle and motorcycle repairman, slight of build, shy, almost apologetic in his body language. As he first welcomes me, I am sure that he was one of the smaller kids where he grew up, and he probably still feels it sometimes.

As a forty-two-year-old adult, Mohammed now labors for eleven hours per day, six days a week, in a space smaller than many American kitchens. Mohammed's work area is crammed floor-to-ceiling with tires, wheels, cogs, chains, motor blocks, and assorted metal bits, but there's an order to the crammery, everything in its place. You can see right away that Mohammed doesn't waste time here. He *works*.

When our conversation concludes, I turn around from Mohammed's garage, facing a half-dozen young men in this working-class part of town.

They are staring at me and speaking to each other in a language I don't understand.

One of them is making a fist.

When I was a boy in Ohio, Morocco was faraway and alluring—Tangier, a pulsing oasis for international spies; Marrakech, where Crosby, Stills, and Nash took the express train with the sunset in their eyes; Casablanca, a place so remote that Humphrey Bogart could try to hide from an entire world war. Even Fez, where the little red hats with tassels came from, felt enticing.

Now that I'm here, it's not quite so beguiling. Casablanca is the size of Chicago, boasting not just Africa's largest mosque but its biggest shopping mall, offering the traditional Saharan pleasures of Sunglass Hut, Pinkberry, and bowling. Tangier just got its second Marjane, the local equivalent of a Walmart Supercenter (boxed Tunisian dates, just 19.9 dirhams per kilo). Morocco's eighteen Pizza Huts are all open until midnight, seven days a week, although the pepperoni is made without pork.

As to Marrakech, express trains still arrive daily—but so do dozens of airlines, all serving the million-plus annual tourists who come here seeking a take-home box of exotic. They wander the souks to buy leather and spices, sit in cafés smoking sweet shisha tobacco, and stroll its main square amid a whirling storm of snake charmers, fruit vendors, jugglers, and fire-eaters. Back home, I may have seen Marrakech's main square as often as the rest of Morocco combined—from Alfred Hitchcock's *The Man Who Knew Too Much*, in which a fugitive spy gets stabbed here, revealing a key secret as he dies, to *The Simpsons*, where it's an obvious place to buy opium or a magic animal paw. In tourist brochures and most popular media, this one city block portrays all of Morocco as soothsayers, incense, and dancing macaques.

No one would imagine that all of America looks just like Times Square. But this is the developing world that Westerners glimpse in pop culture: sensual, colorful, animal, fragrant.

I'm nowhere near any of that.

Instead, I've come to Rabat, a government city where few tourists linger—the main attractions being a mausoleum, a necropolis, and a mosque that was never completed—and rented a room in the medina, not far from the casbah.* I've hired a translator, made local contacts, and traveled at last to a working-class neighborhood unmapped in any guidebook, all just to visit a total stranger named Mohammed.

Now I'm standing in the street near his workplace. Arabic graffiti covers a nearby wall. Strange music pours from a window down the street. A nearby mosque has just sounded a call to prayer. Sweat pours from my body, soaking my shirt. When I first become aware of the young men looking at me, I struggle even to glimpse faces in the glare of the North African sun.

This is the developing world that Westerners often see in the news: indecipherable, alien, menacing. In 2007, bombs were set off outside the U.S. consulate and a U.S.-run school, and the Department of State still dramatically warns that "potential targets" for Americans in public include "clubs, restaurants, places of worship, schools, hotels, movie theaters," and more. Even the Marrakech main square, merry tourist construct it has become, would attract an extremist response, with one popular café and seventeen of its customers blown to bits.

I'm nowhere near any of that, either.

Now all of the young men are making fists.

Mohammed has three children—two girls, fifteen and seven, plus a thirteen-year-old son—and he works these sixty-six-hour weeks to afford to send them to school, get them an education, and try to build a better life for them. That's why Mohammed stands in this small room, his hands, face, and blue overalls covered in oil and grease, for more than half of his waking hours on earth.

He has been guarded since my arrival, unsure what to make of

---

* This is the Casbah of the Udayas, an 850-year-old oceanside fortress. If you're curious, yes, I did rock it, thank you.

this paunchy Midwesterner who speaks little Arabic and has no personal connection to Morocco, but has nonetheless stumbled into his tiny shop from halfway around the world, just to say hello. Out of instinct, I start telling this total stranger about my dad.

James Robert Harris was a manual laborer for General Motors who often did overtime, second jobs, third jobs, whatever, just to put food on the table. I confess to Mohammed that I've never worked that hard in my life—but only thanks to my dad. I also tell Mohammed that I imagine he loves his kids much the same way that Dad loved my sister and me. I understand that this is why he works so hard.

And I am honored to meet a man capable of this kind of love.

This feels like a surprisingly naked thing to say to a stranger whom I've only just met, especially one from a different culture on the other side of the world from where I grew up. But it's the truth. I *am* honored. I *do* see this densely packed tiny garage as a work of love. It's obvious. So the words just kinda come out.

The credit or blame partly belongs to my translator, Bouchra, a young mother of two, bright, strong-willed, and compassionate. I've only known her since this morning, but we've formed an instant friendship, and as I speak, my description of my dad brings a warm smile to Bouchra's face. I catch Mohammed reading her expression, which translates my feelings before we get around to specific words. Encouraged, I go on.

I don't notice the small crowd forming in the street behind me. Drawn by the curious sight of a Westerner, passers-by are starting to stop, ask each other who I am and what I am doing here, and discuss how they should all react.

As Bouchra translates, I start to feel nervous. I may have screwed up. It might be presumptuous of me—a relatively prosperous Westerner, privileged in gender and skin tone and even eye and hair color, a massive winner in the birth lottery despite my parents'

poor Appalachian roots—to compare my dad's story to Mohammed's. It might be more conventional—at least by my own culture's standards—to assume that Mohammed's life must be
inconceivably different, to keep things objective and impersonal,
ask business questions only, to sit quietly, take notes, and move on.

Mohammed has financed his tiny business with microloans,
after all, and those loans are the ostensible subject here. His first
loan five years ago, used to buy equipment and tools, was for the
equivalent of less than $600, repayable at the rate of about $100
per month. As his business has grown, Mohammed now borrows
and repays about $1,700 each year, using the credit to upgrade his
equipment, hire help, smooth his cash flow, and more. Those
numbers and plans were what I'd planned to ask about first. Then
we could discuss what they meant: Without microcredit, would
Mohammed's life be different? Would he have to work longer
hours with poorer equipment, might he be unable to afford school
for his kids?

But here, with this Moroccan bike tinker on one of my first
trips into the field, my intuition has been to tell him about my
dad, see if that connects enough to open the conversation beyond
numbers, and go from there. I'm flying on instinct, however. I'll
just hope for the best.

Bouchra concludes her translation. There is a pause.

Mohammad turns to me, a proud smile forming. *Shukran,* he
says, looking me straight in the eye. This is Arabic for "thank you."

I touch my heart respectfully with my right hand. We stand in
silence, holding eye contact for a second. The need for a translator
momentarily disappears.

The crowd behind me has grown, although I don't know that
yet.

So is Mohammed's business doing well? *Of course,* he tells me
through Bouchra, his tone gently chiding me for the silly question.

After twelve years in business, and after successfully borrowing and repaying seven cycles of small loans over the last five years, Mohammed now does more than shepherd his three kids through school: his shop has grown to employ two permanent staff members, plus several part-time helpers. He has also upgraded and diversified his equipment, enabling his staff to handle virtually any job that comes in. His eighth loan is five times larger than his first, and Mohammed hopes soon to expand his business even further, benefiting not just his own family, but his entire neighborhood.

When I was a boy, this was called the American Dream. Apparently they have something similar here, too.

We talk more about our families, and Mohammed offers to let me work with his tools, maybe spend a few minutes working with him on one of his projects. He seems to assume that since my dad was mechanically inclined, I must be, too. Oh, dear. *Thank you, I'm honored. But I might break something. Possibly my own fingers.*

And then Mohammed and I reach to shake hands.

The palms of Mohammed's hands are covered in grease, so instead of a regular handshake, he presses the back of his hand against mine. It's a polite and playful gesture. I nod and smile appreciatively.

Finally, Mohammad gestures behind me, and I turn, seeing for the first time the large and growing audience I've attracted. Maybe a half-dozen teenage-and-younger males, plus a few passers-by of all ages, are assessing my presence.

Holy crap.

One of the young men steps forward. Bouchra explains that I'm meeting Hamid, Mohammed's son.*

Hamid's hands are also dirty, so when I extend my right hand

---

* "Hamid" is a pseudonym. He's not of legal age and I didn't get explicit permission to write about him, so I'll err on the side of caution.

in greeting, Hamid shyly offers the back of his hand, too, just like his father. I'm still awkward about where to put my own hand in response, so I make a joke out of it, and Hamid and I share a fun moment of goofing around, twisting our hands to mime a half-dozen possible handshakes.

The other boys start to smile.

High five! I suggest, looking back at Bouchra, wondering if this will need a translation. Thanks to the Internet and the global reach of Western media, it does not. Hamid high-fives me instantly.

Small world.

His friends and I exchange a few high fives, too. Those who are unfamiliar with the technique catch on instantly and join in.

Low five! I continue, and we carry on, enjoying the unexpected novelty of knowing how to greet each other in multiple ways.

Fist bump? I ask, making a fist.

The young men's faces turn curious. Howie Mandel's preferred *Deal or No Deal* greeting has not yet reached this part of the Arab world.

I bump my own fists together as a demonstration, saying the American slang word *dap* as I do. The boys smile with a bit of bafflement—*They really do this odd gesture in America? Hokay*—and join in.

Dap, dap, dap, dap, dap. A few of us even start to giggle.

This is the developing world as experienced not through sensational news reports or pop culture stereotypes, but while I've been actually standing in it.

This is why a half-dozen young men came toward me, fists raised, in Morocco.

Because we were having so much fun saying hello.

A small business is nothing more or less than an idea for improving the future. So, numbers aside: Is your work paying off? Is there more food on the table? Are there more books in the hands of children? Does the village have more electric light in the evenings? Is the future improving? *Do the loans help?*

For nearly one hundred million clients of microfinance institutions across the developing world, including some of the world's poorest people, these are supremely important questions.

So I decided to ask.

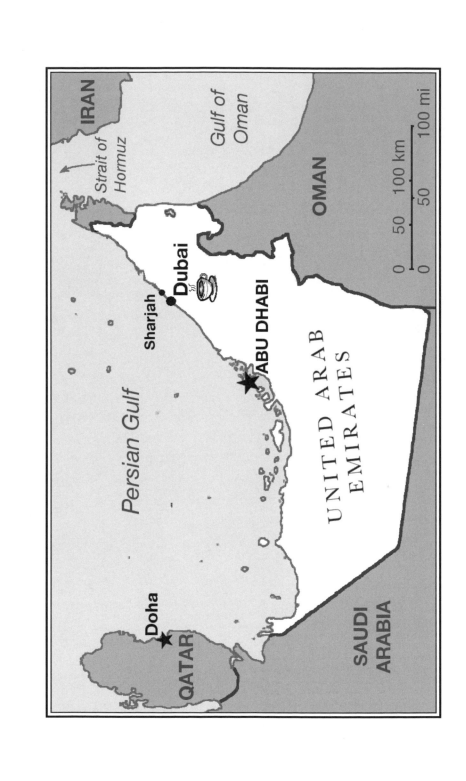

CHAPTER ONE

THE FRENCH RIVIERA, DUBAI, AND THE WORLD

I T WAS AN unexpected journey among the world's richest people
that brought me face-to-face with some of the world's hardest-
working poor.

In 2008, I landed a job writing for *Forbes Traveler*, a luxury travel
website that ran pieces like "London's 10 Best Hotels," "Italy's 25
Best Hotels," and so on.* I'd grown up working-class in Ohio, so
to this point I'd spent most of my traveling life in motels where
you can still hear the interstate. Now I was bopping around the
south of France, sleeping in unimaginably expensive digs and eating impossibly high-end cuisine, composing my refined and gen-
tlemanly opinion of lodgings so opulent that I was often intimidated
even to go inside.

One day, for example, I took breakfast in a bishop's residence
atop medieval ramparts in Carcassonne, where Charlemagne's
dad had once fought off the Saracens; drove to Avignon, then had
lunch at a sixteenth-century palace where Napoleon used to hang
out; and finally spent the evening chowing down on the chef's

---

* ForbesTraveler.com was later folded into the main Forbes.com page, which
doesn't maintain a full archive, but a few of my articles survive on other sites
where they were syndicated. See Sources.

tasting menu on a verandah in Monaco overlooking the harbor.* For several months in 2008, I got *paid* to do that. Every day.

I was just visiting that world, of course. My dad worked in a General Motors factory, and my mom worked part-time in a dime store. When I was little, my sister and I shared one small bedroom, Mom and Dad shared the other, and our one tiny bathroom directly faced the front door, which led to a few awkward moments. But it was home.

Dad passed away almost twenty years ago, but I'll always remember him sitting exhausted on our front steps on steamy August nights, drinking his beer and staring into the middle distance. As I grew up, I slowly realized he was constantly trying to recover from another long day of heavy work, scrounging up the gumption to face another day just like it, and another, and another. Sometimes Mom sat next to him. More often he needed to be alone.

Thanks to their efforts, I didn't know what desperation felt like when I was little, but looking back, I recognize it now on Dad's face. I think Dad would have been proud that I didn't wind up in a factory, too. That was pretty much the main goal. It was never about getting rich—getting *out* would be plenty.

As I walked from my harbourside dinner to the Casino of Monte Carlo, it must have appeared that I had.

The *Forbes Traveler* job evolved unexpectedly after a fellow-writer friend put me in touch with the editor, thinking I might grab a byline or two.† (To survive, freelancers often share contacts the way people on lifeboats share food.) Fortunately, the editor was

---

* If you'd like to ride along, two of the three pieces I wrote from this one day survive online. See Sources.

† While I can never fully return the favor, I can at least introduce Jenn to you: www.wimnonline.org.

far more Traveler than Forbes—a working-class writer named Jeff who had lived in Korea, hitchhiked through Burma, and spent six months with his girlfriend riding chicken buses across Central America. After I wrote a few pieces Jeff liked, we hung out, drank well together, and became friends.* When he needed a few writers to update large chunks of the "Forbes Traveler 400" list of the world's most luxurious hotels, I raised my hand. The destinations had been already chosen, so no expertise would be required beyond the ability to look the part and not break anything priceless. As far as Jeff cared, if I got my facts right, made my deadlines, and didn't cause any diplomatic incidents, the gig was mine.

So there I sat in Hôtel Hermitage in Monaco, supping on Joël Garault's Michelin-starred *gastronomie* and playacting the role of sophisticated luxury travel critic. The next night would bring a different restaurant in another hotel, but the evening specials never varied. An aerodynamically thin waiter would reel off a series of unfamiliar luxury food nouns, possibly at random. I would nod, narrow my eyes gravely, and repeat back the words I could recognize.

One night, after the server listed the specials and departed, I attempted to jot down what he had just said, as close to verbatim as I could. I had to suppress an amused snort at my feeble attempt to reproduce his grandiloquence:

Our starter is mushroomed ennui Al Pacino. The entrée is turbine of Barbasol, drizzled with pumice, garnished with Julianne Moore. Dessert is a chocolate Wallenda piranha. Would you like a moment?

Yes. I would like a moment.

And what wine will Monsieur prefer?

Since this book is about lending tens of thousands of dollars of my own money, you might wonder if I've ever become wealthy. Not

---

* Jeff's work can be sampled at www.fineorsuperfine.com.

in a monetary sense, at least by U.S. standards, although on a global scale the average American is at least upper-middle-class.* I've spent the last twenty-five years mostly self-employed, doing books, TV shows, radio, live comedy, voiceovers, and whatever else I can scrounge, averaging out to a mid-five-figure income requiring a lot of sixty-hour weeks so I'll never be as tired as Dad was.† I may live in Los Angeles, but I'm still a Cleveland Browns fan, I drive a 1995 Geo named Max, I own exactly one nice sport jacket—the same one I've worn all the way around the world, twice now—and my favorite food is still Cheerios, which I am eating dry with my fingers straight out of the box as I write these words at my kitchen table. My Riviera will always be Buick, not French.

I would be financially ruined if those fancy hotel rooms hadn't all been paid for. Most of the suites where I slept would run $500 to $1,500 a night. Just the gift basket usually left in my room, often containing enough fruit, nuts, and chocolates to last a week, would cost more than I'd spend on a hotel. As to the meals, most of these joints would never be so gauche as to put prices on the menus—if you have to ask, go eat some Cheerios—but at the Grand Hotel du Cap-Ferrat, located on the Cote d'Azur on per-

---

*At this writing, the U.S. annual GDP per capita is $49,000, ranked 11th in the world out of 226 countries and territories, once all the data is normed for exchange rates and purchasing power. The pointy tip of the wealth pyramid is $141,100 per person for Liechtenstein (population 36,713, smaller than Grand Island, Nebraska), while the enormous bottom is $400 per person for the Democratic Republic of the Congo (population 73,599,190, almost as many people as the entire U.S. Central Time Zone). See Sources.

†I also had a nice pile of TV quiz show money while it lasted, but that's another book entirely. This was published in 2006, almost became a big Hollywood movie then thankfully didn't, and is already mostly forgotten. If you're curious, Google the words *pudu*, *Bhutan*, and *galoshes*, which form a Venn diagram sufficient to find the book. But let's move on. The money did, at least.

haps the priciest spit of real estate on earth, where people like Prince are quietly spirited in to perform for actual princes, my seaview terrace suite would have cost between $1,600 and $3,300 a night, depending on season; an airport pickup (from Nice, just ten miles away) would run $260, and the cheapest full dinner you could assemble—a piece of fish, some veggies, a chocolate apple for dessert, and plain water to drink—would cost $250 with tip.

Sometimes I was tempted to ask for a side dish of $100 bills, on fire. I'm pretty sure they would have brought one.

I wasn't getting rich doing these articles. The experience was considered a big part of the paycheck. I would clear about twenty grand before taxes from the whole round-the-world trip, along with the lack of health insurance, pension, etc., that goes with the freelance life—but still: I was getting paid to take a once-in-a-lifetime lap around some of the most insanely wealthy places on earth.

Two days before my whole reason for traveling started to change, I was in Abu Dhabi, capital of the United Arab Emirates, sleeping at the $3 billion Emirates Palace, at the time the most expensive hotel ever built.*

I would not have believed everything you are about to read, so let's make a game of it: exactly one sentence on the next page is false. See if you can guess which one:

---

* This has recently been surpassed by Singapore's $6 billion Marina Bay Sands, which has two Broadway-sized theaters, three hundred shops, the world's largest atrium casino, and a convention center capable of hosting forty-five thousand people. If they acquire nuclear weapons, we will be forced to negotiate.

- The Emirates Palace has more floor space than the Pentagon.
- It sits on 100 hectares of land—nearly a third the size of all of Central Park.
- The roof is crowned by 114 domes up to 238 feet high.
- The main gate is just slightly smaller than France's Arc de Triomphe.
- The walls include more than 4 million cubic feet of imported marble.
- The hotel has 102 elevators and 128 kitchens serving only 394 rooms.
- The walk to the pool can be nearly half a mile. The staff needs Segways and golf carts just to get around the interior, and years after opening, some of them sometimes still get lost.
- They have so many custom-made Swarovski crystal chandeliers that it takes ten full-time staffers just to clean them.
- The largest chandelier weighs as much as two Toyota Corollas.
- I would not stand under that chandelier in an earthquake.
- One year, their temporary Christmas tree cost more than $11 million.
- The hotel faces more than a kilometer of private beach on the Persian Gulf.
- Guests also have a private water park and complimentary use of a catamaran.
- They have no vending machines with snacks or soft drinks, but they do have one that dispenses small bars of gold.

Exactly one sentence in the above list is false.

Give up? "Exactly one sentence in the above list is false" is the false sentence. Every bullet point in that list is true.

There's a point where luxury passes beyond any sane human comfort and starts touching lunacy. I met with a PR guy in one of the hotel's forty conference rooms, and he even boasted that they go through five kilograms (eleven pounds) of fresh gold annually just in pastry decorations. Y'know those little sparkly shavings that showoff chefs like to sprinkle on their chocolate Wallenda piranha? The Emirates Palace goes through eleven pounds of that, year after year, and it's all pure gold. Their website brags about it to this day.*

Since gold is indigestible, if you think about the eventual outcome, that's about $300,000 literally flushed away—"disposable income" in the truest sense—year after year.

My dad worked his butt off for thirty-seven years and barely saved up one-tenth of that total by the time he died. So: the lives of ten men like my father. *Whoosh.*

I had not the slightest idea how to emotionally process that thought. The PR guy kept on talking, and somehow my hand kept taking notes, but all that I now remember is overwhelm. Of all the bewildering displays of wealth I had seen, I don't know why my brain took this literal assload of gold so personally. But it did.

I walked out of the meeting in a daze, a sensation enhanced by the Emirates Palace's massive empty echoing halls, many lined floor-to-ceiling with near-priceless antiquities, a cross between *The Shining* and the final warehouse shot of *Raiders of the Lost Ark*. I felt numb and small and brief on this planet.

Swooning under a severe case of wealth vertigo, and partly out of childish mischief, I finally went back to my room, pulled on my swimsuit, hiked out to a quiet spot on the kilometer of private

---

* See www.kempinski.com/en/abudhabi/emirates-palace/press-room/facts-and -figures, where you can also find many of the other statistics cited above, although I did the measurement conversions into units of Pentagons, Central Parks, and Toyota Corollas.

beach, waded in to my neck, slipped off my trunks, and went skinny-dipping in the Persian Gulf.

Ahhhhh. Warm like a bathtub. The Persian Gulf feels outstanding on your nether regions. This was probably a crime in the Emirates, because *most* things that feel good on your nether regions are a crime in the Emirates, but I swam out as far as I dared—not far, maybe fifty feet—bobbed around, and tried to process the anger and smallness and grief I was feeling amid all the opulence.*

Part of what makes intense inequality hard to grasp is the sheer volume of luck involved. Emiratis may prefer other rationales—their inherent goodness, intellect, work ethic, morality, or deity's favor (in other words, the same rationales that you and I might invent if our roles were switched)—but to anyone with eyes, they've mostly just won the birth lottery.

Any child lucky enough to be born Emirati will be wealthier than most of us will ever imagine. But move the birthplace just 130 miles, and the infant's father may be an Iranian salt miner. Timing matters, too: an Emirati baby born before the oil boom might have been poorer than we will ever experience. Fast-forward a century, after the oil runs out, and that same child may be poor yet again.

It's one blind shot at a tiny moving target. Win big at the birth lottery, and you get to poop gold by the kilo. Lose big, and you'll be among the billion without even clean water to drink.

I could feel the value of hard work slipping away. My father's life-time of effort might not amount to a tiny percent of what a sliver

---

* What follows is written in hindsight several years later. Since this book wasn't planned yet, I didn't take notes on these personal feelings, so by now my thoughts on that day may have mixed with later ideas. I've also edited for clarity; my stream of consciousness was obviously not nearly this linear. Especially while committing criminal nudity in a body of water frequented by Iranian warships.

of luck might have meant. Why bother? I thought of Dad on the porch, his body old before its time. For one awful moment, his long labors felt so pointless.

But those labors were what gave his life meaning.

My mom and dad were born in Appalachia during the Great Depression. My father's boyhood home, built by his own father on the side of a hill, lacked electricity and indoor plumbing. My mom's dad was a coal miner. But with hope and hard work on their side, my parents eventually built a better life. Factories were opening in Ohio, so they moved north before I was born, before anyone imagined the size and success of the postwar manufacturing boom. Mom and Dad made my good luck. If my folks hadn't moved, I'd have grown up poor, too. But my folks did their best with the lottery tickets they received, and their whole lives were better for it. So was mine. Dad's constant exhaustion also gave him his pride. Getting through another damn day was a goal he achieved, over and over. It gave his life purpose.

My work makes my life feel meaningful, too, at least when I can do it for people I love. *Aha.* Maybe that's the whole trick: *anything* we do gets its meaning from the reason we do it—usually, the people we do it for. The part of ourselves that we give to others in our efforts—that's where we find our own value.

Maybe life takes on meaning to the degree that our efforts and love are connected.

Maybe the birth lottery can't really change that for anyone. Maybe the world has at least this much fairness: as long as a person can love, their life matters. The sheikhs who built this Pentagonian palace with two-Toyota chandeliers and an ATM that spits ingots? Their lives would have meaning—or not—to the degree that their labor and love intertwine, too. Not one iota more.

It couldn't be that simple, could it? But my own parents—like parents all over the world—had shown it to be true.

I dog-paddled back to the sand, feeling calm and rebalanced. I even remembered to put my swimsuit back on.

If the Emirates Palace is hard to imagine, now picture a city where it would barely stand out. Imagine Las Vegas built by puritan pharaohs with the taste of Elvis. That's Dubai.

It doesn't look like a place where you'd suddenly become interested in helping the poor. If Abu Dhabi is Harold, Dubai is Kumar—living in the moment, never satisfied, endlessly planning the next big score. Until recently, one-sixth of the world's construction cranes were here, slapping together one *burj* after another, the World's Tallest This and the Earth's Largest That and History's Most Expensive the Other Thing.* Dubai seems less concerned with the sustainability of its economy than with making a lasting impression on Google Earth.†

Seriously. Go look at Dubai from space on Google Maps. See those huge palm-tree-shaped islands jutting out in the water, next to a half-melted map of the world? Those are all intended to be

---

* *Burj* means "tower," e.g., the Burj Khalifa, the half-mile-high tallest thing ever built, which is still mostly vacant. *Burj* may be the origin of the word *burgeoning*, which appears in Old French and Middle English near the end of the Crusades, when Western soldiers brought back lots of Arabic words, if not control of Jerusalem. You still use a little Arabic when you eat *sugar* or *candy*, play a *guitar* on a *sofa* or *cotton mattress*, *cork* some *alcohol*, drink *zero*-calorie *lemon-lime soda*, or try *civet coffee*.

† At least one citizen of Abu Dhabi is unwilling to be outdone at excess. Sheikh Hamad bin Hamdan Al Nahyan has had his name carved two miles wide into the sand—HAMAD, it says, visible from outer space (lat. 24.344, long. 54.324, at least until the desert and tides reclaim it), the way six-year-olds scrawl their names onto any flat surface. HAMAD (aka the "Rainbow Sheikh" for his love of bright, childlike colors) also owns more than two hundred cars, which he displays in a pyramid; seven Mercedes sedans, one for each day of the week, each complete with M16 gun racks; and an oversize replica of a Dodge Power Wagon large enough to include four bedrooms. Perhaps you thought I was exaggerating about puritan pharaohs with the taste of Elvis.

giant condo resorts, fantastic and cool when viewed from outer space, something no one on earth can ever do.

They're also built on compressed sand. After the first was completed at twice the projected cost, *Barron's* reported that it was slowly sinking back into the water at a rate of an inch every five years.* Refunds for investors in the second palm island began in 2011, although the project is still officially in development. Dubai still claims to be planning a third one, even larger, although groundbreaking may not begin until the lead investors fly toward the sun on wings made of feathers and wax.

In 2003, Dubai also began spending $14 billion on The World, a group of three hundred artificial islands resembling a map of the earth. These were meant to attract international development, but more than 99 percent remain empty at this writing, and in 2011, these, too, were reported to be sinking back into the water.† The World might soon look less like the Mercator projection than like $14 billion of Play-doh.

I got my first look at The World from atop the sail-shaped Burj Al Arab hotel, whose atrium is large enough to hold the Statue of Liberty without touching the walls. A PR lady was walking me through their observation-deck bar, home of the World's Most Expensive Cocktail, just $7,438 for a whisky in a gold tumbler.‡

Seeing a drink that cost more than my car didn't impress me. It just felt like waste. I took a quiet minute to stare down toward the water, at the nondescript, naked lumps that they dare call The World, trying to understand what it all meant.

---

* "Dubai Sinking—No, for Real," *Barron's*, December 9, 2009. See Sources.
† "The World Is Sinking," *Telegraph*, January 10, 2011. See Sources. In fairness, the developer disputes all reports that islands made of compressed sand could be less permanent than anticipated.
‡ But like buying the giant Coke at Chuck E. Cheese, you get to take the tumbler home.

Fourteen billion dollars could have easily bought anti-malarial bed nets for every man, woman, and child at risk in Africa, with $3 billion more for distribution, training, and maintenance. Since The World had begun, perhaps a million lives could have been saved. Most of them were children under the age of five.*

Instead, they built three hundred lumps of sand in the sea.

I wanted a stiff drink from the bar. But of course I couldn't afford one.

Later that day, I took a drive around Palm Jumeirah, the lone palm island with any significant development. The only visible humans were the men doing the digging and rigging to hold the whole thing together in 105-degree heat.

That's when I first really noticed the workers.

Gaunt. Tired. Defeat in their eyes. Their complexions were varied, but most looked South Asian, maybe from India, Nepal, Bangladesh, Pakistan, or Sri Lanka. A few appeared East African, maybe Ethiopian or Kenyan. A few others were East Asian, perhaps from Indonesia or the Philippines.†

This was strangely and sadly familiar. I live in Los Angeles, where the dirtiest work often falls to the hands of Mexicans, Salvadorans,

---

* Africa's population is at most 1.1 billion. A single bed net donated via charity costs at most $10, an expense that would substantially drop in bulk. The highest imaginable price to net the entire continent, even including wide swaths of northern and southern Africa that don't need it, would be only $11 billion. The real cost would be a fraction of that. For more detail, see Sources.

† Note that Dubai's laborers include Muslims, Hindus, and Buddhists, plus Orthodox, Catholic, and Protestant Christians, and surely a few private atheists and agnostics—probably in about that order. Exploitation of migrant labor anywhere seems rarely related to the faith of anyone involved.

Guatemalans, and other immigrant laborers. The birth lottery reared its head once again.

That night, I was staying in and reviewing an upscale business hotel where the main restaurant had eight separate kitchens, the World's Most Expensive Cognac was displayed in a case, and nothing was particularly interesting about any of it. This wasn't the hotel's fault. It was perfectly schmancy, but after a few days in the Emirates this all just seemed standard. Displays of great wealth are like loud music, spicy food, and swearing: a little can be potent, but too much dulls the senses. I was more interested in fresh air and coffee.

There was no escaping the profane. Not far up the street, it became clear that for those seeking more intimate comforts, there was an excess of options. Prostitution, like alcohol, is illegal in Dubai, but the lure of tourist dollars is a higher natural law.* As night fell over Sheikh Zayed Road, working-class courtesans came out like fireflies, flashing their smiles and brightly covered bottoms, plying their trade in plain view.

I'd never even spoken to a working girl in my life, save one eager matron in Prague who rode my leg for an awkward moment when I got off a train and mistook her for someone I could ask for directions. (To her credit, when I clarified my purpose by pulling a map from my pocket and saying the name of my destination, she

---

*The hypocrisy is amplified by Dubai's draconian legal system. Most Emiratis I've met are open-minded and cool, but the cops may imprison you for debt, having sex or alcohol in the wrong place, having poppy seeds (opium!) on your shirt from a bagel you ate in London before flying in, or having a speck of marijuana smaller than a grain of sugar—something you could acquire innocently by walking in any Western city—stuck to your shoe. The UAE was one of only three governments on earth that recognized the Taliban; the legal system seems almost designed to remind you of that fact.

stepped back, shifted instantly into helpful-mom mode, then pointed out my route. Nobody is only their job.) But here in Dubai, I was blond, blue-eyed, and walking alone with no clear destination. This attracted a small entourage.

The accents and features seemed Russian and Asian. Most faces were young and surprisingly lovely, hardness only intermittent in their voices and eyes. So I stopped and spoke with a few of these ladies, bathed in green light from an electric shop sign, trying to make my lack of intentions clear and simply ask where they were from—as a person first, a writer second, and (as clearly as I could indicate) not a potential client. Their English, however, was limited to price lists, sex acts, and questions to feign interest. These repeated on a loop. There was a quota to fill, a menu of services to choose from, if you please: 500 dirhams (about $136) for the hour-long programme. An oral consult would be half as much.

I later learned that most of these women were probably from the former Soviet republics in the Caucasus region and Central Asia. Communism's collapse had disrupted what little economy existed in struggling villages and factory towns. Some of the girls wound up here. For some, there had been little alternative. Many had been tricked. Others had been brought here by force.*

I walked away wondering how one glass of whisky could be treated as more valuable than the bodies of fifty women along Sheikh Zayed Road.

---

*At the time of my visit, a human-trafficking section of a recent U.S. Department of State report on human rights in the Emirates had estimated that "as many as 10,000 women were sexually exploited for profit in the country." Many young women, often as young as their late teens, had been lured by traffickers with offers of domestic or secretarial jobs, then forced into sexual slavery. The women I met may have been among these victims, or they may have begun this way, then stayed "voluntarily" due to trauma, loss of identity, or dread of returning to their homelands in the aftermath. See Sources.

Shortly after leaving my hotel, I had passed a small group of South Asian laborers, still in their dark blue work clothes, sitting and sweating on the side of the road. It must have been the end of a long day building the next five-star hotel in 105-degree heat. They didn't make eye contact. I'd assumed they were waiting for some kind of ride.

Now, doubling back in search of a pedestrian tunnel—the only way to cross Sheikh Zayed Road's twelve busy lanes—I passed these four men a second time. They were a curious sight. They were silent now, tired. They clearly had jobs, and they seemed at least to have each other as friends. They weren't homeless or alone. But they were still on the street.

The faces of the workers I'd seen earlier, echoes of my father's own face, flashed through my mind. But to be honest, I didn't even break stride. Instead, I ducked into the underpass, heading toward a fancy hotel bar serving *kopi luwak*, the very specific coffee I had been looking for.

Soon to be the basis for my next *Forbes Traveler* pitch, kopi luwak is unique for two reasons: it is the World's Most Expensive Coffee, and it is made out of poop.

Priced at up to $600 a pound, kopi luwak is made from the droppings of a Sumatran cat-like beastie called a luwak civet, which eats wild coffee beans, partially digests them, and then excretes the remainder onto the forest floor. The droppings are collected, washed, dried, roasted, ground, and brewed, resulting in a reportedly complex and mellow drink.

How the Sumatrans figured this out, I do not want to know. Nor do I want to imagine how many other things they tried to drink first. But I'd heard about kopi luwak for years, and now, amid the insensate circus of Dubai, drinking freshly brewed cat poop felt like something to really look forward to.*

The assistant manager personally brewed and served my drink tableside, as if presiding over the opening of a fine wine. Other diners looked on, fascinated like children watching a friend eating glue on a dare.

So how does it taste? *Delicious.* Kopi luwak is, in fact, the single best thing I have ever consumed that came out of something else's bottom.† I drank the whole carafe, had a small sweet for dessert, and then looked at the bill.

All told, this cost me 250 dirhams.

This was exactly the price of an oral consultation from one of the ladies downstairs.

I needed to think. I paid my bill, went back down to the atrium, found a big cushy chair, and let the cat poop digest.‡

I didn't feel guilty, exactly. It's absurd to suggest that people who can afford nice things shouldn't enjoy them, just because there are people in need. History is clear: that sort of thinking is a desire for fair play stretched into madness. (Enforcement would mean totalitarian rule, while utterly devaluing hard work and skill. We'll soon see how well that worked out in Cambodia.) But I'd still felt a strong connection between the ludicrously high price of a tum-

---

*I'd first heard about kopi luwak while writing for one of those TV crime dramas that open with a dead body, police tape, and a grim pun—"Looks like *he* paid through his nose," perhaps, while extracting a roll of quarters from the victim's sinuses. The show's producers had a finely honed sense of the monstrous, so cat-poop coffee was a slam-dunk to include, becoming the key clue that convicted comedian Bobcat Goldthwait of murder. I'd wanted to try it ever since. See www.csifanwiki.com/page/320+l+Last+Laugh.

†This is a very short list.

‡First time for me, second time for the coffee.

bler of whisky and the brutally devalued lives of human beings on the streets below. I could think of two reasons.

First, the price difference is a reminder of the birth lottery. People lucky enough to be born drinking from 18-karat gold Chuck E. Cheese take-home cups rarely wind up turning tricks in the street, and vice versa.

Second, maybe the fancy coffee and booze feel out of whack because they lack humane purpose. Even if my $75 cup of coffee were a hundred times tastier than one costing $0.75, the result is no more than a brief private pleasure. I do have the right to spend money this way, but others have the right to wonder if there might have been a more productive idea—exactly as we all just did while considering $14 billion that did not save a million African lives.

If, instead of a big cup of hot poop, I'd spent that same $75 on malaria netting, buying a meal for ten workers, or helping a street-walker get to a shelter, that would feel much less morally ambiguous, even if I'd overpaid greatly. The love involved, the simple desire to improve someone else's life, makes a difference.

Here we are again: our lives—and our money and actions, too, it turns out—may take on meaning to the degree that our efforts and love are connected.

I was still sorting out these thoughts as I emerged from the crossing under Sheikh Zayed Road.

For the third time this night, I found the South Asian men still in the same exact spot. Barely moving, all four. Not talking, not sleeping. Just staring, exhausted.

One sipped on a drink in a white plastic cup. His face was familiar as he stared into the distance. I didn't know him. But my dad used to have a similar expression, drinking his beer on a hot August night.

This man looked more exhausted than I'd ever seen Dad.

Dubai, on the Gulf coast of the Arabian peninsula, is far hotter than a summer in Ohio. Desert heat mixes with seaborne humidity. Even at midnight, the heat index can reach 110 degrees. Most visitors scuttle between air-conditioned retreats.

These men were apparently sleeping out here all night. Maybe not for the first time.

Perhaps I was feeling guilty about the kopi luwak, or maybe it came weirdly out of missing my father, but I stopped. I said hello. Very awkwardly.

They smiled. Not particularly welcoming, but not hostile. Polite, not quite comprehending my purpose. It might have even been slightly defensive, the sort of nervous smile used by the powerless to disarm tense situations.

I asked if they spoke English. The one closest to me said, "Yes," then shrugged, made a "sort of" gesture with his hand and a sideways tilt with his head, and half-smiled again. I pointed at myself and said, "Bob." No reaction. "Bob" is not a man's name in much of the world.*

I wasn't sure what to do next, so I waved awkwardly and started to turn back to the hotel. I didn't want to impose. I was just some weird friendly foreigner in Dubai. Then again, so were they.

Two of them waved as I left.

I asked at the front desk of my hotel who these men might be. Oh, probably workers who missed their ride back to their compound, I was told.

One way that a construction firm in Dubai could minimize labor costs was by luring immigrant laborers from the poorest regions of South Asia—Bangladesh, Sri Lanka, the southern states

---

* In Indonesia and Malaysia, "Bob" sounds like their word for "pig," which is of course unclean to Muslims. Until I learned this, pointing to myself and saying "Bob" inevitably provoked concern, a curious look, or a delighted laugh at the clueless foreigner. Good times.

of Tamil Nadu and Kerala in India—using middlemen who would make false promises of fair wages, working conditions, and terms of employment. These sales pitches could be so convincing that hundreds of thousands of men actually went into debt to pay their passage to Dubai, hoping to make enough money to send the surplus home to help their families have a better life.

On arrival, the lie would be revealed. The men would find themselves squeezed ten-per-room into labor camps tucked away in desert locations unmarked on maps; forced to work ten- or twelve-hour days in brutal heat, six days a week, for years before release from their "contracts"; helpless to organize due to Dubai's lack of labor laws; imprisoned for any protest; and unable to leave because their passports had been seized—but deported the minute the employer was done with them.*

According to Human Rights Watch and reports from South Asian embassies, nearly a thousand of these men might die annually under the grim conditions. The year before I arrived, more than a hundred reportedly committed suicide.

Survivors might hope to be paid—if they got paid at all, as some employers lacked even the scruples to pay promised wages—the princely sum of about $6 to $8 per day.

The workers still sent as much as they could of that money back home.

They were in this hell, mind you, *because they loved their families.*

I didn't know all this at the time. But that's who these men on the street would have been.

Back in my room, I had notes for an article about kopi luwak. This was no longer interesting.

There was, however, the complimentary gift basket typically

---

* For the seminal Human Rights Watch report on the subject, see Sources.

offered to a *Forbes Traveler* reviewer. This one, however, was of Emirati proportions—a small burj of fruits, candies, and chocolate that could feed a whole family for days. A bottle of sparkling date juice—champagne's placebo, were I an observant Muslim—topped it all off. This now seemed more useful than anything else in the room.

I emptied my backpack, filled it with as much of the burj as I could, threw in some packaged stuff I had lying around, and went straight back downstairs.

This wasn't a big deal. I don't consider it particularly noble or kind or even necessarily the right thing to do. It was more of an involuntary response, a reflex, self-defense. I just couldn't not do it.

If you'd been there, I think you might have done the same thing.

There's not much to tell you about the picnic that followed. The men didn't suddenly perk up, reveal a hidden ability with English, and tell me their tales. If this were a Hollywood movie, one of them might have eventually rewarded me with a wise truism that would inspire me on my quest, or perhaps even joined me as a guide and sidekick from whose simple, noble ways I would gradually learn. Perhaps the spirit of Mahatma Gandhi would have even been present, sagely nodding as we embraced our deep brotherhood and commitment to peace.

But no. We didn't male-bond, show pictures of our families to each other, or even shake hands.

We sat together in silence, sweating and stumbling through the bits of English they could muster, the few shreds of Arabic we had in common, and the place names we could mutually recognize.

America, I said, pointing at myself. *Kerala*, one said, pointing at himself.* And so on. They all tried to share a few details. I learned

---

* At least I think he said "Kerala." His accent was unfamiliar and I was paying more attention to faces, trying to communicate that I was friendly and meant no disrespect.

from hand signals that three of them had children back home. They understood I was a writer. I didn't follow much more than that. Mostly I nodded acknowledgment, which seemed like enough.

We didn't need language for them to understand why I'd brought the food, or for me to know that they didn't mind that I did. It was fine left unsaid.

They didn't eat much. I'm not even sure that they could. The work clothes were bulkier than I'd noticed, covering torsos that were shockingly thin. Everything packaged went straight in their pockets. I'd probably have done the same thing.

All four of them offered to share the food with me at least once. I signaled I was full, but tried to make it clear how much I appreciated their eagerness to share.

The sparkling date juice was a hit. This was passed all around, and I accepted the offer of a swig. It was way too sweet in this heat, and I felt instantly stupid that I hadn't thought to bring water, but they didn't seem to mind.

Looking back, I can't help but notice: I ate nothing, but this was a finer meal than any five-star cuisine.

Stand up, dust off, waves. Slightly bigger smiles. Bye.

Walk away. Back to my air-conditioned five-star hotel. Leave them sleeping outside in the street.

Men like the ones in the street had built these hotels. It was conceivable those very same men had worked on this particular one. And after countless twelve-hour days in blazing heat, these modern indentured servants would never see the inside. While I was being paid just to sleep there.

Process *that*.

There had to be something bigger I could do.

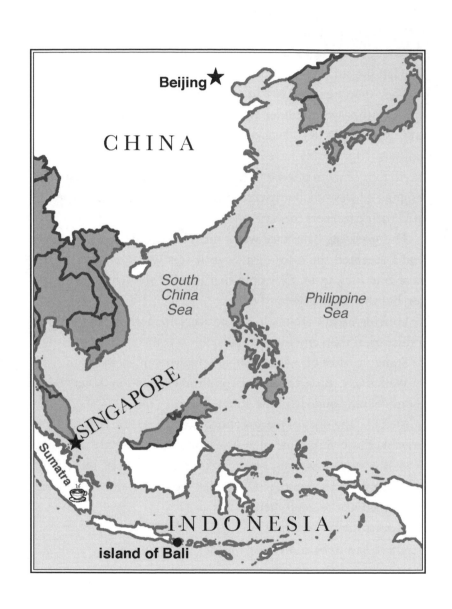

Beijing ★

CHINA

*South
China
Sea*

*Philippine
Sea*

SINGAPORE

Sumatra

INDONESIA

island of Bali

CHAPTER TWO

SINGAPORE, BALI, AND BEIJING

O FFERING FOOD TO four tired men might have been a decent
gesture. It also felt like sprinkling water on a desert and calling it rain. But what more was there? I wasn't rich; I was only playing a rich person in a brief act of round-the-world performance
art. I could give everything I had to some charity, making myself
poor in the process, and even that wouldn't make any visible dent.

How could I have helped those guys—and so many others—in
a more lasting way?

I spent some time on the Internet reading up on the lives of workers in Dubai. The problem was institutional, widespread, and international. If the four men downstairs became millionaires tomorrow,
four more would be lured into their place. Real reforms would take
international pressure and probably a cultural shift among Emiratis,
but even total success would only change things in Dubai. Immigrant laborers would still be lured to wealthy neighboring countries.
In Qatar, just 250 miles west, migrant labor is more than 90 percent
of the population, and they would still face the same hardships.*

---

*The latest number is 94.7 percent, thanks to a pre–World Cup construction
boom. See "The Plight of Qatar's Migrant Workers," Al Jazeera, June 14, 2012,
in Sources. Al Jazeera is headquartered in Qatar, and this article hardly reflects
well on the country. The number is unlikely to be exaggerated.

The real root of the problem was back in India, Nepal, the Philippines, and so on—in the poverty that these workers were trying to escape.

The only long-term solution I could think of was more like a do-over: if there had been opportunities back home, these men never would have signed up for Dubai in the first place. For future generations, the real solution was *there*, not here. And that would also better address the cruelty of the birth lottery.

But that just made my question even more baffling. What could I do, with my limited resources, to make life better in poor villages in countries I'd never seen and knew little about?

The red-eye to Singapore was a welcome relief. Eight hours in coach, watch a movie, fall asleep daydreaming about the flight attendant, wake up in a different country entirely.*

Singapore would feel different from Dubai, I was certain. I'd visited a few years earlier, and it felt less governed than curated: modern, efficient, safe, and spotless. This is all the more amazing given that Singapore is one of the most densely populated countries on our planet.

Imagine squeezing the population of Ireland onto an island half the size of Los Angeles, dividing them with four different languages and a half-dozen religions, and starting most of them out in grinding poverty, with virtually no natural resources. Fifty years later, *that* country now has life expectancy and per capita GDP

---

* A 2011 survey of UK business travelers rated the airline I flew out of the Emirates as having the second-sexiest flight attendants on earth. The winner was the airline I'd flown into Emirates, and third and fourth place were carriers hubbed in the Emirates. Surely this says nothing about the women, but is an accurate portrait of the minds of business travelers far from home in a city where illicit sex is profoundly taboo yet widely available. See Sources.

rates among the world's highest, scoring in most quality-of-life studies ahead of London, Paris, and Milan, and sometimes ahead of every city in the entire United States.* Wealthy, stable, and world-famous for it: everything Dubai wants to be, Singapore has already become.

I felt more relaxed the moment I sat on the plane. Maybe I could stop reeling from the blunt force trauma of wealth to the head. Part of me just wanted to move on, to pretend I'd learned nothing important. Selfishly, I missed the only-mildly-guilty pleasures of the south of France. Maybe what happened in Dubai could stay in Dubai.

The next stop on my itinerary was a new swank-o-rama hoping for inclusion in a Best New Hotels piece. Since I was passing through Singapore anyway to see a more established hotel, my editor asked me to send back my first impression of the new place. It was this:

The instant I stepped off the plane, an attractive young hotel rep recognized my face and greeted me right at the gate— apparently having done Internet research on me and pre-arranged her own presence with security—popped me onto a cart, zoomed me the length of the terminal, ushered me through immigration while barely breaking stride, and plopped me into a limousine at the curb. The limo's engine was already running, and its door was held open by a uniformed livery driver who bowed slightly as I approached.

---

*Examples are in Sources. Keep in mind, economic and health statistics are more easily measured than restrictions on political expression and labor rights, severe fines targeting behavior considered private elsewhere, and a draconian judicial system including harsh whippings with a rattan cane. If the threat of being legally beaten would affect your quality of life, adjust these figures accordingly.

Elapsed time: maybe five minutes.

The limousine, I should add, was a Bentley Continental Flying Spur, a handmade English touring sedan with leather seats that give lumbar massage, optional floor rugs made from lamb's wool, walnut veneers taken only from trees at least seventy years old, and a Manufacturer's Suggested Retail Price more than twice the market value of my mother's house.* The Flying Spur can also do zero to sixty in less than five seconds, despite the built-in refrigerator in the backseat.

I decided to write that the hotel was just fine.

It was about 8 A.M., so we hit morning traffic. With the sun and its heat beginning to peek through the clouds, the driver invited me to grab a cold bottle of water from the fridge. The temperature was climbing toward 90 degrees, with tropical humidity I'd felt in the few steps between the airport and the car.

The car had perfect air-conditioning—four "individually controlled climate zones," in fact—but I took a bottle, drank, and let my eyes relax on the passing scenery, unwinding in a way that I hadn't in weeks. After the desolation of the Emirates, Singapore felt green, lush, bright, and alive. A tourist again, I even pulled out my camera, eagerly snapping up everything new.

We soon slowed for a moment behind a blue Toyota pickup. In the back were three men. I took their picture, too, before a second thought might have stopped me. Two of the men were staring at me. Their expressions looked a lot like contempt.

What? Why on earth . . . ? Then I studied them more closely. Their faces looked Indian.† The one in the middle could have

---

* Not an exaggeration. The car's MSRP as packaged was more than $200,000. The house's estimated value at the time was about $93,000.

† My guess now is that they were Tamils, an ethnic group mostly from India's state of Tamil Nadu, who first came to Singapore as indentured servants under

been the better-fed brother of the first man who spoke to me on Sheikh Zayed Road.

These three men on a hard bench in the back of a pickup were likely heading off to a day of long labor. One of them had covered his head with a red rag, so they might even be working in the sun. Singapore is surrounded by water, barely north of the equator, a place where 90 degrees feels more like 110.* Heat doesn't get more uncomfortably damp.

I, on the other hand, was drinking chilled bottled water in the personal climate zone of a silver Bentley Continental Flying Spur driven by a uniformed livery driver in linen and white gloves.†

In their place, I might have given me a hard look, too.

Even in one of the world's most prosperous cities, it took only moments to be reminded again of my luck in the birth lottery. Of how hard my dad had worked so that I wouldn't have to. Of how he moved from Appalachia to spend his life in a factory in hopes of supporting his family. Of those men in Dubai who were so much like Dad was, and who worked even harder than he did. Of how they might not see their families for years.

It's the way of much of the world, I would come to realize— Albanians in Greece, Mexicans in the U.S., Moroccans in France, Zimbabweans in South Africa, on and on—people do what they must to build a better life. If my dad had needed to cross a border to do it, I am sure that he would have.

---

the British. Some Tamil immigrants have prospered, but not all, and immigrant Tamil laborers are still not uncommon.

* To be exact, Singapore's average 80-percent humidity makes 90 degrees feel like 113.3, according to the U.S. National Weather Service's heat index calculator.

† It also might not please a Hindu that the car's leather interior requires the hides of eleven cows.

The question returned, and now I could no longer escape it: with my limited resources, what could I do to make life better in poor villages in countries I'd never seen and knew little about?

My *Forbes Traveler* cash would be about $20,000, maybe half of my income that year.* I needed to do something good with it, even if it was worth less than three shots of whisky in Dubai. I couldn't get the idea out of my mind, in fact. So in the same little black notebook I'd been using to scribble about billion-dollar hotels, I started a list of what I'd hypothetically hoped my money could do:

- Help poverty in 3rd world (at least a little).†
- Help build an economy, not fix emergencies. Long-term not short.
- Know what happened to $—what it did where.

I felt a little silly making that list. It seemed overly ambitious. But it also felt more exciting than the plushery I'd been wallowing in. Perhaps this was just spiritual money laundering, but the idea of putting five-star cash to use in the no-star world was giving me a new sense of adventure.

---

* After digging out my 2008 tax return—audited by the IRS for all the travel expenses, and accepted with no adjustment—I can confirm that $20,000 was way more than half. Eek.

† The phrase "3rd world" was used only for brevity in private notes. It's a Cold War phrase worth discarding: the West was First, the Soviet bloc was Second, and everyone else was Third. Since that's the vast majority of humanity, the term is falling into wise disuse. Unfortunately, well-known alternatives are few. "Developing world" and its variants are at least widely understood, albeit while implying that poor countries are like teenagers, hoping someday to reach maturity with bigger houses and bosoms and Walmarts. I'd like to disclaim the paternalistic vibe. While we're on it, calling industrialized countries "the West" is equally clumsy, but I've used it here for similar reasons. Apologies to Japan, Australia, New Zealand, South Korea, and so on.

That evening, I went for a long walk down Orchard Road, the city's main commercial boulevard.* At the time of my visit, there were twenty-one shopping centers in less than a mile. Solutions to poverty did not leap to mind.

Then again, a half-dozen decades ago, Singapore was still rife with squatters and slums. Its streets were unsafe, its mosquitoes malarial, its people largely poor and illiterate. Now tourists flock here from Sydney and Tokyo. If nothing else, and regardless of what I might think of its legal system, Singapore has proven that massive improvement is possible, at least.

Straying from Orchard Road, my path was soon flanked with huge public housing developments, ranging from working-class flats to upscale condos. Viewed through the prism of American political ideology, the contrast was impossible—Orchard Road, all international brands, trade, and hyper-capitalism; ten minutes away, massive socialized housing. But this is part of how this tiny island made itself an economic powerhouse. Generations ago, faced with hundreds of thousands of people with no decent place to live, plus limited resources on hand, Singapore's government (a) invested massively in housing, education, health care, and public infrastructure; (b) supported manufacturing with moon-landing levels of government investment; *and* (c) adopted an equally fervent pro-business, free-trade stance toward foreign investment.†

---

* Orchard Road is named for the trees that were cut down to build it. Once you notice the irony, it's visible constantly all over the world.

† To be clear, Singapore's authoritarian rule expedited things, with obvious human and social costs that would require another book to fully explore. I'm not advocating its replication. Fortunately, public goods and infrastructure can be created in thriving democracies, as any American—who presumably has driven on an interstate highway, attended a state university, sought a weather forecast, not died in a fiery crash thanks to air traffic control, survived once-deadly

That's a mixture of policies that no major party in modern America would agree to. But here, these weren't left- or right-wing agendas. These were simply ideas that might work in Singapore, and then did, eventually raising per capita income thirty-fold. The obvious takeaway: ideology can blind us. Anyone convinced that their ideas are the only good ones, appropriate everywhere, should be viewed with caution.

Adding to my notes:

• Might not be left or right. A mix—not a Western idea?

My money might best go into a charity, a for-profit investment, a fund that invests in a mixture of the two, or something unexpected. This narrowed my options to the entire universe of finance and development. *Hmph.*

After an hour, I reached the Esplanade, a glittering waterfront development of theaters, performance halls, and inevitable upscale shopping. On the far side of a bridge loomed a bright-colored circle more than forty stories high: the Singapore Flyer, the World's Largest Ferris Wheel. Take *that*, Dubai.

Speaking of Dubai: in the Emirates, natural resources were the main source of wealth. I'd been thinking of Singapore as lacking any such advantage, but that left out its location—the city was born to be a major port, perfectly placed between India and China. This primo location was why the British showed up in the first place. An export economy was inevitable.* But the Singapore

---

infections made trivial by antibiotics developed profitably due to patent protection, flushed a toilet successfully in most major cities, felt safe thanks to law enforcement and fire services, or enjoyed not contracting malaria, which beset much of the South until a federal insecticide-spraying program banished the disease so thoroughly that not even its memory survives—can see at a glance.

* Singapore is one of "Four Asian Tigers" (alongside Taiwan, Hong Kong, and South Korea) with high-growth export economies. This once led many pundits

model might only succeed in places like Singapore. Try the same policies with a different geography, and the whole thing probably wouldn't have worked.*

Even whole nations can suffer the birth lottery. Another note:

- Can't be just one big idea.

Well, then. *Crap.*

Maybe Bali, renowned island bastion of high-octane exoticism, overflowing with music and dance and traditional crafts, would be more inspiring.

I'll keep this part short. It was not.

Indonesia's thousands of islands are about 90 percent Muslim, but Bali is Hindu, and of a singular type.† Balinese tradition scarcely separates the spiritual and physical worlds. Every detail in life—your clothing, your home, even your personal composure—can be a prayer, and homes and businesses maintain visible

---

to lump them together despite major policy, resource, and political differences, including the advantages of location and history (Singapore has no analog to North Korea on its border, for example, nor Taiwan's political rivalry with China). Some economists (e.g. Paul Krugman, in Sources) also foresaw a ceiling to their expansion far in advance.

* For an exploration of how corruption, internal conflict, being landlocked with bad neighbors, and other misfortunes can overwhelm societies, see Collier, *The Bottom Billion*, in Sources. Later, we'll see the Singapore model attempted in the landlocked African nation of Rwanda.

† Indonesia, in fact, has more Muslims than any other country on earth by a wide margin. There are just over two hundred million Muslims in Indonesia alone—nearly as many as all of the Arab Muslims in the entire Middle East combined. Mathematically, the idea that all Muslims are Arab is only slightly more accurate than claiming that all major league baseball teams are from California.

shrines. Fruit offerings (typically consumed by dogs, eating perhaps on behalf of the gods) abound, and any wrappable object, no matter how mundane—air conditioners, mailboxes, fire extinguishers—may be covered in black-and-white cloth to ward off evil spirits.

It's all so immersive that some visitors come home with wide-eyed tales of wonder and soulful connection. For some, it's a true life-changing experience; for others, it's more like returning from Sea World convinced they can speak fluent Whale. Either way, Bali has reached enough bucket lists that tourism accounts for about 90 percent of the island's entire income.

Unfortunately, these dollars and euro don't remain as rupiah. The owners of many hotels and resorts are overseas, and the proceeds barely brush against Balinese hands. After decades of development and billions in tourist expenditures, at the time of my visit, Bali's per capita income was officially about $4 a day. For those doing menial work, it was less. A hotel maid, I learned just by asking, might clean a whole floor of $200 rooms for just two or three bucks per day.

It would have never crossed my mind to consider the men on Sheikh Zayed Road as relatively well off. Now it did.

Lacking alternatives, young people may pursue any piece of the action. After dark in less upscale areas, *Hey boss!* came the shouts from aggressive male touts. *Taxi? Marijuana? Hashish?* Drug trafficking in Indonesia is a capital offense. So much for deterrence. *Pretty girl, very young?*

Black-and-white cloths do not stop evil spirits.

Ironically, Bali's unique culture has attracted many of its troubles. In some parts of the island, singular beauty has been punished severely.*

---

* I'm not saying don't go. It's still mostly gorgeous, and Bali *needs* tourism now. Just try to get your money to stay on the island, which takes only a bit of online planning. Stay in locally owned hotels with a high percentage of full-time work-

Meanwhile, neighboring islands—Muslim instead of Hindu, less touristed, less developed, poorer but envious of Bali despite what development might mean for their own culture, and so on— face different situations. They have different skills, resources, and histories. A genius idea from Lombok, the next island over, might bump on religions, interfere with local businesses, or depend on traditional skills not practiced locally.

Damn. Uniqueness is a challenge, too. Another roadblock:

- Locals know needs better than outsiders. Outsider ideas may be doomed from start.

In summary: I needed to be open to not one idea, but a vast array, springing from the people themselves in villages all over the world that I knew nothing about.

I kinda gave up. For a few weeks, I tried to stop thinking about it. Then I arrived at Tiananmen Square.

Beijing brought the last of my assigned swank hotels. I had so completely run out of anything new to say about wine lists and pillow menus that my final "Forbes Traveler 400" review reads almost like subtle parody—praising the plants, the activity in the lobby, and the hotel's willingness to repair damaged luggage.* I also snuck in two references to Tiananmen Square, which was miles away and had nothing to do with the hotel, but whose

---

ers; don't deal with businesses owned by the former dictator Suharto's family; buy crafts from the people who make them, not a souvenir stand or a gift shop; and so on. You might also want to take care with the cops, who supplement their tiny incomes by extorting improvised fees; the traffic, which can be preposterous on winding mountain roads; and the water, unless you want to explore the full meaning of the phrase "Bali Belly." You'll have a great trip.

* This review, which I claim with no pride, lives on. See Sources.

historic events we should never forget, especially as long as the current regime is in power.

Spell-checking before hitting "Send," I typed "Tiananmen Square" into Google. My connection to the local server instantly dropped and reset. I tried again, using Wikipedia's search window this time. *Click*, off went the Internet, Page Not Found. After a few seconds, the connection returned.

This was the Great Firewall of China, as it is sardonically called, Beijing's censorship of Internet traffic considered not beneficial to the regime—so strict, in fact, that even using the words *Great Firewall* can get your site blocked. In previous centuries, the Forbidden City was the location of China's rulers. Now, metaphorically, it's information about them.

Tiananmen Square, of course, is a massive open ground created six hundred years ago by the Ming Dynasty. It's Beijing's center of gravity, its National Mall and Red Square. Chairman Mao proclaimed the People's Republic on this spot. He's buried just south of the center.

In the year the Berlin Wall was torn down, Tiananmen Square was the heart of China's growing pro-democracy movement. Then came tank columns, tear gas, shootings of unarmed civilians, media blackouts, purges, and roundups. The movement was crushed.*

This was all fairly recent, yet still before the dawn of the Inter-

---

*Contrary to widespread belief, it now seems that there was relatively little bloodshed inside Tiananmen Square itself. Instead, soldiers fired on civilians along nearby Chang'an Avenue and several side streets, killing more than 150. Meanwhile, as the army rolled into the city from its bases in the countryside, civilians were shot in numerous scattered encounters. In the largest of these, hundreds were killed in Muxidi, a few miles west of the center. Total casualty estimates vary but reach into the thousands. The initial idea that the massacre was *in* the square sprang from early BBC reports that have been contradicted by international witnesses, declassified and leaked documents from both China and the U.S., and in 2009 by the BBC reporter himself. See Sources.

net and cell phone cameras in every front pocket. Little footage exists. The sole iconic image is Tank Man, an anonymous lone pedestrian who appeared simply to be going about his day when his outrage overcame self-preservation. So Tank Man walked into the middle of the street, unarmed, and stared down a column of tanks.

Incredibly, the tanks stopped.

When they tried to go around him, he blocked them again, then climbed *atop* the first tank, perhaps trying to reason with the driver. Once he climbed down, he kept blocking the tanks until two other pedestrians—concerned bystanders? secret police?—ran over and hustled him away.

No one knows who Tank Man was or what happened to him afterward. Imprisoned, executed, escaped into hiding? We may never find out.* What we do know is that one ordinary man, unaware he was being watched by news cameras on hotel balconies half a mile away, gave us all an iconic image of dignity and courage. More people may have seen this lone, anonymous, probably martyring act of defiance than any other in history.†

What we do matters, even if we never see the ripple effects.‡

---

* International concern for Tank Man's fate gave Beijing huge incentive to show that he was still alive, vindicating their now-disproven claim that violence only befell criminals and terrorists. But Tank Man was never identified, much less produced. Sadly, that probably tells us his fate.

† The notable exception, of course, is in China, where domestic censorship has been largely successful to this day. Young people with whom I spoke generally had never heard of the massacre.

‡ Consider the four men I met in Dubai: if even one of them had scowled at me, I might not have sat down. This story might have ended right there, and the last several years of my life would have been utterly different. Yours would be, too, at least slightly, since you would not be reading these words. And yet by now those four men probably don't even remember me, nor would they imagine you reading about them. We may never conceive our own ripple effects. Even one frown or smile at the right moment can change lives.

Frustrated with China's censorious nonsense—blocking "Tiananmen" in Beijing is like blocking "Wrigley Field" in Chicago—I suddenly wanted to find the exact site of Tank Man's protest and pay my silent respect.

Obviously, the location wouldn't be on any tourist map, and there was no one to ask. So I started typing again, looking to bypass the Great Firewall. It took all of two minutes. Before trying a free proxy or even the Google cache, I simply *typed* a Wikipedia URL, rather than clicking a link. Bingo—up came the article in full.* Soon, I found photos of Tank Man's bold moment and news articles that placed it on Chang'an Street to the east of the square. Taking notes of the scenery, lightposts, and other details, I was able to find the exact spot.†

It was just a busy intersection. Unmarked, of course. Tank Man's crosswalk had even been removed. With the Forbidden City just two blocks away, millions of tourists must have passed by this corner with no idea of its meaning. This made it no less inspiring to visit.

I was only here, after all, because that picture had traveled globally within days, via technology that hadn't existed when the man was born. Today, we can now see the same photo almost instantly, even where it is censored, using technology that hadn't existed when it was taken.

Our ability to communicate is accelerating so rapidly that we

---

* I found this shocking. I assume the Chinese government generally implements much stronger blocking regimes. But this is what happened in late 2008. Your mileage may vary.

† As near as I can tell, Tank Man first stood between the northwest and southwest corners of the intersection of Chang'an Avenue and Beichizi Street right on Chang'an's double yellow centerline. According to Google Maps, the exact location is 39.907850 N, 116.403180 E, while Google Earth places it at 39.906362 N, 116.396722 E. I assume this glitch is due to the Great Firewall.

may be too busy keeping up to notice. It took twenty years for the rest of the world to learn even *where* the Tiananmen violence occurred. But with cell cameras and 4G and YouTube and so on, the abuses of the world's remaining dictators are sometimes broadcast worldwide within minutes.

The world has changed fundamentally in just the last decade. An eight-year-old child in Russia—or Thailand, Bolivia, Iceland, Egypt, or much of the planet—may now reach adulthood unable even to conceive of a world where information is not instantly, globally shareable. This new worldview is being adopted by most major human cultures, all at once, with unstoppable speed. Soon, today's wired children will be presidents and prime ministers and CEOs—none of whom have imagined a non-global existence.

Even in Tiananmen Square, now a mecca for tourists, this future could be easily glimpsed. Visitors from every part of the planet were taking pictures and uploading and calling and connecting with their handheld devices. Just within earshot, there must have been conversations with people in a dozen countries. From the middle of China. Five minutes from where Tank Man walked into history.*

That this already sounds almost ordinary is a measure of how rapidly the world can surprise us.

My journeys for *Forbes Traveler* were now finished. Looking back, in this entire voyage through the world of manufactured beauty—

---

*This said, the area is swarming with plainclothes police, e-mails are monitored, and if any of us had shouted slogans of religious or political independence, we might have gotten a chance to meet Tank Man in person. I am not saying China is free or anything remotely like it, just that communications are incredibly better. Greater freedom may take another generation or more, but the flow of information is to dictatorship as leaks are to a dam.

priceless art, grand estates, and fine pillow chocolates on bazillion-count linen, from California to London to Nice to Dubai to Singapore to Kuala Lumpur to Bali to Hong Kong to Shanghai to Beijing—one moment was loveliest by far. And it was totally free.

I was driving in France, running late for my next scheduled froufrou, and I'd made a wrong turn in my rental car, leaving me on a back road in a rural area with no fancy smartphone and a printed map that was nonsense once I'd lost the main highway. The overcast sky had removed any shadow, so I couldn't navigate by the sun. I'd then strayed into a gap between towns, losing even passers-by I might ask for directions. I was utterly lost.

Frustrated, grumpy, resigned to a screw-up, I hurried along, driving quickly and crossly despite having no real direction. My fingers tensed on the wheel, my foot pressed the car forward, my eyes darted from the horizon to the dashboard clock to the speedometer and back again, my brain filled itself with recalculated distances and times and velocities and apologies to people who would scarcely notice my absence. I had no real awareness beyond movement and want.

Then I crested a hill. My view changed in an instant.

Sunflowers.

On both sides of the road, almost to the horizon, on and on, joyful sunflowers, enormous, in fields larger than I'd ever imagined.

There was no way to drive past. I stopped the car, stood in silence, and then started to laugh. No human construction could be nearly this beautiful. I could only feel grateful for all that had gone "wrong."*

---

* I took the cover photo here a few minutes later. If I'd imagined it would ever be the cover of a book, I'd have removed the sunglasses and dopey hat. As to the flowers, they must be just part of somebody's sunflower farm, humdrum to a local. Obviously, that must just be how people grow sunflowers. But I'd never

Sometimes the thing that you're looking for shows up right in front of you, more wonderful than you would have expected.

So now I was standing outside the old Forbidden City, smiling at my tiny victory over the new Forbidden City, and watching Humankind 2.0 interact. People from all over the world were happily taking the same goofy pictures in front of the giant picture of Mao. Over here, three European guys were preening for their camera, posing with their chins up and chests out. Over there, Japanese girls were smiling and making peace signs. To the front, two Americans gave an ironic thumbs-up.

I took a lot of other people's pictures with their cameras and phones—*one, two, three! good? okay, bye*—and let the afternoon go, watching people make silly home movies for YouTube. For a moment my thoughts floated back to the guys in Dubai. *Too bad they can't upload their troubles to Facebook*, I thought.

Wait. Hold on.

What *if* working people trying to get out of poverty could somehow upload their needs to the Internet? What *if* there were a Craigslist or a Facebook for connecting, say, Indian villages and people like me? An eBay where people could log on and do good?

My checklist and warnings started clicking themselves off:

- It would address poverty in the developing world.
- It would build economies, not just fix emergencies.
- With a direct connection, you would know what the cash did and where.

---

imagined it. As to where this was, it had to be somewhere near Mirepoix, but I remained a little confused until finally finding the highway, so I can't be more precise. You might have to get as lost as I was to find it.

- The ideas wouldn't come out of ideology, but just practical needs.
- The ideas would be varied and specific, designed by the people who would know best.
- The ideas would be local, working within community standards. Someone like me wouldn't even need to fully understand the local customs and economy.

I'd been looking at the problem as something *I'd* wanted to solve, or help others to solve, top-down: *Bob* finds a good idea that might work, does a good thing with his money, yay. But the answer was bottom-up: a tradeswoman who works as hard as my dad would surely *know* what would work in her community, so *she* does a good thing with my money, yay. My role would be just to get connected, pitch in, and get out of the way.*

That actually sounded like it would work.

In fact, I was certain that someone was already trying it.

---

* It turns out that this well-meaning but naive urge to see oneself as solving a problem, rather than merely as the helper of people already fixing their own problems, is at the root of a staggering number of development failures. ICT-Works, a group devoted to sharing best practices in bringing information technology to the developing world, recently assembled a list of the top seven reasons that development projects fail. By my count, six can be attributed to insufficient input from the people most affected. See Sources.

"Yes, and"

CHAPTER THREE

CHICAGO, FIJI, AND BROADWAY

I'D ALREADY HEARD about an Internet effort to connect people like me with small enterprises in the developing world. And then I'd moved on, barely breaking stride, much like walking right past those men in Dubai. After that, since it didn't look like what I thought of as charity, it had somehow slipped out of my brain.

Several months earlier, I'd been at one of those conferences where people with Big Ideas have twenty minutes to whack your paradigm, one after another, like speed dating for worldviews.

A neuroscientist explained how our personal moral codes might be related to how our brains are physically wired. My friend Jenn spoke about the sad banality of the exploitation of women. Former presidential candidate John Edwards sermonized on the distribution of wealth, three weeks before it turned out that Edwards was having an affair and distributing wealth to cover it up. The talks about moral codes and the exploitation of women also seemed to apply.

Along the way, I also spent twenty minutes listening to a slender, soft-spoken man named Premal Shah, who distinguished himself immediately by not trying to. Given their brief time in the spotlight, many speakers beseeched and implored. But Shah's voice never rose. His gestures wouldn't have disturbed a grazing deer. He simply smiled and explained how his organization's website—Kiva.org—took a Nobel Peace Prize–winning approach to poverty and made it accessible to anyone with a computer.

This by itself barely dented my brain, since I'd already seen hundreds of charity websites for walk-a-thons, emergency appeals, and so on, not to mention a dizzying number of websites where if you just *Click Here!* once a day, the ad revenue goes to some good cause.

The *Click Here!* sites have always left me feeling a little guilty for every day that I forget. Can charitable giving *be* any easier? All they're even asking for is a mere twitch of my finger, and some flood victim is fractionally closer to not getting cholera. Then on another page, one click, and "1.1 cups of food" goes to "the hungry." And so on. I would imagine myself to be a big advocate for these sites. I'm hugely in favor of food for the hungry. I strongly support not-cholera for all. It seems like you'd have to be cruel not to—literally—lift one finger to help.*

But there are a bewildering number of these things. Plant an Oak Tree, Clear Land Mines, Feed Orphaned Chimps—I've bookmarked and clicked resolutely. I've also Donated Solar Energy, Expanded Nature Reserves, Helped East Timor, Kept Pollutants out of the Ocean, and Saved not only Baby Seals, but Dolphins, Whales, Horses, Abandoned Pets, and Big Cats. If it were possible for one index finger to save all of humanity, mine would sign up. Just tell me where to Submit.

Unfortunately, there's no sense of connection between the cause and effect. You click. Nothing much happens. You just hope that somewhere the 1.1 Cups of Food Fairy will arrive at The Hungry, whoever they are. And it can be surprisingly hard to stay motivated.

I almost wonder if these websites ask too little of us. If my thesis is true—that life takes on meaning to the degree that our efforts and love are connected—we can see why these sites aren't as motivating as we might hope: there's no effort, nor a clear recipi-

---

*These are aggregated at www.oneclickatatime.org. Assuming you have a decent heart, you may also have carpel tunnel by the weekend.

ent, nor any connection. So it feels oddly meaningless, no matter how much real good it might do.

The website that Shah was talking about, however, was unusually personal. You could see the faces of individual people connected to your actions, along with short bios and descriptions of their plans. You'd log in, put in the effort to pick out a Bolivian dentist or a Congolese schoolmarm, and your act of lending would have a specific sense of connection to your affection for their story.

Wait—*lending?* Yes, lending. Not outright giving. That sounded odd.

Kiva.org didn't provide a way to hand out money, but to lend it—in $25 increments to small farms, craftspeople, and mom-and-pop businesses all over the world. This felt counterintuitive: Robin Hood didn't steal from the rich to *lend* to the poor. *How can you lift people out of poverty when they're paying interest?* I wondered.* It seemed almost like a gimmick, maybe an irrational extension of free-market ideology, the sort of unlikely paradigm-yank that conferences like this were designed for.

I might have dismissed the idea out of hand, except that economist Muhammad Yunus and his microlending Grameen Bank in Bangladesh had recently shared the Nobel Peace Prize for reaching millions of the working poor. As a result, I'd read news stories about how Yunus and Grameen had come up with simple, meaningful, and reproducible measures of the economic progress of the world's poorest—water quality, type of bedding and roofing, ability to eat three meals a day, etc.—and developed financial tools to help clients improve their situation through borrowing, savings, and dividend-paying ownership in the bank itself.† Yunus's ambitions of "creating a world without poverty" (the title of his

---

* To be clear, Kiva users don't make a dime in interest, but are simply allowing their funds to be used to provide the capital supporting loans being made by local lenders in the field.

† These "10 Indicators" are supplemented by "16 Decisions" regarding health, mutual support, education, and more. For more on both, see Sources.

then-current book) were praised widely. So was Grameen's near-exclusive focus on lending to women, who had been shown in several studies to particularly benefit, and who were seen as more likely than their husbands to invest in the well-being of their families.* Newspapers and magazines lauded Yunus. Powerful bankers and heads of state sought his counsel. That carried some weight.

So did the surprisingly high repayment rate—more than 98 percent for Kiva in particular. Later on, given the recent struggles of the stock market, I amused myself with some back-of-the-envelope math. At the time, money placed into Kiva loans on the day it went online would have slightly outperformed the S&P 500 index. It was just a quirk of timing, nothing that could continue long-term, but it was fun to contemplate nonetheless: at that point in Kiva's history, Bangladeshi woodworkers and Peruvian farmers had been a safer investment than Wall Street.†

I knew from visiting my parents and grandparents that people can be bright and hard-working regardless of income or birthplace. *Of course* this could work. There's an old saying that if you give a man a fish, you feed him for a day; if you teach a man to fish, you feed him for a lifetime.‡ Microlending, in essence, was one step further

---

* See, of many examples, a 2003 World Bank policy research working paper by Pitt, Shahidur, Khandker, and Cartwright in Sources. Its abstract fairly glows: "Credit program participation leads to women taking a greater role in household decisionmaking, having greater access to financial and economic resources, having greater social networks, having greater bargaining power compared with their husbands, and having greater freedom of mobility. Female credit also tended to increase spousal communication in general about family planning and parenting concerns." As with any working paper, the World Bank did not endorse the conclusions. Other studies have not always agreed.

† To be more specific, Togolese goat herders beat Wall Street by six percentage points. See Sources.

‡ The saying is often attributed to "the Chinese" or the twelfth-century Jewish scholar Maimonides, but its first known use is in the 1885 British novel *Mrs. Dymond* by Anne Thackeray Ritchie.

and less challenging: this was helping someone who already knew how to fish, just by lending a few bucks to buy some new hooks.

As a freelancer, I was always on the lookout for interesting projects, so I bounced an idea off of Jenn: maybe an article about Kiva, possibly including a few client visits, make a cool magazine piece. She egged me on, so I found Shah's e-mail address and pitched him the idea. According to my archives, he replied briefly an hour later and passed me along to Kiva's PR rep, who got in touch the next day. I replied to her that afternoon but received no response.

And as far as I can tell, we all then forgot it entirely.

It would be nice to pretend that I'm not perfectly capable of forgetting important things, but if you've ever seen me on *Jeopardy!* with a clueless stare on my face for a full thirty seconds of Think Music, you know otherwise.*

Freelancing is a constant search for work, and this Kiva idea was just one of many. Since rejection is constant, you learn to hit "Send" and move on to the next thing immediately. And in the rare moment that any idea actually happens, hallelujah, you focus on that one and dive in as hard as you can.

I've made a living this way since my early twenties, when I was

---

Maimonides did, however, state that the highest level of charity, justice, and righteousness (which in Hebrew are the same word, *tzedakah*) to another comes "by providing him with a gift or a loan or by accepting him into a business partnership or by helping him find employment—in a word, by putting him where he can dispense with other people's aid." See Sources.

To Maimonides, the loan was a higher tzedakah than even an anonymous donation, because it did not shame the recipient. Maimonides also stated that health, education, and training should precede such investment. This will be worth remembering when we visit Kiva partners at work in the field.

*I've screwed up Final Jeopardy four times. Those four thirty-second brain-locks, mostly in high-stakes invitational tournaments, have cost me enough to buy two-thirds of a Bentley Continental Flying Spur.

broke, unemployed, and deep in student debt. Out of desperation as much as any real planning, I took a Greyhound to Chicago, moved into a YMCA for a long winter, charged my cheap little room to my credit card when I had to, and took theater classes from Del Close, a legendary improv teacher who taught the words "yes, and" as both a creative technique and a fun way of life.

To "yes, and" is to make agreement your default response to any suggestion ("yes"), with your first goal being to instantly build on any idea ("and"). When everyone onstage is in full "yes, and" mode, trust and creativity overwhelm self-doubt and criticism. Each mind brings new ideas to the mix, and wild invention becomes normal. But if none of us know where we're going, how can we trust that there can be something wonderful right away? *Because we live in a deeply interconnected world*, Del always taught. If you're observant and open enough, you'll start seeing that everything eventually connects with everything else. Complete exercises, taking perhaps forty-five minutes, often turn full narrative circles, in fact, finishing right where they began.

I passed many long evenings soaking up Del's mad-hipster vibe in a dank little bar called CrossCurrents, whose stage was near enough to the Belmont stop of Chicago's elevated trains that the clatter sometimes competed with the sound of Del's voice. No matter: Del's booming baritone hurled encouragement, epithets, and all the truth he could muster against the walls and our skulls, overcoming the ten-ton trains when it had to. I still cherish the memory of that growl.

By the time I met him, Del had "yes, and"-ed his way into being an actor, a comic book writer, a circus performer, a creator of light shows for the Grateful Dead, and most of all an influence on two generations of comedians.* In my twenty-three-year-old opinion,

---

* Del's other students over the years are a *Who's Who* of American TV, film, and live comedy; his influence on the last half-century of comedy is jaw-dropping.

he was the coolest human being I had ever met. It was hard to imagine my own life would be that adventurous or fun.

Del's "yes, and" was where my adult life began. Ever since, and for many years without even realizing his influence, I've managed to make a fun if unstable living simply by saying "yes, and" to pretty much anything that sounds like a good idea, then figuring out the details on the fly.

Looking back at my calendar, in the week where I first heard about Kiva, I was also floating a book idea about the growth of international sport as a mechanism for peace, which didn't pan out; corresponding with Hollywood film producers who were adapting an earlier book for the screen, which didn't pan out (Hollywood, you should know, is like a pit of vipers, but with more vipers); and hoping to get rehired for the third season of a Mexican *telenovela* where I'd worked as *asesor de producción*, which didn't pan out.*

There was also the possibility of a freelance job with a website called *Forbes Traveler. Yes, and* came my instant reply.

I probably stopped thinking about microlending for another reason, too: simple cognitive dissonance. Kiva and microlending just didn't stick in my head as "charity." Any new idea—including objective, testable facts—can be rejected by the subconscious, especially if the new idea contradicts our beliefs or forces us to feel unexpected emotions. This happens instantly, before any conscious processing, even if we're sincerely trying to keep an open

---

I pretend to no place in that pantheon. Were he still alive, Del might not pick me out of a police lineup next to five murderous thugs. Although he could probably get the six of us to do some pretty decent scene work. See Sources.

* This was the Televisa program *El Pantera*. For more, see Sources.

mind. Well-traveled neural pathways are simply hard to over-write. Old patterns of thinking are strong.*

When it came to figuring out what to do with my own money, I'd just spent more than forty years being led to believe that help-ing the poor was primarily a selfless one-way act of giving, and that charity almost always came with one specific, widely repeated set of expectations and emotions.

When I was a teenager, charity was Jerry Lewis staying up late once a year and singing to a small, sick kid in a wheelchair, raising millions of dollars for the Muscular Dystrophy Association, using a literal "poster child" as a visual aid.†

In my twenties, charity was a concert like Live Aid, where fam-ine in Ethiopia (often referred to as "Africa," as if the continent had only one nation; by the measures of population and number of countries ignored, this is like confusing Mexico with the entire Western Hemisphere) was addressed by multi-millionaire musi-cians exhorting viewers to send in $10, the rate of donations sky-rocketing near the end during a video of starving, helpless children.‡

---

* Demonstrations of cognitive dissonance may be what large family gatherings are *for*. Incidentally, when it kicks in, our conscious mind is left to improvise explanations of why the idea was rejected. Since the explanations came from our own brains, we tend to believe them. It's a serious bug in our software, eas-ily noticed with practice. Next time you reject an idea and *then* have to figure out why, or you disagree with someone despite having no real facts you can summon, yet harden your opinion anyway, bingo. It's human. If we were all more aware of it, and it were socially more prestigious to admit cognitive dis-sonance and laugh at ourselves than to protect our own egos and ideology, poli-tics, the media, and a lot of families would be a lot quieter and saner.

† The MDA stopped using the phrase "poster child" in 1993, and its "national goodwill ambassadors" are now typically older, more active, and able to fill a more sophisticated and articulate role. For more, see Sources.

‡ The 1984–85 famine had more complex causes than drought, including a mass-murdering dictatorship, forced collectivization of farms—an idea that had starved tens of millions in the Soviet Union and China—and rebellions in much of the country. *That* was the situation which songs by Kenny Loggins and

In my thirties, charity was Sally Struthers in a series of TV ads, her puppy-dog eyes welling with tears—*won't you please help?*—while shoeless children were shown living in shacks. The appeal was so unvarying and naked in its pity that her very name has unfortunately become a humorous shorthand: *I don't want to go all Sally Struthers here, but I do need a ride to the airport . . .*

For all the real good that these efforts surely achieved, their emotional content was unmistakable: a heavy dose of pity, with side dishes of undeserved guilt or shame. The recipients were rarely held as full equals—creative, smart, strong, and resourceful. Instead, they were stricken, dependent, helpless, imperiled, infantilized.

I think that may be why some people harden against charitable appeals. If we're not up for feeling guilty or sad right that minute, they can feel almost manipulative. Even when we open our wallets, it may be just to stop feeling bad. (*Fine, Sally—here's five bucks for Zambia! Now get off my TV and let me watch the dang game.*) At these times, we may not be acting out of love—even if we want to be—but to make our own least bad choice between helpless pity, personal coldness, or forking over a few bucks to get on with our day.

After forty years of *that* as "charity," somebody tells you that *lending* might work just as well in some places, and sometimes even better? Emotionally—in the realm of cognitive dissonance—it's a complete mismatch. If you're lending to an ongoing small business, what's the disaster you're responding to? Where's the tragedy? Who's the victim?

Of course I didn't think of lending when I first left Dubai.

I'm glad that I didn't. Seeing the no-star world while traveling

---

Adam Ant were meant to remedy. Live Aid–financed relief saved at least a six-figure number of people from starvation, but some of the supplies were also used by the rulers to support the forced movement of millions of people, during which at least tens of thousands died. A quarter-century later, despite a new constitution, even human rights work is criminalized, and millions of Ethiopians remain at risk of starvation and related illness. For more, see Sources.

in five-star luxury put it all in maximally high contrast. If it hadn't worked out this exact way, I would never have been as emotionally invested. And without the paychecks from *Forbes Traveler*, I couldn't have been as financially invested, either.

Finally home in Los Angeles, I fell ill for several weeks (more on that soon) but eventually—near the end of January, 2009—I opened my laptop and took a closer look at this Kiva.org.

Kiva was much as I imagined—a big list of borrowers in dozens of countries all over the world, with photos and bios on every client's page. Impressively, none of these people in difficult circumstances were portrayed with pity, or even as particularly poor. Instead, they were just fellow human beings, their plans for the future described with respect for their ingenuity, work ethic, and dignity. As to the loans, repayment schedules were listed right down to the penny, there was a basket for checkout, and payment could be made via credit card or PayPal. It was basically like eBay, except instead of buying an Afghan, I could lend one $25.

Dozens of faces peered out from my screen. Most were women. Many were mothers of three, four, six, nine. This touched me, too. My own dad had been raised as the youngest of eight, back in that handmade Appalachian home on a hill. My mom was the oldest of six. Large families can be common where birth control is poor, health care is worse, and extra hands can be used on a farm. Moreover, where infant mortality is high and retirement plans are non-existent, a bevy of children may improve the chances of their parents' survival in old age.

The loans were mostly small—the average seemed to be about $400, although I found a couple for as little as $50—and many clients were depicted in something like action shots, posing in mid-enterprise for the camera. Farmers stood next to livestock. Seamstresses posed with garments. Drivers stood at the doors of their taxis. There was dignity in their faces, sometimes even joy—these weren't people looking for a handout, but simply seeking more resources for their own plans.

Some of the jobs were unlike anything I'd imagined, and reading about them was a glimpse of entirely different worlds and ways of life. This is the actual description of a Cambodian borrower:

> Poung T., 39, is a local palm tree climber. With the palm tree climbing, he can tap palm juice from palm trees, boil it to make palm sugar or turn it into palm wine for sale. He is currently earning an average of US$11 a day to help feed his family. His wife's name is Leap Heng, and she is a good housewife. She cooks delicious meals for the family and is the good mother of three children; all of them are teenagers and still under her care.*

Wait, I thought. *Seriously?* Dude is almost my age, and he supports three teenagers by shinnying up and down trees all day? I suppose I could probably front him $25 until payday.

I spent parts of several days just reading the stories before committing to my first loan. Many borrowers had joined together in groups, often with delightfully optimistic names. In Uganda, a shopkeeper named Esther led the eleven members of the Victory Group, borrowing about $370 each:

> This is the 7th loan she has requested on behalf of her group, and she notes that her shop has been doing extremely well ever since she started receiving loans . . . which has thereby enabled her to pay for her children's school fees, purchase cows (which produce milk for her family), and secure a plot of land. She is now seeking another loan to re-stock her shop with additional goods.†

---

* Poung's Kiva page is at kiva.org/lend/85223.
† The Kiva page for Esther's Victory group is at kiva.org/lend/85650.

Seven loan cycles—leading to education, investment in capital equipment (that's what a cow *is*, at least in the developing world), and acquisition of real estate. Esther knew more about how to handle money and run a business than I did.

I poked around the site looking for clients who had already repaid in full. Soon I found Victor, a forty-eight-year-old Paraguayan father of three:

> He plans to use this loan to make more of his most popular product—a leather wristband scented with citronella used to repel mosquitoes. These are popular because the country is plagued by an epidemic of Dengue fever.*

Dengue fever is a mosquito-borne tropical disease. I'd just recovered from it myself. That's what I'd been sick with for weeks. My air ticket home had included a free stopover in Fiji, which is where I must have been infected.† I probably never even felt the mosquito bite that got me.‡ The virus incubated in my system for a week or so, this creature of the developing world secretly reproducing itself in my bloodstream while I flew home to Los Angeles. Two days after my return, it bloomed with a sudden full-body chill that felt like I'd just been immersed in an ice bath. A severe fever spiked rapidly,

---

* Victor's Kiva page is at kiva.org/lend/10611.

† I'd built my *Forbes Traveler* trip around a "Great Escapade" ticket, good for round-the-world travel for as little as $1,600, depending on exchange rate and departure date. For more, see Sources.

‡ This mosquito—probably *Aedes aegypti*, although there are twenty-six known species in Fiji—would have been smaller and sneakier than most of the sixty-odd species I grew up with in Ohio, who were relative hulks and usually dim enough to fly at a swattable height. Most dengue-carrying species are wicked commandoes that sneak up at ground level, dine painlessly on an ankle, then slip away unnoticed.

and the following week felt like the worst flu I've ever had, plus intense, deep aching all over my body. Not surprisingly, local nicknames for dengue often translate to "break-bone fever" and the like.

According to the Centers for Disease Control, up to one hundred million people contract dengue every year. Tens of thousands die. Most of those are children. No vaccine has ever been developed. Nor is there even a recognized treatment for dengue. You just ride it out, take acetaminophen for pain—aspirin or other basic anti-inflammatories are associated with increased risk of capillary leakage, internal hemorrhaging, and heart failure—drink cold water, and hang on for the ride.

There's no way to predict how hard it will hit. I'm a healthy man in my forties, and it took me weeks to fully regain my strength. A lot of people breeze through it way more easily, but some become much more ill, developing full-blown dengue hemorrhagic fever (DHF), especially after a second infection.

With a bit of bad luck, just one small second bite from an infected mosquito can cause your blood vessels to leak, your mouth to turn bloody, blood to flow into your lungs, and so on. If you're near a hospital, this can be treated easily with IV fluids and transfusions, but if you're in a rural area or a country with poor medical facilities, DHF can be deadly.

And yet if you're from North America or Western Europe, you may never have heard of dengue. Thanks to geography, dengue is primarily a poor people's disease. *Aedes aegypti* and other mosquitoes that carry the disease didn't thrive outside of tropical latitudes until recently, so its victims were mostly in the developing world. Big drug companies had little financial incentive to cure it. However, climate change is extending *aegypti*'s range into the southern U.S. and parts of Europe.* Perhaps not coincidentally,

---

* American cases have occurred primarily in South Texas and the Florida Keys. Several other tropical diseases are also starting to appear in the U.S., particularly in the rural Gulf Coast areas of Louisiana, Mississippi, and Alabama.

an expensive vaccine may be available by 2015, just in time for the world's wealthy nations to avoid the disease.

The developing world might receive vaccines, too, although the obstacles involved in bringing patented drugs into poor countries is worth a whole separate book. In the meantime, in Paraguay, Victor and his neighbors are pretty much on their own.

The year before Victor asked for this loan, Paraguay was overwhelmed with dengue, with at least twenty-seven thousand documented cases, and most unofficial estimates surpassing one hundred thousand. The Paraguayan government declared a national state of emergency for two months.

Victor's loan was to buy citronella and leather. His plan was to cut up the leather into bracelet-sized strips, soak them in citronella, and make them available to his neighbors so their kids were less likely to get dengue.*

Victor's entire loan request was just $200.

I was thrilled to see he'd already been fully funded.

Finally, after my visit to Bali, this next client closed the deal for me: a woodcarver named Ni Wayan in the rural west of the island was planning to repay $475 at a little more than a dollar a day, with this explanation (the translation into English was done by an Indonesian volunteer):

> Ni Wayan wants to participate in another loan program with DINARI foundation. This loan is to be used to add her working capital in her business as Sanggah maker. Sanggah is a traditional religious article in Balinese Hinduism faith . . .

Given the areas afflicted, even in America, dengue continues to be primarily a poor people's disease. For more, see Sources.

* At the time, I would have preferred Victor to use DEET, the pesticide in standard use in the U.S. But this was presumptuous of me. Citronella is proven effective against *Aedes aegypti*, and it's less toxic and cheaper. I was still learning to listen.

One Sanggah can be sold for IDR 2 million to IDR 3 million (around USD 190–USD 285) depending on the complexity of the wood carving works. In one month Ni Wayan and her husband can make one to two Sanggah. If she has more orders then she hires extra helps. From this business Ni Wayan can help the family's economy and they are also able to send their children to school.*

Ni Wayan had a workable business model, a track record of repaying previous loans, and a skill firmly rooted in local tradition—everything I could hope to support, even if she lived down the street. But Ni Wayan was in Bali. Her profits would keep her children in school. I remembered what I saw in the streets there when young people ran out of better options. There was no way I couldn't chip in on her loan.

I wasn't sure if Kiva was where all of my three-Dubai-whisky nest egg should go, necessarily. Twenty thousand dollars might still have a wide range of uses. But after reading Ni Wayan's story, I made my first Kiva loans that very night—Poung, the Victory Group, and Ni Wayan among them.

It was a tiny gesture, no bigger than sharing my burj of food in Dubai. The next day, I told my friend Jane about it, and one of us—neither of us remembers who—started joking that I had now officially opened the International Bank of Bob.†

These loans weren't made directly to Poung and the rest. They were made via microfinance institutions (MFIs)—local non-profits, banks, credit unions, and similar organizations that vet and approve clients based on their own criteria. After a due diligence process,

---

* Ni Wayan's Kiva page is at kiva.org/lend/84741.
† Jane is a Hugo Award–winning TV writer, some of whose work you may have already enjoyed. See www.imdb.com/name/nm0260870.

Kiva had chosen to partner with just over one hundred of those in forty-two countries.*

When you lend $25 through Kiva, Kiva forwards the money at zero interest to the MFI, which in turn earmarks the money for the specific clients you've chosen. When the clients repay, the money flows back to Kiva, who credits it back to your account. On first impression, it's a simple bucket-brigade—you, Kiva, MFI, client. Repayment is the reverse—client, MFI, Kiva, you.

That first impression was close, but not exactly correct. Curiously, each loan had three different dates attached to it—"Date Posted," the date it was placed online; "Expiration Date," when it would expire and be removed from the site if not fully financed (or, alternatively, "Date Funded," when it was); and, surprisingly, "Disbursal Date," which often preceded all the others by days or even weeks. One click brought this explanation:

> Each of Kiva's Field Partners operate a little differently, and while some need to wait for Kiva to wire the loan funds to them before they can disburse the loans, others have funds on hand—from savings or working capital—which they can use to front the funds before they receive the wire from Kiva . . . In some cases the Field Partner even disburses the loan before it is funded on Kiva.†

---

* These were the figures in January 2009. At press time, the current numbers are 167 Kiva partner MFIs in 65 countries. For an overview of the wider MFI universe, the MIX Market at www.mixmarket.org is a global compendium of lending and social performance data. In addition to any other specific websites mentioned in these pages, the MIX Market will have a decent thumbnail on any MFI in this book.

† Edited for length. Kiva's description of disbursal has changed slightly but not significantly since I first read this in 2009. For more, see Sources.

In other words, by clicking "Lend $25," I was often backing a loan that had already been made. I didn't mind—I'd much rather see dengue-repelling Victor in Paraguay get financed without having to wait around for somebody like me to pick up the slack. It was easy to see this was probably the only practical way Kiva could work.*

As to the money's safety, Kiva had a five-star system of risk ratings for each MFI, with each MFI's loan volume, default rate, time as a Kiva partner, and contact information all fully transparent. There also wasn't a mountain of unnecessary jargon, although if you were curious, you could find clearly written explanations for virtually anything. I liked that a lot.†

Reading online about microfinance on other sites, in profiles of Yunus, and in news reports, I saw that some of its supporters were praising it almost as a one-size-fits-all "solution to poverty." This seemed a bit over-the-top. Poverty has a *lot* of causes—war, natural disaster, resource depletion, bad governance and corruption, exploitation, and so on. Tiny loans to poor people rarely address these in any obvious way.

Then again, one huge cause of poverty is simply the *cycle* of poverty itself. To take just one issue as an example: poverty often leads to a lack of education. Without education, *everything* is harder—from raising income to solving resource shortages to fighting for better political and working conditions to conflict resolution with others. Breaking the cycle of poverty, therefore, would help make everything else more addressable. Microfinance wouldn't stop wars, end corruption, and create political equality, but if it could put food on the table and get the kids into school,

---

* Later in 2009, pre-disbursals briefly flared as an alleged transparency issue when David Roodman of the Center for Global Development blogged about it under the broad headline "Kiva Is Not Quite What It Seems." See Sources.
† I've tried to avoid jargon myself despite all the political and economic stuff here. A few terms were inevitable. Please hang on and forgive. Jargon should have its own tab on Google Translate.

their kids should have a much better chance with the rest. Giving the working poor better tools for planning and thinking about the future might even break a cycle of despair, regardless of financial outcome. There might be no way to measure any of this with numbers in my lifetime, but it seemed obviously possible.

I was in. I wouldn't make a penny of interest, and my account would eventually lose a few bucks when a loan here or there defaulted. But if the money got into the right hands, did good for people, and then got paid back without causing stress to the clients, fair enough.

Becoming a Kiva lender also means setting up an online profile. Since the clients have pictures on public display, it seemed only fair to post my own, but you can include only as much information as you're comfortable with. Many lenders remain anonymous by posting a photo of an abstract, a favorite location, or a pet.

These pictures of non-humans, I would later learn, can lead to unexpected questions if the page is viewed in the field by a client unfamiliar with the Internet. To wit, in a story I hope is apocryphal: *Why do I have to repay this cat?*

Kiva has no plans to change the rules, preferring that clients, MFIs, and borrowers retain the freedom to find their own comfort zones. Let's just hope nobody using a pig for their profile makes a whole bunch of loans to Muslim clients.

At the time, Kiva already had partners in countries on five continents. I was disappointed, however, to find that India wasn't included yet.

My goal after Dubai was to help the economies where those indentured servants had come from—Nepal, the Philippines, East Africa, and most of all, India. Kiva had partner MFIs in forty-two countries, but not the one I was looking for.

Looking for a way to lend to Kerala, in honor of the Indian men in Dubai, I poked and prodded the Internet for a few hours. It turned out there were at least a dozen Kiva-like platforms to consider.

All of them presented problems. One based in Paris closely replicated the Kiva platform, but setting up an account from America required a bank transfer of funds. Another lent only into China, but you could never withdraw your money, and after your money was lent and repaid a few times, your investment became a donation. Even if you knew you'd never need the money, you'd eventually lose any input as to how it would be used.

Other websites appealed to the profit motive, offering a token amount of interest on my investments. Funds wouldn't be tracked to or from individual clients. Instead, they would be pooled into certificate-of-deposit-like notes to be issued and paid off by MFIs. This practice—called *securitization*, since the loans are turned into sellable securities—didn't quite feel right to me. Would I *really* want to pocket 2-percent interest that might ultimately come out of the pocket of a Guatemalan fisherman? I couldn't see how I could sleep at night. I don't *want* to profit from these loans.

My doubts only grew when I found that these websites were operated as for-profit enterprises. I could imagine a half-dozen possible complications. Granted, a whiff of profit might attract greater amounts of capital to developing-world projects. In fact, a sufficient profit to remain in business may arguably be necessary to make services sustainable long-term. But there's an equally obvious argument—and to my mind, a moral one—that consciously *seeking* to profit from financial aid to the world's poorest people might not be the most noble of enterprises. The balance of mixed motivations could easily fall out of whack. I moved on.

Finally, I came across RangDe.org, headquartered in Chennai. *India! At last.* Rang De (Hindi for "share the colors") was essentially a Kiva clone entirely focused on India, a microlending platform just

for Indians to help other Indians.* Clients were searchable by Indian state—including Kerala, where so many workers in Dubai
were from—with client profiles and photographs as detailed and
personal as at Kiva itself.

I immediately opened an account and made four loans. None
were available in Kerala that evening, but the first loan I financed
was to an incense-stick maker and mother of three named Geetha
in Maharashtra. Credit card, point, click, hurray.

After these first four loans, I took a moment to read Rang De's
fine print and discovered that India has strict laws about the entry
and exit of money, and Rang De was intended solely for Indians to
lend to other Indians. A Westerner like me was never meant to be
involved. That's why I couldn't find any loans to India on other
sites. Now I just hoped I hadn't caused Rang De any trouble.

Kiva it was, then.

I found myself looking back over the loans I'd already made
and trying to imagine the lives on the other end. I wondered
what Poung's trees must be like to shinny up and down all day in
Cambodia, what Esther's shop supplies might look like in Uganda,
and how the rest of her Victory Group might be doing. Having
just gone round-the-world for *Forbes Traveler*—and having just
visited Bali, where Ni Wayan was from—none of them even
seemed all that far away.

I toyed again with the idea of trying to visit some Kiva loan recipients, to see if the loans actually worked. Maybe I could even
find some of my own clients. After looking into so many tired faces
in Dubai, Singapore, Bali, and elsewhere, this seemed infinitely
more rewarding than any other work I could think of.

It seemed like an impossible idea.

---

* Rang De's website is www.rangde.org. Even if you're not in India and can't legally make a loan, it's fascinating to read nonetheless. The name is a patriotic
reference to martyred Indian revolutionary heroes, akin to the American story
of Nathan Hale.

When Jessica Jackley stepped quietly onstage at the USC business school, Kiva had recently received praise from Oprah, President Clinton, *Time*, *Fortune*, the *Economist*, and dozens of other influential figures and media outlets. Most people associated with that sort of press might carry an attitude. But Jessica smiled easily, listened intently, and could have been mistaken for a particularly respectful grad student, were she not the focus of a hundred particularly respectful grad students at that moment, all of them eager to hear how Kiva had become such a success.*

Kiva's own start-up story is as compelling as those of its clients. In June 2003, Jessica and her then-fiancé Matt Flannery attended a talk at Stanford Business School. At the time, Matt worked as a software engineer at TiVo, but he was much more interested in creating a new venture of his own. Jessica, meanwhile, was a school staff member fascinated with what had recently become known as "social entrepreneurship"—the use of business practices to create positive change.

The speaker that night was Muhammad Yunus.†

---

* From here on, you'll notice I've dropped the journalistic pretense of calling Jessica or Matt by their surnames. I like these people, we've become social acquaintances at a minimum, and it just feels dishonest to call them anything else. Likewise, you'll see me call Premal Shah "Premal" instead of "Shah" and so on. This is in fairness to you as a reader. I'll write about Kiva, microfinance, and what I saw in the field as honestly and objectively as I can, I promise, and you'll decide whether this book is a fair report regardless of which name I call anyone. But I'm not a Washington or Wall Street correspondent who plays tennis on weekends with the people he's supposed to be covering, then pretends to be objective on weekdays. That's just dishonest. I know and like these people socially now, and it feels only fair and honest to you to say so.

† Matt describes the origin of Kiva in much greater detail, and very much as you'd hear it from his own mouth, in "Kiva and the Birth of Person-to-Person Microfinance," published in 2007 by *Innovations*, an online magazine at MIT. See Sources.

Six months later, Jessica was in East Africa, working for a non-profit to help them evaluate the social impact of small businesses. She soon realized that business principles taught in Western textbooks are practiced widely as a simple matter of common sense. To a fruit seller outside Nairobi, for example, testing new selections, focusing on the most profitable products, timing purchases of stock to seasons and shelf life, and generating word-of-mouth didn't need buzzwords like Focus Grouping, Core Competency, Just-In-Time Inventory, and Evangelizing. What works, works.

When Matt came to visit, even as a relative newcomer, he observed the same thing—and that one of the greatest barriers for people trying to improve their lives was the difficulty in accessing capital. Local entrepreneurs had no shortage of workable ideas for new businesses; they simply lacked start-up funds. Matt and Jessica began filling their long bus rides across Kenya and Tanzania with discussions of the problem, and when Matt returned home, he set about creating an online solution.

Drawing on his software engineering skills and the expertise of friends, Matt began spending all of his free time writing code for a lending platform. This usually meant working until two or three in the morning, then perhaps grabbing four or five hours of sleep before reporting for his full-time job. This continued for months on end. "Almost the first two years of Kiva, I was also working at TiVo," Matt told me in a later interview. The entire original architecture—the software, the database, the user interfaces for lenders and MFIs, and more—came out of Matt's many long nights.

"That was my fundraising strategy, too: to work [at TiVo] and make money, so I could do this." Matt laughed when he said so, but he wasn't kidding. Kiva's model was almost completely new: Kiva predates Indiegogo, Kickstarter, and virtually every other crowdfunding site, most by several years, and while other online lending platforms were in their early stages, none had attempted anything so specific and personal. As a result, investors doubted Kiva's ability to scale up successfully, and even banks were reluctant to get involved. "I had this period where I would go into banks, and apply for a business banking account," Matt said. "And they would kind of go into the back room to do the compliance part, and it would all get . . . very . . . *slow* . . ."

Matt had to laugh at the irony: His attempts to serve people with no access to banking had no access to banking. When the site first went online, the first loan funds were moved through Matt's personal checking account.

Even the marketing was homebrew: Matt chose the name "Kiva" himself with no market research, simply using an English-to-Swahili dictionary to choose something short, percussive, and punchy like "TiVo."* Matt paid for the logo with his electric guitar.

The very first Kiva loans, arranged in October 2005, were for seven small businesses in Tororo, Uganda, a town of about 43,000 people near the Kenyan border. A Ugandan pastor named Moses Onyango served as the local organizer, supervised by Matt himself over long middle-of-the-night phone calls to Africa. When the site was ready, Matt and Jessica sent an e-mail announcing the loans to about three hundred people on their wedding invitation list.

All seven clients were funded in the first weekend. Kiva was on its way.†

From the start, Kiva also adopted an attitude that the site wasn't really theirs, exactly, but shared with the user community—an idea that Matt, Premal, and Jessica have all often pointed to as essential to Kiva's success. "When you give people a sense of ownership,

---

* *Kiva* is Swahili for "trade" or "agreement," although it's not a particularly common word. Unintentionally, *Kiva* also means "fun" in Finnish, it specifies a religious site in Pueblo tradition, and it's a homonym for "here goes!" in Italian. Depending on the user's attitude, these meanings may be just as valid.

† For more on Kiva's first years—including a forthright recounting of having to deal with a few early cases of overseas fraud before developing sufficient resources for full due diligence, and the steps taken since to assure partner accountability— see "Kiva at Four," Matt's follow-up 2009 article for *Innovations*, in Sources.

actually listening and making changes and valuing their input, then you get a kind of loyalty and word-of-mouth you just can't get any other way," Jessica told the USC crowd.*

Jessica would live up to those words the first time we had lunch.

"It's a real challenge, getting people to see the rest of the world not as faraway or exotic, but just"—and here Jessica sought the right words—"well, *the rest of the world.* Our neighbors."

Jessica was still readjusting to California after some field work in Nicaragua. I'd given her my card at USC and asked for an interview, and despite her fatigue, she'd made time for me, arriving again with the appearance of a casual grad student and a dozen apologies for being five minutes late. The moment the subject turned to micro-lending, however, Jessica instantly became focused and passionate, a fountain of information, ideas, and encouragement.

I told her about Dubai, Singapore, my dad, and my reasons for needing my good fortune to count. Then I broached the idea of possibly following my loans into the field, meeting clients I'd personally invested in, and writing about it.

"Oh, you *have* to do it," Jessica said, with a certainty that surprised me. But she then recited back to me all the reasons that I was appropriate for the task: I'd already been around the world, and was familiar with being alone abroad for extended periods; I'd grown up working class, so I was sympathetic to the clients; I also had a small nest egg to invest that could become emergency savings if needed; and I was able to make a living as an independent writer, free of other responsibilities. "You're probably exactly the person who should."

This lived up to Kiva's give-people-a-stake ethos more than I'd even hoped for.

---

* Matt said much the same thing to me in our first conversation. See Chapter Nine.

Visiting clients all over the world would take money, of course, for travel and hotels and multiple whatnot.* More money than a magazine article could ever pay.

A book, then. This book. I'd written a few before. None of them had really required me to leave my chair, much less go roaming around the developing world, but Jessica's instant confidence had me willing to try.

A few weeks later, I was in New York's famously wedge-shaped Flatiron Building, meeting an editor whose desk is in the narrowest point of the wedge, his chair placing him at a cinematic vanishing point overlooking Broadway.

Paraphrasing slightly: handshake, *yes,* advance, *don't get dengue again, thanks, I'll be careful, do you know how much your office looks like an optical illusion? Seriously, watch the dengue, if you bleed into your lungs or something I might lose my advance, okay, I'll try not to bleed into my lungs, no worries, okay, good luck.*

Now the travel was paid for. This was going to happen.

As I stepped out of the Flatiron Building into the streets of New York, I had no real idea what would come next.

Yes, and.

---

* To conserve cash and keep my lending funds intact, I would eventually redeem virtually all of the frequent flier miles I'd amassed in my life, including a large pile from the *Forbes Traveler* writing. Also, some airline credit cards offer up to 50,000 miles just for signing up and paying an annual fee. I must have burned a half-dozen of those (not to mention my credit score), making it possible to traverse oceans for fares comparable to an airport taxi ride. I also took advantage of overseas discount airlines, which range from terrific to terrifying, and traveled with only a small carry-on backpack and my camera bag, avoiding all sorts of fees and hassles. For more, see www.bobharris.com/bank-of-bob/travel-suggestions.

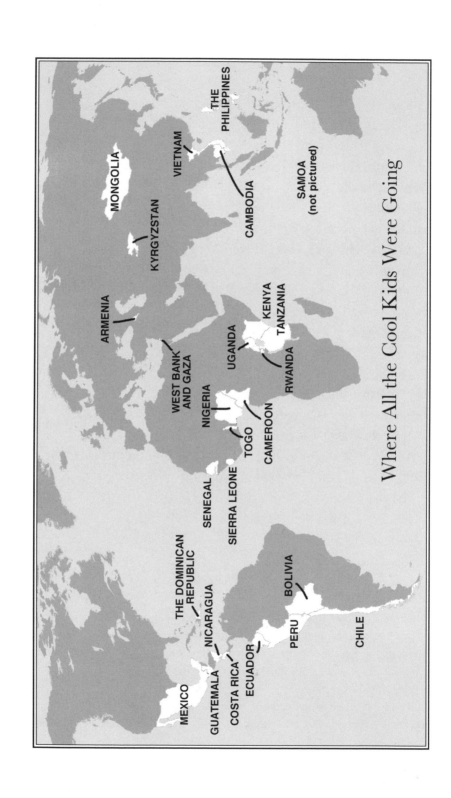

Where All the Cool Kids Were Going

CHAPTER FOUR

THE MISSION

IMAGINE SITTING IN a room with fifty-two strangers. All of you are meeting for the first time. Everyone's one-sentence bio has been put on a sheet of paper and distributed to the entire room. The bios all read like this:

- Created the first women's soccer league in the Kibera slum of Nairobi, Kenya.
- A developer of rich media advertising products for Google who speaks Spanish, Mandarin, and Gujarati.
- Served with European Union peacekeeping forces in Chad and the Central African Republic before working for the Finnish Ministry of Foreign Affairs in Tunisia.
- Recipient of a $10,000 K. W. Davis Projects for Peace Award to carry out HIV prevention and other public health work in Senegal.
- Freaked out in Dubai after drinking cat-poop coffee as expensive as the services of a Central Asian streetwalker.

Okay, the last one was me. I mostly kept to myself.

This was their first day of training as the ninth class of Kiva Fellows, soon to be dispatched around the world to give three months of their lives to help MFIs make loans to the working poor. The fifty-two bright faces around me were all smiling and excited, despite the fact we were crammed into a meeting area that would comfortably seat thirty, all on an unseasonably warm day in the Mission district of San Francisco. This was the biggest space available at Kiva's modest headquarters, so everyone smiled, munched on bagels and water, and made the best of it.

I sat in the back, scribbling notes and trying not to sweat on anything electric.

At the front of the room, armed with an overhead projector, a decade of experience in helping the developing world develop, and an urgent need to upload all that knowledge into fifty-two skulls in less than a week, stood JD Bergeron, head of the Kiva Fellows program.

The Fellows in his charge were all nervous energy, eager to take on the world, or at least help a small chunk of it. They'd gone through a long application process, winning the right to volunteer over hundreds of other candidates, and now they were on the edge of fifty-two separate grand adventures, all while trying to do good for others. Their work and their love might soon be as closely connected as possible.

Some Fellows were stepping completely into the unknown. While most had received assignments in cultures with which they were familiar, a few were going to start the following Monday in countries they'd never seen in their lives. A young woman whose nametag read "Mexico" seemed confident. The guy wearing "Kyrgyzstan" did not. A few Fellows still had no idea where they were going—JD had needed to juggle accepted applications with MFI availabilities, so a few nametags said things like "French West Africa (TBD)." But no one gave off the slightest doubt, fear, or reluctance. The room fairly vibrated with tomorrows and nerves. It was a cross between college orientation and the night before the Normandy landing.

I was included because Jessica had made some introductions, and JD and Kiva had decided this training was the first thing I should see for several reasons. Fellows are the glue connecting clients, lenders, MFIs, and Kiva itself: a typical Fellow files reports to Kiva from the field, trains MFI staff in uploading profiles to the website, adds new information about clients so lenders can stay updated, contributes to Kiva's "Stories from the Field" blog, and more.* Their introduction to Kiva's operations would be a good one for me as well. Also, a few aspects of their training might apply to my own trips abroad, and meeting a few Fellows might facilitate my own contacts in the field.†

JD's first task was to apologize that Kiva president Premal Shah, whom I'd seen speaking a year earlier, couldn't welcome the Fellows in person yet. Premal was occupied that morning, consulting with Secretary of State Hillary Clinton's team about Kiva's rela-

---

*The "Stories from the Field" blog, focusing on the activities of the Kiva Fellows, is at fellowsblog.kiva.org.

†For the record, while I made numerous field contacts with no outside help—Kiva had no partners in Morocco or India when I visited, for example—there were also many cases, such as Lebanon, where it seemed particularly wise to ask Kiva's MFI-relations people to provide e-mail introductions to local MFIs. After some initial reluctance, Kiva became increasingly willing to do so once I'd been in the field for a while and it was clear that I was respectful of the clients' well-being and sometimes precarious livelihoods. Their generosity making in these e-mail introductions is greatly appreciated, but it should not be confused with influence. After those introductions, Kiva had zero influence over anything that followed in the field, no role in choosing which clients I would meet, and no input in my subjects or conclusions here—just a final basic fact-check after the book's manuscript was in copyediting, just before publication. In short, they've had only slightly more input on this book than you have.

tionship with MFIs in the Palestinian Territories. This seemed like a decent excuse.

JD's second task seemed to be to wipe out every expectation of fun.

"Every Fellow says that this training was their favorite part of the process," he announced early, to a room that didn't want to believe him yet. "It's all downhill from here." I've come to doubt it was conscious or intentional, but JD looked directly at me now. "You honestly may have no idea what you're getting into. Part of my job is to prepare you for that."

This shaved just a teensy edge off of the excitement.

"The number of things that are about to change in your lives may surprise you," JD continued. "How many of you are joggers, for example?" About a dozen hands went up. "Probably not anymore. Think of where you're going. You may have traffic, street crime, or pollution. Or if you're in a rural area, think of rabies. Wild dogs consider someone running to be *prey*. People just don't jog in a lot of the world. It can be terribly dangerous."

The room settled in. Still eager, but not quite buzzing as before.

"How many of you expect to be working in another language?" JD asked. About two-thirds of the hands went up. "Those of you with your hands not in the air—you're wrong. Trust me. Communication will often be your biggest challenge."*

JD was giving the opposite of a pep talk. "Some of you are going to countries where the police shake people down, where you'll be charged double or triple just because you're a foreigner, where the heat and the weather can have health implications, where your religious practice, or your lack thereof, is something you'll definitely need to keep to yourself, or where those of you who are

---

*For my own language needs, I eventually found Bouchra in Morocco and nearly every translator mentioned here via www.translatorscafe.com, often on short notice. Highly recommended.

women may not even feel normal walking down the street because of different customs and perceptions."

JD slowed for emphasis. "A lot of you will be in places where the mosquitoes are intense. Some of you might come home with malaria. Probably at least one or two of you. We've had it happen several times."

The Fellows and I would also need to be careful with dengue. In my case, having already been infected once, any trip to the tropics—home to about two-thirds of humankind—would require a good look at outbreak reports, altitudes (dengue mosquitoes can't thrive above about 7,000 feet), weather patterns (mosquito populations fluctuate subsequent to rainy and dry periods), and local medical facilities.

JD went on. "Many of you will be going to places where there are active State Department Travel Warnings, places American citizens are discouraged from setting foot in." JD let this sink in. "Now, we wouldn't send you there if we thought you couldn't handle it and come home okay. But the dangers are real, and we will need you to keep your eyes open to stay safe."*

The Fellows were quiet now, determination and focus replacing the last vestige of giddiness. JD's smile had softened, turning compassionate and encouraging despite the difficult words, like a doctor delivering bad news to a patient.

"I promise you—I *promise* you—you're going to get three weeks

---

* More than half of the countries visited from here on have been the subject of recent U.S. State Department Travel Warnings. Notice that it never comes up. With a bit of research, contacts arranged in advance, and a decent eye on the headlines, I never worried. There are maybe two dozen countries, tops, that I wouldn't currently visit without a Kevlar muumuu and a functional panic button—predictably, Iraq, Afghanistan, Somalia, Pakistan, North Korea, and so on. But those are a tiny fraction of our spinning blue ball, which is generally far safer than the news makes it seem.

or six weeks into this and think this was the single worst decision of your entire lives. You're going to *hate* it."

I thought this was probably true. In describing this meeting room at Kiva in the Mission district of San Francisco, I would not have to specify that we all enjoyed a steady electrical supply, a bathroom down the hall with potable water, a distinct lack of malaria, yellow fever, or dengue, and little imminent threat of dictatorship or civil war. We can assume all of that here. But even after thousands of years of civilization, of the 193 member states of the United Nations, at least one of those assumptions would still be generally untrue in large swaths of at least 130—even with human health, sanitation, and technology at all-time highs.

"It won't be long—you're going to call your families and boyfriends and wives and say you've made a terrible mistake," JD continued. "I see some of you with smiles on your faces, like you think that won't be you. But trust me. It will be."

The room was silent. But I looked around carefully. Not one person was flinching.

"Trust me," he added. "This is really going to suck."

I was reminded of the wizened mentor character in so many boxing or fantasy films, the one who trains talented recruits by breaking down their habits and emotional armor before building new, better heroes. There was a lot in common. Wizened mentors often have beards. So did JD. Wizened mentors have learned from hard experience. JD had volunteered for the Peace Corps and had worked in rural Bulgaria, Mongolia, and Colombia. Wizened mentors offer helpful aphorisms that reveal the nature of the entire struggle to come:

Yoda from *Star Wars*: "Do, or do not—there is no try."

Morpheus from *The Matrix*: "I didn't say it would be easy, Neo—I only said it would be the truth."

JD from Kiva: "Trust me—this is really going to suck."

I almost laughed out loud when he said that, but only from my nervous reaction to its likely truth.

Then, finally—mercifully—JD added, "But you'll adjust, you'll find people you enjoy, you'll know the work means a lot, and by the end, you'll be happy and proud you stuck it out. Almost everyone comes home convinced it was one of the best and most important experiences of their life."

Several of the Fellows audibly exhaled.

After JD outlined the upcoming week's training—every Fellow would have to learn how to function as a liaison, language translator, cultural interpreter, tech support representative, writer, photographer and videographer for the website, and more—Premal finally arrived to greet the Fellows. He and Mrs. Clinton's team had apparently straightened out whatever was troubling Palestinian MFIs in less than an hour.

Premal spoke humbly of his appreciation for the Fellows' three-month commitments, his reassuring tone soothing any residual stress. He then big-pictured the Fellows' contributions with numbers about Kiva's rapid growth: at that point, Kiva had facilitated more than $91 million in loans, and in terms of online traffic, Kiva had more visitors than the Red Cross. This is what the Fellows were making possible, he emphasized. The Fellows spontaneously applauded. Premal smiled broadly if a little shyly, thanked the group modestly, then departed in a rush, presumably to make peace between the two Koreas while calming a panicky squirrel.

The group was given an hour to grab lunch.

The hallways and break room became a clatter of BlackBerrys and iPhones, all last-minute arrangements and things-to-do-befores. There were newspapers to stop, pets to have cared for, and loved ones to talk through the nerves and goodbyes.

Sheethal was headed to Peru, leaving behind a husband in New York. Rebecca was off to Tanzania, where she would also attend grad school in Dar es Salaam. Kimia was going to Ecuador after studying rural clinics in Chile. I envied all fifty-two people, about to be sent all over parts of the world I couldn't yet imagine. I hoped I might see one or two more again, and that my own travels would be nearly as rewarding.

Then again, I had no real idea yet where I was going. Over the previous months, I'd inched about half of my nest egg into loans going to more than forty countries, and MFIs that weren't partnered with Kiva were active in another hundred countries or so. I could have been wearing a nametag that said "Earth (TBD)."

I also had no idea how I'd ever find any of my clients. Kiva wasn't facilitating that, obviously. As JD himself had said to me—twice, to be sure I would see the point—MFIs aren't travel agencies. They're small lenders with an overwhelming number of potential clients and never enough resources to serve them all. They have no time to hand-hold a journalist who isn't fully prepared. I'd have to tread quickly and lightly and listen as hard as I could when anyone finally spoke. In retrospect, I confirm: *always* listen to your wizened mentor.

There was nothing to do now but pick a country and an MFI, kinda throw myself in, and see what I might find.

Okay then. Deep breath.

Time to go.

But first, a quick chat in the taxi as we head to the airport:

Kiva's mission statement is "to connect people through lending to alleviate poverty." If you look closely at that phrase, you'll see lending as only a means between two real goals—connecting people and alleviating poverty.

That should sound familiar: my own goals in Dubai were to find a way to connect to people and try to find something that works. If duct tape had seemed like a great way to connect people and alleviate poverty, this book might have been about duct tape. So as I said earlier, this book isn't about microlending, exactly, but about connecting people and alleviating poverty, about whether and how microfinance accomplishes those goals, and about the people I've met along the way.

I've structured all this as a memoir because the clients' tales are inherently small and personal. There are already plenty of texts with facts and figures and pie charts delving into the workings of microlending. Few of these capture the individual lives, risks, and futures involved in simple human terms. My hope is that you'll see these people and their villages and cities and workplaces and kids more clearly through my eyes than you might have otherwise. I hope you'll see each chapter like a panoramic snapshot, putting the clients and MFI people we meet into the bigger economic and political picture around them at the time, finding whatever lessons there may be.

But while I'm your narrator, and I do learn things and have experiences along the way that I hope you'll enjoy sharing, please don't see me as a dramatic protagonist. When you think about how and why the people we'll meet work as hard as they do, *they're* the heroes. I'm just telling you about it. They're Holmes. I'm Watson.*

Let's be careful about expectations. We're talking, after all, about a middle-class white American traveling the developing world. Too many stories like this—books, TV shows, movies, news reports, you name it—tend to treat non-white people as merely an eye-catching backdrop for the personal growth of the Westerner seeking a truer self in the faraway land. It's so common that on some level, if you've come this far, you might be expecting something similar from here on, too, especially since this trip began when I had a change of heart in Dubai.

If you look closely, many Westerner-abroad tales are actually

---

* Incidentally, I'm braced for claims of "poverty tourism" from people who perhaps misunderstand the phrase. Popping into Soweto or Kibera to tweet an iPhone self-portrait is pure ick. This is the polar opposite: investing-in-people-and-listening-to-their-stories-to-share-them-so-other-people-will-invest-and-make-the-planet-better tourism, if you must. I hope this is abundantly clear.

the same story. Considering films alone: beautifully made as they are, in works as seemingly different as *Dances with Wolves, Avatar, The Last Samurai, Ferngully,* and many others, our hero joins up with exotic strangers in conflict with the West; he gradually comes to appreciate their humanity while realizing the inhumanity of his own culture; and eventually, he becomes *their* hero, his redeeming transformation ultimately aiding his new allies as they fight to save their world.

The standard narrative feels generous and respectful, even subversive—but only if you don't notice that the colonized are *still* being led around by a white dude. Meanwhile, everyone else's own histories, joys, losses, and hopes, whatever they might be, remain subplots or untold.

What follows here is more about everyone else's own histories, joys, losses, and hopes, at least as far as some white guy from Ohio can manage to learn them while traveling, then share them and put them into a meaningful context.* You'll get my reactions and experiences along the way, because I want you to feel like you're actually there, too, but *they're* the important folks here, not me.

The conventional narrative also carries a dangerously false message: that even though the developing world's people may be physically poorer than Westerners, they are inherently purer, wiser, or richer in spirit. That's just reverse racism, a self-serving denial of the birth lottery. Indigenous and traditional cultures deserve full respect and appreciation, of course. But to overdo it into Noble Savage mythology just lets relatively wealthy folks off the hook: we get to learn from poorer people, *and* we don't have to worry

---

* I used the word *white* here advisedly. I grew up in a suburb of Cleveland that the 2000 federal census listed as 97.3 percent European-American. As far as I can determine, this ranked my hometown as the whitest city with a population above 50,000 in the entire United States. Where I'm from, Santa Claus would look ethnic.

because they have a *different* kind of wealth. In the end, it's basically a break-even between being (a) born in or (b) named Chad. We even get to feel more enlightened just because we reached out.*

But the truth is much simpler: poverty sucks, no matter how ancient and rich anybody's culture might be. Poverty is heartbreaking and cruel and unjust. And people in rough circumstances who are striving so hard for better lives can be so much like you and me that to see it all clearly can make your empathy gland swell up until you feel like you can't breathe.

That sense of overwhelm is precisely what racism and reverse-racism exist to protect us from.

Screw that. Let's just try to see the world as it is. If that means overwhelm now and again—and it does—bring it.

So: expect me to stress out, laugh, be surprised, and occasionally learn things. Don't expect me to have some huge character arc, lead a peasant revolt, and come home with my hair in a braid, speaking a clicking language with my one true love. And please don't wait for my wise exotic sidekick—Bagger Vance, John Coffey, Don Juan Matus, Mr. Miyagi—to show up along the way, sharing earthy intuitive magic healing powers and inscrutable

---

* That said, if this book is adapted into a Hollywood movie, these caveats will likely be ignored. The film will probably portray me as a social outcast expelled into a savage wild, where I will be saved and inspired by the purity of the natives. One man in particular, probably a warrior, will hate me, then grow to see us as brothers. He will die to save my life so I can save his village, bequeathing me his headdress, moccasins, or amulet. His sister will be impossibly hot and unobtainable at first, but she will eventually become my feisty but affectionate wife. With her help, and using the knowledge gained in my transition to native enlightenment, I will defeat my home world, although its leader may survive to be the bad guy in the sequel. They will also cast the whitest actor imaginable to play me, assuming they don't just hire a man-sized pile of Cool Whip. This, at least, will be almost accurate. I gotta get to the gym.

truths.* The truth is plenty scrutable: when we meet good folks in hard situations, romanticizing them does no damn good. Simple listening skills will do just fine.

And so the second act of this story begins: Were my microloans really doing the good that I hoped? Would I be able to connect with the clients on a personal level? It was time to find out.

---

* Speaking of Don Juan Matus: if you've read Carlos Castaneda's stuff, by pure coincidence I wrote some of this very chapter in a Coffee Bean around the corner from the suburban home that he turned into the tree-enclosed compound for his New Age mini-cult. It's right behind a Walgreens parking lot. Mystical and transformative.

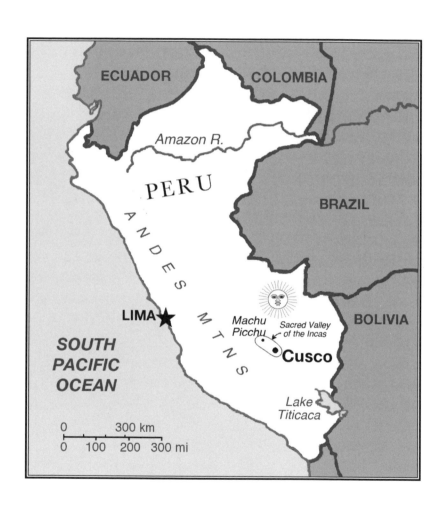

CHAPTER FIVE

THE SACRED VALLEY OF THE INCAS

IRENE HAS HER hand on my leg.*

I had hoped that on my first visit to clients in Peru, I might be lucky enough to receive a friendly response.

It's my thigh, to be more specific. Her hand is on my left thigh. About halfway between my knee and the more interesting bits.

Irene sure is friendly.

I'm unaccustomed to women I've just met putting their hands anywhere on my body quite this insistently, even back home in Los Angeles, where morality rarely even gets an audition. But here I am, in a living room on the fourth floor of a six-story cement housing project on the outskirts of Cusco, and there it is. Hand, leg. Hello, Irene.

I'm really not sure how to react. Especially since Irene and I are hardly alone. We're sitting with nine other people in the largest room of a small apartment, with a TV on one side and a kitchen at the other—all of us in a circle, facing each other. Most of the others are members of Agua Buena, a group of eleven friends who have joined together to borrow seed money for their businesses from Asociación Arariwa, the MFI I'm visiting here in Cusco. With us

---

* "Irene" is a pseudonym. If this book reaches Peru, I see no reason to risk embarrassing anyone.

are Doris, an Arariwa loan officer, and Sheethal, one of the Kiva Fellows I'd met in San Francisco, now assigned here.

This is my first trip into the field, a nervous toe-dip, a test run. My goal for the moment is to get to know the basic operations and rhythms of a typical microlending bank, start developing a sense of how its staff communicates with clients, and generally see if, surrounded at last by people whose cultures and economic situations seem dauntingly distant from my own, I can get comfortable.

Irene seems to be doing her best with the last part. Now she is smiling at me.

I was surprised at how stressed I became when I arrived at these apartments. Back home in America, tall concrete housing projects like these—half-crumbling exterior staircases, rusting fixtures, weeds so overgrown that in some places the sidewalks were covered, graffiti on wall after wall—might be perceived as a fine backdrop for a gang war or a drug-related shootout. But that's pop culture back home.* We're in Peru. I should know better. But it's one thing to be intellectually aware that such faraway images have nothing to do with reality here. It's another to put aside a lifetime of being conditioned by American news programs, movies, and TV programs to fear places like this. My subconscious has been well trained. It was surprisingly hard to walk into an impov-

---

* Income levels and crime actually have only modest correlation, as the U.S. illustrates: despite a sluggish economy, violent crime has continued a decades-long decline. Crime actually has a dizzying array of correlating circumstances— from obvious factors like unemployment, population density, educational levels, and (perhaps most significantly) the percentage of young males in a community, to statistically real correlates like maternal smoking and hot weather. Whether any of this is *causative* is a messy question. Little about the subject seems to fit neatly with left-right ideology or pop culture assumptions in any case.

erished Peruvian apartment block and sit down in a crowded roomful of the working poor for the very first time.

How would they react? Would they resent my relative wealth as an American? Would they see my skin first and judge? Would they expect me to know things I didn't? I had no idea what sort of emotions were coming.

"Awkward over the degree of physical affection being shown" had not been on my list. But Irene clearly has her own plans.

I'm hoping Sheethal doesn't notice. I can just imagine her telling Kiva that within seconds of arrival, I seduced an Andean woman in front of the MFI representative and an entire group of borrowers.

But what should I do? Should I gently move Irene's hand away? Or would that call attention to it and seem offensive? This could just be a cultural thing. But I've had multi-year lovers who weren't this comfortably affectionate. And I've known Irene for about as long as you've been reading this chapter. You're reading my thoughts pretty much in real time here. One of which is: *shit.*

Unable to decide, I sit perfectly still, trying to act nonchalant, like my thigh is public property. Microlending is all about sharing, after all.

I'd chosen Peru as my first stop for a bunch of reasons, none of them involving my left thigh.

Microfinance has a long history here. John Hatch, founder of the Foundation for International Community Assistance (FINCA, also a Spanish word for "farm"), gained his first valuable experiences in Peru. Hatch eventually pioneered the practice of what he dubbed "village banking," a system that brings together perhaps twenty members of a community, usually women, to self-administer what amounts to a tiny branch of a central MFI. The MFI can thus back numerous village banks, which in turn can offer simple savings and small loans with lower interest to the client and lower costs for the bank than any available alternative. Village bank loans require no collateral, since the members essentially co-sign for each other as a group, which also creates a mutual support system. When Hatch first tried the system in Bolivia, hundreds of villages signed up in just the first few weeks.

Three decades later, FINCA now works in more than twenty countries, its repayment rate hovers around 97 percent despite working in many of the world's poorest areas, and its model has been replicated in at least seventy more countries, including Peru, which now has one of the most developed microfinance infrastructures in the world. As a result, I'd have a great chance of meeting experienced people who could provide useful guidance.

I'd also needed to choose an urban environment to minimize any imposition on the local lender. I couldn't expect an MFI to worry about whether I could find their office or where I would sleep. Cusco was perfect—as the jumping-off point for tourism in the Urubamba Valley and Machu Picchu, this ancient capital of the Incas had grown to roughly the size of Cleveland.

Even better, the local Kiva partner, Arariwa, had served more than fourteen thousand low-income entrepreneurs over a wide swath of southeastern Peru, with a strong emphasis on lending to women and providing education services to every client. I'd lent to about two dozen Arariwa clients, and Sheethal was about six weeks into her assignment here.

Best of all, despite its tropical location, Cusco is one of the highest cities in the world, sporting an altitude more than twice that of Denver.* Dengue mosquitoes can't survive at that height. I wouldn't

---

* Cusco is 1,152 feet higher than Apple's listed maximum operating altitude for the MacBook I'm writing this on. *That's* how high Cusco is—component manufacturers worry that the thinness of the air can interfere with cooling, make the hard drive spin out of control, or allow the CPU to be wrecked by cosmic rays. (Cusqueños still use laptops all the time, no problemo, the same

have to worry about a second dengue infection and bleeding into my lungs. *Bonus.*

Irene's hand was still attached to my thigh.

Irene was dressed head-to-toe in traditional Andean female garb—braided hair, a soft shoulder cloth over her sweater, a simple *pollera* skirt—and she'd smiled sweetly at the sight of me when I first arrived. I'd returned the smile, just trying to be friendly, grateful to be welcomed. When I sat down to observe Doris and her clients, Irene sat down next to me, and she had bonded with my left thigh as if mind-melding with my femur.

Fortunately, no one had noticed. Instead, after a bit of socializing—which seems to be one of the major side benefits of group loans—everyone was focused on the free hour of financial instruction being given by Doris, Arariwa's loan officer. This regular class with Doris—who would also collect payments, update ledgers, answer concerns, make financial suggestions, and otherwise address every banking need of the group—was why eleven people were jammed shoulder-to-shoulder into a tight circle between fluorescent lights and a checkered linoleum floor.

The walk to Arariwa's office had been a stroll through local history. Spanish colonial buildings near Cusco's center were built directly upon Inca foundations. Look up, and it's all rounded archways and baroque façades, but at street level, ten-ton stones interlock in jigsaws so perfect that in many places you can't slide an index card in between, despite centuries of earthquakes so frequent that one version of Jesus here is El Señor de los Temblores, the

---

way that eating an expired box of cereal doesn't always make you sick. But still. Gives you a sense of altitude.)

Lord of the Earthquakes.* It's as vivid a metaphor for colonialism as may exist: the European finery rises directly atop the Incan foundation.

Further on, the streets and buildings became newer, reflecting Cusco's recent growth—all bustle and enterprise, much of it informal. Just up the road from Arariwa was a long line of stalls selling all manner of goods: car parts, electric bits, cell phone and camera clackery, electronic cables, thick rope. Here, a Toyota pulled up, the driver popped the trunk, and two waiting teenagers grabbed a large motor and lugged it away down the sidewalk. Twenty yards into their journey, a bicyclist nearly toppled them. Just beyond, two men hustled giant bags of potatoes into a restaurant, stepping over two yapping dogs. Everywhere, constantly, was the thrum and honk of Tico taxicabs scurrying to and fro.†

I arrived at Arariwa already convinced that the work ethic in Cusco is strong.

Arariwa is the Quechua term for a wise elder who oversees the

---

* Incidentally, this local title for Jesus may be a leftover from pre-colonial worship of an earthquake deity. New World Catholicism gradually incorporated local traditions in ways contemporary Europeans wouldn't have recognized. In Peru, the Trinity is often portrayed as equal triplets—heresy in Rome, but sensible in a polytheistic culture—coca leaves show up as a sacrament in art, and the Last Supper as portrayed in the big cathedral here includes a corn beer called *chicha* and local rodents served as meat. Mary is often portrayed in the triangular shape of a mountain, reminiscent of the Incan earth mother Pachamama, and she carries Jesus in an Andean wrapping. (Compare this to the Aztec-influenced Virgin Mary of Guadalupe, who seems to have absorbed some attributes of the local Nahua goddess Tonantzin.)

†The Daewoo Tico was a Korean subcompact built in Romania and Poland that never caught on in Western Europe, was never sold in America, and hasn't been built in ten years. Nonetheless, it has somehow become spectacularly common and popular in Peru.

harvest, the traditional means of planning for the future.* The name fits perfectly with Arariwa's work, which includes a wide variety of non-profit services—agricultural education, business training, nutritional and reproductive health counseling, the promotion of savings and financial planning, and more. Founded in 1977, they've survived some extremely violent and chaotic years in Peru (see below), and they started microlending in the early '90s, before the chaos had even subsided. Today they have four offices across the Cusco region, they conduct monthly job fairs in a downtown square, and are building strategic alliances with international funders, including Kiva.

Arariwa's headquarters is a simple space with a large outdoor waiting area just beyond large locking gates. Perhaps a dozen men and women—clients, judging from their work clothes—were doing the milling-around killing-time thing, waiting for classes and meetings. A few had children in tow. Before I could say hello—or rather, before I could make myself comfortable enough to introduce myself—Sheethal bounced downstairs, greeted me with a big smile, and gave me the nickel tour.

In a room just off the main waiting area, a client meeting was under way. Training is a large part of Arariwa's mission, and simply familiarizing potential clients with their options takes some instruction. In addition to loans, Arariwa also supports interest-bearing savings accounts through the hundreds of village banks it

---

* Quechua languages descend directly from those of the Incan Empire five centuries ago, and are currently spoken by about ten million Andean people, mostly in Ecuador, Peru, and Bolivia. Quechua bears no resemblance to any language you probably speak—"hello," for example, is *rimaykullayki*—but you use some Quechua almost every day. Granted, you may not frequently kick up your *Pumas* and enjoy a *Pisco* sour while snacking on *jerky* with *lima* beans while a *condor* drops *guano* on your *llama* carrying *quinoa* and *quinine*. (If you do, you have a cool life.) But anytime you order *Coca*-Cola, you're speaking a little Quechua.

serves.* I was curious what sort of discussion was going on, so I leaned my head in for a look.

Instantly, the room fell silent. Two dozen heads turned and peered back at me, startled. *Oh, hey, sorry. Maybe being interrupted by a big gringo is kinda off-putting when you might just be getting comfortable here. My bad.*

Laughing gently at my awkwardness, Sheethal ushered me upstairs to meet a few of the senior staff. They were all busy for the moment, so I had a few minutes to look around. The offices were unlike any bank I'd ever set foot in. American banks consciously seek to project wealth, power, and success: Roman columns, hardwood desks, leather chairs. Here, the décor was simple, functional, with only a few local paintings and the odd potted plant.

Arariwa's services include both individual loans and the village banking model, and Agua Buena was the first of these village banks I could visit. The upside for Agua Buena would be access to funds that they couldn't qualify for individually (borrowers at the bottom typically have virtually no credit a regular bank would acknowledge), with a built-in support system, some flexibility in repayment (given that the group can cover for each other), and an interest rate far lower than they could find any other way. For the lender, group loans also keep administration costs down and minimize risk by spreading it across a large number of people.

---

* Banking regulations in most countries make it far easier to set up an institution that lends money than one that holds money for the client. As a result, microfinance has spread through the practice of lending, so much so that the general term micro*finance*, referring to any small-scale financial service, is often used to mean the much more specific micro*lending*. However, as you can imagine, the ability to save and even earn interest is often of as much use to the working poor as credit, and saving is obviously safer for the client. Fortunately, many MFIs have been successful enough that they have been able to gain licensing and expand into offering savings accounts as well. Grameen itself now has a larger savings portfolio than lending. The eventual facilitation of savings may be one of the more positive and underappreciated benefits of microlending's growth.

On the downside, however, peer pressure and existing power dynamics within groups might occasionally be exacerbated. People are people, and if things go south, some clients may suffer not just financially, but socially. Screw up a group loan, and word gets around. But if things work out—as they usually do, or Arariwa wouldn't still be growing after twenty years—the group strengthens, everybody learns from each other in their regular meetings, mutual trust and support deepens, and over time, everybody wins.

Agua Buena certainly did not lack for trust.

As the meeting began, everyone's repayments had been dropped loosely on a table near the kitchen end of the room. There was no laptop computer or high-tech accounting. Peruvian nuevo soles were just tossed on the table—clumps of banknotes with no rubber bands, no neat stacks, no real concern for whose cash was credited where. Everybody knew everybody. *The money's over there,* generally, and that seemed to be close enough.

To my American eyes, this wasn't *banking.* No, banks have surveillance cameras and security systems and guys with guns and radios to call more guys with guns and radios, plus high-tech computers and counting machines that go *fif-fif-fif-fif-fif-fif* and an electric take-a-number sign that goes *boong* when it's your turn to encounter an actual unarmed human, all on the rare occasion you're not just diddling with computerized cash machines or banking online, deploying secret codes and arcane p@55words to keep invisible but ever-looming bandits at bay.

Money crumpled on a kitchen table was weird enough. Nobody even *looking* at it, much less counting it—that was truly unusual. Also, encouraging. Instead, everyone was listening intently to Doris, who was beginning a class on how to calculate, track, and achieve financial goals.

Many microlenders offer and sometimes require basic classes in financial literacy. This is more than simple charity; it makes financial sense, since successful clients lead to a more profitable bank. Doris was therefore part banker, part teacher, and part motivational speaker. Dressed neatly in a black sweater and slacks, Doris projected competence and success without any unnecessary flashing of wealth, giving the impression of being a part of the community and yet slightly more successful, a walking aspirational example.

Given the recent massive scandals among Wall Street banks, I was charmed by the sheer George Baileyness of it all. It was striking to see that small banks could still view their clients as *customers*, with individual hopes that need nurturing, instead of just faceless revenue streams. Helping clients to believe they can succeed can be a big part of an MFI's mission.

Looking around the room, I wanted to know what sort of plans Agua Buena's members had in mind. Did they each have specific long-term goals, or were they just trying to turn a short-term profit with some borrowed cash? I was also on alert for any unhealthy group dynamics, perhaps a leader pressuring the others. But they seemed to be perfectly comfortable with each other. Just as Irene was perfectly comfortable with me.

I should mention that Irene was perhaps seventy years old.

It's hard to be sure, given my unfamiliarity with the aging effects of equatorial sunlight at 11,152 feet. Two miles of atmosphere that would filter the sun's rays at sea level are simply missing here. At noon on a clear day, the sky feels almost radioactive, and you can understand why the Incas regarded the sun as their most important god, Inti, patron deity of the entire civilization. His face still peers out from the national flags of Argentina and Uruguay, and the results of his UV power are visible in most faces you encounter.

Irene had surely spent years of her life working outdoors, and Inti had lined her face so deeply that her every expression was framed and emphasized by the creases. She might have been sixty.

Or eighty. I really couldn't tell. Asking would have been rude. Besides, we were becoming so close.

I'd met Inti myself. I'd budgeted time to acclimate to the thin air, but the urge of tourism rushed me into taking a train to see Machu Picchu, a five-hundred-year-old ruin the size of Times Square. Perched 8,000 feet high between two bullet-shaped mountains, it's so far into the Peruvian jungle that Spanish conquistadors never found it. While a few local roads exist, none connect to the rest of the country. The train, the river, and your feet are the only way in and out.

Nobody really knows how it was built. The Incas lacked a written language, the wheel, and draft animals bigger than llamas, but somehow they managed to carve and arrange a bazillion granite slabs into a city where the aqueducts still work. Nobody really knows why, either. Maybe it was a retreat for the emperor Pachacuti, a religious site, or something else now long forgotten. And as to why it was abandoned—maybe famine, war, drought, disease, or some other reason—nobody knows that, either. The only thing anyone really does know, in our century, is that it's spectacular.

Since this was the wet season, the place was surprisingly vacant. I spent a happy afternoon scrambling up and down ancient stairways nearly alone in a hot plastic raincoat, soaking myself in pure wonder. After about two hours, the sky suddenly cleared with the speed of one stiff breeze, *whoosh*, and the blue was immense. A rainbow even formed in the valley below. So I took a second lap to see it all again in the brilliant sunshine.

And then my legs suddenly felt remarkably shaky. Of course: I'd just spent four hours using a vast Incan ruin as a high-altitude StairMaster with a reduced oxygen supply, all while covered in a hot plastic raincoat. That's how beautiful Machu Picchu is: enough to make you lose common sense. Now I was dizzy, and my left eye seemed on the verge of developing an independent agenda.

I have a rule about avoiding major neurological events where there aren't even roads for an ambulance out, so I caught a bus down to the tacky tourist village at the bottom of the hill—imagine an interstate truck-stop city on a river in the Andes, if you can—found a hotel, took my temperature (102.0 and climbing), and hurled my increasingly cedar-hued body into a cold shower. Of the following twenty-four hours, my main recollections are the fetal position, bottled water, and the sound of a distant flute band serenading passers-by with the mellow hits of ABBA.

I soon recovered from the heat exhaustion, if not the music. Lesson learned: Inti is nobody to mess with.

Doris unfolded a large plastic visual aid and hung it on one wall with masking tape. It was a simple goal-setting grid, with rows labeled with the Spanish for *Personal*, *Family*, and *Business*, and columns labeled *Goal*, *When*, *Money Needed*, and *How to Pay Back*. Doris was about to lead the group through their own personal examples, using dry-erase markers and industrial-grade encouragement.

Irene wasn't paying much attention. She wasn't a client herself, but simply the mother of one of the borrowers. Besides, Irene spoke only the local form of Quechua, so she couldn't follow Doris's *presentación* if she'd wanted to. Instead, Irene looked softly around the room, yawned, gave my leg a squeeze, and smiled at me mischievously. I smiled back, not wanting to disrespect her. But my eyes darted around the room, making sure our forbidden love had remained secret.

Someday I will learn the Quechua for *your mother seems flirtatious and I feel socially awkward*.

Doris next led everyone in a goal-setting exercise, asking each client what they would do with a windfall of cash. The answers came haltingly, with long periods of silence. For good reason.

Only twenty years ago, poverty was so rife in Peru that a pair of brutal rebellions—one Maoist, one Marxist, for those keeping score—could control much of the country and terrorize the capital, at least when not fighting each other.* The government responded with its own balaclava-clad killers, and human rights violations became so widespread that in the early 1990s, the U.S. State Department travel advisory flatly told Americans to "defer all travel to Peru until further notice," using language nearly comparable to that currently used for Afghanistan.† Throw in attempted coups, forced sterilizations of at least two hundred thousand indigenous women, death squads, and an ultimate toll of perhaps seventy thousand people in the conflict, and you get a sense of the chaos.

As to the economy, anyone over the age of thirty here can remember periods of triple-digit (and even quadruple-digit) inflation. The local currency, the nuevo sol ("new sun," currently worth about three to the dollar) replaced two previous currencies, the sol and the inti, which both collapsed due to hyperinflation. When the sol fell apart, it was replaced in 1985 by the inti, worth 1,000 soles. In 1991, the same thing happened—*squared*: the nuevo sol was worth 1,000,000 inti. Considering inflation and exchange rates, if you're a Peruvian over the age of forty, you've seen your currency fall by a factor of about three hundred million.

---

*The larger of the two, the Maoist Partido Comunista de Perú, more widely known as El Sendero Luminoso ("the Shining Path") viewed—and still views, in its active remnants—violence as a positive good. Its founder rejects the notion of human rights as "bourgeois" and "imperialist," has spoken of the "quota of blood" necessary for his revolution, and casually puts the price of triumph at "a million lives." This would mean killing about 5 percent of the entire country. When polls often showed Peruvians supporting the government even at the height of repression, their alternative was even more frightening. For more, see Sources.

†Peru: State Department travel advisory of August 7, 1992. Compare this to the State Department advisory on Afghanistan, June 27, 2012: "The Department of State warns U.S. citizens against travel to Afghanistan."

Mercifully, Peru's autocratic leader successfully cracked down on the rebels, and then a massive corruption scandal forced him into exile. Both sides of the vice that had gripped the nation were suddenly gone. In the decade since, a fairly stable democracy and expanding economy have finally begun to emerge. Granted, the growth is built largely on the export of raw materials and agriculture, so the benefits accrue first to the mining and agribusiness companies and their CEOs and shareholders. But the gunfire has quieted, the economy is now one of the fastest-growing in Latin America, opportunities do exist that were unthinkable just a generation ago, and microlending is so widespread that billboards for competing MFIs are a common sight.

Given all that, the puzzled faces of Doris's clients make sense. Imagine being an adult who came of age during decades of ongoing crisis, and now your loan officer is trying to convince you that simple goal-setting and math might now help summon your own business into existence? But Doris was in full Tony Robbins mode: *Todos tenemos un sueño del futuro,* she says. *We all have a dream of the future.*

I could see in these faces what a challenge even this can be.

Clotilde Amable is Arariwa's director of education, the officer in charge of how Doris and scores of other loan officers encourage and train clients to start building those dreams. I learned right away how instinctively she believes in other people. Sheethal introduced us in Spanish, so Clotilde, who also speaks Quechua but only a little English, assumed I was fully fluent in Spanish, too. When I told her in Spanish that my ability with the language was meager and rusty (*necesita hablar conmigo como con un niño confundido*—"you need to speak with me as with a confused child"—were my exact words), and that I might need her to speak a little more slowly, Clotilde just smiled warmly and dismissed it with an encouraging wave of her hand. *Aprenderá* ("you'll learn"), she said, and then proceeded to continue speaking almost at full speed, playfully encouraging me to catch up.

I'm pretty sure that's part of how Clotilde does what she does. She wasn't being rude or oblivious. I'm sure she just sensed that I wasn't ready to push myself, so she did it for me. Thankfully, Sheethal (who speaks five languages: English, French, Spanish, Portuguese, and Kannada, the language of her youth in Bangalore) filled in when the gringo needed more than encouragement.*

Sheethal explained that I was writing a book that might raise awareness of microfinance in America. Clotilde replied with a positive *bravo*. I found this humbling to the point of discomfort. Clotilde has been working with the rural poor six days a week for nearly twenty years. I was just writing about it. She deserved all the bravos. But in the first few minutes of meeting her, this was her second example of being generous and encouraging as a first instinct. I was pleased when the conversation stretched into a second afternoon, with a friend of Sheethal's helping to translate my bad Spanish into good. And so I asked:

Change is difficult for anyone. Is it difficult to address the psychology of the poor, to get them to believe they can start or grow their business successfully?

"Oh, yes, and this is very important," Clotilde replied. "But we can. We have a lot of experience with this. *First*"—and here she paused, letting the word *first* sink in—"comes their vision of the future, and their ability to change their situation. Next comes the training. But above all"—another pause for its importance, this time with extra eye contact—"we must help them to believe

_____

* All quotes here are from my notes in English, which were a mixture of my immediate translations and Sheethal's. Any errors are mine alone. This will be the rule in interviews throughout the book.

in themselves and their group, and in their right to live a dignified life. *Then* comes work on their finances."

How do you stay motivated, after all these years, when there are so many people in need? I asked.

"We always get new ideas from working with our clients," she replied. Arariwa often holds focus groups with its customers, making sure that their programs are actually responding to their needs. This matches the respect that Kiva projects for the clients on the site, and what I felt for the guys in Dubai. "We are always learning new things, and seeing new ways to help. So of course you want to try—and when you see someone succeed, then of course you are encouraged, because you know the next woman can, too."

How did you start doing this work? Microfinance didn't exist when you were a child. Is this close to what you thought you would do, growing up?

"I always, always loved working with children," Clotilde said. "Since these are families, this work is very much the same."

I didn't really understand this last answer. Not yet.

The first client of Doris's who was willing to talk about her dreams was Matilda, a fortyish matron across from me. When she finally spoke, it took me a moment to tune my *telenovela* Spanish to her accent, but I realized she was listing personal items she would like to buy—her answer, in essence, was a shopping spree. A short-term dream. Nothing more.

The next volunteer was a man who had sat by the door with his arms and legs crossed for the first thirty minutes. I didn't get his name, but between his feet was a large plastic bag, which he had been sitting over like a nest egg. Now he opened it at last to display a jumble of calendars, ashtrays, playing cards, and other small sundries, all bought in bulk for resale. His windfall would be invested in buying more stock. A medium-term dream, just a small improvement.

Doris was patient but subtly dissatisfied with both answers. She wanted everyone to think bigger, looking for long-term goals, talents they could develop, new businesses they could cultivate to serve and diversify the community. "More shoes" and "more calendars" won't change the local economy.

Another woman, perhaps thirty-five, finally spoke of her family and her desire to build her cooking business so that her children would have more money for education. At last, Doris was pleased. This was a long-term goal she could encourage. *Yo se que lo puedes hacer*, she said emphatically, *I know you can do it.*

The woman agreed, adding that she would need her faith—a long dramatic pause here, with a nod to the Virgin Mary watching over us from a portrait mounted high on one wall, above an electric devotional candle, facing a paper print of Da Vinci's *The Last Supper*—and a *lot* of hard work. A laugh of recognition spread around the room.

Hard work is at least as constant as faith. Four members of this group couldn't attend the meeting, as they were still at their jobs well into the evening. Leaving work even to attend to their own finances would be prohibitively expensive.

And what would "prohibitively expensive" amount to? This group of eleven adult clients was making their second set of repayments on a six-month loan totaling about $500. Do the math, and each client here was reasonably hoping to finance their small, growing businesses with just over 25 cents per person per day.

Twenty-five cents is more here, of course, than it is back in Los Angeles.

Today, laborers around Cusco might commonly make 4 soles ($1.50) an hour, plus or minus. A farmer, a craftsperson, or any skilled tradesman might make a little more, while part-time, domestic, and informal help surely make a lot less. So the tiny amount that the members of Agua Buena had borrowed per person still works out to the equivalent of a week's income for a working parent. Possibly more.

Before the meeting with Agua Buena, I met Sheethal in a big town square so we could share the taxi. I was a little surprised that she instructed me never to pay more than three soles for a ride within town. Four would be too much. This was quibbling over the equivalent of 35 cents, something she would never dream of doing back home. But after a couple of months in Cusco, she had realized that paying more would inflate the price for everyone—including locals unable to afford it. So even tipping had serious implications.

Sheethal's generosity was never in question, of course. She was braving long hours, strange food, harsh sun, and thin air, while leaving behind loved ones and career—she's the founder of Leap Work, a New York consultancy handling social networking for non-profits—all on her own dime, just to help a non-profit in America support a non-profit in Peru.

As a thank-you for her help, I bought dinner at a nice restaurant in the touristy part of town, the kind of place that would barely register in New York but was fancy enough here to be beyond a volunteer's budget. We ordered alpaca—which looked like beef and tasted like Tico exhaust*—and I asked if the gig was as rough as JD had warned.

---

* Regarding other exotic comestibles: coca tea, a centuries-old and effective traditional medicine, is made just by boiling loose coca leaves containing the tiniest trace of stimulant. It's not only legal in Peru, but extremely helpful to visitors adapting to the thin air. It should not be confused with its hardcore distant relative: coca tea is to processed cocaine as a cozy fireplace is to a methane explosion. The kick felt roughly equal to one strong cappuccino plus half a Vicodin. After an hour of walking, I'd be short of breath, tired, and achy, but with one pot of coca tea, my feet would stop hurting, my head would stop hurting—heck, my whole childhood would stop hurting.

Chicha, on the other hand, is cheap homebrew beer made from corn, its fermentation accelerated by adding the maker's own spit. *Pass.* (This is not to be confused with fruity non-alcoholic varieties retailed in much of South America.

"It's not the Riviera," she said dryly. "My apartment here is, um, challenging, let's say that. But I'm doing all right." Now came a smile. "I like the people at Arariwa. And I know I'm way better off than a lot of people. You see them come in the office, and it's good to know what I'm doing will help." As JD had predicted, a lot of her work was simply the training of Arariwa's junior staff in the routines of getting financing via Kiva—taking photos of the clients, writing up their stories, uploading them onto the site, and so on. Few sources of funding for MFIs are nearly this personal or labor-intensive, but Kiva's contribution to Arariwa's lending budget was making a difference in the lives of hundreds of clients.

Another of JD's predictions had also been true: Sheethal was in touch online with many of the other Fellows, and in places like Nepal or Cambodia, daily life was much harder. Two of the other Fellows had already contracted malaria. Sheethal might have been having the easiest time in the group. Did Sheethal miss home? "Yes, but my husband is about to visit. My family is coming, too. Plus, I speak the language, and I have some friends I can hang out here with now, so that helps." In fact, Sheethal eventually stayed in the field for an additional three months, taking another fellowship in Bolivia, spending more away from her family so that strangers could better provide for theirs.

Doris took down the goal-setting poster and hung a new one in its place: *El Camino de las Metas Financieras*. The Road of Financial Goals. A female icon—which made sense, since 72 percent of Arariwa's loans are to women—was portrayed walking a six-step road toward

---

We're talking about the stuff brewed by some dude in his living room who signals it's ready by raising a plastic bag on a pole on his roof. *Yes* to cat-poop coffee for me, *no* to chicha.)

a starburst of financial prosperity. Along the way, the icon had to compile a checklist that helps prioritize spending, saving, and investment. And so the next exercise began.

My mind wandered. On the door to the next room, just to one side of Doris's starburst of financial prosperity, hung an old calendar with a picture of cute dogs. On the opposite wall, another expired calendar displayed a photo of a reed boat on the cobalt waters of Lake Titicaca near the Bolivian border. My mom used to hang calendars if she liked the pictures, too.

To my right was a bedroom door decorated with a large poster of Tweety, the Warner Brothers cartoon canary. Here, Tweety was portrayed not in a cage, but lounging on a tropical island in a sun hat made from the Inca flag, exhorting the viewer to smile and keep hope in the presence of God. From behind Tweety, on the other side of the door, were children playing quietly in what must have been a communal bedroom. There were four or five distinct voices—at least—but they shushed themselves frequently so as not to disturb the adults, doing their best to be good. They knew the parents' meeting was very important.

From my left came a soft snore. Irene had fallen asleep.

Shopping-spree Matilda glanced toward Irene and me, seemed to instantly grasp the weirdness of my situation, and smiled reassuringly, crinkling her nose for good measure. *Oh, that's just Irene,* Matilda said to me with her eyes, as clearly as if she were speaking English. *She's a little grabby, but it's okay. That just means she likes you. You're sweet to deal with it like that.*

Oh. Good. So, um, we're cool, then. Thank Inti.

I gently moved Irene's hand from my thigh and placed it in her lap. Her lips made a slight sun-baked smile as I did. Now I wanted to know the Quechua for *your mother is incredibly welcoming, she probably just sensed my nerves and wanted to calm me, and I feel remorse that I worried that anyone could have misunderstood her simple affection for a stranger.*

I can't be the only visitor to Peru who might want to say that someday.

The conversation turned to the group's Christmas basket, a means of pooling resources over the holidays, buying in bulk to save money and share leftovers. The focus became five-kilo bags of rice and sugar, large supplies of milk and cooking oil, who would do the shopping, and where the best deal might be found.

And with that, the meeting wrapped. Coats on, everybody up, thanks for coming. Everyone had a long day of work in the morning. Doris gathered up the money from where it had sat for the last hour, plunked herself down at the kitchen table, and entered the repayments on a ledger. The four members of the group who weren't present would need to come to the Arariwa office to make their payments, but that, too, was no big deal. Doris was confident that they were good for it. Back home, I'd seen fantasy baseball leagues more concerned about payments than this loan officer was.

Irene awakened, arose, and practically bounced out, all waves and bye-byes, her step far more sprightly and young than I could have expected. I will smile when I think of Irene for the rest of my life.

Finally, Sheethal and I gathered our things and waited for Doris at the kitchen table. Behind her, on the refrigerator, was a paper plate that a child had apparently decorated with a macaroni face. *Hey, I made one of those when I was little*, I thought. *And Mom's kitchen had a linoleum checkered floor.* Suddenly, I was seeing my own childhood. Or at least a snapshot of it.

Photographs have a way of replacing the memories they're meant to record. I don't remember the moment at all, for example, but there was a day in the mid-1960s when I was a pudgy little boy in Ohio with a round face wearing a pale blue rugby shirt and sitting on Mom's linoleum checkered kitchen floor. It's the only photo I have from those years, so it's the only picture of my own early childhood I carry in my head. My teeth were crooked back then, and I was already self-conscious, so it took a lot to get me to smile. I'm smiling in that picture.

Just as I was remembering all this, a pudgy little boy with a round face emerged from the bedroom with Tweety on the door. He stopped when he saw me standing on his mom's linoleum checkered kitchen floor. I stopped, too. He was wearing a T-shirt almost exactly the same color blue I'd just remembered, much as if my childhood memory had summoned him into the room.

I was a little spooked, to be honest. *Nobody told me I had a doppelganger in Peru.* He seemed a little unnerved, too, albeit probably for a different reason. *Nobody told me there was a white dude out here.*

Before I could say hello, he turned away shyly, then disappeared back into the bedroom, giving up on whatever had caused him to emerge. But I could see he'd been curious about me, so I looked out the window for a while, letting him sneak back out secretly, at his own pace, giving him time to take in the big gringo and get comfortable. Eventually, I looked back and nodded a hello.

The boy gave me an enormous crooked-teeth smile.

When Doris asked this group to talk about their dreams, there seemed to be none. All of their responses were only about business, money, providing for the family, maybe a nice possession or two. Nothing more. The most ambitious idea in the room was one guy who wanted to start a printing business, but not because he liked printing. It just looked profitable.

I don't write this as criticism, but from recognition. My own father worked for thirty-seven years to put food on the table and help his son and daughter have a better life. That *was* his dream. And now, the same thing here: aside from tiny differences—language, religion, clothing choices, and so on—the people in that living room in Cusco could have been my own aunts and uncles.

Microcredit didn't look like it was going to make any of those parents rich, obviously. But a blue-shirted boy with crooked teeth who makes macaroni faces on linoleum floors gets *food. Clothes. School.* And someday, maybe, *dreams.* An upgrade on the birth lottery.

Something clicked for me here. So far, I'd only put about half of my nest egg into these loans, and they were already starting to pay back, like clockwork. It seemed selfish to begrudge a single dollar that I wasn't putting to use if it could be down here, helping my doppelganger learn to read and do math. I decided that all $20,000 and change that I made from traveling the five-star world— every penny—would go into at least one cycle of loans.

That issue, at least, was now resolved. But now I had even more questions.

Peru was still recovering from economic upheaval and civil insurrection, and it was one of the more stable places on my itinerary. What might happen where ethnic tensions, poor governance, or the threat of war might make group lending difficult? And on a personal level, how does anyone even cope in the face of such severely difficult circumstances—how do people keep working, raise their kids, and hang on to hope, so something like microfinance has meaning? How does one not just go insane?

The people I would visit next had stories to tell.

CHAPTER SIX

WELCOME TO SARAJEVO

Y OU JUST KEEP going," Seida says with a shrug.
She exhales slowly, searching my face.

Seida Saric is the director of Žene za Žene ("Women for Women"), the Kiva partner MFI in Bosnia.* We're in an upstairs conference room, and we've been talking for almost two hours. Seida's group is part of an international organization that operates in some of the world's most challenging environments—Afghanistan, Iraq, Sudan, the Democratic Republic of the Congo, Nigeria, Rwanda, Kosovo, and here, Sarajevo, the site of the longest and most deadly siege of a city in fifty years, where we sit.

I understand Seida's words, of course. Her English is nearly flawless. But emotionally, I've got no experience remotely like what she has faced. I'm sure it shows. So, for emphasis, she adds, after a pause: "You just *do*."

Her tone carries emotions that I've never heard mixed: resignation, defiance, pride, and even a note of surprise—as if to say, who knew one *could* survive?

In the 1990s, Bosnia was the scene of the deadliest European conflict since World War II, with approximately one hundred

---

*The website for Women for Women in Bosnia is www.womenforwomen.org /global-initiatives-helping-women/help-women-bosnia-herzegovina.php.

thousand people killed and two million forced to flee their homes. In the aftermath, Seida has spent much of her adult life helping survivors, especially women. Žene za Žene has offered job training, placement services, agricultural resources, education on their legal rights, and simple emotional support, not to mention microloans and other financial tools. Under Seida's watch, Women for Women has reached nearly thirty thousand women here.

But it's still just a fraction of what needs to be done. And the underlying causes of the war are still not fully resolved. Fear and hatred could strike again. Much of her life's work could be undone by further conflict.

While I'm in Bosnia to learn more about microfinance, I'd also like to learn how people persevere, finding the strength to reach out to others with love and support, without allowing bitterness, rage, fear, or depression take over.

So I've asked. *How do you keep going? How do you find hope? How do you—if not forgive, I guess—how do you move on and see the future?*

Seida studies my face. Some things are beyond communicating in words. Still, she tries to explain. But human endurance doesn't have an explanation right this minute.

"You just do," she says again.

I had no idea how isolated from the rest of Europe Bosnia would feel, but the first lesson came on the flight in.* I was nearly the only passenger.

---

*The country's full name is "Bosnia and Herzegovina," but it's usually just "Bosnia" in practice. "Herzegovina" ("Land of the Duke") is a southern region once controlled by a fifteenth-century duke, but there's no current political boundary. It was joined to Bosnia in as early as the sixteenth century, and "Bosnia and Herzegovina" came into use in the nineteenth century. Despite Herzegovina's own varied history, in current usage, "Bosnia" now usually refers to all of Bosnia and Herzegovina as one. We'll go along with that here.

My flight was on the flag airline of Bosnia and Herzegovina, B&H Airlines, which had exactly five planes in its fleet. This one was an ATR-72-200, a funky old prop plane from the late 1980s that American and Delta both used for short hops in the early '90s, at least until they learned that cold climates led to icing problems that could make the planes do something other than fly. The ones that survive are mostly now rattling around the developing world. It was a warm day in Vienna, so I was hopeful that the plane would stay convincingly in the air.

Also encouraging: the flight had a full crew, baggage attendants, and everything you expect—except other travelers. For a while, I was the only non-employee in sight. A few other customers eventually trickled aboard, but I sat over one of the wings, right in the middle of the plane, and the half of the cabin in front of me was completely empty.

The in-flight magazine was weirdly cut off from the world, too. Of its dozens of ads, exactly one was from an international company. The rest were all for local restaurants, car repair shops, building supply dealers, and so on. Not one had a translation into any language besides impenetrable Bosnian.* It was as if Bosnia's own international airline expects no one but Bosnians ever to visit.

I found this hard to fathom. The Dayton Peace Accords were

---

* Bosnian is a Slavic tongue so closely related to Serbian and Croatian that they are not only mutually intelligible, but sometimes barely distinguishable. Prior to the 1991 breakup of Yugoslavia, all three were usually considered one language, and in casual use, minor differences may go unnoticed—at least until somebody signals their ethnicity. Then, in the verbal equivalent of peeking at Schrödinger's cat, suddenly you're speaking Serbian, I'm speaking Croatian, and a few phonemes and usages signal a deep cultural divide, unknowable a moment ago, now an unchangeable fate. A fourth version, Montenegrin, was summoned into existence in 2009, when the newly independent government of Montenegro added two letters to the standard alphabet and proclaimed that the same exact words everyone had always used were now a new and distinct national language. We may consider this a preview of much that follows here.

signed in 1995, so the shooting stopped long ago. In the age of the Internet, I just couldn't imagine a city almost as large as Cleveland, just one hour by air from Vienna, being so disconnected from the rest of the world. Could the war still affect things that much? As the plane landed, I wondered how many visible signs of the war would remain.

It would take only moments to find out.

The airport grounds were virtually deserted. It was only 6:10 P.M., but there were no taxis, no buses, nor even private cars from whom to thumb a ride. Just a nearly-empty parking lot, the distant sound of vehicles on the main road, and the *whish* of a humid breeze. The fellow travelers from my own flight seemed to have simply vanished.

A distant Volkswagen hatchback was marked POLICIJA, so I wandered over, jabbered at the cop in polite touristese—*zdravo, američki? taxi, hvala?* ("hello, American? taxi, thanks?"—hereby exhausting my Conversational Bosnian)—then waited as he kindly used his cell phone to call me a ride. Five minutes of polite silence later, a cabbie rumbled up in a rusting BMW. Off we went.

Almost immediately upon exiting the airport, we passed a tall apartment block, perhaps eight or ten stories high, its walls Swiss-cheesed with bullet marks and shell craters.* I assumed this was a relic, something that would be torn down when there was money to do so. But no. In a window, a woman was folding laundry. In another, a young man was calling down to a friend in the street. On the sidewalk, two young lovers were out for a walk, and a married couple was pushing a stroller. Children played soccer next to concrete walls deeply scarred from explosions. It all seemed as ordinary as birdsong.

You just do, Seida would say.

---

* I can only estimate the building's height because my eyes simply got stuck on the bullet holes.

I asked the Two Dinos. *Seriously, guys—how are you not completely insane?* They laughed and said they didn't know. But the specific way that they laughed was at least a part of the answer.

The Two Dinos were lifelong best friends who came to my hotel one morning to help introduce me to a microlending client not associated with Kiva in any way. I'd decided to visit a number of MFIs unrelated to Kiva, partly out of curiosity to see any detectible difference, and partly to eliminate any concern from readers trained to be cynical that somehow my client visits could be cherry-picked. (Kiva doesn't even have a partner in Morocco. The visit to Mohammed and his lender, Al-Amana—"honesty" in Arabic—sprang from the same see-it-all rationale.) So my assistant had looked online for press reports of local microfinanced businesses and found a blog entry by one of the Dinos. The first Dino had brought along the second Dino, and together we were about to meet Tiro.

Both Dinos were now in their early twenties, but they'd grown up trapped in Sarajevo for the duration of the siege. At the same ages when most American kids go from grade school to middle school, the Dinos spent nearly four solid years hearing the whiz of bullets, falling asleep to the sound of explosions, and wondering how the carnage would ever end.

One day, they told me, they were outside, playing soccer— *Wait, what were you doing outside playing soccer?* I asked. The snipers had gotten into a rhythm, they replied, and the shooting stopped after lunch for a while, and you eventually just got used to taking a risk every day anyway, so—*Expletive!*, I interrupted again. So one day, they were playing football outside, the way kids do, and a shell suddenly hit very close. Fortunately, it didn't explode, or both Dinos would have been maimed or killed, for sure. *Long colorful expletive!* I repeated.

So—and this was the money question—*growing up with all that, the stress, the anger, and everything that had to be part of it*—seriously, *guys—how are you not out of your minds?*

They laughed at the question, but not right away. The Dinos first looked at each other, searching for words, then laughed at having nothing really to say about it. It began as the sort of nervous laugh you make when you're feeling several strong emotions at once, the laugh that might vocalize like *oh-h-h-h man, wow, whew, geez, I dunno*, and then it grew into more relaxed laughter as they recognized each other's reaction.

In that moment, you could see shared memories, instant empathy, and a similar sense of humor. And they both took strength from that, and then laughed. There was my answer. The Two Dinos had not gone insane, at least in part, through their friendship.

The Dinos and I took a taxi to Breza, a small river village maybe twenty miles outside of Sarajevo. Breza was remarkably like the Ohio town where I was born, about twenty miles outside of Cleveland—cloudy, small, on a river, and filled with Eastern Europeans. I felt more at home than I would ever expect you to believe. A few of the Dinos' friends joined us when we arrived, and together we descended on Tiro's sports bar.

Tiro greeted us with open arms, a big front-teeth-missing-but-who-cares smile, and cold Sarajevskos. A fiftyish man dressed perpetually in the Dodger-blue jersey of his favorite team—Željezničar, "the Railworkers," nicknamed Željo, pronounced like "J-Lo"—Tiro had dreamed for most of his life of opening a Western-style sports bar where he could entertain his neighbors.

After years of saving, he finally had a location, equipment, furniture, and a staff ready to go—but that was in 1992. Then came the war. Tiro fled to Austria, leaving everything behind. Six months after the Dayton Accords, he returned to find all of his belongings either stolen or destroyed.

Tiro rebuilt from scratch, thanks to a series of small loans from the local office of Partner, one of the country's largest MFIs. It took nine years, but Tiro's new tavern grew from just two small tables in a tiny space to two full seating areas comprising about 1,000 square feet, plus a full bar, big-screen projection TVs, a kitchen serving hot food, and an upstairs billiards room. Tiro's loans totaled about 4,000 Bosnian marks —the equivalent of less than $3,000.

We raised a Sarajevsko to his success, and Tiro started rummaging around for his favorite Željo souvenirs, showing them off like a kid with his favorite toys. We posed for photos with his soccer trophies, then spent the rest of the afternoon enjoying a game on the big screen. Eventually, the Dinos didn't even need to translate. There's no need for language in football, after all, when beers and high fives will do.

Watching the game with Tiro, the Dinos, and a few of their friends, I could find no emotional difference between watching Željo in Breza and the Browns back in Ohio. Although Željo is more likely to win a Super Bowl.

You'd never have known just from looking that all of my new friends were Muslim, survivors of a war where that accident of birth could have gotten them killed.*

From the start, Yugoslavia was more an alliance of neighbors than a unified nation. Tellingly, when the country finally emerged in the early twentieth century, it was called the "Kingdom of Serbs, Croats, and Slovenes," a variety pack right in the name. Not mentioned were the people of its smaller territories, including Bosnia, a triangular region nestled squarely between the more powerful Serbia and Croatia.

---

* *But Muslims don't drink!* some readers might say. True—the same way Catholics and Jews never break dietary laws, Buddhists never get testy, and atheists never say "God!" under stress.

Ottoman rulers converted much of Bosnia's population to Islam at about the time Columbus was landing in America.* However, about a sixth of the population were Catholic Croats, mostly to the southwest, and nearly a third were Orthodox Serbs, mainly to the north and east. Clear lines were never drawn, however, and in densely populated areas, Serb-, Croat-, and Muslim-majority sections were highly intermingled.

During the Cold War, the government of Josip Broz Tito kept a lid on ethnic politics, but once Tito was dead and the Cold War was over, politicians rose to power not by appealing to cooperation, but by stoking ethnic nationalism. Eventually, "Yugoslavia" split into six separate nations—a process filled with conflict and tragedy.†

The farthest-flung sections, Slovenia and Macedonia, seceded with relatively little bloodshed. Montenegro and Kosovo would remain under Serbian influence for several more years.‡

As the rest of the nation fractured in the early 1990s, what remained was governed from Serbia by Slobodan Milošević, who

---

* Bosnian Muslims are often called Bosniaks, which has recently become the official term. However, no Bosnian Muslim I met ever used it in my presence. When I asked about this, I was told it was either from habit—under Yugoslav rule, the word was viewed as ethnically divisive—or because they didn't like when their own politicians used it to play to ethnic pride. Out of respect for the preferences of individuals who were gracious to me, I use the longer term here.

† Seven countries, if you count Kosovo, as 91 UN member nations do. The other 102 members do not.

‡ Montenegro gained independence peacefully in 2006. However, Kosovo, which Serbian nationalists regard much the same way that Texans think of the Alamo, had become mostly populated by Albanian Muslims as early as the nineteenth century. The 1999 war that led to Kosovo's current status is worth an entire separate book.

rose to power by stoking historic Serbian grievances with their neighbors. Bosnian muslims were derided as "Turks," alien invaders in a land they'd inhabited for five centuries, while Croatians were scorned as *Ustashe*, named for the pro-Nazi secret police of previous generations.

On the other side of Bosnia, Croatia was led by a similar nationalist, Franjo Tuđman, whose plans for separation from Yugoslavia were met by the secession of his *own* Serb minority. Croatia's independence came at the price of tens of thousands of lives, Croats and Serbs alike.

In between all this sat Bosnia, its north and east considered Serbian by Serbs, its southwest considered Croatian by Croats. Before their own conflict, Milošević and Tuđman had even discussed how they would carve up the territory. Eventually, tragically: ethnic cleansing, genocide, and the systematic mass rape of tens of thousands of Bosnian women as a weapon of war.

Sarajevo, Bosnia's capital, was blockaded and placed under siege for nearly four solid years. An average of more than three hundred shells hit the city every day. At least ten thousand Sarajevans were killed, and between five and ten times that figure were wounded, including more than fifteen thousand children. Zetra Stadium, proud host site of the 1984 Winter Olympics, gained a new purpose—as an enormous bullet shield, behind which its parking lot could be used to safely bury and mourn the dead.

To simply fetch water from a well—necessary for survival, since the city's infrastructure was virtually destroyed—was to risk your life. The snipers in the hills knew where the wells were, too.

During my visit, every person I spoke with at length (and with whom I felt comfortable broaching the subject) had either lost a close relative, been shot at and survived, or escaped shortly before the encirclement and spent the entire war as a refugee. And all of this was simply to rearrange territorial boundaries between groups who, I was told with near-unanimity, might struggle at first even to distinguish each other by appearance, accent, or dress.*

And now I would ask them how microfinance was assisting in their rebuilding. Given the horrors most people had been through, I was afraid the question would seem trivial.

It was anything but.

Sead is already angry with me.

Sead has a two-day beard, grime on his fingers, and a full inch of ash permanently attached to the thick Drina cigarette that seems to never leave his hand. His olive-green shirt carries the demented inscription "Curling for men!" on its breast, the apparent result of a Canadian wartime charity donation. He speaks sharply. I don't need to wait for Amra, my translator today, to tell me that I've managed to tick Sead off within thirty seconds of meeting him.

We're in the living room of his home at the top of a dirt road that branches off of another dirt road in the hills outside downtown. Not far away is the Zetra Stadium, whose converted purpose I can't get out of my mind.

Amra and I have driven here with a loan officer from Partner. Now we're sitting on a couch in Sead's living room, and Sead is gesturing grandly, letting me know that I have done him wrong. As he waves his right hand emphatically, the cigarette between his middle and index fingers retains its full inch of ash no matter how violently it moves.

---

*The consensus of what I was told, at least: people can usually tell each other apart (a) by their names; (b) if they self-identify with religious symbols, speech, or garments; or (c) by the license plates on their cars, which indicate which part of the now-mostly-segregated country they're from. There is no physical marker like lighter skin or different features. On some occasions the choice of words can give the speaker away, although the accent itself may not.

My offense: I have accidentally brushed one of my shoes against one of the couches in his living room.

Before you judge: Sead is right. I have been careless, and I do owe him an apology. The couches in Sead's living room aren't just décor—they're his livelihood.

Prior to the war, Sead was an electrician, and his wife Munira was a graphic designer. They managed to get out of town just before the siege and spent the war years as refugees in Germany. When they returned, everything they'd had was gone or destroyed. They had children to feed, no health insurance or societal safety net of any kind, no market for their skills, and few possessions other than a decent bed.

What they did have, however, was ingenuity. Realizing that as Sarajevo rebuilt and more refugees returned, there would be a growing market for decent beds like their own, Sead and Munira took theirs apart, studied its design and assembly, back-engineered the whole thing, and began to make homemade copies to sell.

When I brushed my dirty shoe against Sead's couch, I messed up merchandise he and his family had made with their own hands. I apologize, of course, and fortunately the dirt wipes away with just a moment of labor and worry. Meanwhile, Amra does a great job of translating my admiration for their resourcefulness and creativity. Sead's pride overwhelms his disdain, and soon he brightens, lights another Drina, and relaxes. We're good.

Sead tells more of his story. Soon, he and Munira expanded into other kinds of furniture, eventually teaching themselves to make all manner of sittable things, from the simplest white hassock to custom-made leather corner sofas in imaginative shapes and wild colors. Today, if the kids pitch in, the family can make five sofas in a single day, and their business is growing as fast as they can keep up. Large furniture companies have offered to buy their business several times, but Sead isn't interested. "Their price is too cheap, and the quality would go down," Sead says. "No, this is ours. I will not let them skim my milk."

I ask where they would be without the small loans that helped them get their business off the ground. Sead pauses, looking for words. "I don't know," he says, as Amra's voice rises in the translation, just as his does, for emphasis. "They were a big help. A very big, *big* help."

Munira, wearing a matronly wool sweater and with her hair pulled into a tight bun, brings out a service of thick 10W40 Bosnian coffee on a silver tray. We all sit amid bare walls and unshaded light fixtures, sipping and chatting. Munira lights up a Drina, reclines toward a heavy-duty Pfaff sewing machine behind her, and tells me about her days. She has four males to feed, she says, detailing endless days of cooking and cleaning and tending an acre of land while also stitching the furniture fabric for hours on end. She is proud of her endurance, seeing it as a part of her Balkan heritage, the measure of being a strong wife.

The boys are twenty-one, sixteen, and nine now, she tells me. Good workers, all of them, but half of the money from the business must go to their education, of course.

"True wealth is in educating your children to fend for themselves, to not use drugs or spend too much money on things," Munira says. "The war was proof that we can always lose things. Eternal wealth is giving your children a better life."

Sead nods and looks adoringly at Munira when she says this. She glances back and touches his leg affectionately. They've been through hard decades, but now even in their late forties, they still sometimes flirt like teenagers. I have a good camera with me, so I offer to take their picture and e-mail it as a small present in exchange for their hospitality. Maybe I can create a nice portrait that would look nice on the wall. Munira hops comfortably onto Sead's lap, they pose, and we laugh.

Smiling, relaxed, and clearly glad to be together, these two former war refugees now share a successful business and a healthy family. They are home.

Amra, who translated with Sead and Munira, was eight years old when the war started. She and her family fled just before the siege began, escaping through Croatia to Germany and eventually Kenya, where they rode out the war.

Coming back wasn't exactly easy. Bosnians who managed to escape have often been resented by those who were left behind or chose to stay and fight. Survivors of the siege carry scars, physical and emotional, that returnees might never fully share, and they don't always feel as respected as they might like. It's a small but ongoing source of friction that still surprises Amra when it comes up.

Amra is blonde, like many women here, and could pass for a northern European—a fact more noticeable because she doesn't wear a headscarf. Few Muslim women here seem to, so I ask her about it.

"Of course we don't," she explains with an amused shake of her head. "We're Muslims—but we're European Muslims. We live like Europeans, because that's what we are. People in the West have all these weird ideas. It's no big thing . . . To some of us, it's very serious, but to a lot of us, it's like how some Americans are Christians and some are Jewish, but you don't worry about it. I think when people expect big scarves and head coverings, they're thinking of Arabs or Asians. Muslims in the Arab world, they dress like Arabs. In Asia, they dress like Asians. In Africa, they dress like Africans. I mean, what else would you expect?"

As we sip our coffee, I can't help but think about how Milošević and his followers would have demonized Amra as a "Turk," irreconcilably different, acceptable as a casualty, for nothing more than growing up as her parents' daughter.

Back in Ohio, my niece and my nephew have both reached adult-hood, so my empty-nest sister had time on her hands. Curious about her own identity after two decades as *Mom!*, she took an interest in genealogy, hoping to learn more about our proud Irish-American roots.

Our parents told us that we came from Ireland, as did their parents, and so on, so it had to be true. For the first forty-six years of my life, I was Irish-American, less for the ethnic kitsch—cable-knit sweaters, the Chieftains on iTunes—than the sense of the underdog: escape from famine, British oppression, Bloody Sunday. To be Irish is to imagine yourself plucky and literate, fond of music and poetry, and able to drink like we have a few extra livers. But we're loyal and passionate and take joy in sheer language. We'll fight you at dawn, write a ballad about it at lunch, buy the beer to make nice, and at sunset, we'll French-kiss the Blarney Stone.*

And then my sister found out:

We're *English*.

Not just a little, either. Full-on *pip-pip, cheerio, blimey, God save the Queen, tally-ho*, and *smashing*: straight up my paternal blood-line, my father's father's father's father and so on, I am the spawn of three generations of knights and at least one sheriff of Essex.†
I'm the oppressor, at least through the Irish-American lens. I'm the Royal Dragoons, I'm the Black and Tans. I dither about cricket whilst my manservants subjugate Rhodesia. I arrest Gandhi.

---

* Something I've actually done. Not recommended.
† Notice that somehow along the way, we Harrises went from a century of noble knighthood to a new life as Appalachian dirt farmers. Real estate may not be our greatest talent. As if to emphasize the point, our heraldic family coat of arms doesn't include any lions, swords, horses, or the usual symbols of noble landed gentry. It's just three small hedgehogs on a blue background. Fear our power.

Well, dang.

Then again, it's not like I had much to do with my "identity." I turned out English-speaking, Baptist-raised, blue-eyed, and balding. None of that was my call. I also didn't choose my first language, my nationality, my religion growing up, my appearance, or my own social customs. Pretty much the only things we *do* get to choose are how we treat others and conduct ourselves in the world. Are we honest? Are we caring? That's who we *are*.

But every Bosnian I met had been defined by identities they never chose. Many of their loved ones had died because of them.

Amra had met me in my hotel, a charming family B&B called the Pansion Harmony, where the manager, a good-humored fellow named Tariq (but whom my mouth kept calling "T-Rock"), had supplied me endlessly with cold Sarajevsko beers—these Bosnian Muslims sure know how to drink—and hot *ćevapi*, a dish of minced beef with onions on bread that tastes almost exactly like White Castle. The Harmony was such a comfortable place to stay that I could easily forget where I was: the hills near Grbavica, a district on the south side of the river, the scene of some of the heaviest casualties in the siege.

I walked down the hill one drizzly morning. Nearly fifteen years after the cease-fire, many streets, sidewalks, and apartment buildings were still perforated with bullet holes and shell craters, in some places so thoroughly that it seemed inconceivable that the buildings could still be structurally sound and people could still live there. But they did. A few balconies even had fresh flowers, often local roses, which grow here in such quantity that Sarajevo has sometimes been known as the City of Roses.

Walking downtown, I found one of the shell craters had been filled in with red resin—making a circular pattern of crimson, symbolic of the bloodshed.

This, too, is known as a Sarajevo Rose.

About a mile away, I reached the city's main rail station. The large metal WELCOME TO SARAJEVO sign is still riddled with dozens of bullet holes. Two blocks from there, I passed a large shell crater in the pavement right next to a children's playground. The sight makes a noise in your head. One you'd rather not hear.

Later, I took a rainy afternoon and walked in the other direction, heading up from the Harmony to the crest of the hill. At the top, I found an enormous metal sign:

Добродошли у Републику Српску

WELCOME TO REPUBLIC OF SRPSKA

This was the dividing line, then.

The Bosnian War and the siege of Sarajevo ended by splitting the territory of Bosnia into two entities—the Federation of Bosnia and Herzegovina, mostly populated by Muslims and Croats (who had made an earlier peace with the Muslims, eventually allying against the Serbs), and the Republika Srpska (RS), a Serbian-majority state bordering Serbia itself. The Federation and the RS each has its own capital, flag, national assembly, police, and holidays, but together they comprise the Republic of Bosnia and Herzegovina as a two-state nation.

I was standing on the imaginary, invisible line drawn on the ground that convinced people on one side not to kill real, visible people on the other.

I'd stood on lines like this many times before—between the Koreas, the Irelands, the Berlins, and so on. They're everywhere, if you notice. (Even Ohio and Michigan once almost went to war over Toledo. Had they *been* to Toledo?) The oldest surviving peace treaty on earth, the Treaty of Kadesh, once even promised that an imaginary line between the Egyptians and the Hittites would guarantee peace across the Middle East "forever." Its crumbling fragments now sit almost forgotten in a Turkish museum, while the Middle East makes more crumbling fragments.*

Now I straddled another such line, segregating lands that will now be claimed and defended by the "Federation" and the "RS," maybe for centuries and possibly again until death, until both imaginary constructs—just like the "Hittite Empire," "Yugoslavia," "New Grenada," "Rhodesia," "East Germany," the "Vermont Republic," "Tanganyika," "Czechoslovakia," "South Vietnam," "North Yemen," "West Florida," and eventually every set of invisible lines—change or disappear.

Down the hill, near the Harmony, were the grassy slopes from which snipers and artillery killed thousands of people much like Amra and Sead and Munira. From my own hotel room, the streets of Sarajevo would resemble the view held by gunmen who turned any open roadway into Sniper Alley.

My heart started to pound almost audibly. I had to steady myself by grabbing onto the sign while a large truck sloshed past. It took me a moment to realize what I was feeling—anger—and then try to let it go. War crimes were committed by all sides, I reminded myself, and narratives of victimhood can be framed by each faction.†

The anger surprised me. In retrospect, I guess I expected to make friends on all sides, imagining that I would merely resign myself to sad bafflement at their conflict. *Can't we all just . . . get*

---

*Historians now argue about whether or not it was a peace treaty. If this debate ever devolves into a fistfight, humankind as a species will have crossed into parody.

†For those keeping score, here's one measure, at least: the International Criminal Tribunal for the former Yugoslavia indicted a total of 161 people, including 94 Serbs, 29 Croats, 9 Albanians, 9 Bosnian Muslims, 2 Montenegrins, and 2 Macedonians, among others. Some independent observers might say this ballparks the relative level of atrocities committed, but this (a) depends on whom you ask, of course, and (b) perpetuates ethnic hatreds simply by asking the question.

along? So I kept walking into the RS, looking for the first place where I could talk to people, maybe learn the name of a good bar on this side of the hill. There was a gas station on the right with a Western-style convenience store attached—not exactly a consulate, but a start—so I lightly popped in.

Dobar dan! ("Good day!") I said to the lady at the counter. *Zdravo!* ("Hi!"), she replied. Cheerful, friendly, sweet. To my eyes—which may admittedly have missed subtle clues—her clothes, accent, and manner were not remotely different from those of the people less than a mile away on the other side of the hill.

I think that's what got to me. If she'd spoken a different language or been clad in some exotic garb, I think I would have remained calm. But silent rage now flashed through my body.

Fifteen hundred children, I suddenly wanted to shout. Not at the nice gas station lady, of course. Just into the air.

Fifteen hundred children had been killed in the city on the other side of that hill, right *there,* just a short walk away. Hundreds of thousands of people were terrorized while men stood for years firing explosive hot metal down onto innocent families—all just so that people on *this* side of the hill could perhaps take the city, and thus feel incrementally safer, perhaps more righteous in an unchosen heritage and an imperceptibly different *dobar dan.*

But I held my tongue, fixed a smile on my face, picked up a soda to feel normal, and flipped through a couple of newspapers while waiting to pay. On the RS side of the line, the papers were in Serbian. One had a weather map still showing Serbia, the RS, Montenegro, and Kosovo as essentially one country, a unified Greater Serbia, regardless of accepted international borders or how many lives these notions destroyed. It was as if nothing had been learned from the carnage.

What I felt was considerably more than sad bafflement.

And this wasn't even remotely my fight.

What I felt could only be a tiny fraction of the fury that many people here—on all sides—must still live with and swallow daily.

How does anyone live through what everyone here lived through? How do you not go insane?

A few days later, I led Amra on a hunt for Nermina, a crafts-woman whose skill had attracted a bit of press indicating that she, too, had built her business with microloans. After a bit of sleuthing, we found her at work in a small rented space in the five-hundred-year-old stone central market in Sarajevo's Old Town.

Nermina's boutique was twenty feet deep but only five feet wide (*slot* might be a better word than *boutique*), crammed to the gills with lustrous handcrafted glass and porcelain goods—vases, clocks, earrings, trophies, abstracts, you name it—all produced by Nermina herself. The color and light turned this half-millennium-old stone slot into a fragile, luminous wonderland.

After my literal *faux pas* with Sead's couch, I was afraid even to step inside, lest I exhale and destroy half of Nermina's inventory. Since it was nearly closing time, I waited a few feet away until her last customer had gone, then introduced myself via Amra. This petite redhead in her late fifties was eager to chat—surprisingly so, since we arrived with no advance contact or notice—and she led us to a café a few blocks away where the food was acceptable and the quiet was excellent.

Nermina's English was good enough that Amra would often trans-late my questions into Bosnian, but Nermina would reply directly in English, sometimes slowing her words for emphasis in a way that took her thick Bosnian accent closer to Bela Lugosi territory.

Before long, we had somehow begun talking about the war without any of us raising the subject. It was implied at all times, I was learning. When the conflict began, Nermina hoped the in-ternational community would somehow force peace. "I wished maybe Rambo would come," she said, elegantly turning an unrea-sonable hope that became great disappointment into humorous self-deprecation. "Someone will stop this, I hoped—bullets and shelling are *verrry* bad for glass," she added with a laugh.

But Rambo never came to the rescue, so Nermina fled to Denmark, raised two teenagers while working at a bilingual newspaper, then returned to Sarajevo to pursue her personal mix of art and business. "The most important thing in life is to love what you do," she instructed, lighting her second cigarette and relaxing back into her chair.

Her glasswork was like nothing I'd ever seen, so we talked a good deal about her techniques, all of them self-taught, and her major supplies, which are often simply discarded bits of glass that she scavenges from other people's trash. But since the work is all freelance, her income can be unstable, and sometimes her best creations go unsold. On this, Nermina and I bonded.

Talk of income logically led to finance, and Nermina emphasized the importance of planning and being conservative with her funds. Yes, she started her business with microfinance after the war, and yes, it was indispensible—without the loans, she estimated her business would be "half!" in one of her direct English responses—but of late she had grown large enough to seek loans from conventional commercial banks.

She added this last casually, not realizing its significance to this project. In microfinance terms, successful growth into a thriving, sustainable business with full credit is arguably the industry's best-case scenario. Nermina's story—like Tiro's, and like Sead's and Munira's, and like Mohammed's in Morocco—was a perfect example of microlending achieving its goals, the sort of canon story that might promote the practice universally.

I felt satisfied and excited. I could see why microlending had such a vogue after Muhammad Yunus and Grameen Bank had been awarded the Nobel Peace Prize.

Then Nermina leaned forward. In the most cinematic way you can imagine, the overhead light was now behind her, darkening her face, smoke curled from her thick Drina cigarette, and her raspy voice resonated with heavy Mitteleuropa angst.

"Budt Bob," Nermina intoned somberly, speaking to me directly in English for emphasis, giving me the full Bela Lugosi again. "Jou must promiss me sometink."

Sure, Nermina. What's up?

"Jou mussst alzo write about dee *darrrrk* side of meekrofeenanz."

The dark side? Wait—what do you mean?

"Too menny pipple, it cause terrrrrible problems. Jou mussst luke into dis, Bob—doughnut forgeet dee *darrrrk* siiide."

A clap of thunder would have added to the suddenly somber effect. But not much.

So much for microfinance as an easy, one-size-fits-all solution. *Crap.*

Dee darrrrk siiide of meekrofeenanz, as Nermina elaborated her genuine concern, turns out to be exactly what we might expect, once we start thinking of the working poor in developing countries—even the world's very poorest people—as really no different from you or me.

In America, anybody with a credit card can get overextended, especially if we're not well educated about our finances. People sometimes also find themselves borrowing for a one-time personal expense—to help with a wedding, say, or an emergency medical issue—important enough to merit a long period of debt. If things get bad, it's then possible to pay off one credit card with another, and another, starting a potential spiral of debt.

Meanwhile, banks can hurt people by charging high interest rates or outlandish fees. If you've used an automated teller machine in the United States, you know that even some big, stable, highly profitable banks may decide to charge their customers whatever they can get away with. And anyone who was alive in 2008 knows that the financial world sometimes attracts greedy people. In the worst case—think of America's recent home mortgage crisis, for example—banks might start juicing their short-term profits by extending credit to people who shouldn't even qualify for a loan.

To understand dee darrrk siiide of microfinance, just imagine all of those possibilities as they might look in a poor country, perhaps one emerging from tragedy or war.*

Clients might begin with more unstable incomes, poorer education, or greater risk of serious health issues. Lenders might not communicate with each other through a centralized credit bureau—one might not even exist, in fact—making it difficult for an MFI to measure creditworthiness. Weak or unstable governments might have little or no regulatory power. The society might lack the social safety net that exists in most industrialized countries. The lending institutions might be corrupt, exploitative, or simply too poorly managed to do anything but strong-arm their customers to make a profit.

The dark side of microfinance, then, would simply be the dark side of banking, period, amplified greatly by the context.

In Bosnia, once the war ended, microcredit grew exponentially. The total value of loans at a major MFI called ProCredit quintupled between 2001 and 2007. Another MFI grew by a factor of eighteen.† But with little regulation, a bubble soon formed. Some MFIs incentivized their loan officers with commissions, so the pursuit of profit trumped the welfare of clients, many of whom should not have received loans, and perhaps a quarter of whom became severely overextended.

---

*After 2008, up to 58 percent of Bosnian borrowers had multiple loans, and 15.8 percent were delinquent more than thirty days. Of those with multiple loans, the average was 2.3 each. See Sources.

† Roodman, chapter 8. See Sources.

Clearly—just like with American home mortgages—the bubble would burst, and it did.*

"Yes, people taking too many loans, people making too many loans—this was a very big problem."

These were my translator Amra's words, summarizing a response that sounded five times that long. We were sitting with Adisa Mujkic, an executive with Partner—the large MFI who had financed all of the Bosnian borrowers I'd met so far—in her office in a strip mall about a mile from downtown.

I'd have liked to meet with clients whose lives had been negatively impacted, but obviously no MFI would make those introductions, and there was no press I could find naming failed borrowers I could track down.[†] Even if I did, I suspected that few clients would be likely to discuss their hardships. So instead, I was at Partner, asking what they and other MFIs were doing to prevent the problems from recurring.

Adisa sat behind an IKEAoid desk, a new HP laptop, and a tray of business cards. Her suit was as spotless and neat as the rest of the office, whose décor was the same Dodger blue as Tiro's sports

---

*Also comparable to American subprime lending: a strong case that at least some of the bankers responsible knew very well what they were doing to a criminal extent. See Bateman, Sinković, and Škare in Sources. The downturn in the West was a small but contributing factor affecting clients' ability to repay. See Chen, Rasmussen, and Reille in Sources. The collapse in Bosnia was severe enough that Kiva decided to suspend lending to Women for Women, giving them a "paused" status on the website which remains as of this writing.

[†] I actually did find one such borrower just by asking around—microloans were that ubiquitous in Bosnia—eventually meeting him at a sidewalk café called Club Bill Gates. However, after talking at length he got nervous about publication and asked me not to use his story, even with a pseudonym. Rest assured, it conforms closely to what this section describes—money too easily available, over-indebtedness, borrowing from Petar to pay Pavle, and eventual default.

bar. As we sipped tea served by a young assistant, we slipped into a routine: I would ask a sentence-length question, Amra would translate this as a sentence-length question, Adisa would respond with a Greek epic tale or possibly any two Faulkner novels, and Amra would translate this back into a sentence-length answer.

Adisa wasn't babbling or evading the question, Amra explained. Adisa was just making sure every concern was addressed in Homeric detail. To summarize: yes, some MFIs had recklessly glutted the market with loans, seeking only profit. Bosnia's crisis had also been partly caused by a lack of any mandatory national central credit bureau. Instead, there had only been a World Bank–funded registry. Unfortunately, since local banks did not have to provide data, this system accomplished very little.

In its place, Bosnia was now developing a Central Registry of Credit, with which all banks were required to share their client information. A 2007 law had also given the Bosnian government expanded oversight powers to regulate the entire industry. Hopefully, Adisa believed, this would prevent the problem from returning. Hopefully.

Still, while I barely glimpsed dee darrrrk siiide of microfinance in Bosnia, it had affected many lives for the worse. If it had happened in Bosnia, it must have happened elsewhere, too, and might still again. I'd keep an eye out in my travels.*

---

*Among the hundred-plus countries where microfinance is active, similar excessive-lending cycles have also played out in Morocco, Pakistan, Bolivia, India, and Nicaragua. In the latter case, too-rapid growth, the global economic downturn, and grandstanding by president Daniel Ortega led thousands of rural clients to stage a *No Pago* ("no payment") movement. A 2011 law allowed borrowers to renegotiate their loans, but the movement still occasionally flares. The most notorious crisis, in the Andhra Pradesh state of India, will be explored shortly.

Is ethnicity ever a problem? I eventually asked. *Would a Serb not want to owe money to a Croat, or would a Muslim not want to work with a Croat loan officer?*

Surprisingly: "No," said Adisa, without hesitation. Then, without the slightest irony or humor I could detect, she added: "Money has no religion."

Adisa stated this as a casual mention of obvious fact. Given the tragic history still visible on almost any street, I found this both optimistic and disorienting. Monstrous wars that had killed tens of thousands of innocent people weren't enough to inspire enlightened self-interest. Tiny loans, on the other hand, were.

Money has no religion. For the first time in my life, I could imagine the inherent selfishness of people as a kind of hope.

At Women for Women, Seida Saric's hope isn't tempered with cynicism. It's more about overcoming deep wounds with kindness.

I'm reluctant to ask about her own war experience unless it seems relevant, but of course it is, and it comes tumbling out:

"In the war," Seida remembers, "someone would go for water, you would pray they would come back." She lived in a tiny circle of people near the airport, and they initially thought the war wouldn't last. "Later, here you thought, another week, okay, another, another." This lasted for nearly four years. To this day, she feels a special bond with the people who shared her experience. "When we get together," she says, pausing for a moment to find the words, "we communicate in a special way."

She credits her sense of equality to her father, who raised all four of his girls to think of themselves as fully equal with anyone, regardless of gender, religion, ethnicity, age, and so on. This Muslim woman in Eastern Europe has a more finely developed sense of justice and equality than most Westerners I've met.

I tell Seida about Munira's pride in her ability to never stop working, to feed and care for her furniture-making family virtually around the clock. Seida laughs and nods with rueful compassion. " 'Equality' here is still based on a gender role—being a good mother, a strong wife, and so on," she says. "This is not equality. Respect for doing a role, yes, but not real equality, where there *are* no roles."

A statement like that would be considered feminist even in many American circles, I point out. It must be a fairly revolutionary thought in rural Bosnia. "These people were raised under socialism," she replies, "which doesn't involve a lot of thinking for yourself, economically or politically. That's why they need rights education. They need to stand up for themselves, and know that they can, and should." And so tens of thousands of Bosnians are now helped by Women for Women's eleven offices around the country—3,500 women are in the core program at any time— with thousands of successful microloans just a part of the services.

Seida's voice softens when discussing one particular kind of client.

During the war, many thousands of women, including girls as young as twelve years old and mothers as old as sixty, were systematically raped. Some of the abuse descended into torture so depraved that simply reading the case summaries may be difficult.*

Almost two decades later, many of the victims are still recovering from the trauma. But rural Bosnia lacks any counseling infrastructure, and seeking psychological help still carries a cultural stigma. For many women, their initial contact with Seida's group has been the first time anyone has listened to their stories. Simply being recognized and heard can be life-changing.

---

* Online links are in Sources. Not for the faint of heart.

"You can see it is sometimes the best thing in their whole lives," she says, more with joy and empathy than any noticeable pride. "I have seen faces brighten in six months. One girl who was in this office, you would swear she is a completely different person."

Seida finally smiles—broad, beautiful, even contented. I suggest that perhaps Seida herself is still healing by doing this work, and that helping others is part of her own emotional recovery. "Yes," she says. "I think this is probably true." But she pauses for only a moment to consider this, then returns to others, preferring to keep the focus on the women.

"But some women, when they get stronger, they are still taken by their anger." One client, for example, returned to her small village along the Drina River near the border between Bosnia and Serbia. That town, Srebrenica, was where Serb forces slaughtered more than eight thousand people, a massacre that the International Criminal Tribunal considered a genocide. It's now a part of the Republika Srpska, and Seida tells me its police force now includes some of the same paramilitaries who committed unprosecuted war crimes there. Seida's client went back just to *spite* them. "It is just to say 'you didn't win!'—so she walks past the killers every day." Seida feels sorry for her. "So young! But the need to defy them is defining her life. She must let it go, but no."

How do you not go completely insane? I would ask Seida. But she has just given me her answer. In a sense, Seida is a prisoner of the past, too, her work defined above all by the war—but her work is what frees her as well.

Our lives take on meaning to the degree that our love and our actions are the same.

As my meeting with Seida eventually ends, I've almost given up on meeting any of my own Kiva clients. It just feels unlikely, and too much to ask. But I wrap our interview by mentioning that I would love to meet any microlending clients she'd like me to meet, and that I did make a few loans to some of Seida's clients myself.

Instantly, eagerly, brightly: "You have names?"

You mean my own clients, specifically? Yes. Yes, I do.

Seida is smiling now, her sharp mind already racing ahead of the game, and at least as intrigued as I am. "You want to meet them?"

Yes, and.

The previous summer, I'd contributed $25 toward a Kiva loan to a livestock trader named Zagorka.* Her Kiva photo showed her laughing next to a large pig, and something about the look on her face reminded me of my mom. Now I was suddenly on the road to Tuzla in a last-minute rental car with a new translator, heading north to meet Zagorka and a few other clients face-to-face.

The car rental, incidentally, was not from Hertz or AutoEurope or any of the big multinationals. It was from a friend of T-Rock, the guy at the front desk of the family B&B where I was staying. I told T-Rock I needed a car, he called some dude, and the next morning the guy showed up with a one-page piece of paper to sign, which I took to be the Bosnian for "really, I won't steal your car." I handed the guy 50 euro, he handed me the keys, we shook hands, and I was off. *Of course* I would return the car with a full tank and on time. We didn't need more than a handshake. We were both friends of T-Rock, after all.

Whatever you might think from seeing the TV news, much of

---

*A pseudonym. On her fifth cycle of loans, Zagorka missed a payment, and when a client falls behind even slightly, Kiva's policy realizes that maybe the client wouldn't want to have that fact broadcast all over the Internet, so they anonymize the listing. Only Zagorka's occupation, nationality, and loan details remain visible on the page for her Kiva loan. Out of respect for Zagorka's privacy, I'm concealing her real name here, too.

the world is still on the Honor System—it has to be, just to function at all.

My new translator was Ajla, a twenty-five-year-old Bosnian woman who works professionally in five languages, primarily for visiting businessmen and government ministries. As a translator dealing with every faction in Bosnia, she knew a lot about the perceptions on every side.

Ajla was nine years old when the siege began. Her older brother was thirteen. At nine, she said, you still don't know what is normal and what isn't. Ajla told me many difficult stories that day about things that were definitely not normal. Since I was an outsider about to get on a plane, perhaps she could somehow open up to me in a way she often couldn't with many people in her daily life—but the one story I will never forget is this:

Parents rarely traveled together, for the same reason that the U.S. president and vice president never do: if one gets shot, you need the other one alive to keep things going. But one nice day, the guns in the hills were fairly silent, and Ajla's parents decided to risk a trip for water together.

A few minutes later, Ajla and her brother heard a shell explode in the direction of the well where their parents were headed.

My heart sank. I wanted to pull the car over to express my sorrow properly, but traffic wouldn't allow it. Ajla continued, matter-of-factly, in words I will always remember:

"My brother and I just looked at each other. The strange thing is, there was no emotion. We just started talking about who would do what: I can cook, you can go out and find work, we can ask my uncle for help . . ."

Her voice trailed off.

Nine years old. And already she was so used to seeing people murdered around her that she could remember feeling nothing in the moment.

"The good news is, my parents were okay—they had decided

to go somewhere else at the last minute." Ajla went on to describe her own puzzlement at her lack of emotions during the war, the numbness and overload. "I will always remember it," she said twice.

And yet, driving to Tuzla with me, Ajla had grown into a lovely, funny, thoughtful, open-hearted woman, close to her parents, deeply caring for her brother despite friction, madly in love with her fiancé Mirza, and a professional at catching nuance in five languages.

So now I asked Ajla: *how are you not completely insane?*

She smiled and thought about it, amused at first.

"Maybe I am," she replied, with a laugh that became a sigh. "I don't know. I think some of it is that we all were in it together, so we all remember, and we know it wasn't just us." Ajla thought aloud for another minute or two, but kept returning to how her friends and family all shared the same emotions together.

Friendship, support, connection: this is what the Two Dinos showed, what Seida talked about before I even asked, and now what Ajla answered with, too.

In Tuzla, Ajla and I met Nela and Jasminka, the local Women for Women loan officers, and I passed along the one final request I would have for the day (and would continue to have while meeting every client in this book): *please, don't anybody tell Zagorka or any client we're visiting that I put $25 into financing their loan.* Were I asked point-blank, of course I'd admit it. Otherwise, no—let's never let the client know I was a lender.*

---

* To be clear: I was there to understand more about their lives, see if the loans did any good, and offer friendship—not to cause some icky indebtedness angst. My contribution to the loans was small and fungible anyway. They'd have probably gotten financed without me. Besides, for the client: how much more friendly and empowering would it be to realize that some American has come all the way to your doorstep just because you're interest-

Everybody was cool with that (and will be everywhere for the rest of this book). So: on to Zagorka's house. I'd finally meet my first Kiva client.

There's a reason Zagorka seemed a lot like my mom in her Kiva profile. It's because she *is* a lot like my mom: friendly greeting, almost a hug even on first meeting, but eyes that still measure you, making sure that you're safe enough to open up to. Can I get you something to drink? Sit down on the porch, here, let me get you some coffee while we talk.

Out comes the 10W40 Bosnian coffee, followed by stories of children, then grandchildren. Then neighbors, and children of neighbors. Her whole world opens up if you sit still and listen. So I do.

Zagorka has three grown children—two daughters abroad and a son who still lives at home. He takes care of the house and helps with her business, which is buying pigs and poultry and reselling them at a profit.

This brings us to her microloans. *Have they been a big help?* Definitely—Zagorka is on her fifth loan cycle, re-upping to invest more every time, and her son has added a bathroom and insulated the entire house with the profits. After twelve years in the same house, she's happy for the extra room. *Is the interest rate ever a problem? Or the fees?* Zagorka looks puzzled that I would even ask. Of course not. Otherwise, why would she keep going back to the same lender?*

---

ing, and he wants to know more about how your life is going? This was the truth, after all.

A client found out exactly once, in Tanzania, where a loan officer in Dar es Salaam let my status as a lender slip to a client named Lucy. When I arrived, the mood was deferential, measured, and a little uncomfortable. It took half an hour before it got pretty close to normally pleasant, but we never got anywhere near just hanging out. I felt lousy about accidentally causing any stress.

*I asked nearly every client I met their opinion of their interest rate, out of

Not everything feels quite like home. Zagorka's husband remains indoors, shy and invisible. He has war-related medical problems that Ajla doesn't specify in translation. I let the subject drop.

I do the math and realize that Zagorka and her family would have moved into this house shortly after the war. I assume she's a refugee who returned like Sead and Munira, so I ask her if she still feels any tension with the Croats and Serbs. Ajla doesn't translate this.

"But Bob, Zagorka is not a Muslim," Ajla tells me. "She is Croat."

Oh. Right. Maybe her business in *pork wholesaling* might have been a clue. I withdraw the question and compliment the coffee. Ajla passes this along.

---

earshot of any MFI employee, at every opportunity. To keep from repeating their responses throughout the text, I'll summarize the virtually unanimous replies here. To my great surprise, the answer was rarely anything but dismissive, much like Zagorka in Bosnia and Mohammed in Morocco, ranging in tone from *not particularly, why do you ask?* to *don't be ridiculous, I can do math and make decisions, thanks.* Much more frequent, and confirming that the clients felt unafraid to speak their minds, were desires for grace periods, interest-bearing savings accounts, and the ability to re-borrow before full repayment if an opportunity came up, similar to conventional revolving credit. Even if rates sometimes seem high to Western eyes, I've rarely met a client who was particularly concerned about interest. Some of the short answers as to why: inflation tends to run higher in the developing world than in the U.S., which unavoidably tacks on a few percentage points (up to fourteen in Tanzania, at this writing); clients usually understand that a high volume of small loans can be more expensive for the MFI to administer than the smaller volume of larger loans made by a conventional bank; nonetheless, MFI rates are frequently not much higher than local conventional bank rates; and the sole alternative to an MFI loan may be black market rates vastly higher. All told, interest rates tend to be reasonable in local circumstances and are often manifestly *not* high. In 2012, for example, the inflation rate in India was over 7 percent (see www.bbc.co.uk/news/business-19252730, for example), but Rang De still administered education loans at 9.02 percent APR (see www.rangde.org/frequently-asked-questions.htm#43). For more, see www.bobharris.com/bank-of-bob/interest-rates.

But the fact that Zagorka is a Croat answers my question about tension. During the first years of the war, Croatian forces conducted ethnic cleansing against Bosnian Muslims throughout the Lašva Valley, southwest of here. Thousands were killed, and the Croat leaders were convicted of crimes against humanity. Every single person on this porch is old enough to remember this.

And yet here we sit, talking easily, laughing like old friends. I watch closely for any sign of tension in eyes or body language. I see none. These are loan officers and a client with a business, people who have known and worked with each other for years. Maybe Adisa at Partner was right: perhaps money has no religion. And maybe small bits of business like this actually help create common ground.

As recently as the 1980s, millions of Americans viewed Russia—and Russian people themselves—as a deadly looming menace. Now we trade with Russia, and the fear has subsided. China, same thing, if less so. If it works on a bloc level, maybe it works on a block level. I see every reason to think so here.

As for my own project, I'd been worried about MFIs cherry-picking which clients I might see, so I might only witness success stories. But I chose Zagorka, lent her $25, then came here and asked for myself how things went—exactly what I'd set out to do. Not only were her loans building her business and family home, they were helping in their own tiny way to heal a war-torn community. And now we're sitting and chatting almost like any two neighbors.

Zagorka asks about my own family, so I tell her about my mom in Ohio. Zagorka smiles, all mom-like, and asks how long it has been since I called her. Two minutes of banter later:

Hello . . . Mom? Hi. Um, good. I'm in Bosnia, actually. Yeah, Bosnia, that one. It's pretty nice, actually. How are you? Yes, yes, I know this call is expensive . . .

Up the road, we next visit Admira, a married mother of two whose Kiva profile described the start of her seventh loan cycle, financing a small retail clothing business at a market downtown.*

Admira and her extended family greet us in what now seems a familiar Bosnian routine. Chairs, coffee, cigarettes, stories.

Unfortunately, the story here is not the success I'd seen many times on this trip. I was sad to learn that Admira's business was now closed. Her father had died, and I gathered that he was not her only intimate loss, although I did not press the question. The time and emotional energy required to handle her situation, plus health and funeral expenses, meant that Admira and her family were now going through a tough period. But they were still optimistic.

In Bosnian, Nela and Jasminka from Women for Women speak in reassuring tones. Nela's English is decent, and she tells me later that Admira's loan will be restructured if necessary so that the family will not be unduly burdened while they get back on their feet.

I wish my bank treated me like that. Sure enough, Admira was able to repay the loan in full less than six months later.

Admira's mother-in-law Hajida is, coincidentally enough to beggar belief, another of my Kiva clients.† She comes out to join the discussion. Wow. Small world. Suddenly very small.

While Hajida and I chat, Admira's eight-year-old daughter emerges from the house in full Strawberry Shortcake regalia. The clothes might have been twice as old as she was, perhaps purchased secondhand or culled from Western charity donations during the war, but still: *awwww.*

---

* Admira's Kiva page is at www.kiva.org/lend/114725.
† Hajida's Kiva page is at www.kiva.org/lend/118455.

Hajida's enterprise is a small sideline—buying poultry in bulk, fifty chickens at a time, selling half at a profit, and freezing the others for food. Her business is struggling, too, which she attributes to a downturn in Bosnia's economy caused in part by the global economic pullback. I'd wonder if the world system was really so fully globalized, but Strawberry Shortcake here makes a strong corroborating argument.

I ask if Hajida or Admira has any trouble with the interest rate. "It is the only way," Hajida says while Ajla translates. "People working understand what they are doing," Admira adds. "It is good, okay, it is business."

We sit as a group now and chat about inflation, which is high here, and climate change, which the grandparents are emphatic about—"I used to go to sea on June second of every year," says an older man, "but now it is *impossible*, every year, because the weather has *changed!*"—and smile fondly at Strawberry Shortcake as she skips and struts and slyly seeks our attention.

Ajla's face lights up when she watches the little girl. You can see how much she will love being a mom.

Unexpectedly, this is what I find most encouraging about having lent $25 toward dozens of random Bosnians, then meeting a handful in person—that Ajla will be a mother someday.

Let me explain.

In a sense, the war in Bosnia is still far from over. Even if not one more bullet is fired, the wounds remain deep and will take generations to heal. Seida's work will last for as long as she does, and for many years after. Someone will need to help counsel the forced children of the rape victims, and then their children after that. The horror will echo for generations, until the memory of the memory is gone.

But those generations will come.

While I was writing this chapter, Ajla married Mirza, and

together they began a new life. A few days later, she posted nearly two hundred wedding photos on Facebook, where we're still in frequent contact. She and Mirza look giddy and thrilled, exactly the way young newlyweds should look. It's almost hard to imagine the nine-year-old Ajla, so shell-shocked that being orphaned seemed a typical fate. A whole world has changed in less than one lifetime.

And in that new world we'd sat—this grandson of a Baptist farmer, with Ajla and two Muslims on a Croatian Catholic lady's front porch, slurping coffee and laughing while I called my mom in Ohio—all connected by little deals and bits of business.

Peace may not have fully arrived in Bosnia, but it exists in small pockets all over the country. If Ajla's children are never to know fear as their mother did, I have to believe that personal exchanges like this will help.

Money has no religion, Adisa had said. Neither, of course, does an open heart.

To see this here gave me hope that it might be possible almost anywhere.

CHAPTER SEVEN

THE GREAT RIFT VALLEY AND NAIROBI

CHAIRMAN ISAIAH STANDS before the fourteen of us. We're assembled in a handmade wooden home nestled among rolling green hills.

The room is lit only by streaks of blue sky sneaking down between the timbers. When I first stepped out of the daylight and into this little square room, it took my eyes a few moments to adjust. But now I can see that I am facing a wall covered with newspapers, the only decoration the owners seem able to afford.

Here in the Bureti district, not far from Lake Victoria at the western edge of the Rift Valley Province, farmhouses like this one dot the landscape, many far from even the bumpiest back road. I've traveled here by riding along with Fred Koskei, head of the local branch of Juhudi Kilimo, a Kiva partner MFI serving farmers across Kenya, and Nathan, one of Fred's loan officers.* Nathan has told me that much of his workday consists of long walks to these farms.

Each member of the group we're visiting has entered this home in near-perfect silence, all smiles and respectful nods and gentle Kenyan handshakes (the grip is relaxed; to emphasize your

---

* Juhudi Kilimo's website is www.juhudikilimo.com.

pleasure to meet someone, use your left hand to support the bend of your own right elbow)—but no spoken words. In the twenty minutes it has taken us all to assemble on our doily-covered hardwood seats, I have heard not one word spoken aloud.

This handmade home has taken on the mindful hush of the southern Baptist churches I remember from my youth. Sure enough, my eyes find the words "The Rapture is About to Come" written on the far wall, and I realize that everyone is indeed wearing their Sunday best. The men's jackets are slightly frayed, however, and one lady's skirt has a loose hem. This may be the one good set of clothing that everyone owns. But we are here, and there is joy.

Instead of a hymnal, on the table before me is a handwritten pledge signed by every member of this Self-Help Group, swearing their mutual loyalty. Most Self-Help Groups are comprised of neighbors too poor collectively even to start with an MFI, so they pool their savings until they can share their first loan. Every adult now assembled has paid an initial fee of 10 Kenyan shillings—about 15 U.S. cents. Even this echoes the coin rattle of the collection plate.

Finally, the Chairman rises, and the air falls perfectly still, save for the distant braying of a goat in the hills. He begins with a short prayer.

The Chairman bows his head, closes his eyes, and raises his hands to chest level in praise. Everyone here knows what the Chairman is saying, but the silence remains.

This is the Bureti Self-Help Group for the Deaf.

Together, they are calling for God's guidance while thanking him for a chance at a better life. Fred and Nathan, who have both walked many miles through these hills to help poor farmers like these, bow their heads modestly, respectfully, honored to be here.

As am I.

The nearest town is Litein, population 2,300. The main road to the north leads to a rural border with Uganda near Lake Victoria, while the highway to the south runs toward the Serengeti. Both are closer than Nairobi. If you're a Westerner, those place names probably invoke certain images in your head—the East Africa that Western eyes know mostly through British colonialism, Hollywood, and safari tourism.

And yet my whole body tells me I'm in Rose Hill, Virginia.

Both of my parents grew up on farms near that small Appalachian town, a speck on the map near a break in the mountains called Cumberland Gap. About a mile north of Rose Hill, on the other side of the hills, is Harlan County, Kentucky, famous for the labor unrest of its coal miners. My dad's parents came from there. To the south, there's not much until Sneedville.

As of the 2010 census, Rose Hill's population is exactly 799.* The closest hospital or dentist is nearly twenty miles east, in the big town of Jonesville, population 5,280. According to Rose Hill's own website, fewer than half of its citizens age twenty-five or older have a high school education. More than 40 percent of the town—including more than half of the children—lives below the poverty line.† To think that America and the developing world are inherently two separate things requires a great lack of knowledge about both.

In the 1930s, when my parents were kids during the Great Depression, subsistence farming and Jesus kept bodies and souls together, and if the work wasn't done by Sunday, Jesus might have to wait. My dad's house, built by his father by hand, never had indoor plumbing or running water, and no electricity until he was twelve years old. And while both of my parents attended a one-room

---

*This Rose Hill should not be confused with the Washington, D.C., suburb of the same name, also in Virginia, whose population is almost twenty times larger. See Sources.

†One enterprising local has a thriving e-commerce business at www.roadkill BBQsauce.com, where you are encouraged to "Eat More Possum." See that you do.

schoolhouse—that's where they met, of course, when he was in third grade and she was in first—Mom wasn't there for long, since her dad was a struggling coal miner and they had to move frequently. Dad had to drop out after eighth grade because his older brothers were off fighting the Germans. He was needed on the farm.

I didn't witness any of that personally, of course. By the time I existed, both sides of the family had worked their way up to owning livestock as a source of financial stability. My mom's dad, all red sunburn and crooked hands in my memory, had built a whole pasture of cows by the time I was ten. Their milk went to market and came back as tools, fertilizer, seed, clothes, electricity, and more. The extra income helped feed and clothe Mom until she met Dad again as a teenager.

That's what dairy cows can do.

That's why the Bureti Self-Help Group for the Deaf hopes eventually to work up to owning cows. And it's why Juhudi Kilimo provides loans to buy them.

Symon and his wife Jenn are showing me their new cow the same way a taxi driver might show off a shiny sedan.*

We're on a small single-family farm near the city of Murang'a, to the east of the Rift Valley and about two hours north of Nairobi. Symon is dapper in his double-breasted jacket, and Jenn is cheerful in a pink shirt and skirt. The couple is posing with the cow next to a large stockpile of dried grasses and leaves, encouraging me to take a photograph.

---

* Symon's Kiva page is at www.kiva.org/lend/202103. Note that Symon fully repaid his loan, but the Kenyan shilling declined against the dollar during repayment, so I and other lenders took a one percent currency loss—twenty-five cents on a $25 loan. This is a rare event, but it happens. The effect is pretty small. In my own portfolio of more than 5,000 loans, the total currency loss has been 0.01 percent—the equivalent of one penny per hundred dollars.

The cow, however, isn't cooperating, stomping around in the mud like a child who doesn't want to meet the newcomer in the living room. As I snap several photos, Symon and Jenn alternate between posing proudly, stumbling out of the way of the lurching animal, and laughing at the silly moment, big grins on their faces. Finally, Symon pats the cow's head and gives its neck a little push, and the cow obligingly turns her head toward the camera, too, as if to say, "Fine, you win, let's get this over with." *Click.* As group portraits go, it's as sweet as they come.

The cow's name is Grace, which feels ironic, since she moves like a cow. Still, the name is no surprise, since the Central Province is mostly Christian. For every African first name I hear, there may be a half-dozen Peters and Marys and Matthews.

Grace is a Guernsey hybrid capable of producing roughly twice as much milk per day as any local species.* By purchasing Grace on credit, Symon and Jenn can sell the extra milk at a tidy profit, even after you deduct the cost of additional feed, water, and miscellaneous cow-care supplies. For the first year, the additional profit pays off the loan. Afterward, the additional income is Symon's and Jenn's, free and clear, and it can be used to pay for tools, fertilizer, seed, clothes, or electricity—exactly like my grandfather's dairy sales did half a century ago—or simply the capacity to own more cows, the same way a real estate investor uses apartment rents to buy more property.

Additional sources of income are a necessity here. We're taking

---

* East African cattle—mostly hump-backed Boran and Zebu—are hardy and well suited for the flat plains of Masai country, the arid Somali border region, or the desert-like Turkana district, from whose early inhabitants you and I both descended. Many Masai, Turkana, and other peoples of Kenya still maintain a lifestyle built around nomadic husbandry of these species. While the milk is sufficient to feed the owners, it's not nearly enough to cultivate a dairy business. That said, the dairy model can only work in the cool highlands. A Guernsey like Grace wouldn't last a week in the heat.

these cow-and-family portraits in Kenya's lush Central Province, an area with the size and population of Connecticut and the most fertile farmland you can imagine. A local joke says that you could stick your finger in the ground and it would grow. These hills have been farmed well for centuries, but growing families mean that inheritances must be divided into smaller and smaller plots of land, which still must be made profitable to feed the next generation. Symon inherited this square of land from his mother, whose inheritance was only a third of her parents' holdings.

After raising five children, Symon and Jenn now find themselves with a bonus "gift" child late in life. They also now help care for the family of Jenn's sister, all while anticipating the medical issues we all face as we age. Extra milk income would make a big difference. A fancy hybrid cow would be just the thing.

But where can a rural farmer in Murang'a, Central Province, borrow 63,000 Kenyan shillings—about $825 in U.S. dollars—to finance a fancy new cow?

Juhudi Kilimo (Swahili for the decidedly unexotic "Agricultural Effort"; in conversation, it's just "Juhudi") serves rural clients from seven field offices across Kenya. Unlike the MFIs we've already seen in Peru and Bosnia, Juhudi doesn't focus on working capital for craftspeople, furniture makers, or other small service businesses. Instead, Juhudi focuses on asset financing—think of a car loan—on cows, goats, poultry, pigs, rabbits, and other livestock capable of generating income. As we've seen, once the loan is paid off, the client is left with both the asset and a steady source of income. On paper, at least, it's a great deal for the client, and for the lender, it's scalable, simple to implement, and almost impossible to overextend to individual clients.

It's a model with tremendous potential. Eager to see it in a rural setting, I first stopped in Nairobi, East Africa's largest city, where Juhudi makes its headquarters.

Nairobi is a tough town.

A 2002 UN study found that more than a third of the city's three million residents had been robbed in the previous year alone. Nearly a third of all homes and businesses had been burglarized, about one resident in five had had their car stolen, and a similar number had been physically assaulted.* The website of the local United Nations office, meanwhile, warns you to "never walk at night in the centre of Nairobi even for a short distance," that carjacking is a "fairly common crime," and that even "street children can become violent."†

On the day of my arrival, I picked up a copy of the *Standard*, the oldest newspaper in the country. Respectably august—its reporting is hard-hitting enough that masked gunmen armed with AK-47s raided the place after a story embarrassing to the president—it was nonetheless filled with insane tabloid violence. The first nine pages of the paper included a slashing, a stabbing, an armed robbery, a carjacking, the burning of a home by vigilantes, theft of a baby, and a summary execution committed by police.‡

Part of the problem is that the leadership is notoriously corrupt. One global study of government transparency ranked the current Kenyan administration at 154th on the planet, below even the lunatic Mugabe regime in Zimbabwe.§ With funds misallocated

---

* *Crime in Nairobi: Results of a Citywide Victim Survey*, UN-HABITAT, September 2002. See Sources.

† Security advice of the United Nations Office at Nairobi as of October 2010. See Sources.

‡ There was also an article decrying the popularity of Judge Judy, Tyra Banks, and the Kardashians. This newspaper became my favorite in Kenya.

§ See Transparency International's 2011 Corruption Perceptions Index in Sources. No perfect measure exists of actions meant to be hidden, but this one is widely accepted. Only fifteen governments ranked as more corrupt than the current Kenyan government. Five were in active war zones.

and bribery widespread, law enforcement is barely existent, and a culture of impunity has developed among criminals, along with a sense of helplessness for everyone else.

So infrastructure teeters under the strain of a growing population, crime runs almost unchecked, and people who can afford it hire full-time guards. More than two thousand private security firms operate in Kenya, albeit often to little effect. Throw in the 1998 bombing of the U.S. Embassy, ongoing terrorist activities from a Somali Al-Qaeda offshoot called Al-Shabaab, and the occasional aid worker or two kidnapped in the north and hustled off to Somalia for ransom, and not many Americans would see an exciting career path in moving to Nairobi to run a small upstart MFI.

Nat Robinson did.

I find the CEO of Juhudi in their national headquarters, a converted residence in the relatively quiet suburban Ngong neighborhood of Nairobi. From the outside, this microlending bank looks like just another family home. Given the security situation—shortly before my visit, four unidentified gunmen carjacked a Juhudi vehicle, tied up the guards, kidnapped and robbed the driver, and only released him when a BMW came along, providing a more lucrative target—blending in seems like a good idea.

A tall man in his thirties, Nat carries a boyish energy and not the slightest hint of self-importance, despite Juhudi's self-declared mission of helping a hundred thousand farmers to improve their lives. Most people I've met carrying that sort of goal can project an earnestness field twenty feet thick. But Nat was raised in a small town in Colorado, where pretense probably violated some sort of local ordinance. Even as we discuss value chains and market segments, the vibe feels more like two dudes talking baseball at Vanderbilt, where Nat got his MBA.

Nairobi seems like a bit of a jump from all that. Does he miss home?

"Nah, not really. It's a pretty big adjustment, but I get to go back fairly often. And I worked in Shanghai for a while, and I've traveled a little"—here, Nat's being modest; he has traveled to more than forty countries—"so I'm used to being overseas. And you live here and do this work for a while—for all the problems here in the city, most people are great, and when you get in the field and see what we're doing, it's really rewarding.

"Plus," he adds, breaking into a huge grin, "when I speak Swahili, it totally blows people's minds."

Nat runs me through some numbers about the "smallholders" (a British term for family subsistence farms on small plots) whom Juhudi serves: about half of the clients are women, and more than three quarters live on less than $4 a day. These farmers make up 75 percent of Kenya's entire workforce, but three quarters of them are still unserved by MFIs.

Seeing the obvious need, a Swiss non-profit, working in cooperation with the R&D wing of a large Kenyan MFI, developed the concept of financing livestock and farming assets in much the same way that Western businesses acquire capital equipment. After all, if your upgraded business computer can pay for itself in increased productivity, so can the cows on even a poor rural farm.

One key to successful microlending, as in any business, is for the product to be carefully designed to fit the customer: shopkeepers whose stock turns over rapidly may do well with short-term loans; craftspeople may have only seasonal income, and would need to repay accordingly, with longer grace periods; large farmers may need multiple cycles, one for seed and equipment, one for hiring day workers for the harvest; and so on.

Juhudi's dairy loans, designed to be profitable to the customer after the first year, are so well structured—even including a small bit of insurance, so that if the cow gets sick, the customer isn't hurt—that Juhudi has never even had to advertise. Word-of-mouth is plenty: "We've got more demand than we've got money to lend," in Nat's words. In fact, one of Juhudi's biggest early challenges was simply managing their own growth. New offices and staff cost money, after all, especially given Juhudi's extra expense in providing personal business training and technical support to every client. As they grew, Juhudi needed to attract their own new capital from larger investors.

The world's thousands of MFIs receive funding from a variety of sources, depending on their environment and goals. Non-profit MFIs tend to be funded more by foundations, government and international development agencies, non-governmental organizations (NGOs), charities, private grants, and the like, while for-profit lenders tend to be backed by commercial funds, investment firms, larger banks, and even initial public offerings of stock (IPOs), but there's some variation and overlap, particularly as an MFI grows.*

And how could Juhudi, a small for-profit upstart working in a challenging environment, prove to investors that they were worth taking seriously, gaining funds to expand? Kiva.

When Kiva chooses to partner with an established MFI, list some of the MFI's loans online, and then provide lender funds at zero interest, they never provide more than 30 percent of that MFI's

---

* This is not an exhaustive list, obviously. At this writing, the MIX Marketplace currently lists 248 sources under "Funders" at mixmarket.org/profiles-reports, and even this is surely incomplete. (Kiva, for example, is not listed.)

While we're on it, Kiva's own funding breaks down like this: in 2011, 52 percent of revenue came from online donations, 16 percent from foundations, 13 percent from in-kind donations, 10 percent from corporations, 8 percent from individual contributions, and I may have dropped a twenty in the elevator when I visited. Their biggest corporate donor is VISA, and the biggest institutional donor is the eBay-related Omidyar Network, about which you'll later learn more. See Kiva's annual report at annualreport.kiva.org/ and financial reports at www.kiva.org/about/finances.

total funding, and typically only about 5 percent, give or take. But to a small MFI, working with Kiva can have benefits other than money. "Being able to point to our relationship with Kiva definitely helped us develop our financing," Nat says. "They do enough due diligence that if you're working with them, people can see you're legit."

I compare passing Kiva's current due diligence process to the Good Housekeeping Seal of Approval, and Nat smiles. "Yeah, definitely. It was a huge help."

Interesting. This is an important benefit of Kiva that I hadn't thought of—one that virtually no lender at home ever gets to see so directly. By supporting the clients of these MFIs by making a loan through the site, visitors are also supporting the MFIs themselves, enabling new services to grow and reach more clients.

There are numerous other challenges, too, as Juhudi grows and tries to reach those hundred thousand farmers.

Local black-market moneylenders, for example, don't always appreciate it when a legitimate MFI rolls into town and starts offering more reasonable terms. This can be true anywhere, but in Kenya's current climate, more than one loan officer has been surrounded by thugs, many of them politically connected and therefore untouchable, and forced to write off a few loans. But in this, Juhudi was assisted by the 2008 election of Barack Obama, whose partially Kenyan ancestry gave an instant credibility boost to Western organizations here. "The lady in the lunchroom up the street still insists that she's his cousin," Nat says with a laugh.

Donor fatigue is another issue, as it is for any non-profit in the developing world. Any fresh earthquake or tsunami or a volcano explosion tends to shift the focus of big-pocket donors to emergency aid. The day-in, day-out process of building an economy from the very bottom up doesn't attract square-jawed reporters and the TV entourages, so long-term solutions can have trouble remaining funded. This is why Nat's steering Juhudi Kilimo toward self-sufficiency. "That's one of the advantages of trying to solve poverty through a business model, as opposed to relying on grant money," Nat explains. "If you're making a profit while you're helping people, you're not relying on funding that can dry up."

As a final challenge, cow loans can only work if farmers can get a fair and consistent price for milk. So far, this hasn't been a problem, given that most of the milk from these loans is sold directly to Kenya's largest dairy. But Nat foresees the eventual need to expand into larger loans to build private milk-chilling plants and other processing and distribution equipment.

What Nat's trying to address is a major concern in development work, conceptually simple but difficult to overcome. Even if you create a truly efficient model for creating wealth—and these cow loans are a zesty example—if you're only helping people generate one commodity, the means to distribute that commodity has to develop, too. And even if it does, should too many people create the same business in the same space, the price will come down. Without creativity in distribution and in developing different, complementary businesses, a cookie-cutter approach is inherently limited.

This limitation is hardly unique to microlending. An Ohio neighborhood with eight lemonade stands would have the same problem, as would a suburb with too many shopping malls or a smartphone market with too many kinds of handsets. When markets saturate, prices come down, and somebody goes out of business.

The stakes are unimaginably higher in the developing world, where losing your shirt is a more literal term. Bankruptcy to the most challenged of the working poor can mean hunger, lack of medicine, and worse. So even when an innovation brings growth and success, clients, MFIs, and everyone involved all need to think constantly about coming up with even more new ideas.

Symon is another farmer in Murang'a.* His Juhudi loan for a dairy cow is one of the loans I helped refinance via Kiva. Symon also grows coffee, and Symon has poultry, and Symon is expanding into bananas, and Symon will happily talk your ear off with all of his plans.

We're scrambling around his farm on an overcast afternoon. He's ten years older than me, but I can barely keep up. I certainly can't write down everything he's telling me as he shares an almost microscopic knowledge of his land.

"These leaves, from my coffee? These are also good fodder. These I cut up and give to the cattle. It is very good for their bones, lots of calcium." Suddenly Symon is thirty feet away. "Over here, this is where I put in the piping to irrigate my coffee." I write this down. Now Symon is twenty feet behind me. "These, these are the racks where my coffee is dried." *Scribble, scribble.* I look up, and he's gone again. "Want to see my manure pit?" *What? Oh, there he is.* "I can sell this manure for profit." *I bet you can,* I think with amusement and respect.

I am joined on this hopscotch by Nelly Njoki, Juhudi's regional manager, Rachel Brooks, a former Kiva Fellow who has worked with Juhudi all over Kenya, and the Grace-the-cow-owning Symon, who is a friend of this Symon. The four of us trail along like the tail of a comet, often at some distance. Grace-owning Symon is a heavy-set man pushing sixty, Rachel has just had her third child, and Nelly is so visibly pregnant that I've winced every time our car has hit a pothole.

Any protective instincts are completely wasted here, however.

---

* Not to be confused with the Symon who posed for a photo with his wife Jenn and prize cow Grace. The Kiva page of Symon the coffee farmer is at www.kiva .org/lend/226038.

Our conga line snakes around Symon's farm for the better part of an hour, and I'm the one who tires first. Grace-owning Symon has a farmer's endurance, and Nelly has worked with Juhudi from the beginning, usually late into the evening and often on Saturdays, motivated by her clients' successes. Nelly's unborn child is probably enjoying the ride like a snowboarder.

For her part, Rachel has been answering my questions about microfinance in Kenya since just after 7:30 A.M. Nairobi's morning rush hour makes Los Angeles freeways feel downright bucolic, but we eventually swerved and panic-braked successfully through a parade of overpacked *matatu* minibuses; a group of Muslim teenage girls walking to school in British-style uniforms and Islamic head coverings; and at every stoplight, swarms of men selling every small item imaginable—razors, newspapers, vegetables, candy, and (once) goldfish in small plastic bags. Through it all, Rachel has briefed me on zero-grazing units (purpose-built shelters for cows where there isn't land for them to graze) and chaff cutters (hand-cranked feed cutters that look like steampunk meat grinders), and a typical sequence of borrowing: first loan, cow; second loan, zero-grazing unit for multiple cows; third loan, next cow; and so on. Rachel's seminar has also covered the local impact of the 2008 economic crisis (severe); the kinds of loans other Kenyan MFIs specialize in (*boda-boda* loans, for motorcycle taxis, are popular); and the Merry-Go-Round, a savings model used by the very poor, where everyone chips in a small amount weekly—maybe the equivalent of 50 cents each—and takes random turns borrowing against the pot, giving everyone fair access to working capital.

Merry-Go-Rounds are popular in the Kibera slum of Nairobi, where about a quarter-million people live without basic services. While Rachel was talking, I realized that the simple fact that Merry-Go-Rounds exist—that in those conditions, people still organize, support each other, and try to find creative, practical means for improving their lives—made me feel both inspired and a little bit grief-stricken: no one so resourceful should be so hammered by the birth lottery.

While Symon describes his work routine, the sun comes out, so our conga line ducks under the shade of a banana tree. At 7:30 A.M., when Rachel and I first got into the car, Symon had already been awake for three hours. He rises daily at 4:30 A.M., milks his cows at 5, takes the milk to a cooling shed from about 6 to 6:30, moves the cows' dung to his manure pit until 7, and only then finally sits down to breakfast with his wife and elderly mother.

This is humbling to imagine. Symon shovels dung for a half-hour before breakfast every day. I can't make myself go for a jog.

Nelly listens with impressive care to Symon's plans, asking open-ended questions. Back home, banks have knowingly made bad loans, packaged those bad loans into fraudulent securities that bilked a second group of people, pocketed the bailout money once the whole thing collapsed, and are still foreclosing on homeowners, generally treating people like the stuff Symon shovels before breakfast. But here Nelly stands, under a banana tree, miles from her office and within olfactory range of a manure pit, despite being so pregnant that her child may walk right out of her womb, just so she can listen to a client.

And Symon's goals are impressive. The cow that my $25 helped to finance is a means for Symon, not an end. Symon has a plan. Cows, you see, provide cash flow for his longer-term investment in coffee, which recently paid off with a million Kenyan shillings—about $12,500—in its very first year. Symon has reinvested that money, convinced that his operation can be five times larger in a few years.

If so, maybe I'll ask *him* for a loan.

A few days later, I'm heading northwest, toward the highlands again, and then westward into the Rift Valley. The roadside slowly changes from cinderblock homes—incremental housing, built over the course of years, as the residents save up for each new addition—to red-flowered flame trees, lush purple jacarandas, Australian blue gums imported by the British to dry this once-swampy area, and the spiky euphorbia plants used by the Masai to burn skin for tattoos.

Next comes Lake Naivasha, a fifty-square-mile lake at an altitude one thousand feet higher than Denver, home to hundreds of species of birds, including a stand of flamingoes large enough to attract tourists all by themselves. Unfortunately, Lake Naivasha is also home to industrial-strength floraculture, with daily flights bringing fresh flowers from here all the way to Europe for sale. On Valentine's Day, about one in three roses given in the UK will have been grown here in Kenya.*

Unfortunately, these giant flower farms, and the population boom that resulted from their success, are slowly polluting the water with pesticides and waste. The fishing industry is dying, farmers here can no longer rely on the lake for irrigation, and the whole kaboodle—flowers, jobs, and the life of the lake itself—may well be dead in another twenty years or so.† But in the global economic system as it currently exists, the short term is the only term that matters. And so, as with diamonds and chocolate, when we Westerners give roses to our sweeties (a typical bouquet costing more than a week's wage for a flower worker), these tokens of even our gentlest, most life-affirming love can be bound inextricably to cruelty and waste.

To fully know humankind might feel like befriending a madman.

The modern flower industry is really just a variation on a theme.

These same lands were so coveted by the British a century ago

---

* See "Drained of Life" by Ogodo and Vidal in Sources.
† See *Lake Naivasha* by Food and Water Watch in Sources.

that the British East Africa Company not only seized them all, but assigned them entirely to white settlers, some of whom built vast wheat and cattle and coffee plantations. This chunk of Africa soon became explicitly known as the "White Highlands," and Lake Naivasha became a luxury retreat for the "Happy Valley set" of wealthy philandering expats who looked like *The Great Gatsby* but behaved more like *Jersey Shore*.

The Swahili word for "white person," *mzungu* (plural form, *wazungu*) means "he who wanders," implying rootlessness, idleness, and a lack of identity, with a detectable note of disdain. The Happy Valley set weren't why the word was invented, but they were wazungu of the first magnitude. The locals, meanwhile, were mostly reduced to laborers, herded into "native reserves" on inferior soil, subject to imprisonment and occasional killing if they didn't quietly just go pick the beans.

If you're familiar with Baroness Karen Blixen's memoir *Out of Africa*, you've seen colonial life portrayed as nearly idyllic. Damn straight: for colonists like Blixen—whose holdings were so extensive that her former coffee farm is now an entire Nairobi suburb, named "Karen" in her honor by the white developer—yes, things were swell. But for the locals whose land had been taken by force, many of whom were compelled to live in "native reserves," not so much.*

---

* Even Kenya's borders were never determined for ethnic, linguistic, or historic reasons, but simply by lines drawn by colonists. Check out the 1885 Conference of Berlin, convened by European powers to decide which pieces of Africa each would have exclusive "right" to colonize, and the Scramble for Africa that followed. Among other lunacies, the conference affirmed an area three times the size of Texas, now known as the Democratic Republic of the Congo, as the personal property of Belgium's King Leopold II. No Africans were represented, although millions soon died under Leopold's brutal rule. (See Sources.) The following year, the governments of Queen Victoria in England and Otto von Bismarck in Germany finalized a border between their East African claims, drawing mostly straight lines across hundreds of miles of land inhabited by

From Naivasha, we head northwest through Nakuru, then west—passing the great Mau Forest where politically connected Kenyans have taken land, only to lose it shortly after becoming politically less connected—and watch as the land turns to rolling green tea plantations. Finally, we reach Litein, a town of only three thousand people, but the capital for a district of more than three hundred thousand farmers, tea workers, and tradespeople—thousands of whom now have microfinanced livestock, equipment, and creative small side businesses.

Charcoal flavored . . . ? Really? Charcoal is a flavor? Um . . . sure. I'd love some.

We're discussing yogurt, by the way. Charcoal-flavored yogurt. I'm about to put some in my mouth.

I'm sitting with Fred and Nathan of the Litein office of Juhudi. We're on the bare-wood porch addition to a small family restaurant owned by Mercy and her husband, who is so busy cooking in the back that I never get a chance to meet him.* The couple has four children under the age of twelve, and Mercy's day begins by making them breakfast at 5 A.M. After that, she milks their cows, stores the milk, and works in the family restaurant until evening.

It was in that restaurant that Mercy realized that some of her milk could be made into yogurt to sell to her customers. Juhudi cow and capital equipment loans have helped this family build their farm, establish their restaurant, and acquire a freezer for

---

pastoral and nomadic peoples who had scarcely heard of Britain or Germany. Those arbitrary lines remain the basis of the official border between Kenya and Tanzania to this day.

* "Mercy" is a pseudonym to save anyone (myself included) from embarrassment, for reasons you are about to appreciate.

their yogurt. Now Mercy has generously offered me a sample of the product.

Fred and Nathan seem amused that I've never tried charcoal yogurt. It's a common flavor here, inexpensive, made from the shaved bark of the wattle tree, a multi-pronged cactusy thing. *I did not know this?* they ask. *No, I did not know this.* Not wanting to seem fussy, I nod and accept Mercy's offer.

Mercy has big plans, I learn while awaiting my fate. The restaurant is profitable, as is the yogurt, so her family is eager to borrow and plan for more cows, more land, you name it. Fred and Nathan, knowing her track record, are supportive of her ambitions. She hands me a yellow mug of the yogurt, which is the texture of lumpy ooze.

I try to delay the inevitable by bringing up Obama. *Oh my, yes! It is great he was elected, we are big fans, very happy for your country.* Mercy waits, expectantly, as I am about to sample this beverage substance. Fred senses my slight distress and smiles. Nathan takes my camera and snaps a photo of me, looking down at the yogurt like Socrates contemplating a hemlock frappé.

In many books where a white guy visits Africa, this is where the yogurt turns out to be a magnificent treat, and the narrator ruefully regrets his cultural biases and narrow Western palate, the reverse-racist Noble Savage myth stretched to cuisine. And I would love to write something like this, if only because I would prefer a pleasant memory.

But oh, dear, no. It was ghastly. I'm sure if one is raised with charcoal yogurt, it's perfectly delightful, just like a thousand other regional delicacies. But this is me, Bob from Ohio, whose favorite food remains Cheerios. Even a year after the event, sitting here in Los Angeles, I can still feel the sensation of runny bovine secretions, bitter charred bark, and dry lumpy sludge. My throat started to close in panic before this first sip of mucus was halfway to the back. For a moment, it was all I could do to keep breathing.

Somehow I managed *oh my, yes, that's um, really good, thank you.* Once again in Kenya, a *mzungu* was lying. Fred's and Nathan's amused faces were priceless. Mine was probably pretty good, too.*

Still, it was great to see Mercy's business doing so well.

I'd first met up with Fred at the Litein office of Juhudi, which he runs.

Litein is tiny, but all bustle: motorbikes, cars, trucks, tractors, bicycles, and donkeys pulling sledges share the streets with skipping kids in green school uniforms, workmen in Liverpool soccer jerseys, women of many shapes balancing packages of many more shapes on their heads, and the occasional cow. Right on time, a thin, stylish man in a black suit and crisp white shirt walked up and extended his hand. *How ever did you recognize me?* I joked. "You looked lost," Fred replied, already teasing me gently in the first moments of our friendship.

Fred is from Bomet, a slightly larger town about twenty miles away, where he first learned about microlending in college. His initial experience was with a village bank whose total assets were only 60,000 shillings—about $750. "It was small, but I liked it right away," Fred explained. "You could see it as something that people can really do for themselves."

---

* I also soon developed diarrhea of psychedelic intensity and realized that the yogurt may not have been pasteurized to the industrial extent that my bowels comprehend. God bless whatever intestinal flora allow the locals to digest Mercy's cow goo, but I lacked them entirely, with results that were probably audible in Uganda. Fortunately, ever since a bad beverage in China led to a case of *Crouching Tourist, Shooting Dragons*, I always travel with at least two kinds of antibiotics, prescribed in advance by my travel doc. A week-long blast of Levaquin turned off the fireworks. Lesson for the traveler: trust your instincts. If you recoil, your subconscious is trying to keep you out of trouble.

Later, Fred worked for two years with another MFI in nearby Kisii, but for six months along the way, Fred worked in the Kakuma refugee camp, in the far northwestern desert, where the average daytime temperature is 104 degrees. Even its name tells you how remote this place is—*Kakuma* literally means "Nowhere." Nonetheless, roughly eighty thousand refugees from wars and instability in virtually every nearby country—Sudan, Somalia, Rwanda, Ethiopia, Eritrea, Uganda, Congo, the Central African Republic, Zimbabwe and more—have sought Nowhere as an upgrade on what they left behind.

However, once newcomers are safely ensconced in this township of tin, thatch, adobe, and other improvised housing, Kenya does not allow the freedom to leave without special passes. Nowhere becomes both a sanctuary and a functional prison. Tens of thousands of people remain stuck for years amid dust storms, poisonous snakes, and the never-ending heat. And even if things improve in their home countries, the refugees may still be unable to leave. The trip home may simply be too expensive.

For six months, Fred lived there by choice, trying to work out a lending architecture that would enable refugees who could return home safely to finance the cost of the trip by paying off their loans with their existing skills in farming or small business. "It's not as bad as you'd think," he told me. "They do business with each other, they trade, there's a sense of community."

It never crossed my mind to ask Fred how he handled the stress. Where others saw despair, Fred saw skills and abilities, not to mention the resourcefulness that helped these people survive in the first place. Fred saw the people, not their situation.

There's good reason for optimism, even for people stuck hundreds of miles away from any financial infrastructure. Thanks to technology, as long as there's a phone signal, there's potential access to finance.

In 2007, Safaricom, a division of the UK telecom provider Vodafone and Kenya's largest cell phone provider, launched M-PESA (the *M* implies "mobile"; *pesa* is Swahili for "money"), a service that allows customers to deposit, withdraw, and transfer money using simple text messaging. Physical cash can be securely deposited or withdrawn for a small fee at more than thirty thousand retail outlets across the country, and money floating on your phone can't be stolen, because cashing out requires ID and a secret PIN. It's easy to use, secure, and most of all, fast.

Maybe you're my brother in Mombasa, and you need me to send you emergency cash to cover a medical need. Or maybe you're a retailer, and I want you to sell me anything from a gallon of milk to a Holstein cow. If we both have basic cell phones and there's enough cash in my M-PESA account, we can do the transaction in seconds without even touching our wallets.

M-PESA's transfer fees are also cheaper than existing services from banks, the post office, and bus companies, so in a country where three times as many people have cell phones as bank accounts, the service has been adopted with astonishing speed. By the time you read this, about half of all Kenyans will be using M-PESA, which already accounts for more than 5 percent of the cash economy nationwide. Virtually every neighborhood I passed through, even the most ramshackle village, had at least one green M-PESA sign marking a retail outlet where cash could be uploaded or downloaded. In some places, it was common to see a half-dozen M-PESA signs within a five-minute walk.

The service is mainly used by migrant workers in Nairobi to support their rural families—"Send money home" was the original marketing slogan*—but customers constantly devise new ways to use the service. Things you'd write a check for in the U.S.? M-PESA.

---

* The first TV ad is at www.youtube.com/watch?v=nEZ3oK5dBWU.

Purchases you'd make with a debit card? M-PESA. Pay utility bills at the bank? M-PESA.

M-PESA's original purpose, however, was to facilitate microfinance by bringing the cost of reaching clients in the field down as close to zero as possible. The savings could then be passed on to the clients through lower fees and interest rates. To Safaricom's credit, they've never lost sight of that goal, and in 2010, they teamed up with Equity, a commercial bank with the largest customer base in Kenya, to launch M-KESHO (*kesho* is Swahili for "tomorrow"), an M-PESA-linked bank account. M-KESHO offers an array of services that the working poor can use to take control over and protect their financial well-being: short-term microcredit, inexpensive microinsurance covering emergency medical or funeral expenses, and fee-free savings accounts with no minimum balance that pay up to 3 percent interest.

Watching M-PESA and M-KESHO in use, it feels strange to realize that nothing comparable exists back in the United States. But innovation is often a local phenomenon, and the developing world sometimes skips ahead a step or two in implementation— bus routes blossoming where train tracks were never laid, wireless computing spreading rapidly where dial-up modems were scarcely installed, and so on.*

Where hard-wired telephone networks were not already in place, mobile tower construction and mobile phone use have exploded: among humankind's seven billion people, there are now more than six billion mobile subscriptions—five billion in the developing world.† Signal presence and strength are often remarkable.

---

* In the former Soviet republic of Estonia, Wi-Fi has become considered a basic right, and schools, trains, hospitals, government offices, and even park areas offer free connections. Their view of Internet access as an essential public good like electricity is pioneering, but as local economies demonstrate productivity gains, it may become common sooner than we currently imagine.
† See World Bank report, July 2012, in Sources.

The ancient Motorola Razr I've taken on these travels—cheap, durable, easily replaced, charged by USB and with an extremely accessible SIM card, and compatible with at least one mobile network frequency in use virtually anywhere on earth—has worked almost instantly almost everywhere; the weakest reception has been at home in Los Angeles.* New uses for inexpensive phones are likely to accelerate on a track strikingly separate from Western smartphone development—especially where their use can make life easier for people in rural and developing areas. As inexpensive handsets from India and China spread through the developing world, applications that assist in agriculture, health, employment, inventory, marketing, commodities trade, and even basic governance are already becoming the leading edge of locally powered development.

Naturally, Juhudi Kilimo and other MFIs across Kenya are now exploring mobile banking as a means of bringing down the costs of their own services to the client. "It's definitely a big part of everybody's future," Nat Robinson told me back in Nairobi. "When we opened the new Juhudi office in Eldoret [a rapidly growing city in the Rift Valley Province, north of Kericho and Litein], something like fifty farmers came for the launch. None of them knew how to use an elevator, but all of them already knew how to use M-PESA."

Mobile banking is spreading rapidly around the developing world. Vodafone and its subsidiaries already offer M-PESA in Tanzania and Afghanistan, with plans for India and Egypt. The South African mobile giant MTN is in the game in a half-dozen African countries with more on the way, and France Télécom is planning similar services across West Africa. Even Grameen, the mothership of microfinance, has started Grameenphone mobile banking

---

* If you're curious, my U.S. carrier was T-Mobile, owned by the German multinational Deutsche Telekom. I chose them specifically for the widest international compatibility. The only country that I can recall where my Razr was a total brick was Japan, where apparently no reciprocal agreement existed.

The Marrakech main square, a common Western image of the exotic. The Argana Café, at center rear, was blown up by religious extremists ten months after this visit.

There is actually a job where you get paid to sleep in places like this. Carcassonne, France.

An immigrant laborer, reportedly paid as little as six dollars per day
for working ten or even twelve hours, six days a week, in the desert heat.
On the glamorous Palm Jumeirah. Dubai, United Arab Emirates.

Kopi luwak, allegedly the world's finest coffee, brewed from the roasted poop of
an Indonesian civet. Served here on an ostrich leather tablecloth. Stay classy, Dubai.

Three men in a work vehicle beginning a long day in tropical heat, viewed from a chauffeur-driven Bentley worth more than twice as much as my mom's house in Ohio. Singapore.

Sometimes the signs are right in front of you. A portentous road marker near Gatwick Airport. London, United Kingdom.

A long day's labor concludes for an unknown fisherman. Bali, Indonesia.

A spot where a marker should be near Tiananmen Square, Beijing, China.
Tank Man began his protest very close to where the bus is passing.

Perhaps not the best place to realize you may be on the brink of a major neurological event.
Machu Picchu, Peru.

Tiro (left), me (right), the Two Dinos (one on each side), and two friends in Tiro's bar.
Breza, Bosnia and Herzegovina.

Fresh thermal glass and flowers on some balconies.
Life goes on, fourteen years after the end of the siege. Sarajevo.

Symon the coffee farmer, near Murang'a, Kenya. His cow loans facilitated coffee investments that turned profitable in the first year.

Symon the dairy farmer and his wife Jenn show off Grace, the gorgeous Guernsey they purchased with an asset financing loan from Juhudi Kilimo. The extra milk pays off a cow loan, then can be sold for years at a profit.

Attempting to enjoy charcoal-flavored yogurt, while Fred of Juhudi offers moral support. Photo taken by Nathan, who managed to keep his hands steady on my camera while trying not to laugh at my expression. Near Litein, Kenya.

At the end of our visit with the Bureti Self-Help Group for the Deaf.
The little girl is still eyeing me suspiciously.

Shishura Baguhereze! means "Scratch and Win!"—a mobile phone airtime card promotion from
Rwanda's biggest carrier. Mobile technology is revolutionizing banking in much of Africa.
(The bottle of "Nil" at upper left is named for the Nile River, not conceptual nothingness.)
Along the road to Kabarondo, Rwanda.

An officer of the Negros Women for Tomorrow Foundation (NWTF) displaying a guide to "honorable vows" for clients on the island of Cebu in the Philippines. Photo © 2011 Devra Berkowitz.

Hanging out with the gang at the NWTF field office in Cordova on the island of Mactan.

A child drives a toy car festooned with logos from
NASCAR, Valvoline, and a half-dozen other
Western companies. At the foot of a statue of
Vladimir Lenin. Hanoi, Vietnam.

Nary works full-time in a tourist hotel, plus several
hours each day in her own roadside sundries shop.
Near Siem Reap, Cambodia.

Song's home near the Tonlé Sap, with two of her plates on display. Our conversation took place where the young boy is sitting. Photo © 2011 Devra Berkowitz.

Bo prepping her morning glories in the afternoon sun. Near Phnom Penh, Cambodia.

The Cambodian fishing village where Mom lives. Photo © 2011 Devra Berkowitz.

Kathmandu, Nepal, outside the former royal palace. Women chip cement by hand.

Kathmandu, the brochure abstraction. Prayer cloths outside the Buddhist stupa of Boudhanath.

Rollerbladers enjoy a Saturday night on the seaside corniche. Beirut, Lebanon.

Detail of the statue in the center of Martyrs' Square, Beirut. The entire
statue is perforated like this. Some of it has been blown to pieces.

Lebanese members of humankind's first interconnected generation. Jeita, Lebanon.

The eyeglasses of Mohandas K. Gandhi. Framed in the room where he slept his last
night on earth, a few months after composing his talisman. New Delhi, India.

in Bangladesh. At this writing, about one in four of all transactions in Kenya is through M-PESA, and the BBC reports that by the time you read this, perhaps 150 separate mobile banking systems will be in place around the world.*

Granted, there are regulatory and technical kinks still to be worked out, and nothing ever goes quite as planned. (One surprising snag: what happens when you decrease the cost of moving money? Money itself is less expensive—which fuels inflation.†) But that doesn't change an exciting reality: anywhere a cell tower can be built and cheap used handsets can be distributed, it should soon be possible for even the world's poorest to have much improved access to savings, credit, and insurance.

Even in the middle of Nowhere.

"My ten-year-old wants to be an engineer," Kipkirui says proudly. "She is number one in her school." Kipkirui has been slightly reserved since I arrived in his small print shop/office supply/M-PESA services store near the center of Litein. But now, talking about his middle child, he is suddenly beaming.

"I have an older girl, fourteen. She wants to be a nurse," he tells me. "My boy is just four. He doesn't know what to be. Right now, he is happy being four."

Kipkirui's kiosk is just one of his businesses.‡ He also travels to schools to sell stationery and art supplies, and he and a hired helper work his grandfather's land—an inherited family farm that produces milk, vegetables, and tea for sale.

The milk comes from a dairy cow financed by a Juhudi loan for 60,000 shillings (about $750 when the loan was made). The profits from the milk help feed his three kids, pay their school fees, care

---

* See BBC report by Jane Wakefield, *Mobile Banking Closes Poverty Gap*, in Sources.
† See Will Mutua, citing Africa Development Bank research, in Sources.
‡ Kipkirui's Kiva page is at www.kiva.org/lend/226271.

for his extended family, and improve his home. Kipkirui's next loan will finance a zero-grazing unit to care for this cow and the others he plans to finance—once he has five cows, in fact, he will feel sure that all of his children will get a full education.

He seems happy to share his ambitions with me, but he also looks tired and short of time. Which, of course, he is. His routine is like others I've learned about here—up at 5, feed the kids, handle the cows, then go to work, day after day after day. I clear out of his little office quickly. As I see how hard Kipkirui works for his kids, the $25 I chipped in toward his cow loan feels more like a privilege than a favor.

Fred has accompanied me up to Kipkirui's office, and on the way out, we hop back in the car with Nathan to visit a few more clients. Joining us are Mosbei, another loan officer, and Chris, our driver. Soon, the five of us are careening again through the hills, bouncing through a linear arrangement of potholes where a road once must have been. I worry about the suspension of the old car under the weight of five grown men. Finally, there is an odd tinny *thlawk* from behind and below, followed by a draggy scraping noise.

The exhaust pipe, already rusted and crumbling, has almost completely separated itself from the car. I suspect that it simply got tired of all the shaking and decided to lie down. Back in the U.S., you'd call AAA, get a tow, hope the repair shop can fix it in a day or two, maybe have to rent a car in the meantime, and mentally budget a couple hundred bucks for parts and labor.

Here, however, Fred and Nathan and Mosbei and Chris just go totally *yes and*, instantly surrounding the problem, kneeling and climbing around and under the car until they yank the whole dang pipe clean off. I stand to one side, a total *mzungu*, offering help which they clearly don't need. In a few moments, we're all back in the car, bouncing more loudly through the potholes, driving back into town with the entire muffler and tailpipe balanced precariously between us through the windows.

Soon, we arrive at a whole city block of guys with welding tools and car parts, men whose entire living is built around keeping ancient vehicles intact by any means necessary. Tires roll by, as do doors, axles, and whole engines on small pull cars. Some guy carries a windshield down the street. You're missing a this? I've got one of these, or most of those are just like it. *Yes, and* could be Litein's city motto.

We pull over and scramble out, but before Fred engages any repairmen, I am requested to go stand somewhere else entirely. Why? Because a *mzungu* is perceived as rich. It will cost three times as much if I'm seen as part of the transaction.

So I go stand twenty feet away, not part of any particular group, and with no obvious purpose in being there. I glance back after just a minute, and the legs of two mechanics are already protruding from under the car. Ten minutes later, all done. Total charge, non-*mzungu* rate: 250 shillings. About three bucks.

In the meantime, this *mzungu* is indeed "he who wanders," rootless and idle. Most of the repairmen are too busy working to give more than a curious glance, but children stare as they walk by. I wave and smile. They wave back but keep staring.

In this globalized world, I'd assumed there wasn't anywhere left you could go where you'd be somebody's first white guy. But later, I ask Fred and Nathan, and sure—I could have easily been a kid's first *mzungu*. Fred still remembers the first white people he ever saw, in fact: growing up in Bomet, tourists in buses would pass on their way to view wildlife. "It was such a novelty," Fred says. "People would wait by the road just to see them go by."

"Hey, look!" Nathan adds, playing the child he once was, watching the white people with wonder. "One of them waved!"

Suddenly I'm trying not to laugh. Nathan's voice has just

perfectly mixed childhood awe, adult self-deprecation, and a rueful appreciation of absurd social distance. The finest actor couldn't nail that line with the nuance that Nathan just showed.

Nathan is in his mid-twenties and came to Juhudi straight out of college. As a loan officer, he has a workday as endless as that of his clients, hopscotching from dawn to dusk between the office and clients, often walking miles between farms, constantly supporting and motivating and educating when he arrives. It takes a person of great humor, enthusiasm, and compassion to do what he does. My notes say this about him, verbatim: "Nathan awesome. Quiet sharp funny cool."

We conduct this conversation about *mzungu* sightings in hushed tones, however.

We are speaking quietly because Fred and Nathan and I are sitting in a small living space inside bare wooden walls, with sunlight peeking down between the slats. We are waiting for the start of the meeting of the Bureti Self-Help Group for the Deaf.

The *mzungu* discussion was prompted by the first thing that happened when we arrived at this small home.

Outside, during our first silent greetings with the members of the group—smiles, gentle handshakes, appreciation shown with our eyes—we were interrupted by a small girl, perhaps two-and-a-half years old, adorable in her bright yellow dress, screaming. BECAUSE IT'S A MONSTER! A MONSTER! A GIANT WHITE MONSTER!

This would be me.

These weren't her actual words, of course. She wasn't saying anything specifically in English or Swahili or anything else one could translate. It was more of a nonverbal mélange of polytonal full-throated cacophony. WHAT IS *WRONG* WITH YOU PEO-PLE? HE'S GOING TO KILL US ALL!

My pale English-American skin requires a thick layer of sunblock. In a place like Litein, practically right atop the equator, my dermatologist likes me to carry a tube of Neutrogena with an SPF of 85, one notch below Liquid Paper. Plus, since I've already had dengue, in most parts of the world, I also need to wear an additional coating of insect-repellent DEET, which glistens on top of the sunscreen.

In other words, as the two-and-a-half-year-old girl in a bright yellow dress best explained in her horror, IT'S . . . IT'S . . . *SHINY!*

I was two-and-a-half years old once. I used to be afraid of the kitchen faucet. It made a whiny noise I didn't like. This alone could make me shriek in terror. I can't imagine what it would be like when everyone you've ever seen is the same soothing dark brown, the color of *people*, and then all of a sudden there's this creature who doesn't look human, and your own mom doesn't even seem to realize the danger.

BLEAAAAAAUUUUGGGGH! and I really don't blame her.

I'd never imagined that a visit with deaf people could possibly be this loud.

Before the meeting begins, as the members settle in, we can't help but chat. For translation, we've set up a bucket-brigade: I will speak English to Fred, who will speak Swahili to a member of the group with some hearing, who will translate into sign language, and then the reverse, back and forth, a large swerving circle of chit-chat.

But there's no need. Deaf-mutes spend their whole lives learning to communicate without words. So the man two chairs over asks *are you married?* by miming a ring on the finger. I gesture no. But he is, happily—*and with three children*, he shows me, showing the number and gesturing their heights with one hand. This is easy, and the conversation begins to flow. *I work as a digger*, another member tells me, tossing invisible dirt over one shoulder. My reply, *I'm a writer*, needs just the mime of a pen. Even in sign language, my job is less strenuous than his.

We keep it simple, of course, but I've had conversations in my own language that were more difficult to convey. This feels like a holiday at the home of a distant relation you're surprisingly comfortable with.*

On the table in front of me is the group's manifesto:

MANIFESTO

a) improve welfare of the members
b) initiate activities to improve the living standards of deaf and general disables
c) to unite all disables and empower them to fight for their rights
d) to educate the members and general public of HIV/AIDS and its prevention
e) to network with government agencies and other organizations and work together
f) finally, to show the community that the deafs and disables are like any other human. *They can also do!*

Indeed they can.

Finally, as the Chairman begins with a prayer, the room falls still. All eyes focus on his hands as they circle and dance in the air, sending up signals to God. The Chairman vocalizes slightly, a murmur—words not as I would know them, but as he does. It takes a moment to recognize, but the cadence is that of the classic Lord's Prayer.

———————————

* Which, in the long view, is precisely accurate.

Every member of the Bureti Self-Help Group for the Deaf faces exceptional challenges—economic, physical, political, and more—but they have come here to offer each other love and support and hope and comfort against trying times. And now they raise their hands in silence, hoping an almighty being will indeed help those determined to help themselves.

Fred and Nathan, heads bowed, are here to help answer those prayers.

There's a reason this feels like a church. If this place isn't holy, I don't know what is.

DEMOCRATIC
REPUBLIC OF
THE CONGO

UGANDA

VIRUNGA

MTNS

●Ruhengeri

●Gisenyi

RWANDA

*Lake
Kivu*

KIGALI
★

Kabarondo

●Gitarama

Gikongoro
●

●Cyangugu

●Butare

BURUNDI

TANZANIA

0   20   40 km

0   20   40 mi

CHAPTER EIGHT

RWANDA

Yvonne has motioned me to sit on a hard wooden stool against a cement wall near the front door of her two-room home.* Five feet away is the glass dime-store counter where she works for twelve hours a day. A few feet beyond is the far wall.

Yvonne's stock-in-trade—vegetables, sugar, baking supplies, razor blades, ballpoint pens, small candies, chewing gum, and fruit—sits atop, below, inside, behind, and in front of the counter, overflowing all the way out to the porch. Sweet potatoes are stacked near the doorway, next to a three-foot bunch of stout Rwandan bananas. A *Thriller*-era Michael Jackson poster is the sole decoration.

Yvonne is a client of Urwego ("ladder," as in climbing out of poverty) Opportunity Bank, one of Kiva's partner MFIs in Rwanda. I have found her by tagging along with a loan officer named Daniel, a focused young man who exudes confidence and efficiency in three languages. In America, Daniel might be a rising star at a

---

* "Yvonne" is a pseudonym, as are all client names in this chapter. Rwanda is a small country with no independent media, and the language barrier was sometimes formidable. I am not completely certain that the purpose of every interview was universally clear. Given the local history, I prefer to err on the side of client privacy.

Fortune 500 firm. Here, he sits beside me on a plastic chair in this modest section of Kigali, translating our conversation.

Yvonne is giving what Daniel calls her "testimony"—a rolling stream of Kinyarwanda* that Daniel translates into English every thirty seconds or so. Her voice is flat and careful, and when Daniel translates, her eyes dart from his face to mine, seeking reassurance that the emotions being conveyed match her own. There is a faint but perceptible note of reluctance. She is careful with her words, unsure what to think of me or my intentions.

Yvonne is a compact woman of perhaps thirty, dressed in a wrap skirt circled by the fanny pack that serves as her cash register. Her T-shirt is a Western donation festooned with a random non sequitur, a common sight throughout Rwanda. (¡NO PROBLEMO! her shirt chirps.) Yvonne's children are also in donorwear, currently including T-shirts with logos from Speed Racer and the Broadway show Annie. All three kids are hovering near the doorway, nervously stacked between the sweet potatoes and bananas, listening intently to their mom's chat with this big shiny American. They dare not come closer. I might bite.

The best way to make Yvonne feel comfortable is to feel comfortable myself. I focus on the children peeking in through the door, remember my own niece and nephew at that age, and mentally retreat to my sister's house in Ohio. The small boy wearing Speed Racer finally smiles back, then abruptly disappears, overloaded by

---

* Kinyarwanda, a Bantu tongue spoken only in Rwanda and parts of Uganda, and directly related only to a Burundian dialect called Kirundi, bears no relationship to Indo-European languages and surprisingly little to most of its African neighbors. With ten noun and ten verb classes, it is wildly challenging for English speakers and vice versa. That so many Rwandans have learned English in adulthood deserves tremendous respect, especially with translation materials so hard to find. The best phrasebook I could find in Kigali is just thirty-two pages long. Disturbingly, the writers of this thin volume thought it useful to include not just standard tourist phrases, but warasaze ("you are crazy"), umushyo urihe? ("where is the knife?"), and aka n'akaga n'ibyago ("this is unfortunate").

the glossy Caucasian. When I laugh affectionately, Yvonne finally starts to relax, and her story begins to flow more easily.

A year and a half ago, Yvonne and these three kids were sleeping on a mat in a tiny unpowered shack that she rented for the equivalent of 5 U.S. dollars per month. Thanks to a series of tiny loans, now she has a proper home and owns this small but growing business, and her children sleep on a real bed under a good roof.

But how did Yvonne manage this so rapidly with almost no education, not much help, and six-month-long loans smaller than an American business lunch? I can't wait to hear. My admiration for her as a hard-working single mom grows by the minute.

As she murmurs in Kinyarwanda, Yvonne's face softens. Gratitude and hope peek through, especially when she glances toward her kids in the doorway. Her voice becomes more expressive and natural, so the children inch into the room, gradually more comfortable with this luminous weirdo. The comfort feeds on itself. Yvonne loosens up enough to smile while she talks, fiddling absent-mindedly with a box on the counter while sorting through her memories.

My own mom used to do the same thing sometimes.

Mom worked at a dime store called Newberry's in the Ohio town where I grew up. She spent thirty years arranging and sorting a motley pile of sundries much like this—candies, small boxes of gum, a deck of cards—and when you'd stop in to say hi, she'd sometimes fiddle with the stock while talking about her day. Exactly the way Yvonne is doing right now. I can't help but think that she and Yvonne would have been friends if the birth lottery had worked out differently.

The boy wearing *Annie* begins playing with a marble at my feet, rolling it back and forth, and I realize that my mind has wandered away from Yvonne's story. I catch myself just as Daniel begins the next burst of translation.

"Yvonne came from Gikongoro," Daniel says, thinking nothing of it. Daniel then explains that Gikongoro is a small town to the south, perhaps two and a half hours away. Daniel assumes that I have not read about Gikongoro.

I have heard of Gikongoro, I say softly.

I have heard of Gikongoro because in the second week of April 1994, tens of thousands of people there were huddled in churches, fearing for their lives. Large numbers of the Hutu majority had begun killing members of the Tutsi minority in Kigali, the capital, where we now sit. The violence was spreading rapidly, with Hutu militias attacking Tutsi all over the country. Previous massacres had happened often enough that a sudden shift in the air toward murderous hatred had gathered its own nickname: "the Wind."

Fortunately, churches and schools had always been places of sanctuary. No one would kill in a place of worship or where everyone's children are educated. So when the violence reached the area around Gikongoro, tens of thousands of local Tutsi sought refuge in their churches—at least until they were told by their clergy to move to an unfinished technical college at Murambi. There, these innocent people—men, women, children, the sick, the elderly, everyone—hoped to ride out another Wind.

They could not. On April 21, 1994, Hutu militia overran Murambi in a slaughter that lasted for more than seven hours. Those who escaped fled to a nearby church. The next day, they were killed, too. Many of the killers were also members of the very same church, killing their fellow congregants. The local bishop was eventually indicted for war crimes for his role in the killing of his own flock.* An exact count will never be known, but perhaps twenty-seven thousand Tutsi were at Murambi on the morning of April 21.† Fewer than thirty are known to have survived.

---

* Jurisdictional issues derailed his prosecution, however. See Sources.
† This figure is from the Kigali Memorial Centre; most sources give higher numbers.

Yvonne came from Gikongoro, Daniel has just told me.

I am no longer sitting in a front room of a growing convenience store with an increasingly relaxed mother of three whose family is warming to my company. I am in *Rwanda,* the one in the newspapers.

I keep my eyes relaxed and smile at Yvonne, but I cannot help but think it:

Are you Hutu? Or are you Tutsi?

The question rips into my feelings for her. I don't want it to. And yet it is unavoidable.

This very question almost destroyed an entire nation. I know this. And if I can't get it out of my mind, how can anyone expect ten million Rwandans to? I feel ridiculous. What can my tiny investments mean *here,* of all places?

The three-month Rwandan genocide was one of the most gruesome periods in human history. Hutu members of the Interahamwe ("those who kill together") militia searched house-to-house, killing their own neighbors in every city and village, attacking not just the Tutsi minority, but moderate Hutu deemed sympathetic to the Tutsi. Civil society simply ceased to exist. Doctors, lawyers, and teachers joined in the slaughter of their charges. In mixed families, some Hutu men even killed their Tutsi wives. Survivors lived on the run, hiding in caves, forests, or deep in the marshes, trying to evade the killing teams on their trail. Most could not hide long enough.

Analogies to explain the sheer scale of the violence are so stunning as to trigger disbelief. For one example: when the genocide began, Rwanda's population was roughly the size of Manhattan. Try to imagine Manhattan taking the death toll of more than three hundred September 11ths—one at breakfast, lunch, and dinner for more than three months—along with the frequent rape of the female survivors. The numbers, at least, are comparable.

Compounding the senseless enormity, the very notion of ethnic identity in Rwanda is historically fictional. Hutu and Tutsi have been essentially the same people—speaking the same language, practicing the same religions and traditions, intermarrying, etc.—throughout known history. For centuries, the words *Hutu* and *Tutsi* were class markers, with *Tutsi* signifying the upper-class minority. As recently as 150 years ago, a Hutu who acquired ten cows became an instant Tutsi. The Wind, in essence, is arbitrary, the birth lottery run completely amok.

Even Rwandans can't tell who's who with real certainty. It's generally held that Tutsi are taller, thinner, and more European-looking than Hutu, but like faces in clouds, the differences are only clear if you talk yourself into seeing them. Genetic studies find virtually no difference. The notion only solidified in the 1930s, when Belgian colonists needed locals to administer their rule, and it was natural to their minds that Rwandans with slightly more "European" features should be in charge. Similar ideas about genetics would plunge Europe into its own deadliest era, but that was still a few years away.

The Belgians, armed with calipers to measure facial features and a veneer of pseudoscience, lined up every Rwandan, decided who was whom, enshrined their phony distinctions with ID cards, and endowed the 15 percent of Rwandans decreed as "Tutsi" with the power to rule everyone else. Never mind that the necessity of ID cards labeled "Hutu" and "Tutsi"—even during the genocide— has always proven that the difference doesn't rise even to the level of cosmetic.

The Catholic church in Rwanda supported the madness, spreading a pseudo-Biblical "Hamitic" explanation so nutty that it sounds like something invented from whole cloth, which it is: British explorer John Speke, who had no training in history or anthropology, once suggested that some barely-more-caucasoid Rwandans weren't precisely *African*, see, but descendants of Noah's son Ham. As a Biblical character, Ham was perceived by Europeans as a part of their civilizing traditions—despite the fact that Ham was a Levantine outcast who would never have been allowed in the country club—and so therefore, everything good in Rwanda came from the black people who were really secretly kinda white. The idea, unbelievably, stuck.*

But by 1959, Belgium could no longer afford to manage the colony, so they bailed—but not before deciding that "reform" should bring the Hutu majority to power. Once in charge, frustrated Hutu inevitably sought revenge against their former Tutsi rulers, even turning the Hamitic theory back on the Tutsi, treating them as non-African invaders, "cockroaches" to be expelled from Hutu land.

That's when the Wind first started to blow.

Rwanda was poor before the genocide, and sixteen years later, at the time of my 2010 visit, it was still poorer than Burma or Bangladesh, ranking just barely in front of Afghanistan.† Life expectancy is shockingly low, even by developing-world standards. Palestinians born in Gaza, for example, will live an average of sixteen years longer than a typical Rwandan. Even North Koreans live seven years longer. And for every car, communal van, or motorcycle taxi plying Kigali's new roads, perhaps fifty pedestrians roam the sidewalks, many heading to or from long

---

*This "Hamitic" theory also spread to the U.S., where it was sometimes used to justify racism, slavery, and segregation. My own grandfather, for example, was a literalist Baptist minister, and when I was eight years old, I made a black friend at school. Grandpa disapproved; my new friend's skin bore this "Curse of Ham." Even to an eight-year-old, this carried no moral logic. Today, collective punishment of this kind would now get any human leader a comfy seat in The Hague.

†CIA World Factbook, per capita GDP adjusted for purchasing power parity, 2010. See Sources.

days of work. In the countryside, sparsely traveled roads serve largely as magnificent footpaths for hours-long walks to distant markets.

At least one argument seems obvious for Kiva loans here: $25 might go farther in Rwanda than almost anywhere on earth.

Yet despite its continuing struggles, Rwanda had also become a darling of the development world, its prospects for growth trumpeted in the international financial press, its society and government stable enough to attract aid and investment from China, India, the EU, Japan, the U.S., Saudi Arabia, and others. The streets were safe, crime was rare, and new buildings were rising. In a growing economy, microfinance was also spreading rapidly.

Curious how such a transition was possible, I came to Rwanda hoping, in essence, to see hope—to see Rwanda through a lens other than its past. If microfinance clients could build new and better lives here, of all places, then there might truly be hope anywhere.

Kigali is certainly one of the neatest cities in the world, partly due to a nationwide system called *umuganda* ("contribution"). On the last Saturday morning of each month, the entire country—every able-bodied person over the age of eighteen, from the lowliest villager to the president himself—turns out to do mandatory chores in their community. Businesses close, houses empty, order is kept. All of this is overseen by a hierarchy of neighborhood, district, and national officials, linking the smallest hamlet to the president's inner circle.

This would be inconceivable in most countries, but Rwanda's rolling hills created a world of isolated farming villages where everyone simply had to depend on each other. A simple theft could be stopped (and usually still can be; I'd walk across Kigali alone at night a thousand times before trying it once in Nairobi) just by shouting *mwezi* ("thief"). Neighbors are so obligated to respond that staying home would imply complicity in the crime.

So: a culture of mutual support and suspicion, uniquely blended as one.

And we grasp how the genocide spread so rapidly. The irony could not be more perverse: why were more people killed by Rwandan machetes than even the Nazis managed in any three-month period? Because Rwandans had a stronger sense of community.

Today, umuganda is more organized than ever, with attendance checked by a hierarchy that reaches all the way to Kigali. It's not paranoia to think that the government knows where you are: they keep attendance records. A local joke states that two Rwandans may speak privately, but if three Rwandans talk, one is working for the government.

Yvonne was being generous even in telling her story.

If there is one set of eyes watching over this nation, they belong to Paul Kagame, the Tutsi general who stopped a genocide, rallied the exiles back into their homeland, and has led Rwanda into its future ever since.

When Kagame surprised me by agreeing to an interview via the Internet, my first question was a softball: I asked what he would most want to tell Americans about his country. His answer was 161 words long, covering—*inhale*—peace and security, unity and reconciliation, good governance, health care and education, the building of infrastructure, agriculture and investment, and global cooperation—and *exhale*. President Kagame is an extremely serious thinker, "serious" being a high compliment in Rwandan culture.

Kagame's own story is half Capra, half Kafka: after his parents fled Rwanda when the Wind blew in 1960, Kagame grew up in a Ugandan refugee camp during the brutal dictatorships of Idi

Amin and Milton Obote. As powerless a child as any on earth, young Kagame nonetheless set an impossibly ambitious goal for himself: to lead the return of liberated Tutsi exiles to Rwanda.

Kagame soon displayed an intellect and daring usually found only in fiction. After training with the Ugandan army, Kagame changed sides and joined a Ugandan rebel group. After gaining the trust of its leaders, Kagame and a fellow Tutsi exile named Fred Rwigema then began recruiting more Tutsis to join the rebels, quietly forming a Rwandan cell within the Ugandan uprising. Finally, a few years after the uprising took power in Uganda, Kagame and Rwigema simply took their Tutsi faction of the Ugandan military, ran off, and invaded Rwanda with it.

Stop for a second and consider—who *does* that? Who creates a whole rebel army in the middle of some *other* guy's rebel army, so that when you're done fighting off one horrible dictator who isn't even your main enemy, you can then steal your own guys away and go fight the bad guys you're actually after—hoping that the first army doesn't get ticked off and attack you, too?*

This 1990 invasion of Rwanda by Kagame's Rwandan Patriotic Front (RPF) was repelled by the Hutu government, so Kagame led his men high into the Virunga Mountains, home to Dian Fossey's primate research station, which now had guerrillas in its midst. Kagame then began a hit-and-run campaign that by 1993 was able to force the Hutu government into a power-sharing agreement. Kagame's lifelong goal was at hand.

The agreement could have led to a peaceful, power-sharing gov-

---

* To be exact, Rwigema led the invasion while Kagame was in an officer training course for foreign soldiers with the U.S. Army in Kansas. When Rwigema was killed on the third day, Kagame immediately returned to Rwanda and assumed command. It is plausible that the Ugandans might have quietly supported Kagame's invasion, maintaining deniability in case the invasion failed. However, no such deal has been acknowledged as far as I can find. There would be little reason to hide it now.

ernment, but Hutu extremists viewed the deal as a sellout to Tutsi invaders. Two days before the treaty would have gone into force, the Hutu president who signed the peace deal was assassinated, and the genocide began.*

Finally, one hundred days later, Kagame's army defeated the Hutu militias, ending the genocide and allowing the Tutsi exiles to return home.

Kagame's gaze now emanates from seemingly half the interior walls of the country—offices, stores, restaurants, homes, you name it—including the Kigali headquarters of Urwego Opportunity Bank. Yvonne from Gikongoro is one of their thirty thousand clients, and Daniel, who translated, is one of their most valued officers. Now I'm sitting with Jeffrey Lee, Daniel's boss, Urwego's enthusiastic president.

Jeffrey gives off not a whiff of CEOitude. His own story is a classic American immigrant tale: despite humble origins in Korea,

---

*There were multiple contributing factors to the genocide, of course. Extremism often flourishes amid economic pressure, and a 1990 IMF structural adjustment program often receives some blame. However, Rwanda's traditional subsistence farming had long been converted to an export economy—in this case, mainly coffee—creating vulnerability if the coffee price dropped. And when the Cold War ended, the West no longer saw any need to fight the Red Menace in Latin America by propping up its large coffee-exporting economies. When price supports were removed, the value of coffee plummeted everywhere, including Rwanda. Western newspapers trumpeted this as a victory for consumers able to snag a cheap tub of Yuban, but farmers in the Rwandan hills suddenly saw their incomes disappear. The price of coffee did not increase significantly again until April of 1994, after the killings began, as global supply was about to narrow without Rwanda's usual contribution. ("Pests in Colombia and massacres in Rwanda helped make this the second year of bad harvests," noted *Fortune* on June 13, blithely equating genocide with troublesome insects.) The swinging of machetes is actually visible on the commodities chart.

he eventually reached a luxurious Manhattan office as head of U.S. operations for Korea's second-largest bank. He could easily be living a life of limousines, Broadway shows, and skating at Rockefeller Center. But nine years ago, Jeffrey made a promise to the Lord. Jeffrey is now a born-again Christian who considers his time here "life tithing."

This momentarily kicks up my firewalls. My grandfather, the racist minister, taught me to be careful around anyone claiming Truth on their side. But it's also soon obvious that Jeffrey and I are here for the exact same reason, even if I don't invoke any deities. We both saw ourselves as fortunate, and we both felt a deep need to share our good fortune with others. Jeffrey grew up working-class in Korea and never changed. My dad unloaded boxcars for GM in Ohio. *Got it.* I soon start to like Jeffrey a lot.

Urwego's offices are modest compared to the imperious towers that Chinese investors are building downtown, some with ten-foot metal gateways more appropriate for Montgomery Burns of *The Simpsons.* Here, Jeffrey doesn't even have air-conditioning. This bank president is content with a pedestal fan.

"Watch—Rwanda is going to be the first African 'tiger' economy," he says, comparing Kigali today to Seoul thirty years ago. Jeffrey is qualified to make the comparison, since he grew up in South Korea during its postwar dictatorship. "They will privatize what they can, but they also invest in public infrastructure that benefits everyone, business included." That's largely the Singapore model, which makes perfect sense: as a small country with no real industry, transforming itself into a trading hub may be Rwanda's only real shot at rapid growth.

Maybe the vast mineral wealth just over the Congolese border can bring a literal gold rush to Kigali, assuming the eastern Congo ever stops being one of the most unstable places on earth. Accordingly: Rwanda is to have new hotels, a rail line through Tanzania to the Indian Ocean, a new airport, a stock exchange—which ultimately opened in 2011 with three listings—and even a giant convention center. It's almost a "Field of Dreams" approach to third-world development: *if you build it, they will come.*

I asked Kagame about this strategy. "One thing is clear," he wrote back, "the many billions of dollars in aid that have been spent on Africa in the last 50 years of the 20th century have not resulted in a developed continent." This certainly echoes the sentiment of a growing number of economists and aid workers. "We understand our context better than anyone else and know what we need to move Rwanda from poverty to development and prosperity. We therefore have to do the hard work first, develop and own our policies, and invest our own resources and efforts in implementing these homegrown ideas . . . The results are very visible."

True. Major players pop into Rwanda all the time. Starbucks and Costco now buy about a quarter of Rwanda's coffee. Tony Blair's charity has sent full-time development advisors, and Bill Gates's foundation is building a new medical center. None of this is the same as a Fortune 500 company building a manufacturing plant or even moving its African headquarters from Nairobi. All in good time, perhaps.

"I know it may sound like a longshot," Jeffrey tells me. "But who would have thought the same of Singapore, or Seoul, or Taipei thirty years ago?"

When I ask about Urwego's own plans, Jeffrey grabs a laptop and zips me through PowerPoint slides. Pie charts and jargon fly by, but the basics are clear: despite six hundred new accounts a day, Urwego still serves only about 5 percent of its potential clients. Enormous growth is still possible. Urwego is also expanding to include microsavings and microinsurance, hoping one day to offer its clients almost the same range of financial planning tools that any conventional bank client might have. Plus, M-PESA-style cell phone banking is coming. They're even turning a truck into a complete mobile branch able to reach anywhere the country has roads. "Come barefoot" is their welcoming slogan.

To help prepare clients, all applicants must first receive Urwego's free training in business, household, and health management. More profit-driven MFIs would view all these efforts as hindering the ability to increase the number of customers and maximize return. But Urwego is doing the opposite: planning its own future success by investing in its customers' well-being.

So far, I've visited four Kiva partner MFIs—Arariwa, Women for Women, Juhudi Kilimo, and Urwego—on three continents. I've chosen all four virtually at random, knowing nearly nothing in advance about their business models, based mostly just on whatever contacts I've been able to develop in urban destinations where dengue fever isn't currently active. So far, all four Kiva partners have seen free education as a fundamental part of their mission. Coming from a culture where profit is often considered inherently noble, simply part of an "invisible hand" magically coalescing millions of selfish choices into accidental wisdom, I feel saner in Jeffrey's office than I've ever felt while watching CNBC.

In fact, Urwego's return on investment is capped—by charter—at just 7.5 percent. This is a bank explicitly *not* about maximizing profit. Any funds above that figure must be channeled into lowering the costs to clients, increasing outreach, or improving employee benefits. This seems in keeping with Muhammad Yunus's own belief that profit in microlending should be capped.* There is virtually no chance of Bosnian-style overreach for profit here.

There is always, however, the specter of chaos.

Downstairs, I passed one of Kagame's soldiers sitting guard near the door. Even on this half-empty street on an ordinary Tuesday, his rifle was poised in both hands, his right index finger just an inch from the trigger.

---

* Yunus laid out specific recommendations in a *New York Times* op-ed. See Sources.

After assuming power, Kagame installed a Hutu as titular president, insisting that his was a government for all Rwandans. But Hutu militia who had fled across the Zairean (now Congolese) border didn't buy it. Instead, the Hutus regrouped, transforming refugee camps into a resupply system for Hutu soldiers. Even after stopping a genocide, Kagame was still faced with ongoing war. Ultimately, Kagame ordered his troops to go into the refugee camps, take down most of the Hutu Power dead-enders, and push nearly all of the Hutu who had fled back into Rwanda— where instead of vengeance, most received welcome as fellow Rwandans essential to the nation's future. Only 135,000 suspected killers were imprisoned. (The word *only* is worth a moment of reflection.)

Unfortunately, it was impossible to put 135,000 accused killers on trial. Who would guard them? Who would pay for their custody? How could so many trials be held? Witnesses, evidence, juries of their peers—the breadth of the tragedy rendered ordinary justice numerically impossible. Imprisoning this many able-bodied men would also leave the fields fallow, dooming the rest of the country to hunger. Even vigilante justice would condemn innocent people to starvation.

So while harsh punishments were handed out to a few national organizers and local ringleaders, the vast majority of "ordinary" murderers—let us pause over that phrase—were left to face only *gaçaça* ("grass") tribunals, facing their former neighbors in the manner of traditional village councils, often sitting in the shade of a graceful palaver tree. As with the Truth and Reconciliation project in South Africa, punishment would be light in exchange for full disclosure. There was no other choice.

Today, the official line is that nobody is Hutu or Tutsi anymore. Everyone is simply "Rwandan," and in public, the subject is now a social taboo.* Thousands of "ordinary" Rwandans who butchered their neighbors now roam the streets freely. Life goes on.

How long will it take for a new national identity to form? Kagame was optimistic: Rwandans are "reverting to the old culture," he wrote. "Whatever language, religion, or culture colonialism brought could only be constructed on top of the Rwandan language, religion, or culture that already existed"—and here he got ambitious— "restoring unity should take less than two generations."

I want to believe him. But I come from a country where some people still defiantly fly the Confederate flag almost 150 years after Gettysburg.

Hoping to better imagine reconciliation, I took a long morning stroll to the country's primary museum, the Kigali Memorial Centre, passing twenty-foot billboards for wall paint, corner stores adorned with signs reading ELECTRICITY FOR SALE,† and scores of Rwandans walking to and from church in their Sunday best.

Inside the museum, you find a history of Rwanda, displays about several other genocides, and physical remnants, including a collec-

---

* Sadly, one fairly reliable way to tell if you're talking to a Hutu or a Tutsi: visible scars. I met my first definite Tutsi, for example, in an elevator. A dignified businessman in a finely pinstriped white shirt, gold-framed glasses, and shiny leather shoes, he would not have attracted a second glance on Wall Street—save for the five-inch machete scar running from his right temple to just over his right eye. We passed the ride between floors exactly as anyone does: *Might rain later. Hmm, yeah, we could use it.* Then—*ding!*—he wandered off to his meeting on Two, carrying a memory I would not have the heart to invoke with a question, and would not need to, the scar telling his story in rough contours.
† This is a scratch-off card scheme that allows low-income people to power their homes where conventional banking and billing don't reach. Still, I couldn't help but picture a big box of loose volts shooting sparks on a shelf, a sparkly pouring process, and happy customers trotting home with glowing plastic bags in each hand.

tion of more than two thousand family photos of the victims as *people*, as they were in life: smiling, playing, picnicking, playing, graduating, marrying, dancing, working, holding their children. Many photos have personal inscriptions in Kinyarwanda or French: *"Je t'aime et je t'aimerai toujours et je ne t'oublierai jamais dans ma vie."* ("I love you and I will love you forever and I will never forget you in my life.")

Outside, there's a courtyard built around huge brown cement slabs. It takes a moment to realize: these are burial vaults. In case you don't figure it out, there is a helpful sign:

PLEASE DO NOT STEP ON THE MASS GRAVES.

A set of stairs leads down a hillside, where you find yet more enormous brown slabs. These are expansion vaults. As Rwanda rebuilds, it's common for construction teams to unearth undiscovered remains. These extra mass graves are to handle the overflow.

When I was a boy in Ohio, the Holocaust was the only genocide ever discussed. The words "never again" seemed like a shared oath for humanity. But just in my brief years on this earth, full-bore slaughters have taken place in Indonesia, Bangladesh, Burundi, East Timor, Cambodia, Guatemala, Iraqi Kurdistan, Sudan, Bosnia, and Rwanda, plus massacres that many would argue as genocide in Argentina, Equatorial Guinea, Sri Lanka, and more. Every populated continent has had at least one mass killing just in my lifetime, save Australia, and they haven't always been swell with their own native neighbors.

I wondered: *maybe the Wind is just part of being human.* It is the worst thought I hope ever to have.

And I stood on this hillside, surrounded by 258,000 people, watching life go on in the distance. Groups of women in bright clothing were walking to church, workers were ambling home, young men were talking with friends over a beer, kids were kicking a soccer ball.

People were still going on with their lives.

How?

Walking back to downtown, I spent every moment with the realization that virtually everyone I brushed against over the age of about thirty-three was either (a) a survivor, or (b) a supporter or an active participant in mass murder. I couldn't stop searching the eyes of every adult, silently screaming: *are you Hutu or Tutsi?* I was thankful that no one could hear.

Forty-five minutes later, I was back in the city center, passing the country's largest shopping complex, surrounded by thirty-foot beer ads, a buzzing swarm of motorcycle taxis, and enough people wearing donated non-sequitur T-shirts (ROCK ME SEXY JESUS) to compel a wan smile. It was a relief to return to mundane mind-numbing commerce. Next door to the mall, I ducked into the luxurious Hôtel des Mille Collines, which you might know by another name. Thanks to Hollywood, it's also called the Hotel Rwanda.

This is where more than 1,200 Tutsi survived despite the presence of death at their literal doorstep. In the movie, credit goes solely to a plucky hotel manager, Paul Rusesabagina, whose heroic savvy and half-Hutu blood bought him the wiggle room to save lives. In reality, Rusesabagina was also aided by the influence of his high-profile guests, courageous protection from a handful of UN soldiers, and (by some accounts) Hutu concerns that Tutsi forces would kill Hutu prisoners if the Tutsi in the hotel were harmed.

Regardless, the film was shown proudly in Rwanda's largest soccer stadium, and the former hotel manager became a national figure. But when Rusesabagina used his fame to insist on a greater Hutu role in the government, he became *persona non grata*. Rusesabagina now lives in exile in Belgium. I could find his name nowhere in the hotel, at the Kigali Memorial Centre, nor any official marker of the genocide.

Official reluctance to allow ethnic politics to re-enter acceptable debate is understandable. Germany still doesn't allow Nazi symbolism nearly eighty years after Hitler's ascent—and they don't still have hundreds of thousands of "ordinary" killers walking freely. You can understand why Kagame might try to keep the country on message.*

I sat in the small courtyard of the Hotel Rwanda, trying to imagine the days of the Wind. But the scene in front of me made it almost impossible. Local businessmen chatted up deals by the pool. Men and women flirted over cocktails. Tourists enjoyed a pit stop on the way to a gorilla trek. A four-piece band near the bar began to play honky-tonk, possibly Hank Williams's "Born to Boogie" in Kinyarwanda. It seemed as if everyone was just trying to move on—not just here, but outside, on the long walk to and from the museum, and everywhere I'd been in the country.

And that's when I realized: *That's the whole point, isn't it? This entire country really is just trying to move on. I only don't recognize it because it's new to me. These people aren't over it, but good lord they're trying.*

I'd wondered on arrival how a country could move on from such horrors. But signs of rebuilding had been everywhere. I just hadn't seen them for what they were. Twenty-foot ads for wall paint: *rebuilding.* The small corner stores offering ELECTRICITY FOR SALE: *rebuilding.* Even in the Hotel Rwanda: the poolside business deals, the new relationships forming, even the tourist business

---

*As strong as the let's-not-have-another-genocide rationale may be, the government's strict control over local media is often criticized. At the time of my visit, Reporters Without Borders rated Rwanda as less free than Cuba, Libya, or Saudi Arabia, ranking it with North Korea and Burma as the "most repressive countries in the world" for journalists. That said, I never hid the fact that I was writing in and about Rwanda, and I carried a highly visible camera with no worries except near government or military facilities, which is common sense in much of the world. I never had the slightest trouble.

schlepping people out to see wild gorillas? *All part of a nation re-building.*

Yvonne and her three kids? *Rebuilding.* Yes, $25 does go as far here as almost anywhere on earth—and comparing the business climate here to Burma or Zimbabwe, probably much more so.

At last I could see why Jeffrey Lee was so excited.

I am sitting on a hard wooden stool against a cement wall near the front door of Yvonne's two-room home.

Here is the rest of her story.

Fourteen months before my visit, Yvonne and her three beauti-ful children were sleeping on a mat in a space they rented for five bucks a month. Yvonne's husband had been in and out of jail, met another woman, had other children, and fled to Uganda.

A single mom of three with no skills, Yvonne at least had per-sistence. So she learned from friends how to buy sweet potatoes, sorghum, and other staples in bulk, then transport them home to be sold to her neighbors at a profit. Her series of loans from Urwego, overseen by Jeffrey and administered by Daniel, have helped her grow this trade; move to a better home; feed, clothe, and care for her children; show her neighbors the example of a successful small enterprise; and begin seeing her future with hope.

Yvonne's business model is very much the same one used by 7-Eleven and other convenience stores across America. I tell her this—about shops just like hers on street corners in every city, playfully suggesting that she has the beginnings of an empire. She laughs, and for a moment, I can see the young girl she so recently was.

Her first loan was for 70,000 Rwandan francs—the equivalent of just $140. (Just six $25 Kiva loans to another Urwego client might do the same for anyone like Yvonne.) Prior to the arrival of microfinance here, local banks required five times as much just to open an account. A loan for Yvonne would have been inconceivable.

Next year, Yvonne now says with visible joy in her eyes, her children will finally begin school. Back in America, Kiva has a separate category called "education loans." But almost every borrower I've met has kids, and the loans support businesses that help get their kids into school. Most Kiva loans, it would seem, are education loans.

The little boy in the *Annie* shirt accidentally rolls his marble under my stool. Without even looking up, comfortable with me now, he crawls to my legs, parts them like barn doors, and crawls through.

I bet you just forgot to wonder whether or not Yvonne and her children were Hutu or Tutsi. I certainly did.

Yvonne would have been about fourteen at the time of the killings. Either by a miracle she's a Tutsi survivor in good health, or (much more likely) she came from a family whose men were among the killers. But she was a *kid*. She didn't start it, and she couldn't have stopped it. Now she's just trying to get by in the aftermath.

Later, Daniel and I and a driver named Wilberforce—the surname of a British politician who fought to end the slave trade, still sometimes used as a given name in his honor—ride toward the Tanzanian border. We listen to gospel music praising *Yesu* (Jesus) while we chat. The melody is soothing, and the three of us chill out, looking out the windows at ladies in traditional wraps walking under colorful parasols, children with a soccer ball skipping on the sidewalk, and workers wearing donorwear jerseys from the Green Bay Packers and Ohio State.

An hour from Kigali, we reach Kabarondo, where an Urwego representative is hosting classes for several lending groups in a small brick and cement rectangle a hundred yards from the road.

Afterward, twenty-eight Urwego clients join me on benches and chairs under the shade of a graceful palaver tree.

During the genocide, a reported 1,700 Tutsi sought refuge in church buildings just a short walk from this tree.* Hutu militia killed them all—men, women, and children—with machetes, arrows, gunshots, and grenades. But that was in 1994.

This same tree would have been used for the local *gaçaça* tribunal. But those began in 2002.

This is 2010.

We sit, not-Hutu and not-Tutsi, plus one curious Ohioan, and we talk about their future.

How many of you work at least six days a week? Every hand goes up.

Seven? Nearly every hand stays up.

The language barrier is difficult, even with Daniel's help, and Rwandans are reluctant to speak too openly, so summaries are all I can gather.

Claude, from the Twunguke ("Profit") group, has a wife, a young son, and the air of a man on the make. He glances at his cell phone three times during our chat. As he describes hustling his way into owning a barbershop, a tire shop, and a moto taxi, he tries not to let his pride show, but it sneaks through. I will not be surprised to learn someday that he has two dozen employees, all of them glancing at text messages and trying to focus on two things at once, just like him.

Theo, from the Gyanumukyo ("Take the Light") group, has built a primary school out of profits from running a DJ business. His own daughter attends, as do some of the other clients' kids. I think he might be a fine music teacher someday, since it would

---

*This number is taken from the genocide charges against Onesphore Rwabukombe. At the time that we sat under the tree, Rwabukombe was under arrest in Germany, awaiting trial for supervising and participating in this and two other massacres. At last notice, that trial was still underway.

combine his two passions. He laughs when I say so, but it looks like he is already considering it.

Chantal, wearing a vivid blue wrap, is from the Umurana ("Faithfulness") group. She puts her kids through school out of profits from her bar and a moto taxi. The bar carries homebrew *urwagwa* beer made from bananas and sorghum, plus bottled soft drinks and Congolese beer.

All afternoon, I struggle to accept the fact that some of the men I am laughing and sharing stories with here may be murderers.

Rwandans have no choice. They have to accept it.

If I want to help them rebuild, I have to, too.

As we're all talking, two children watch my every move from a distance. An *umuzungu* (the local way to say *mzungu*) doesn't descend on Kabarondo often. Even more rarely do two dozen adults sit under a palaver tree and talk with one.

When the meeting is over, I spy the pair eyeing me curiously from fifty feet away. Their voices have a sly playfulness. I can't understand the words, but it looks and sounds exactly like this:

I dare you to touch him.

No way. You do it!

Uh-uhh. I dared you first.

Okay, fine. But I'm cooler than you, then.

You are not. Because you're not gonna.

Watch me. Just watch.

Finally, the one on the right pulls together his nerve and marches over, stopping about two feet away and staring up at me with his best attempt at manly bravery, as if to say, "All right, *umuzungu*, here I am, what's your deal?"

I smile and say *muraho* ("hello") and *amakuru* ("how are you"). Visibly startled to hear friendly Kinyarwanda from an *umuzungu* mouth, the boy simply squeaks. Unsure what to do next, he runs back to his friend. Both are laughing now, so I say goodbye, figuring they've both had their fill.

They have not.

Feeling bolder, the other kid marches on over, pauses, and then suddenly hugs my left leg, a big full-body hard climbing-on-your-uncle hug. His friend, not wanting to seem less courageous, grabs my right leg and does the same thing.

For one beautiful minute, these two kids are squeezing my legs and laughing and looking up at me like the whole world could be friends. I did not see this coming.*

So I stand there thinking maybe this kind of innocence and trust is hard-wired in each new generation. Even here, even where some of the worst things in human history have happened, literally *right on this very ground*, among these very families—these innocent hugs are still part of who we are.

If the Wind is part of being human, these children—and their natural impulse to welcome, hug, play, and laugh with a total stranger—are part of who we are, too. The best of who we are still endures—even after the worst Wind we can conjure.

I came to Rwanda looking for hope. It is hugging my legs.

That said, it's unclear if Rwanda's attempt to create a unified, peaceful culture will work. The risks and challenges are enormous. The wounds of conflict and fictions of ethnicity may be too strong to overcome. Kagame or a successor may eventually

---

*I am fully aware that it is cliché for the Western traveler to feel touched by African kids. This is also a provocatively paternalistic image. But what can I do? It happened—and it was sweet not because they're African, but because they're *kids*. You'd melt, too, if two curious Norwegian kids ran up and hugged your legs in Oslo, or Chinese kids in Shanghai, or whoever wherever. This was that, only with the added context of unspeakable horror already rushing into the past.

grasp power too tightly. Nearby conflict in the eastern DR Congo, where Hutu and rival militias continue to shed blood, could spill back into Rwanda, or the mineral wealth of the region could simply lead to a future conflict that saps Rwandan resources and international investment.* The list of possible bad outcomes is long.

Whatever headlines may follow, they will carry much of Yvonne's future with them.

Microfinance clients in the developing world often have much greater external risks—political, economic, or physical—than the same business would elsewhere. When Yunus and Grameen shared the Nobel Peace Prize, microlending was sometimes trumpeted as a revolutionary solution—by itself—to poverty. This had always sounded like overstatement, ignoring political, environmental, and social factors like war, resource availability, population density, and so on. One visit to Rwanda makes this abundantly clear: the growth of Yvonne's front-room convenience store may depend on factors entirely outside her control.

So is Yvonne's grocery a better or lesser candidate for lending than a comparable shop in a country with a less tragic past and unsettled future? It depends on our criteria.

One way to perceive the difference between rich and poor, in any country or context, is to consider the amount of risk in everyday life. If a microbial infection, a broken axle, or a drought would

---

*The Rwanda-adjacent eastern provinces of the Democratic Republic of the Congo are rich in minerals used in high-tech gadgetry. Coltan, for example, is the source of tantalum, an essential element in high-performance electronics. When the price of coltan rises, so does the likelihood of conflict over control of the mines. Despite laws against trade in "conflict minerals," there's a fair chance that your laptop or mobile phone contains tiny bits of the eastern DR Congo as you read this.

be merely a hassle, a few days or weeks of inconvenience, you're in the middle of the world's economic spectrum, regardless of your currency's strength. You're doing okay. But if any of those could threaten your life or livelihood, you're poor. Poverty alleviation, in this sense, can be simply about lowering risk.

By this measure, Yvonne's family is currently somewhere in the middle, having escaped from the bottom in just the last few years. She can get medicine, find resources to help with capital and emergency expenditures, and lives in a society with access to trade and reserves to handle widespread calamity.

By continuing to make capital available to her, Urwego—and in turn, Kiva lenders—can lower her family's risk even further. She can buy supplies and use the profits to help her family as needed, sometimes even dipping into the borrowed capital temporarily if circumstances require it.* Even if Yvonne's business never grows beyond her one little store, the availability of this capital lowers day-to-day risk, a kind of wealth that may be difficult to measure in academic studies but is nonetheless utterly real.

The little boy in the *Annie* shirt will soon be able to read the word *Annie* because of his mom Yvonne's business, whether it grows further or not. Literacy breeds knowledge, understanding, and peace. That's good enough for me.

My personal choice, then, is to eagerly fund loans to people like Yvonne in countries like Rwanda, grateful to feel confident in Jeffrey and Urwego, while letting governments and politics do whatever they're going to do.

---

* This informal repurposing of loan funds is common, and easy enough to understand. When I was broke in my twenties, I sometimes charged my room at the YMCA to my credit card, grateful to have an alternative to not paying at all. Income streams are unstable in many small enterprises—including my own for the last twenty-eight years—and so this "income smoothing" is a logical measure. Some observers have a problem with it; I can only assume they've never had to juggle their own bills.

In a country as poor as Rwanda, allowing the profit motive to reign supreme could cause great harm. Credit, after all, *is risk*. Making it available without a focus on client education and safety could raise risk levels dramatically—and by that measure, make poverty even worse. So I also take reassurance in Urwego's self-imposed ceiling on profit. A non-profit model, dependent on fundraising and striving to minimize losses, might not be sustainable. By operating at a modest and limited profit, Urwego can serve its customers reliably long-term with minimal risk of exploitation.

As I boarded a flight to my next destination, I didn't even want to think about what would happen if an MFI were poorly managed or had been set up with no ceiling to its own profit.

As it happened, I was about to visit my first MFI in serious financial trouble. Elsewhere, the profit motive was about to have a terrible impact on one of the poorer parts of a country with more people in poverty than any other.

CHAPTER NINE

DAR ES SALAAM, ANDHRA PRADESH, AND A WALK TO THE SEA

YOUR BACKSIDE CAN get a lot of friction on a Tanzanian minibus.

So can your front. Also, your upper middle back, shoulders,
forearms, and shins, all of which may be engulfed in the elbows,
knees, torsos, bosoms, and bottoms of dozens of other fellow passengers, all of whom have been forced by circumstance to regard
this as utterly normal.

There is no guarantee that you will be sitting down. Or standing. I spent much of my first minibus ride in a semi-vertical, slightly
bent position, mostly in the aisle but partly in the lap of a small
bald man, with a teenager and a skinny matron sharing my lap in
turn, all of us positioned like the faceless bent dancers in a Keith
Haring poster. This kind of minibus is called a *dala-dala*. My initial
assumption was that *dala* was Swahili for "butt cheek," so that
dala-dala would simply be a physical description of each ride.*

There really should be a warning on the door of each minibus:

_____

* I was wrong. The term supposedly comes from the price charged by van operators before their business became legal: 5 Tanzanian shillings, equivalent at
the time to 1 U.S. dollar. Conductors would shout "dollar, dollar . . . ," and the
phrase became the name. I still like my explanation better.

CAUTION: PREPARE TO BECOME STACKABLE

Dar es Salaam (Arabic for "Abode of Peace"), Tanzania's largest city, is near the equator on the east coast of Africa, facing the Indian Ocean. Its climate is downright Miami. So riding a dala-dala can also mean sharing sweat, aromas, and exhaled carbon dioxide with the dozens of people pressed up against you.

"You okay, Bob?" Anganile asked, peering up through a teenager's armpit.

"Yeah, sure, no worries," I told him, expelling the exact same puff of air that Anganile had just used.

Minivans like these are a common form of public transport in much of the developing world. I'd known since I began this project that I would wind up climbing into a few. Now I could only wonder how anyone ever gets out.

Our destination was the headquarters of SELFINA, a Kiva partner MFI where Anganile worked as a loan officer. I'd helped finance several of SELFINA's loans via Kiva. The money in turn was invested in inventory for small informal groceries, a stationery business, a small restaurant, and a pub.

SELFINA's offices are in a residential area, twenty minutes from downtown by butt-cheek butt-cheek.* I looked out the window and watched enormous billboards for Tusker lager, Vodacom phone services, and the permanently ruling government go by. It was sham-election season, so there were more ads for the ruling party than anything else by far, although the Tusker came close.

Ari zaidi, nguvu zaidi, kasi zaidi, said the government. "More dedication, more power, more speed."

---

* Dar es Salaam is also served by plenty of moto taxis, which allow you to get around cheaply by hopping on the back of somebody's motorcycle and hanging on for dear life. No thanks. As to air travel, the national carrier is called Precision Air, named for something it has little of, the same way that some people in Hollywood have the word *creative* in their job titles.

Wakati bora, marafiki bora, bia bora, said the beer. "Best time, best friends, best beer."

The two platforms sounded equally good, although I suspect they were both disappointing in practice.

Soon, Anganile motioned for me to follow him out, so I oozed and contorted myself through the bolus of passengers. I'm pretty sure that when I finally squeezed out of the dala-dala, there was an audible *Pop!* as the flesh closed behind me.

Five minutes of walking down the crossroad—passing two more huge billboards (*Kujenga uchumi imara,* "Build a strong economy," said the government; *Ladha halisi, chupa mpya ya kipekee,* "Real taste, unique new bottle," said Guinness)—led us to a four-story building housing a variety of business and aid groups: the Social Action Trust Fund, Women in Development, the House of Quality Furniture—and SELFINA.

Victoria Kisyombe, the founder and managing director of SELFINA, greets me with a warm, almost maternal smile, dressed not in business wear but a bright floral caftan. We sit together near a broad window facing brilliant sunlight and the tops of swaying palm trees. I feel more like I'm in New Orleans than East Africa.

Twenty years ago, Victoria was a happily married veterinarian with four children and a practice near the Zambian border. After the death of her husband, however, Tanzanian custom dictated that his family could reclaim all of their marital possessions, save a single cow. Suddenly Victoria was forced into a decade-long lesson in the challenges facing single Tanzanian women.

That cow, named Sero, was Victoria's sole asset, essential to her family's well-being. As her own children got older, Victoria began to look for ways to help other Tanzanian women finance income-producing assets that could help them stabilize their lives. In 1995, Victoria founded Sero Lease and Finance Limited, named for the cow that kept her family going, with five fellow widows as the first clients. In the years that have followed, SELFINA (an acronym of the original name) has opened ten branch offices nationwide, reaching more than twenty-five thousand clients, many of them widows, young girls, and other women who would never have been able to start a business any other way, indirectly affecting more than a hundred thousand lives for the better.

A few months before my visit, this Masaai widow from a small town near Lake Malawi was recognized by the World Economic Forum as one of Africa's five social entrepreneurs of the year in a ceremony featuring an appearance by President Jakaya Kikwete, head of the ruling CCM, the *Mtu wa Watu* ("man of the people") on billboards across Dar es Salaam.

Our conversation spends virtually no time on her award. Victoria plunges directly back into the work that drives her. "We have a lot of traditions that make it very difficult for women to get credit or own land, I'm afraid," Victoria admits wearily. She has surely earned the right to sound tired. I've read and been told several times by others that she has built SELFINA by working seven days a week for virtually an entire decade. "The problem is very big. If we had the funding, we could do a lot more—we could reach ten times as many women, I am sure."

Like every other Kiva partner MFI we've visited so far, SELFINA sees education as a major part of its mission. "We train in money management, business management, HIV/AIDS and health awareness," she says, counting each subject of education off on her fingers like a grocery list. "We also train in women's rights, political rights, plus dealing with domestic violence, issues of inheritance . . ." Her voice trails off. The mere act of listing the number of challenges still facing hundreds of thousands of rural Tanzanian women seems a reminder of Victoria's lifetime of work still ahead.

It's a fabulous story—but with one small problem. Not long before our visit, Kiva had "paused" SELFINA's ability to raise funds on the site, suspending the appearance of any new SELFINA loans that Kiva users might fund. This was explained at the time only by this short note:

This organization has been paused pending a Kiva examination into SELFINA organizational issues.

Kiva soon posted a second notice, which began with this:

SELFINA remains paused as we seek to better understand the current situation at the organization.

Finally, just before I sat down with Victoria, this:

SELFINA remains paused since there has been no resolution of the situation. Kiva has not received payments owed by SELFINA for two months . . . Kiva is in contact with SELFINA and its other creditors to monitor the MFI's progress to resolve the situation.

Wait—*what?* SELFINA isn't paying Kiva back, and so much so that Kiva had to stop offering their loans to protect their own lenders? I'm hoping there has been some sort of mistake, a simple oversight, or a minor problem to be easily fixed. But Victoria looks a little uncomfortable when I ask. "We are 'paused' because of some changes we have had, caused by the way we have grown," she says. "But we have consultants now to sort out some extensions."

I ask for specifics, and Victoria goes on to explain that Kiva and other international funding make up only about 20 percent of SELFINA's funding, and the money from Kiva is really appreciated, and for women in rural areas, this kind of work is really their only support. None of which answers my question, exactly. Victoria also explains that SELFINA has expanded their outreach nationwide, listing the many field offices from the Coast region all the way inland to Ngorongoro. Then she describes the truly useful and needed services—electrification, irrigation, etc.—that SELFINA works to finance. Still, she hasn't quite answered my question.

And then, finally, we get to it: setting up all these branches *was* the problem. "We have of course had to train, equip, provide electricity— even standby generators—at each branch. We have had to put a M.I.S. [Management Information System] at each branch . . ."

Overexpansion was the cause of SELFINA's troubles. But unlike in Bosnia, it appears this wasn't selfishness or profit-seeking, just a desire to do more good for more women too quickly—literally the best of intentions. Victoria's ambition to do good had simply outpaced the ability to build infrastructure to keep up with it—all surely complicated by the financial crisis in the West.

Victoria's fifteen years of outreach to disadvantaged clients might be unusual back in America, but her organization's financial situation was not. In 2009, the year after the 2008 financial crisis, 140 American lending institutions failed—a 460-percent increase from the previous year.* In 2010, the year of my visit to Tanzania, that number increased to 157, and the total number of U.S. bank branches dropped by nearly 1,000, primarily in the most economically challenged areas.† The crisis sent ripple effects of bursting bubbles and cascading delinquency all over the world.

As I leave SELFINA a few minutes later, all handshakes and warm smiles, I am unsure what will happen next with SELFINA, despite its past success. I take Victoria at her word that she is doing all she can. But the look in her eyes tells me that things may not go well.

Anganile and I spend the rest of the day visiting clients around Dar es Salaam. We're driving now, and I confess relief. Not every dala-dala would be so crowded as my first, but stackability takes endurance. I'm happy to save my energy for meeting clients.

We visit Jayne, who does handicrafts—beautiful hand-painted baskets and carvings and jewelry boxes. We say hello to Lizbeth at her boutique. She does Masaai- and Western-influenced paintings and other artworks, including delightful Christmas ornaments in which the traditional triangular evergreen shape extends out from a Masaai warrior in traditional garb.

"Jayne" and "Lizbeth" are pseudonyms, however, because Kiva

---

* Figures here are from the FDIC. See Sources.
† See Schwartz in the *New York Times* in Sources.

was eventually forced to mark every loan from SELFINA as defaulted. The clients were anonymized, and the lenders' portfolios (including mine) all took a small loss. As Kiva's page on SELFINA explains:

> Sero Lease and Finance Limited (SELFINA) has been a long-standing partner of Kiva's for three years, successfully paying back over $757k in loans since the partnership began in May of 2007 . . .
>
> As part of an upgrade of its backend systems, SELFINA initiated a major program to transition from manual loan tracking to computerized management information systems. This process uncovered a number of problems. After thousands of SELFINA's loans had been entered into the computerized system and a portfolio report was run, the portfolio at risk greater than 30 days was calculated to be well above 50% . . .
>
> With the much higher levels of delinquency, SELFINA was unable to mobilize continued debt financing and faced significant strains on its cash position and liquidity . . .
>
> Kiva has learned that since June of 2010, SELFINA has not been able to pay other creditors to the organization. In addition, they have been unable to consistently offer repeat loans to those clients who are repaying, and have faced serious strains upon their equity (the internal funds used by SELFINA to cushion the organization against financial shocks) . . .
>
> Kiva has been forced to conclude that continued repayment from the organization is doubtful at this point. Accordingly, Kiva has defaulted any remaining active loans from SELFINA and has closed the organization as a Kiva field partner. Kiva will continue to pursue recovery of funds on these loans and apply funds proportionally to lenders if and as funds are received.*

---

*These quotes are all from Kiva's field partner page for SELFINA, www.kiva .org/partners/90.

SELFINA turned out to be a good illustration of how those few defaults do tend to occur: roughly half of Kiva's unpaid loans have resulted not from individual clients failing to repay, but from the partner MFI itself breaking down due to adverse economic developments, poor management, or some other external cause. Fortunately, it's a rare occurrence, more so as MFIs establish longer track records and Kiva hones its techniques for due diligence. Kiva's default rate has been steadily shrinking for years and seems poised to fall below 1 percent. Kiva lenders who prefer to stick to the most reliable MFIs will likely have something closer to 100 percent repayment.

SELFINA's clients would be able to find funding elsewhere, at least. Tanzania had several large and stable MFIs they could turn to, including BRAC Tanzania, the local affiliate of the largest nongovernmental development organization on earth, and Kiva partner Tujijenge Afrika, a Tanzanian non-profit whose thousand-plus Kiva loans had suffered not one default.* The loss to Kiva lenders like myself would be minimal as well. Kiva's overall repayment rate was still easily above 98 percent, and my own portfolio's rate was 99.3 percent.

I felt bad for Victoria, however. I tried to imagine how it would feel to rise from being a rural widow who owns exactly one cow to receiving international acclaim for your work—and then to see

---

* BRAC, founded in Dhaka and originally known as the Bangladesh Rehabilitation Assistance Committee, operates in some of the world's most challenging environments, including Afghanistan, South Sudan, and Haiti. Most branches offer much more than microfinance, including health services, agricultural assistance, financial training, and research support. See Chapter Twelve. BRAC Tanzania's website is www.brac.net/content/about-brac-tanzania.

Tujijenge Afrika is Swahili for roughly "let's build ourselves Africa." Their website is www.tujijengeafrika.org. The no-default statistic was true at the time I was in the field; updating the figures before print, of the 1,347 Tujijenge loans financed on Kiva.org, 4 have defaulted, a non-default rate of 99.7 percent.

your good efforts collapse so rapidly that you're unable even to pay your own bills.

At least Victoria's ambitions had been principally selfless. This was sadly not so in a case that was soon to gain international notoriety. Nermina's warning about the dark side of microfinance was coming true, four thousand miles away from where she had warned me—in India, the very country I'd originally been most interested in helping.

In October 2010, the southeastern Indian state of Andhra Pradesh (commonly called "AP"), a hotbed of microfinance with more than a hundred MFIs in local operation, experienced a severe crisis. Microlending had grown so explosively in the preceding few years that as early as 2009, some observers already foresaw a Bosnia-style bubble. In the prescient words of international microfinance consultant Daniel Rozas:

> Frankly, the numbers there concern me—AP has more microfinance clients than any other country in the world except for Bangladesh . . . Most disquieting, the state was already at 6% over-capacity a year ago. Explaining these numbers without allowing for extensive multiple borrowing is indeed a challenge . . . I would argue that these areas show vastly increased sector-wide risk, and thus, significant probability of a large-scale crisis . . . In their pursuit of growth, many MFIs have continued to add large numbers of new customers in Andhra Pradesh and other highly saturated regions—I believe that is irresponsible . . . [This] puts short-term gain not only above the long-term financial soundness of the sector, but, more importantly, above the long-term interests of the very poor the MFIs are seeking to serve.*

---

* See Rozas, "Is There a Microfinance Bubble in South India?" in Sources.

This was complicated by an unusually intense focus on the profit motive by local MFIs, most notably SKS Microfinance, founded by a former Yunus acolyte named Vikram Akula. A month after Rozas's prophetic article, SKS was gearing up for its 2010 initial public stock offering—a chance for those with ownership stakes in the company to make enormous sums of money—by launching a massive drive to expand the number of loans it made. Called "Incentives Galore," the program offered prizes to field agents including TVs, home appliances, and bonuses worth up to ten times their annual pay—all in exchange for signing up as many borrowers as possible. In the frenzy that followed, SKS could call itself the world's fastest-growing microfinance company—just in time for its IPO.

According to a later investigation by the Associated Press, one field agent signed up 273 groups in a single month—more than twenty times the recommended volume for client safety.* The well-being of the clients might appear to have become secondary, if not completely irrelevant.

For Akula and SKS's investors, the IPO raised $358 million. SKS founder Vikram Akula made more than $12 million himself.†

To many observers (myself included), the notion of making millions from lending to $2-dollar-a-day earners sounded inherently ill-conceived, if not worse. Yunus and Grameen and FINCA and the other pioneers of microfinance had never intended the gross enrichment of lenders and loan officers. Thinking back to Clotilde in Peru, Seida in Bosnia, Jeffrey in Rwanda, or Nat and

---

* See Kinetz, "Lender's Own Probe Links It to Suicides," in Sources. In fairness, SKS's response is at sksindia.com/downloads/SKS clarification on the Associated Press report.pdf.

† See Datta, "Lunch with BS: Vikram Akula, SKS Microfinance," in Sources. ("BS" here stands for *Business Standard*.)

Nelly and Fred and Nathan in Kenya, profit seemed to be the very last motive for most in the industry—or at least anyone I'd met with whom Kiva had partnered.

As the IPO approached, one didn't need to be an expert in microfinance to see trouble ahead. It took only two more months for the reports of suicides—"suboptimal outcomes," in the jargon of an SKS board member—to begin.*

For bankers and investors to make money on their big bets, SKS would have to come through with its revenue. When loans made under the above circumstances began to default, some local field agents reportedly began to take coercive measures against the clients, ranging from persistent pressure to harassment to outright intimidation. To some clients, the only escape from the group-loan community obligations and debt might be suicide. Early reports placed the number of suicides in the dozens; some estimates of the toll ran even higher.

An outraged Muhammad Yunus has frequently characterized aggressively for-profit institutions as "loan sharks" ever since, even urging them publicly to stop using the word *microfinance* at all.† SKS denies wrongdoing to this day, but two different investigations

---

*The speaker is Ashish Lakhanpal, quoted in Kinetz. "Suboptimal outcomes" for client suicide has to rank with "collateral damage" (Pentagonese for the deaths of innocents) and "controlled flight into terrain" (FAA-speak for a plane crash) for euphemism.

†See Sources for examples, including Yunus's op-ed in the *New York Times* and his vocal public denunciation as reported in "Profit-focused MFIs Are Loan Sharks: Yunus," staff reporting with no byline in the *Times of India*. Yunus's criticism of foreign-investor-owned and IPO-driven microfinance did not begin with SKS; he had previously been almost as vocal in his criticism of Compartamos, the largest MFI in Mexico. One common defense of SKS was that it was forced to seek funding different from Grameen because of India's distinct regulatory environment. Obviously, this may rationalize funding through an IPO, but no other behavior described.

reported by the Associated Press point to coercive behavior by field agents as directly related to some of the suicides.*

The suicides were publicized widely by Indian officials with their own interest in promoting local Self-Help Groups, which borrow from government-owned banks, not MFIs, and which were starting to default as members under duress rushed to repay their MFI debt first. The officials didn't wait for careful investigation as to how many deaths were directly related to SKS's actions.† Instead, they rapidly seized the populist high ground and passed a state law that made it cumbersome for MFIs to operate at all. Almost instantly, all of microfinance throughout the region—including the work of perfectly good MFIs unrelated to anything described here—was shaken by the fallout, similar to the way a run on one failing bank in the West can cascade into a crisis across the financial system.

The crisis attracted global attention. In the West, the reputation of microfinance after Yunus's Nobel Peace Prize was hit by the media's grand pendulum, swinging backwards and hard: *India's Major Crisis in Microlending*; *India Microcredit Faces Collapse from Defaults*; *Discredited*; *Suicides in India Revealing How Men Made a Mess of Microcredit*; and so on.‡

Despite the obvious fact that hundreds of non-profit and responsibly profitable MFIs all over the world had *nothing whatsoever* to

---

* Kinetz, cited above.

† Left out of the news-making, for example, was the horrifying fact that thousands of Indians commit suicide due to extreme poverty every year, did long before the SKS crisis, and continue to do so. The main causes are debated, but the causes most often suggested are the urbanization and corporatization of India's farm system, climate change affecting monsoonal rains and harvests, and the introduction of genetically modified crops. The topic is worth a separate book. See Sources.

‡ Headlines from the *Wall Street Journal*, October 29, 2010; the *Economist*, November 4, 2010; the *New York Times*, November 17, 2010; and Bloomberg Newswire, December 28, 2010, respectively.

do with Andhra Pradesh or any Indian lenders—operating with different goals, services, internal structures, and environments—the global reputation of microfinance took a serious blow.

I wonder if the words *microfinance, microcredit,* and so on might best be discarded as stand-alone terms. Bundling everything from SKS to tiny non-profits in the popular term "microfinance" is as imprecise as blurring Bank of America, the Small Business Administration, and Moe's Pawnshop into "American lenders." This cannot be helping anyone.

I don't pretend the expertise to suggest the most workable alternatives. The degree of non-financial services, the sources of funding, or just sheer dang size might be worth denoting somehow. But perhaps "microfinance" should mean that only money is handled, so "for-profit microfinance" would be clearly different from "non-profit microfinance," and MFIs like Women for Women offering a wide range of client services might be called "non-profit microservices." Urwego, perhaps, could be "capped for-profit microservices," and a for-profit megalender like SKS might be an "MF-IPO."* Changing the terminology might seem impossible this late in the game, but devising a simple way for the media and the public to understand who does what will ultimately just help the clients. If more accurate terms had existed when the Andhra Pradesh crisis began, small non-profits half a world away would not have seen their reputations affected.

For a time, even Kiva's reputation suffered by association, despite having no partnerships anywhere in India at the time, nor any

---

* These are only proposed as what TV writers often call the "bad version" of an idea, meant as a verbal first draft to help others think of better versions along the same lines.

partner on earth even alleged to engage in similar strong-arming. Of course, many American readers had only heard about microfinance once before, perhaps when Yunus was featured on *Oprah* or *The Simpsons.* If the only two flying objects you'd ever seen were the Goodyear blimp and the Hindenburg, you might suddenly worry about anything big and aloft.

Years later, with time for retrospect, Akula told a conference at Harvard that "Professor Yunus was right . . . Bringing private capital into social enterprise was much harder than I anticipated."*

Unfortunately so.

Yunus's prestige has also taken a large hit, and not just from the above. His home country of Bangladesh has long suffered under one of the more corrupt governments on earth.† In October 2006, just as Yunus received his Peace Prize, the country's two major political blocs were fighting bitterly for control. When a round of planned elections fell apart, riots, violence, and eventually an official state of emergency followed. It was in this context that Yunus spoke out against the established corruption and proposed a third, more populist party (to be called the Nagorik Shakti, Bengali for "Citizen Power"), calling in the country's largest English-language newspaper for secular governance focused

---

* See Neha Thirani, " 'Yunus Was Right,' SKS Microfinance Founder Says," *New York Times Global Edition*, in Sources.

† At the time of Yunus's award, for example, Transparency International's "Corruption Perceptions Index" ranked Bangladesh the eighth-most-corrupt place in the world, behind only Chad, the Democratic Republic of the Congo, Sudan, Guinea, Iraq, Myanmar, and Haiti. Meanwhile, of the world's twenty most populous countries, the World Bank currently rates Bangladesh near the bottom in almost every measure of honest, lawful, and uncorrupt governance. See Sources.

on alleviating poverty and empowering women. This did not go over well.

Yunus's ideas were a sharp rebuke to the political class, and his increasing status posed a potential threat to their own, especially if some military leaders might prefer Yunus in charge, as was rumored at the time. Ever since, any allegation against Yunus, regardless of its truth, has been repeated by prominent Bangladeshi political figures seeking to drive Yunus out of the public eye and seize control of Grameen itself. Despite consistent debunking and refutation when the charges were examined independently, the allegations generated constant headlines, and any observer not directly interested might have gained the impression that Yunus is somehow to blame.*

One charge might have stuck. Bangladesh's finance minister eventually got Yunus on a technicality: he had passed the mandatory retirement age of sixty.† Yunus continued to fight and appeal, but he finally resigned after the head of the Grameen Bank Employee Association was arrested and tortured.

Finally, in August 2012, the ruling party rewrote Bangladeshi law in a fashion that essentially gives control over Grameen to the government. Despite international outcry, a bank almost entirely owned by millions of poor Bangaldeshi women may soon be turned into a prize of private patronage. Barely six years after Grameen shared a Nobel Peace Prize, its destruction by Bangladesh's political class may now begin.

Yunus's immediate response, published by the same newspaper where his call for democracy, secular governance, and an end to

---

* Friends of Grameen, a group chaired by former UN High Commissioner for Human Rights Mary Robinson, has assembled the clearest summary of the many allegations, with links to objective debunking. See Sources.

† Yunus was seventy when the issue was raised, so the minister had apparently not noticed for a decade. Perhaps the oversight can be excused, however: the minister himself was seventy-seven years old.

corruption ignited the campaign to destroy his influence: "a black day in the nation's history . . . I can't summon words to express my sorrow."

While nothing described here had anything to do with Kiva—whose MFI partners in fact were not even breaking even, operating at an aggregate loss for the year—the news was depressing nonetheless.* So was the increasing realization that the early studies about the effectiveness of microfinance weren't exactly as definitive as had been generally accepted.† And the evolving vendetta against Yunus, with one soon-to-be-debunked headline after another, was an undeserved black eye for the whole industry. Microfinance had a powerful enemy, it turned out. And exactly where I should have expected.

In fiction, a compelling bad guy—Moriarty, Darth Vader, the Joker—is often strikingly like the hero, someone blessed with similar skills, power, and resources, but whose response to circumstances is the opposite of heroic. In purest form—Mr. Hyde, Tyler Durden—the nemesis *is* the hero, or rather what the hero would be without kindness, love, responsibility, and the positive attributes we value most. This resonates because the stories often represent our own struggles between our best and worst selves.

---

*The most recent figure puts the aggregate profitability of Kiva's MFI partners at -0.7 percent.

†The short version: the rigor of early studies has been questioned, economists barely agree even on how to create controlled studies of the effects of microloans, most broad-scale studies don't conclude much of anything, and there's disagreement over how to read those and what to study next. Sometimes I think that if two economists in a burning airplane had to flip a coin to decide who got a parachute, they'd argue over the coin as a statistical model. For more, see Sources.

The failure of microfinance in Andhra Pradesh was a near-perfect realization of true nemesis. Where responsibility should have stood, there was recklessness. For wisdom, short-sightedness. For generosity, greed. Amid executives, investors, lending officers, and government officials—everywhere in the crisis—our nemesis stalked every step.

Almost any human tool can be used for good or bad, depending on whose hands it falls into: the same compound can be medicine or poison, depending on dose; our hands can be used for a caress or a punch; even a lie can be used to hide child abuse or beautiful birthday presents. When a hammer can be used to build a house or slay a neighbor, nobody argues over whether the hammer "works." It depends on who is using it, their motives, their carefulness, and their level of skill.

Of course microfinance can fail when its own people fail. Just like investment banking, air traffic control, ski jumping, soufflé making, or Cleveland sports for the last forty years. A vanishingly high number of people in banking are honest and kind, but bankers and savings and loan operators have committed fraud many times. Microfinance has differed only in the depth of hope attached to it and the vulnerability of lives in the balance.

That sense of urgency had only gotten more intense in my travels. It's one thing to be intellectually aware that billions of people have lives massively more difficult than yours, all through no fault of their own. But it's another to actually dive in full-body, to play with cute kids amid the nightmarish backstories of Sarajevo, Kigali, and Six Flags Over Yugoslavia. On a personal level, it was difficult for a while to remain optimistic about humankind, having seen tiny slices of hunger, infant mortality, and other conditions easily preventable if humankind weren't more interested in building and/or blowing up monuments to ourselves. It was hard to take heart in the successes I'd seen at Arariwa, Women for Women, Juhudi, Urwego, and elsewhere. Once I was home, it was even a challenge to stay emotionally connected to the warmth and friendship that had been obvious everywhere I'd gone.

Los Angeles, with its potable water, microwave popcorn, satellite TV, insects free of malaria and dengue and Chagas and chikungunya, good Wi-Fi, distinct lack of shell craters in the sidewalk, and Fatburger, was almost as disorienting as my first night in Dubai. After dala-dala rides, Sport Utility Vehicles looked more like Personal School Buses. Turning on the TV could be even more confusing. After listening to stories of genocide, hard work, and restored hope, it was hard to feel connected where human value seemed to be measured in units of Kardashian.

I found myself oddly stressed for a couple of weeks. I even tried getting drunk a few times. Not surprisingly, this didn't sort anything out. So I tried harder for a while.*

Soon, I found myself reaching out to stay in touch with as many people whom I'd met on this project as I could—translators, MFI employees, Kiva Fellows, volunteers working with other charities, and eventually, fellow lenders from all over the world. And making loans became an appointment on my calendar.

Since clients frequently repay on the first of each month, the funds usually make their way back to Kiva and are credited to lender accounts on the fifteenth. I'd quickly adopted the habit of checking my account in the middle of each month and redistribut-

---

* This is mentioned only because I don't want to falsely portray myself as some jut-jawed do-gooder able to zip around the planet, look poverty and tragedy straight in the eye, and not even flinch. Heck, no. I flinched pretty darn good. For a while I downed more bourbons than the French Revolution. If you think you might flinch, too, that's only normal. But please also feel confident that you'd probably adjust to it at least as well and quickly as I did, probably by connecting to other people, too. This is the only mention you'll hear of my own personal stress. Billions of people have serious struggles. My problems came simply from feeling overwhelmed as an observer. Not really in the same league.

ing the money. Since I'd eventually invested more than $20,000, in most months, at least $2,000 would reappear in my account. This I would happily redistribute to eighty more clients. Because the payments were partial, one couldn't say precisely that the exact dollars from *this* bicycle delivery person in the Philippines were going to *that* student in Guatemala, but reinvesting still felt like running my own tiny foundation.

After my experience in the field, many client stories felt more compelling than ever. The Makiese Plus Group, for example, is a group of thirty-two neighbors in the capital of the Democratic Republic of the Congo (DRC). Various parts of the DRC have been subject to deadly conflict for nearly two decades, including a 1998–2003 civil war virtually unknown in the West but by far the deadliest conflict on earth since the end of World War II. To this day, more people die of malnutrition, injury, and preventable disease in that war's aftermath than in all of the other active war zones on earth combined. Conflict continues in a Pennsylvania-sized area along the DRC's eastern border, with no end in sight.*

Keeping that history in mind, here's how the Kiva page describes the Makiese Plus Group leader: †

Wivine M., 47, . . . sells fried dough and sausages and eggs. Her present working capital amounts to about US $200 . . . Her initial capital was US $40 . . .

In 1993, Wivine fell victim to the pillaging in Kinshasa and lost all her merchandise . . . Thus, from 1994 to 2004, she tried selling cases of soap without success. In 2003 she was caught off balance at the death of her husband. She changed her business in 2005 to begin selling spices which brought her to a

---

*This is generally the same mineral-rich part of the country that will need to achieve peace if Rwanda is ever to become truly stable.

†The Kiva page for the Makiese Plus Group is at www.kiva.org/lend/100987.

significant capital of US $2,400—which sadly was stolen by robbers . . .

Wivine took up selling fried dough again with the insignificant working capital of $20, a business she has continued until this day. Her business is growing rapidly and producing a profit of US $30 per week. The loan that she has received has allowed her to buy 1 sack of wheat flour, 1 jerrycan of 25 liters of refined vegetable oil, sugar, and other ingredients for making fried dough.

To which I remember thinking: *Jeebus. All this woman is asking for, after years of war, death, and repeated ruin, is to get enough flour and oil to make more than $30 a week?*

After seeing neighboring Rwanda with my own eyes, stories like this made my innards churn like never before. Hell yes, I clicked the "Lend $25" button, chipping in so that Wivine and her thirty-one partners could borrow an average of about $100 each to get their hopefully non-pillaged businesses off the ground.

But I'd be lying if I told you that I fully read and considered every profile I lent to. Not even close. In truth, it became time-consuming to sort through hundreds of profiles just to find the eighty most compelling. After a while, depending on my own mood, all of the stories might seem almost equally inspiring—or, on a bad day, equally depressing.

So instead I began to lend with more arbitrary criteria. I started lending more and more to clients in countries I was likely to visit. Relatively peaceful Armenia got priority over Afghanistan, while dengue-free Georgia got preference over Ghana. Urban areas also got my focus, since I'd be more likely to meet an MFI that could help me find my own clients. So my loans to Mongolia, say, wound up going more to taxi drivers in the suburbs of Ulaanbaatar, the capital, than to a ger-dwelling yak herder from rural Bayankhongor.

This felt capricious, but most lenders' choices wind up being a bit arbitrary, whether they realize it or not. At the first Kiva Fellows orientation session, JD, wizened mentor and accurate forecaster of temporary suck, had noted with some chagrin that most Fellows soon learn exactly which kinds of photos tend to attract funding—and which do not. Much of this is predictable: a clear photo does better than a blurry one, a smile outshines a frown, and an action pic of the client at work is more eye-catching than a nondescript portrait taken in the MFI office.

Other factors, however, speak to Western perceptions of poverty: a thin black Ghanaian woman holding a child, for example, might attract lenders at light speed compared to a grizzled white Ukrainian man, even if on close inspection the white dude has seven kids to feed and a wife dying of cancer. The thin black woman simply looks more "poor" to Western eyes, so her loan probably gets refilled faster. As Matt himself once put it, "A female African fruit seller? Funded in hours. Nicaraguan retail stand? Funded in days. A Bulgarian taxi driver? Funded in weeks."*

The birth lottery echoes again, if somewhat in reverse. Damn.

Some of the Kiva profiles occasionally reminded me of some of the more difficult lottery results I'd seen in my travels. There were times I felt fairly overwhelmed. I briefly even considered abandoning this project.

Just over the next hill, however, there were sunflowers.

Kiva "lending teams" are self-selected groups of lenders, usually gathered around a location, an ideology, or a specific cause: Team Virginia, Unitarian Universalists, and Animal Lovers were all among the first teams formed on the site.

The software enabling lenders to organize themselves into teams was launched shortly before Labor Day of 2008, not long

---

* Flannery, "Kiva and the Birth of Person-to-Person Microfinance," *Innovations*, cited above, p. 50.

after I first heard Premal Shah speak. By the following spring, there were more than six thousand teams active on the site.* The two biggest teams:

- Atheists, Agnostics, Skeptics, Freethinkers, Secular Humanists, and the Non-Religious, with 3,725 members raising $465,525
- Kiva Christians, with 1,794 members raising $370,000

A spirited ideological argument was being carried out in competitive good works. As to who was winning, the Atheists could claim more members and a higher loan volume, but the Christians could claim higher loans per member. Either way, the whole argument was over who could be kinder to total strangers. This may be the best disagreement that humans can have.

After those two, the top ten teams included Team Obama, Team Europe, the self-explanatory KivaFriends.org, Poverty2Prosperity.org (a lending group focusing on economy-building projects in agriculture, health, education, renewable energy, and safe water, as opposed to funding just any mom-and-pop business), Australia, Belgium, GLBT (Gay, Lesbian, Bisexual, Transgender) Kivans, and Team Germany, all of whom had raised more than $100,000 in these $25 loans. The Late Loaning Lenders, for their part, invested solely in loans nearing expiration, keeping thousands of loans fully funded.

Impressive. But I wasn't in a joining mood. Besides, I was sure that I'd personally make the same number of loans regardless of any team memberships. I didn't quite understand why so many lenders enjoyed it.

A few months later, a fellow lender named Aaron e-mailed to

---

*The Kiva Community page as of May 2, 2009, viewable at web.archive.org /web/20090502023835/http://www.kiva.org/community.

inform me that he was a fan of my work, supported my book, and wanted to suggest that I should start a team to support my own loans. I'd never met Aaron, but his lender page made him appear to be a working-class Midwesterner who, like me, had gotten an education and was trying to do something good.* Still, I let the suggestion go.

Aaron, unsatisfied, wrote again, now telling me he'd started a team anyway. There was *going* to be a team of my friends in this world, and that was that. And so, on June 16, 2009, Friends of Bob Harris was officially born.† Aaron was captain by default, but he invited me to take over whenever I liked. It took about a month before my inner control freak decided that if there were a team using my name, I'd want my hand on the steering wheel.

I still didn't think anything would come of it.

By that time, Kiva had over 100,000 loans being funded by 6,500 lending teams, and the Atheists had just cracked the $500,000 mark. What good could result from a tiny team of maybe a dozen or two people I didn't even know, organized by a guy I'd never met, when I wouldn't even have much time to encourage them? At the time, there was also a team called Women Who Lend To Shirtless Men, devoted to choosing loans based on inadvertent beefcake in the client photos. Women Who Lend To Shirtless Men was just as big, and they had far more reason to feel excited.‡

Surely this was a waste of my time, I secretly grumbled to myself, still trying harder sometimes. But due to an unlikely confluence of four unrelated factors, Friends of Bob Harris unexpectedly started to snowball.

In its first year of existence, the team had made less than $100,000 in loans, one-fifth of which was my own $20,000 cycling

---

* Aaron's lender page is at www.kiva.org/lender/aaronx.

† The team page is at kiva.org/team/bobharrisdotcom.

‡ The team page is at www.kiva.org/team/women_who_lend_t_shirtless_men.

through for the first time. But in late 2010, the team suddenly raised about $50,000 in a single month, and the next month, more than $65,000. Meanwhile, a growing stream of new members—almost all of them people I'd never met, from all over the world—started joining and lending like their lives depended on it.

What the . . . ?

I took to watching the discussion board in genuine astonishment. The people joining were funny and friendly and cool and kind—exactly the people I'd most want to remind me why I'd started with all this myself.

So now Katie, a schoolteacher in Adelaide, was touting a clothes seller in El Salvador. Patty, a soapmaker in Queensland, joined right in with her. Ramona from Berlin, Abdulaziz from Riyadh, Edith from Brookyn, and Petra from Delft all piped up. My real-world friends started inviting each other, too, eventually diving in by the dozen. Paul in Denver and Leslie in Helsinki and David in Miami and dozens of others—all of these and many scores more were suddenly all in the same cyber-place, all supporting my work, all cheering me on.

I cheered back. It was breathtaking to watch so many people I cared about all rallying at once, none of them with any knowledge that I particularly needed support, but providing it exactly when needed.

And what they did, most of all, was *fun*. Friends of Bob Harris (now casually calling themselves FoBH) competed good-naturedly with other teams—*look out, Team France, we're coming through!*—and cheered every time a new milestone—*8,000 loans! Yay, us!*—was reached. FoBHs started doing "lend-a-thons" on the first day of every month, seeing how many loans they could make in the first twenty-four hours, thrusting the team to the top of Kiva's monthly standings for the first several days of each month. Almost everyone got excited whenever Kiva partnered with an MFI in a new country—*hey, everybody, we can make loans in Timor-Leste now!*—

racing to get their $25 in before the new loans were filled.* And several times every week, a half-dozen FoBHs would get excited about a particular loan simply because of the person's story, their cute kids, or simply just their smile.

It was impossible not to marvel at the faith and goodwill on display. Hundreds of people on this one team alone had put their hard-earned money where their heart was, sending it halfway across the world, worried less about repayment rates or portfolio yield than just trying to do good for people they would never meet. This was indiscriminate generosity, trust as a default emotion, eagerness to bet on total strangers all over the world, innocent joy at the hope for their success, over and over and over.

By the start of 2011, FoBH had surged to more than 250 members, who had collectively made nearly 10,000 loans totaling just over $250,000 to clients in more than 50 countries. Not having any idea how it happened made it feel all the more wonderful.

Everyone should have a total stranger start an online group where hundreds of strangers join together to call themselves your friends, all just to be nice to more total strangers. I couldn't help but feel like one of the wealthiest people on earth.

So how did this happen? As near as I can tell, several strands of good fortune colluded in less than two weeks.

A few of Kiva's most active individual lenders, who join and lend via dozens of teams—including one anonymous mega-user who has made more than 64,000 loans and goes by the pseudonym Good Dogg†—joined FoBH at the same time, causing a small surge in loans credited under the team's name. This, in

---

*This "country collecting" is a source of pride for many Kiva lenders who want to distribute their funds as widely as possible. Long-term users have often made loans into fifty countries or more. As this goes to press, I'm personally up to sixty-five, visible at www.kiva.org/lender/bobharris.

†His Kiva page is at www.kiva.org/lender/gooddogg1.

turn, made the team just large enough to appear for the first time in Kiva's monthly list of its top ten teams.* And FoBH showed up on this list, becoming easy to notice on the site for the first time, just days before Oprah Winfrey mentioned Kiva as one of her "Ten Favorite Things" for 2010, sending a huge burst of new traffic to the site.

When new visitors looked through the top 50 of Kiva's 20,000-plus lending teams, they saw 49 teams that represented locations (Team Europe, Team Canada), religions (Kiva Christians, Kiva Baha'is), political viewpoints (Team Obama, Women Empowering Women), and so on, all represented with little logos or flags. Exactly one team was represented by an actual human face. This happened to be mine.

People join Kiva to connect with other human beings. You can guess which team they frequently joined.

I wish I could take credit for that kind of foresight, but my face was attached to Friends of Bob Harris only by default. I'd always assumed there would be a better idea eventually. Sometimes the simplest idea is the best.

One other key event in the growth of FoBH preceded the others: a few months earlier, a Kiva lender named Jonathon Stalls had started a fundraising walk with his feet in the Atlantic Ocean. By the time I met Jonathon, he was crossing the Golden Gate Bridge, having traversed the entire United States to raise money for Kiva.

In the hours before I met Jonathon (spelled, yes, "–athon," his actual birth name, prophetic for an endurance athlete), I flew into town and cabbed it at dawn to the north end of the bridge. I was a wreck, but Jonathon, who had just walked 3,018 miles, didn't seem remotely fatigued. Instead, this twenty-eight-year old, who

---

* The top ten list is at www.kiva.org/community.

had just exercised for ten hours a day for eight and a half months, was positively buoyant.

He had every right to feel excited. It was a crisp blue morning, San Francisco was gleaming across the bay, the smell of the ocean—his ultimate goal—was drifting in from the west, and he was surrounded by a dozen friends and well-wishers who had joined him for the last two days of his journey.

As we shook hands, it dawned on me that we'd be walking eight miles, ultimately returning to the neighborhood I'd just left. My feet already ached at the idea. Jonathon had already walked 3,010 more miles than that, much of it across vast empty spaces in Kansas, Colorado, Utah, and Nevada.* Along the way, Jonathon had sometimes camped out, but more often he was offered a place to sleep by a local Kiva supporter, an Internet couchsurfer, or just a friendly family. The blog of his travels is a portrait of America painted at a long, slow stroll.†

For all of the terrible social conflicts our evening news emphasizes, the United States, it turns out, is full of people ready to welcome a passing stranger. Even more encouraging, Jonathon found that American small business owners can completely connect with the struggles of independent entrepreneurs in the developing world.

Joining Jonathon on this day were several friends and Chelsa Bocci, Kiva's Director of Community Marketing, a job title that indicates her main function as lead organizer of users, lending teams, and social media. In practice, Chelsa's role is much greater. With Jessica Jackley now running another business, and CEO Matt Flannery and president Premal Shah both frequently off meeting with partners and policy makers, Chelsa often serves as Kiva's institutional memory and organizing hub, sloshing enthusiasm on

---

*There's a route map of Jonathon's walk at www.kivawalk.com/wp-content /uploads/2009/12/rough-route-map.jpg.

†The Kiva Walk blog is at www.kivawalk.com.

anyone who shares her current velocity. A more accurate job title would be Glue.

Together, we crossed the Golden Gate and zig-zagged through the city to Kiva headquarters, where Jonathon shared a slide show of his journey. Sunsets and highways and faces rolled by. Supporters had started a Kiva Walk lending team, and Jonathon shared the statistics of its success—its four-hundred-plus members had made more than $400,000 in loans, enough to fully fund at least one small business loan for every day of his journey.

The value of Jonathon's walk wasn't just in the money raised for Kiva, however, nor the publicity it generated, nor perhaps anything related to microfinance. It was more: for tens of thousands of people—for the readers of his cross-country blog, the lenders inspired to share their good fortune in support of the walk, and the countless diners and shop owners and families he met on the way—Jonathon had made the world smaller, friendlier, and more connected.

The ripple effects would never show up in an academic study, but they may be the most profound. Jonathon surely met teenagers with dreams of seeing the country. He met small shopkeepers who'd never realized that their worries were similar to those of people halfway around the world. And Jonathon surely met young people who dream of work that connects to a world greater than their own. Jonathon had changed all of those lives for the better.

The final leg of Jonathon's walk, reaching from the bay all the way across town to the ocean, began on a cool Saturday morning. Many of Kiva's staff were along for the day and excited for the walk. My feet, calves, and butt were decidedly not, but my pride would have been sorer if they hadn't agreed to join in.

Soon, I found myself keeping up with JD, my wizened mentor, the longtime head of the Kiva Fellows program. He looked younger and more relaxed than I'd remembered. This was probably be-cause this was the first time I'd ever seen him when he wasn't try-ing to focus, train, and scare the crap out of a roomful of eager strangers about to become far-flung.

JD, it turned out, had a new title: Senior Director of Social Per-formance. Translated into English, this meant that Kiva had recog-nized the need for more wide-ranging analysis of the economic and social impact of Kiva's hundred-plus MFI partners: which partners were (or weren't) especially supportive of new businesses, effective at innovating better services, or particularly strong at alleviating poverty? Kiva also wanted to develop the means to objectively quantify each MFI's impact for visitors in a way that would be clear at a glance.

Executing all this sounded impossibly complex, but as the head of the Kiva Fellows program, responsible for their placements around the world, JD had as much active experience in communi-cating with MFIs worldwide as anyone in the industry. JD seemed truly excited. "It's a lot to take on, sure," he said—and his eyes showed that he really did feel a bit overwhelmed—"but the whole industry is developing better metrics and sharing best practices . . . It can only make what we're doing more effective."

Yes, okay, I get all that intellectually, I replied. *But how do you actu-ally do that? How do you quantify a whole planet of different social and economic contexts?*

"Ask me again in another year or so," JD said, laughing. "I should know by then."

I made a mental note to hold him to it.

Late afternoon brought perfect blue sky as we trooped around the Presidio, through pine trees and dirt paths and salty fresh air. I found myself walking with Matt Flannery, Kiva's CEO. It was the first time we'd ever had a chance to say more than hello.

I asked him how it felt to have inspired somebody to walk the width of the country. Matt demurred. "I didn't. The entrepreneurs and the lenders did that." His humility seemed completely genuine. And then he changed the subject to ask me about what it was like to be on *Jeopardy!*, pleasantly shifting the topic onto someone else's perceived proud moments, not his own.

This exchange was a preview of Matt's modesty and curiosity about others. Given the opportunity to accept praise, he measured it, decided it was unearned, and politely rejected it. He'd also done his homework and knew what to ask that might draw me into a conversation instead of an interview. This wasn't dodging a question. I got the idea that Matt really would rather hear one of your stories than tell one of his own.

I poked again a few minutes later, trying to get him to admit being proud of what he'd had such a huge hand in creating. "Well, I can't take that credit," Matt replied. "It wouldn't have happened without a lot of other people. Everybody here, everybody out there, it's really theirs." This wasn't false modesty—there was even a gentle edge of admonishment in Matt's voice, as if I needed to reorganize my view of the world in a less top-down fashion.*

So I asked Matt instead about the mistakes along the way. If he were deflecting questions or holding anything back, it would now become clear, but Matt's modesty filter allowed this data stream through. "Oh, we had a *lot* of struggles early on. Most of the people we worked with were good, but a couple of the partners turned out to be outright frauds. That was just"—and here Matt trailed off,

---

* I later learned that when Kiva moved into its first rented office space, Matt assembled furniture for the staff himself, by hand, the night before. Later, when Kiva moved into its current, much larger offices, Matt declined any opportunity to take a corner room with a closing door. The CEO's work area was placed in the middle of traffic—open, ordinary, equal. The humility is consistent enough that when this book is published, I almost expect him to complain about this footnote.

searching for words, then cut directly to the lesson gained—"we had to clean that up, learn from it." *

Wow, I said, exhibiting my finely developed vocabulary.

"But we did," Matt continued, with a *no-big-deal* voice and *of-course-we-did* shrug. "And now it works better, and we'll keep learning."

The ocean.

Jonathon didn't say anything when it first came into view. He just started walking a little faster. And then a little faster.

Cameras out. Try to keep up.

After more than three thousand miles of walking, Jonathon Stalls stripped off his shirt, started running, and dove right in.

We all stood in a half-circle and applauded.

For Jonathon's project, completion.

Once Jonathon's own journey finished, he later suggested that members of the Kiva Walk team might consider joining mine. Many loans Jonathon first inspired are now re-lent through FoBH, and I believe that Jonathon's recommendation was the initial factor in starting the FoBH snowball. Then came Good Dogg and many other lenders, visibility on the Kiva page, and the surge after *Oprah*, and FoBH has been growing ever since, carrying Jonathon's walk onward.

As I watched Jonathon rejoice after walking three thousand miles, my recent doubts now appeared only foolish. People do impossible things all the time.

---

*A list of the MFI partnerships to which Matt was referring, along with what they were caught doing and links to their Kiva pages, is in Sources.

Right here in front of me, Matt and Premal and Chelsa and everyone at Kiva had already created something that had never been imagined before. Simple crowdsourcing hadn't even been attempted when Kiva began, much less deployed to connect people all over the world. Now it all works so smoothly that we take it for granted.

Grameen and FINCA and others had already pioneered new opportunity for millions, not to mention an industry in which thousands of people all over the world work full-time to help build their communities, with ripple effects I'd seen for myself. And from Mohammed and Tiro and the two Symons and Yvonne and so many others, I knew firsthand that these small loans can make a big difference.

The next step was simply to learn more about where and why microfinance works best, what its shortcomings are, what other programs effectively alleviate poverty and create opportunity, and how microlending fits into the broader puzzle.

These are massive and ongoing questions. They would not be solved on my next series of trips. But thousands of good people are looking for answers.

Some are finding them.

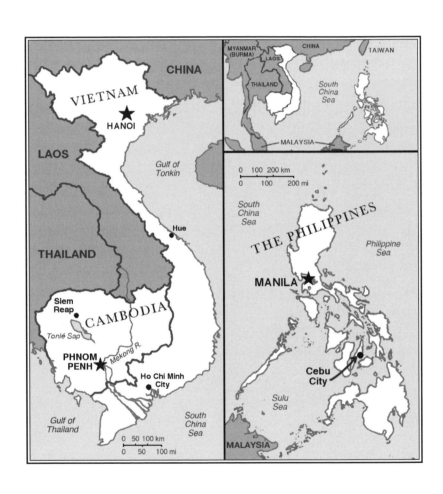

CHAPTER TEN

MAGELLAN'S CROSS, HANOI, AND CAMBODIA

I'VE MET A lot of people who work hard in these travels—eleven hours a day is common, and even twelve or thirteen no longer surprises me—but this may be a record.

In a hilly neighborhood near the town of Compostela on the island of Cebu in the Philippines, Jinifer gets up at 3 A.M. Every morning. Seven days a week, fifty-two weeks a year.* On the day that you read this, Jinifer has been up that early. She'll often get an hour or two of rest in the afternoon, when her mom and other family members pitch in to relieve her, but most nights, she doesn't get to bed until around 10 P.M. Her basic routine is a nineteen-hour day.

Jinifer and her family live near a quarry, and at around 5 A.M., men from her neighborhood start to walk past Jinifer's house on their way to work. Many of them are hungry. Seeing a market opportunity, Jinifer started getting up at 3 A.M. to prepare hot meals by the time the workers pass by.

There aren't a lot of weather statistics for Jinifer's specific town, but in booming Cebu City, maybe fifteen miles away and with a nearly identical climate, the mean temperature is 83 degrees, with an average relative humidity of 78 percent. At any given moment,

---

* Jinifer's Kiva page is at www.kiva.org/lend/273110.

the average heat index is 90 degrees. Even in the cool of the morning, the average low is 77 with sticky high humidity.* Jinifer cooks hot meals in that climate for several hours each day.

Jinifer makes twelve dishes every morning—pork chops, *dugo-dugo* (a stew made from pig's liver and blood), vegetables, various soups, *bola-bola* (a kind of meatball), and so on—offering something for anyone's taste.† Jinifer keeps the breakfast meals available all morning, and since workers on break also like soft drinks, snacks, and various sundries, Jinifer also works the family's *sari-sari* convenience store.‡ In the afternoon, Jinifer's elderly mom pitches in, so sometimes Jinifer gets a nap, but the sari-sari keeps offering beers, snacks, and much of what you'd find in a 7-Eleven. Between keeping customers happy, caring for Ginver, her beautiful two-year-old son, and otherwise maintaining the home, it's 10 P.M. before Jinifer knows it.§

I sit with Jinifer and her husband Bernie on their porch one afternoon, my shirt so drenched in sweat that I'm afraid I'll ruin the

---

* Located just 10 degrees north of the equator and surrounded by other islands in every direction, Cebu is remarkably consistent in its steaminess. The lowest temperature ever recorded was 66 degrees. In contrast, Havana's record low is 41 degrees, Honolulu's record low is 52, and even Tahiti has gotten down to 61.

† Personally, I'd want the vegetables. The only *dugo-dugo* recipe I've found begins this way: "simmer pork for 30 minutes and remove scum that rises . . ." See Sources. *Bola-bola*, however, are like a pure pork version of American meatballs and Spanish *albondigas*, reflecting the two Western powers who colonized these islands. The Spanish name *albondigas*, in turn, comes from Arabic, reflecting Spain's own colonization more than a thousand years ago. In one meatball, you can eat three empires.

‡ *Sari* is Tagalog for "miscellaneous," so reduplication into *sari-sari* implies a wide variety of mixed goods—a convenience store. Reduplication for emphasis is common in Malay, Tagalog, and other Austronesian tongues, but in English this sort of usage, while hardly a hush-hush no-no, is only so-so.

§ I can't promise that the boy's name is correct. I triple-checked it verbally, but it sounded so much like Jinifer's name that I still wonder if there was some confusion. If so, my bad.

furniture. The buzz of three-wheeled motorcycles and single-stroke scooters and open-wheeled jeepneys crossing a distant bridge almost drowns out the sound of the dog snoring at my feet. I lean forward to focus as Jinifer and Bernie talk about their dreams.

"We have three people who work for us now," Jinifer says, pride and fatigue fighting in her voice. "They sell our meals house-to-house, on commission, and we hope to hire more. Eventually, we hope to have a delivery service." The ripple effects of Jinifer's sari-sari feel inspiring to imagine.

We move off the porch and talk by the sari-sari, standing next to shelves lined with cooking oil, ketchup, paper towels, packaged snacks, bottled water, and mobile phone cards, stock that was financed in part by the $350 Kiva loan I'd invested in. "We hope to be able to continue to improve the business," Bernie says. "Maybe renovate the house, keep hiring more people, send our boy to school and to college." Bernie smiles, his black mop of hair perfectly matched on the head of the two-year-old boy in his arms.

Jinifer and Bernie have been speaking to me in Cebuano, the island of Cebu's most common language, one of at least 120 languages used throughout the Philippines. Raymond Serios, the head of special projects for the Negros Women for Tomorrow Foundation (NWTF), the Kiva partner MFI here, translates.* Like many lending executives and loan officers all over the world, Raymond speaks three languages as part of his job.

Raymond is from Bacalod on the island of Negros, so while his

---

* *Negros* is the name of the nearby island where NWTF was founded. I'd like to add that the word has nothing to do with the twentieth-century American usage of the word, but the island gets its name from the word Spanish explorers used for the darker-skinned locals, exactly as they did in sub-Saharan Africa. The origin is identical.

work brings him to Cebu frequently, he sees it with new eyes every time. As we drive along the main road toward the island's biggest city, the buildings grow steadily and become newer on both sides of the road. Raymond marvels about Cebu City's recent boom. "It's like a second Manila, almost," he says, precisely as a three-wheeled *trisikad* (a kind of bicycle rickshaw with a sidecar) darts into view from behind a parked bus, causing an oncoming car to veer briefly across our path. "Have you seen the malls?"

I have. Cebu—one of the fastest-growing cities in Asia, now more populous than Boston, although with a greater metro area only half as large—boasts several vast state-of-the-art multi-level shopping malls, complete with multiplex movie theaters and almost as much security as a typical airport. One of these meccas was a ten-minute walk from my hotel, and I was surprised to be separated by gender and frisked up the inseam just to buy a chicken sandwich. Then again, a few islands south of here, several Islamist insurgency movements are responsible for bombings, kidnappings, beheadings, and so on.* There's also a long-standing but low-simmering communist movement called the New People's Army that still pops up occasionally, although lately it's more about shaking down rural farmers than any grand anti-imperialist action.

I ask Raymond about all the security and the rebellions, and his response is compassionate. "If people are joining the rebels, most of the time, it's really about economic reasons," he says. "If you're young, on a farm, and you're not making it under this system, yeah, sure, you might rebel. Everybody needs hope. That's why we're here."

NWTF's programs serve more than eighty-five thousand clients

---

* The most active group, devoted to creating an autonomous Muslim homeland in the country's south, is the Moro Islamic Liberation Front, or MILF. This acronym existed long before the film *American Pie* was conceived. I have no idea if the movie has reached Mindanao. I kinda hope not.

in five mostly rural provinces. The average loan is just $130. Their flagship program on Cebu, Project Dungganon (*Dungganon* means "honorable" in the Hiligaynon language of Negros) brings lending and education to rural women in the poorest 30 percent of the population. Other programs include microinsurance, education loans, utility loans, asset loans—financing a motorized tricycle, for example, a kind of local taxi that can transport up to ten or even twelve people profitably if not very safely—scholarship programs, and larger programs for successful clients who can use greater capital.

The stories of these clients, in turn, are used as much as possible to inspire people just starting out. "It's *hard* to get people to dream," Raymond observes, affection and frustration bulging the word *hard* into audible italics. "People always just naturally respond in their comfort zones. If they've been poor all their lives, that can be their comfort zone. So we give examples of other members' successes whenever we can." Change a few words, and I'd heard the exact same thing from Clotilde at Arariwa in Peru.

I ask if communications are a problem in the Philippines, where thirteen different languages have at least a million native speakers.* What good is an inspiring story if it can't be understood? Raymond concedes that it's a unique obstacle of local geography, complicated by cultural differences and the physical isolation of having clients on four separate islands. Fortunately, new clients come primarily by word-of-mouth, so if NWTF staffs its field offices with locals fluent in the subtleties of their clients' cultures, the challenges are easily solved.

After our next clients—two more sari-sari owners—we stop at a field office on the nearby island of Mactan, whose name you

---

* These aren't just dialects, although the word is sometimes misapplied. Here's the same word in the four languages on NWTF documents (Cebuano, Waray-Waray, Tagalog, and Hiligaynon), plus Spanish, spoken by some elderly clients, and English, spoken by most visitors: *iro, ayam, aso, ido, perro, dog.*

might have heard in middle-school history lessons. It's where the explorer Ferdinand Magellan was killed.

I don't know what they taught you in school, but my teacher fuzzed over most of the details, leaving an impression that Magellan represented civilization, exploration, the human desire for adventure, and Christianity—after all, his flagship was named *Trinidad*, for the Holy Trinity. The people who killed him, unnamed savages of no distinct ethnicity or history, must not have comprehended the sheer nobility of the enterprise. Almost as bad, they kept him from circumnavigating the globe, which was—as I was taught, anyway—the whole point of his grand adventure.

What I wasn't taught in school was that the actual purpose of the trip was to make Magellan a literal boatload of cash. The Spanish king, hoping to gain economic leverage over his Portuguese rival, had promised Magellan and his partner that if they could colonize the Spice Islands (now part of Indonesia), they'd get 20 percent of the voyage's profits, a ten-year monopoly over the route so they could gouge future travelers, local governorship over the islands, a private island to live on, and 5 percent of Spain's take from the new colony—wealth beyond imagination, in other words. Magellan, for his part, wasn't exactly an idealistic explorer corrupted by royal ambition. He was only able to convince the Spanish king that he could pull this off because he'd already been part of something similar in what we now call Malaysia.

This was somewhat less noble than the version in my schoolbook.

When Magellan got to Cebu, the local chieftain agreed to convert and cooperate, and Magellan ordered a large Christian cross to be erected on the site. On Mactan, however, chief Lapu-Lapu replied that his people had enough gods and wealth, thanks. Magellan responded with an attempted landing of forty-nine men armed with crossbows and axes. Unfortunately for Magellan, Lapu-Lapu had about 1,500 men on his side, all simply waiting on shore while Magellan's soldiers, covered in metal, struggled to wade in from the sea. Magellan, not the greatest tactician ever, never again set foot on land. In some accounts, the large cross Magellan had erected on Cebu was symbolically destroyed.

Today on Mactan, Lapu-Lapu is considered a local hero, and the biggest city is named in his honor. Magellan is remembered with only a dilapidated shrine. In Cebu City, however, a tourist-friendly display of "Magellan's Cross," accepted by many as authentic, attracts a steady flow of curious visitors. This is admittedly another piece of wood entirely, a mere replica of the actual cross, which is said to be protectively hidden inside the display. The authenticity of the unseen wood is a matter of faith, and irrelevant as long as tourists and their wallets are engaged by the experience.

Magellan's Cross feels symbolic of much of the developing world, at least as it exists for Western eyes. The exoticism of Marrakech, the gleam of Dubai, the spiritual purity of Bali—like Magellan's Cross, maintaining an outside perception has become an integral part of the local economy. But the thing that visitors come to see, believe that they see, and return home believing they saw may not be the full story of what was actually there. If the reality is more complex and less enticing, it may also be more familiar, human, and fragile.

In Mactan, modern visitors often decamp directly to beachfront resorts where rooms go for up to $600 a night. The hotel's Cebuano workers get paid about 2 percent of that per day. Alternatively, a newcomer may head straight to do business in Cebu City, whose booming growth is a source of local pride but where the economy is in large part built around twenty-four-hour call centers serving overseas clients of multinational corporations. Many local families now have at least one son or a daughter working late into the night, caring for the flower delivery or airline reservation needs of long-distance Westerners.

So who won, really, between Lapu-Lapu and Magellan?

We arrive at NWTF's Mactan field office, located in the town of Cordova, after 7 P.M. I'm surprised to discover that the entire staff is still in the office.

Because they live here.

Unlike any of the other MFIs I've visited, these loan officers work, relax, and play together, sharing a home almost like family. My visit is a major and welcome break from routine, so we sit together in the main living room, sharing pizza and telling stories and getting to know each other. I meet Randy, Irene, Vanessa, Mary Jean, Jacob, Hope, and more, all from either Mactan or Cebu. It only takes about ten minutes until they make me feel so comfortable it's like we're hanging out in a college dorm. But these aren't kids, of course—they're adults with families to support who consider themselves fortunate to have found stable office jobs doing work they believe in, with housing costs defrayed by NWTF.

Many of the staff go home on weekends, but some can't very often because it's too far. Charlie has a boy and a girl, five and three years old. He misses them audibly just in speaking their names. A few others have spouses who also work, so they pay for a *yaya*—a nanny— to raise the kids. Vanessa has a four-year-old boy named Ivan and a three-year-old girl named Princess. Her husband is in Saudi Arabia, working for a year on contract. So the whole family is split up, trading time and this vast chunk of their lives together for the hope of better days down the road.

These folks are sleeping at work, putting in long hours, missing their kids for weeks at a time, but cheerfully making the best of it—just like their clients, and as we've seen everywhere, in the loving hope of giving their own children a better life.

We're still just a fifteen-minute ride from those $600-a-night luxury beach resorts. A few years ago, I'd have been paid to sleep there, to write about them. I'd have looked into the distance from a balcony window and wondered what life was like for the people who live here but whom I'd never really see. I'd have wondered if they'd be friendly, or hostile, or if the difference between us would feel too weird to overcome.

I'm laughing with my mouth full of pizza. I don't wonder anymore.

While we were in Compostela, Raymond also took me to a field office, where I met several more loan officers, another dozen or so clients, and a branch manager named Dancer.* We also met a few people in the field. The occupations of the clients:

- Sari-sari owner
- Cheesemaker†
- Sari-sari owner
- Manicurist
- Candle seller
- Drinks-and-cigarettes seller next to a village cockfighting pit‡
- Sari-sari owner

---

* Not really. Actually, he introduced himself as "Dan, sir," and I misunderstood so utterly and for so long that it's just more true to what happened if you hear it that way for a while, too.

† Specifically, *kesong puti*, "white cheese" made from water buffalo milk, wrapped in banana leaves and served with warm bread.

‡ Cockfighting is not only legal in the Philippines, it's enjoyed with gusto by thousands of people in large arenas, advertised on billboards (often with close-ups of psychotically angry birds that look ready to peck your face off), and reported in the sports section of the newspaper. Kiva briefly allowed cockfighting loans on their site, allowing the marketplace to decide whether to finance the loans. The volume of outraged users made it clear that the marketplace was saying *no*.

Three more sari-sari owners meant that more than half of all of the clients I'd met in Cebu ran sari-saris. That seemed like a lot.

Certain microenterprises seem to thrive all over the world: on any given day, transportation services, cosmetics sales, clothing resale, car repair, barbershops, and food prep might comprise a quarter or more of all of the loans on Kiva. Stores like Jinifer's sari-sari are also especially common: on the day I write this, for example, six Filipino MFIs currently list a total of 353 loans on Kiva, 132 of which—more than a third—are sari-saris.

It's great to see a business model that seems to thrive anywhere, and for largely the same reasons that it flourishes in the U.S.: convenience stores, despite sometimes charging a high markup, add value to a community. The word *convenience* accurately describes the primary product: people everywhere are often eager to pay for the time saved in not having to seek goods in several different markets—time that can be used in more profitable or personally important endeavors. Across the developing world, where workdays can average twelve hours or more, it's an essential commodity.

But you also couldn't build an entire economy on convenience, nor on secondhand clothes reselling, taxi transport, bicycle delivery service, nor several of the other microfinanced business models that tend to succeed anywhere.

Jinifer's sari-sari is successful primarily due to her incredibly hard work, but partly because it's the only sari-sari in the neighborhood. It's not hard to imagine, however, that Jinifer's success could convince neighbors to open competing businesses. This might be successful at first, but the ceiling on neighborhood growth is obvious.

In the U.S, we see superficially similar competition almost anywhere we look. In the Midwest, if two freeways cross, there's usually a gas station, and if it succeeds, there's a second one. Competition means prices stay fair for the consumer, which is appropriately viewed as a good thing. But this only works because of high liquidity and an open system—e.g., a fairly fixed level of demand due to a steady volume of traffic from outside the community, with profits available for investment either locally or far away, whatever benefits the business most. If the gas stations offer competing yet complementary services, both may even attract additional customers, thriving alongside each other. Competition can actually create more than one winner.

But what if it's a rural village, people are on foot, and money spent largely comes from and stays in the community? Different ballgame. There are only so many *bola-bolas* a neighborhood can want to eat, and the profits can only travel around in the community circle, buying *bola-bola* ingredients. Open two sari-saris, then three, then four, and all could easily become unprofitable. Competition can actually create more than one loser.

Obviously, MFIs and investors need to encourage economic diversity by continuing to innovate loan products and training tailored to complementary sectors. Just as the success of cow loans in Kenya has led Juhudi Kilimo to consider funding large-scale milk-processing operations, one might also imagine loans tailored to cheesemaking, retail, and every other cow-related business we can dream up. On a neighborhood level, lenders must also evaluate projects with the same commonsense approach that any commercial lender in the U.S. would take. Want to open a gym right next to two other gyms? To get a loan, you'd have to have a pretty convincing business plan. The same idea is even more important in developing economies.

Happily enough for Cebu, NWTF seems to exercise enough care that none of the sari-sari-owners I met—nor any entrepreneur in any field—seemed to suffer from neighborhood competition. The Filipino government is also actively seeking to keep sari-saris from struggling in isolation. One program, Hapinoy (a portmanteau of *happy* and *Pinoy*, the slang word for "Filipino") specifically assists more than a thousand sari-sari owners by setting up regional distribution centers and providing bulk discounts to local store owners, boosting their profits.

That said, the Hapinoy website notes that the Philippines now have more than seven hundred thousand sari-sari stores comprising more than 30 percent of all retail in the country.* I'm sure nearly every one of those sari-saris is run by hardworking people who are eager to grow their businesses. But *can* they—all of them, at once? Not indefinitely. Instead, in the best case, local sari-saris might grow large enough to buy their competitors, exactly as happens in any maturing industry. This is surely a good outcome— but it's simply changing the way a pie is sliced.

The next step in building the economy would encourage the entire supply chain of the sari-saris—encompassing processing, packing, delivery, storage and other large-scale grocery services. These, however, would be loans far larger than anything we'd currently consider micro. A set of transition services bridging between micro- and full-size financing thus seems essential.

And now I start to wonder: how many microfinance business models are actually scalable? Plainly, many are not, at least without improvements in infrastructure. For Jinifer's sari-sari to grow, keep hiring, acquire more physical space, and eventually become a major grocery, she would need not just dedication and intelligence, which she has in abundance, but also moderately skilled labor, a physical transportation and power infrastructure better than the one in her town, and of course financing tailored to her growth.

At some point, successful poverty alleviation will often require support for small and medium enterprises, too. Microfinance, in this context, is neither the cure-all some of its more triumphalist supporters have imagined, nor the non-solution its critics prefer— but a key rung in a ladder.

---

*This figure is from the Hapinoy website, www.hapinoy.com/about_storepro gram.html.

My next stop was Cambodia, another "mature" market like the Philippines, where financial services for the poor are evolving more from the best practices of large MFIs than the innovations of small start-ups. Along the way, I stopped for a week in Hanoi, Vietnam.

I was born in 1963, so my early memories of television include somber news about the Vietnam War, and later, the bombing of Cambodia. For anyone my age or older, the words *Hanoi* and *Phnom Penh* are inherently ominous. Since Vietnam still proudly flies the communist hammer-and-sickle more vigorously than any other country left on earth, I wondered if Hanoi might feel authoritarian, repressed, even hostile.

My very first impression only confirmed my biases: as I boarded an inbound Vietnam Airlines jet, a flight attendant handed me a copy of the *Viet Nam News*, an official state media organ. Its bold headline: "Party Leader Emphasizes Unifying Function of the Fatherland Front." The sheer excitement of that prose gave me goosesteps.

And then I looked up from the paper and started noticing everything else.

Shortly before takeoff, the attendant pulled a curtain to separate first class and coach. *Wait*, I thought—this is the state airline, owned and operated by the Vietnamese government, surely meant to accurately reflect Vietnamese values. Isn't communism supposed to at least attempt the appearance of a classless society? But no—on landing, the flight crew kept us economy-dwellers in our place, on the wrong side of a drawn curtain, until all of first class had disembarked. So much for dictatorship of the proletariat.

The flight attendants, I should add, were dressed in hip-hugging silk pants and traditional *ao dai* tunics slit high enough to flash more taut tummy skin than I've ever seen on a Western airline. So much for communist post-gender prudery.

Nearly every time a Vietnamese citizen found out I was American, the response was immediate warmth: "Thank you for the visit," "Please enjoy our country," "I am happy you are here," and so on. So much for hostility.

Even during a brief layover in the Ho Chi Minh City (formerly Saigon) airport—the airfield where the last two American soldiers died in fighting during the Vietnam War, shortly before North Vietnamese forces gained control of the entire city—a hard-charging capitalism was on display. Duty Free stores, exactly like you'd see in the most acquisitive city on earth, were flanked by floor-to-ceiling display ads for Calvin Klein perfume and Ferragamo shoes, while large wall displays offered eight-foot illuminated ads for a Vietnamese bank in English and an American bank in Vietnamese. *Bring Prosperity to Customers*, saith the Vietnam Bank for Agriculture and Rural Development; 50 *Hãng Hàng Không Sẵn Lòng Phục Vụ*—"50 Airlines at Your Service"—replied the CitiBank MasterCard.

Signs of fierce nationalism remain, inevitably—a large TV monitor, for example, was playing the movie *Black Hawk Down*, about a failed U.S. military operation that resulted in a humiliating American defeat, unlikely to be a coincidental choice. But Western-style commercialism was on constant display. In Lenin Park, parents rented their children rides in motorized mini-cars emblazoned with NASCAR, Valvoline, and other American racing logos, directly under a statue of Vladimir Ilyich himself. Vietnamese national TV regularly broadcasts a letter-perfect *The Price Is Right* knock-off, right down to identical sets, games, and music—but with more product placement than the U.S. equivalent. And at the Hanoi Hilton, the prison where Senator John McCain's grueling years of torture and confinement began, there's a gift shop selling the very symbols of communism itself, already converted into consumable kitsch: Ho Chi Minh T-shirts, red-and-yellow-star jewelry, hammer-and-sickle beer cozies.*

However, while streets have transitioned from bicycles to scooters to motorcycles to cars, and the economy has physically accelerated, Vietnam's turn to capitalism hardly means progress is guaranteed. The highway to the airport, for example, was lined with massive billboards for high-end luxury items—but beneath those signs were massive rice paddies, where people living at the level of feudal serfs still continue to harvest by hand. The middle class is vulnerable as well, thanks to the inherent risks of becoming dependent on international trade. Profits from small export manufacturing—often in "craft villages," where former farmers have organized to create pottery, jewelry, artisan paper, and so on—have been whomped by the global pullback that began in 2008. After years of rapid growth, a whole class of Vietnamese workers was rapidly threatened with a new kind of unemployment.

Worse, political power remains vigorously centralized, large economic decisions are still centrally planned to a degree orders of magnitude beyond the basic regulations that U.S. pundits exaggerate as "socialist," and human rights scarcely exist. Never mind organized opposition: merely signing a petition is enough to land you in jail. The fate of the country's poorest people—the intended recipients of microfinance—will inevitably be at the mercy of a self-interested government that shows little sign of sharing either economic or political power.

Obviously, without the development of democratic institutions, there's a visible lid on how much good any attempt at poverty alleviation can do. That's not to say that a loan to a client in

---

*This sarcastically nicknamed "Hanoi Hilton" should not be confused with the actual Hilton, which opened several miles away twenty-six years after American POWs were released.

Vietnam or Zimbabwe or any other one-party state is a waste. Hell, no—it's probably desperately needed. But those lives are simply going to need a lot of external factors to change, too.

Microfinance needs human rights and transparency to thrive.

My first visit to a Cambodian client is a voyage into the "developing world" in a literal sense: the sealed pavement gives way to rutted dirt roads that snake through recent constructions of cinderblock, cement, and wood. Electric wires are strung overhead with an improvisational flair, enabling the whir and squeal of power tools next to bare open fields. Here on the outskirts of Phnom Penh, the national capital, living standards are changing, but the struggle forward manifests itself as a few bricks, a stack of cinder blocks, a new tin roof at a time.*

On the far side of the road is a modest building where Bo currently lives.† It's too large and solid to qualify as a shack, but that word certainly carries the flavor. Nearby, Bo is kneeling on a thin cloth mat at the edge of a field, her back to the road, cutting and bundling morning glories.

Bo is a client of Hattha Kaksekar Limited ("Helping Hand for

---

* The gradual construction of new homes—often one floor, room, or wall at a time, accomplished only over the course of years as funds become available—is called "incremental housing" in development-speak. To the eyes of Westerners who think of houses as ready-made products built by real estate companies and contractors, the disorder can be hard to process, but it is a sign of devotion, resourcefulness, and hope. Naturally, incremental housing is often microfinanced. To see examples, go to www.kiva.org/lend, look down the left-hand side, and select the little button labeled "Housing." On the day I write this, 186 loans are available for finance in nineteen countries, from Mexico to Mongolia, from Kenya to Kazakhstan.

† "Bo" is a pseudonym. This lady has been through enough, and while I can't see any reason that giving her real name here would cause a problem, I make mistakes, and my instincts simply tell me to be cautious.

Farmers" in Khmer; "HKL" for short), an MFI that focuses on women in low-income rural areas in almost every corner of the country.* Cambodia is another mature market, with twenty-three licensed microlenders serving about a million Cambodian families. Given the local average family size and a national population of only fourteen million, about one Cambodian in three is in a family whose future is entwined with microfinance.

Bo is tiny, about sixty years old, a mother of four and a grandmother of two, and has been working in the Cambodian sun for hours. But she rises to greet me, we exchange a *sampeah*—the hands-in-prayer greeting universal in this part of the world—and she welcomes me with an openness that I doubt I could offer in her place.

Bo is old enough to have lived through the "Killing Fields" period of Khmer Rouge rule, a radical spasm of violent, cultish communism that drove all of Cambodia literally back to the Stone Age. Cities were evacuated; money was abolished; schools, hospitals, and historic monuments were destroyed; people with skills—doctors, linguists, actors, singers, anyone with an education—were targeted for extermination; and the entire country was turned into a labor camp where resistance, fatigue, or even picking a piece of fruit to salve your hunger—"private enterprise," by Khmer Rouge standards—was a death penalty offense.

The Wind blew hard for nearly four solid years. In a country of eight million, about two million died from starvation, execution, or simple exhaustion. One person in four.

If it's hard to conjure a real feeling for the joy, energy, and buoyant good humanity lost—and those may not be words you initially associate with Cambodia—download the music of Sinn Sisamouth from iTunes or some other source. He was Cambodia's most popular singer, and his music is a time capsule of what Cambodian

---

* HKL's website is www.hkl.com.kh. Click "Branch Network" to see a map of Cambodia covered in little successful dots.

mainstream culture sounded like before the rise of the Khmer Rouge—'60s-R&B–infused beach pop that could have poured out of any nightclub in L.A., save the Khmer lyrics. You'll want to dance with an umbrella drink in your hand. And then, when you realize he was probably killed *because he could sing,* consider two million more people like this, gone.

Bo probably listened to Sinn's music as a girl. And then came the bombs, and the Wind, and a war in the aftermath. That would have been her young adult life.

And now she's here, cutting morning glories in the brilliant sun, welcoming me, hands steady, with a grandmotherly smile.

Through my translator, Top—a forest engineer with three kids who speaks Khmer, English, and Russian thanks to attending college in St. Petersburg—Bo dives happily into her finances, perfectly open and eager to share. Her only bashfulness is about her poor teeth, which she covers shyly whenever she speaks or might smile.

The morning glories are a great little business, it turns out. She pays $5 for seeds, but this species grows tall enough to cut in just over two weeks, and she can sell them at market for $40. So she plants and cuts almost every day, rotating through her land, making enough money to invest in other activities, too. Bo's first loan with HKL was for $500 to help open a motorcycle shop with one of her sons. A second loan helped open a second shop. Bo has used those profits to buy two-and-a-half acres of land about a kilometer away. That's where she intends to build and live someday. And the land is now worth five times what she paid for it, so borrowing against it to build should be no problem.

This tiny Cambodian grandma picking flowers by the side of the road has built a more robust business and retirement portfolio than at least half the Americans I know.

Back at HKL headquarters, Hout Ieng Tong, the president and CEO, and Toch Chaochek, soon to become HKL's VP and chief operations officer, join me at a large table. After perhaps five seconds, Chaochek gets up, turns on the AC, and offers me water, possibly because I am already transforming into a puddle. Dengue fever is common here, so I spend every day slathered in a thick syrup of sweat, sunscreen, and insect repellent, all of which eventually starts to pour down my arms and legs. I must look like I'm melting.

Tong is an MBA who has traveled to three continents to study best practices in the field. I ask if the devastation of the genocide and the war years makes the task here much harder than he has seen elsewhere. "Actually, my hopes have been met beyond any expectation," he says proudly. "Yes, the majority of people are still very poor. So what we do is very important for them, and we have no problem reaching them—and we hope our American friends will help on this issue and invest more," he adds. I would have expected a wink from most people in Tong's shoes, a half-ironic acknowledgment of directness, softening the moment of pure selling. But this wasn't sales. This was simple sincerity.

More than half of all visitors to Cambodia bypass Phnom Penh and fly directly to Siem Reap, the tourist springboard five miles south of the Angkor Wat, a spectacular twelfth-century temple complex that was once the center of the Khmer Empire. As ornate as anything the Greeks or Romans ever imagined, and currently covering a footprint the size of Lower Manhattan (if we include the nearby Angkor Thom grounds), the temple complex is the most visible remnant of a thriving city that once may have had up to half a million people—ranking it as possibly the largest city on earth at the time—sprawled over an area the size of Los Angeles.* Like nearly all empires, Ankgor enjoyed a few good centuries at

---

* See "Map Reveals Ancient Urban Sprawl," BBC News, in Sources.

the top of its game, but drought, war, and the inevitable excesses brought on by its own sheer power eventually did it in.

Six hundred years later, the surrounding area is a mix of jungle, struggling rural settlement, and booming tourism. Siem Reap is now the fastest-growing city in the country, even if it's still smaller than Providence, Rhode Island. You can see the influx of tourist money simply by driving in from the airport. Initially, and farthest from the complex, the road greets you with local accommodations: the Chreuk Leong Guesthouse, the Princess Angkor, the Lotus Resort and Spa. Pass through the small city itself and approach the park, and you find the hotels wealthy Westerners prefer, cutting the fifteen-minute ride to the park in half: the Sofitel, Le Meridien, the Raffles Grand. In the downtown in between, both groups of visitors converge on Pub Street, lined with pubs, and enjoy the evening promised in the name.

Not surprisingly, Siem Reap is also home to one of HKL's fastest-growing field offices.

Nary works full-time in one of the luxury hotels for about eight-and-a-half hours a day. I don't ask how much they pay her, but the walls of her home are made of corrugated tin, and the couch on her porch is the front seat of a car.

She supplements her income by working a roadside stand almost every morning, selling drinks, gum, and other sundries to passers-by on their way to work. She borrows from HKL to finance supplies for her stand, and it's going well enough that she hopes to keep getting more and larger loans so her business can grow. Nary's husband is a driver who also does pest control, and between their four jobs, these two twenty-nine-year-olds hope to be able to start a family and a wholesaling business, although I didn't catch in which order.

Nary tells me of her endless thirteen- and fourteen-hour days—

work she is glad to have—while wearing a pink T-shirt that says SMILE in English, with a big heart over the E. And she does.

Song doesn't work in a hotel, but she has found her own way to profit from the influx of tourists.* Song and her husband live near the Tonlé Sap, a river that turns into a lake during the rainy season, where tourists often come for a boat ride. Song has invested in a camera and a small color printer. When visitors board a tour, she takes their photos, and when they return, the photos are mounted on simple souvenir plates for sale. Song is part of a four-woman group loan, using her share of the $800 they borrowed to replenish her stock of these souvenir plates. If the tourists don't buy, the stickers are removable. Song keeps at it from dawn until dusk.

Modern Cambodian pop music, which to my middle-aged ear sounds exactly like Britney Spears singing backwards, plays from a nearby home, and we settle onto a wooden bench to chat. (I realized later that I forgot to remove my shoes, a *faux pas* that I was later told was roughly on par with farting loudly. Song, if you ever read this, I apologize.) After two years and four loan cycles, Song is confident enough in her business that next she'll ask for a bigger, longer-term loan, so the lower rate will improve her profits.

Song's husband—the boy next door when they were growing up ("better a near business than a far one," she explains sweetly)—makes about $5 a day as a boat driver, and with two young sons to provide for, the extra income is handy. Some nights after work, they treat the boys to a trip to a local arcade. Song says her kids hope they'll become mechanics someday. She doesn't have to add that she hopes so, too.

---

*The Kiva page for Song's group loan is www.kiva.org/lend/186034. "Song" is her surname and not what I called her in person, but I am using it here to keep her full name private.

These families are wealthy compared to the next folks we visit.

Our dirt road hugs the bare-dirt banks of a small brown river. Between the road and the river stands a long line of wood and tin shacks, one or two rooms each. The sides facing the road are propped open with sticks; during the rainy season, these sticks will be removed, closing the wall to provide shelter. On the river side, small boats are tied up. It's from here that the subsistence fishermen who provide for these families leave for work every morning and return every night.

Considering that we're on the edge of a river at the edge of a jungle, there is shockingly little vegetation. The ground is bare and brown. The air smells of fish, smoke, and dust, with occasional sniffs of rotting refuse. Here, just a short drive from hotels charging hundreds of dollars a night, the reliability of even basic nutrition can be an issue. When there are no fish, the children may not eat.*

At the far end of the far end, the road stops, crossed by a small creek. You get out of the car—a giant shiny spaceship, compared to the surroundings—and cross to the other side via three narrow fishing boats, bobbing crossways in the water side-by-side as a temporary bridge. One step, catch your balance, second step, whoa, third step, jump. It feels like crossing the tracks to the wrong side of town on the wrong side of town.

This is where I found a mother of five named Mom.†

---

* Having enough to eat on a reliable basis is called "food security" in development-speak. I don't use the term because to Western ears it sounds like having a lock on the fridge.

† *Mom* means "beloved" in Khmer, the kind of sound-symbolism linguistic congruence that reminds you that all human brains seem to process simple sounds similarly: *ah, ooh, whee, mmm,* and so on may be as universal as a heartbeat. I

As I arrive, Mom is cleaning the hardwood floor of her home with a large thatch brush, literally beating any dirt out of the house. I pass a pen of baby chicks, greet her and her husband with the prayer gesture and a well-intended failure to pronounce Khmer diphthongs, then promptly forget to remove my shoes again. Nonetheless, the couple welcomes me warmly, we sit beneath an old TV and a picture of Cambodia's king, and we talk for almost an hour outside the ears of any loan officer.

Mom's husband does almost all of the talking. He's muscular, lean, and energetic, thanks to twelve hours of physical labor a day, and he speaks softly but with a simple intensity. This family's loan, $300 repaid over the course of a full year, has bought new fishing equipment—traps, nets, lines, and so on. "It's a big help," he says, several times, when I ask if the loan has made a real difference in their lives.

At the beginning of this project, back when I made my first loans, I'd considered the not-ancient proverb stating that if you give a man a fish, you feed him for an hour, but if you teach a man to fish, you feed him for a lifetime—and then added that microlending went one step further by helping a man who already knew how to fish, simply by lending him a few bucks to fix his boat. The reality of this thought is suddenly right before my eyes.

I ask the couple what they would have done if they hadn't been able to get the loan to buy new fishing equipment. There is a silence, a moment of thought, a slight shake of the head. I'm sure they both understand the question. The answer doesn't seem to be one they want to think about. I tell them I understand and we change the subject.

The conversation turns to children, as it always does. Their five—one daughter and four sons—are all old enough for school,

---

have not included her Kiva page here because doing so would disclose her full name, and I respect her privacy.

so Mom can help with the fishing labor during the day. The oldest will be dropping out after ninth grade in order to help with the work and eventually start his own boat business. My father, as a teenager in Appalachia almost seventy years ago, growing up in a home his father built, did the exact same thing.

Eventually, the afternoon wears on and there is work to do. Handshake, thanks through our translator, respect in my eyes.

Crossing the three boats again—step, balance, step, whoa, step, jump—I now carry a difficult thought: by global standards, even this family is not truly poor. They often make around $5 a day.

Half of humankind lives on $3 or less.

I couldn't leave without hiring a guide for one day and seeing the Angkor Wat while I was there. My guide was named Sam. He was more memorable than the temple.

Sam grew up during the Cambodian-Vietnamese war, which began when Vietnamese troops entered the country to dislodge the Khmer Rouge. When he was a boy, Sam's family sheltered Vietnamese soldiers fighting the Stone Age genocidal lunatics, an act that could have gotten them all killed if misfortune had led to discovery. Fortunately, they survived, and after the war Sam made a living by collecting bullet casings from the ground and selling them for scrap metal. Again, his luck held: despite often coming close to stepping on a land mine, he never quite did. But he still has nightmares about it sometimes.

Some of Sam's best days of scrap-hunting were on the grounds of the temple complex. This massive relic of human creativity was a frequent site of not just fighting, but rifle practice. The skills of killing were cultivated in the physical shadow of the holy.

And as Sam told me this—literally as the words were coming out of his mouth—he crossed my path and stepped about fifteen feet to my left. His practiced eye had spotted a shell casing on the ground, where it may have remained undisturbed for more than twenty years.

After showing the casing to me for confirmation, Sam casually dropped it back to the ground, continuing our conversation. The bullet now carried no meaning. We went on with our day.

My translator in Siem Reap was named Prim. He also grew up during the war, frequently frightened by the sound of shelling. His father, a doctor, kept AK-47s in his home and office for emergency self-defense. Fortunately, the need never came.

We were driving through a rural area as Prim told his story. I sensed no anger in him, no repressed trauma, and I was reminded of Sam and the shell casings. Prim's whole childhood had been terrorized by war and violent lunatics. How could he not still be angry, at least a little? Once again, I had to ask: *how are you not just completely insane?*

Prim seemed to dismiss my question as that of a child, its answer obvious:

"We have to move on," Prim said simply. Then, gesturing at his heart: "If we seek revenge, it never ends."

This is exactly what I was taught to believe in Sunday School. Halfway around the world, it was practiced under conditions my own soul might not have endured.

As Prim spoke these words, we were crossing a bridge over a large shallow lake, surrounded on both sides by a wide field of lotuses. Endless flowers extended far toward the horizon.

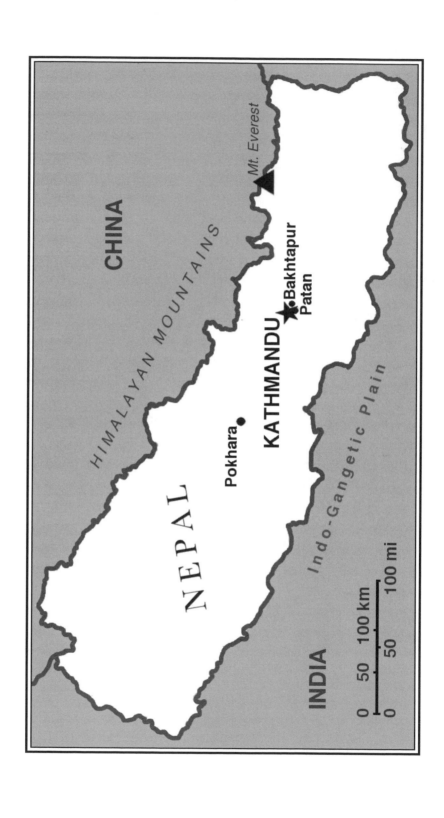

CHAPTER ELEVEN

KATHMANDU

I LIKE YOU," Ganesh says, gently touching my chest. "You— happy man."

Ganesh is a thirty-ish Nepali family man with a thousand times more English than I have Nepali. We're waiting next to each other in line for our flights out of Kathmandu, and we've started talking to pass the time.

Isn't this kinda backwards? I think to myself. The version of Nepal that Californians discuss is all incense and hand-wavy enlighten- ment, a big mug of organic chai tea with extra chakra sauce. Nepal is where you *go* to find happiness. Not where people are supposed to envy how happy you are.

But after a week in Kathmandu, only one thing about my con- versation with Ganesh will be a surprise. And it will be a big one.

I've stopped in Kathmandu on my way to India. I was hoping to meet clients of the local Kiva partner, Business and Professional Women (BPW) Patan, a local chapter of a major international women's rights and advocacy organization.* BPW works to help

---

* BPW Patan's site is www.bpwnepal.org.np/chapter.php?id=2&name=Patan %20Chapter.

women sustain themselves economically through a wide range of services in ninety-five countries, including some truly difficult environments.

But the meetings didn't work out. The clients I'd lent to were hard to reach, both physically and electronically, given Kathmandu's crumbling infrastructure. Electric power is often only available for perhaps just twelve hours a day, and even that is frequently interrupted by blackouts. This must be brutal during Himalayan winters. There are no street addresses, so you may need to bring someone along who knows where they're going. And Kathmandu is not a small town: it's physically about the size of Manhattan, with two-thirds of its population. That doesn't include another million-plus people in nearby communities, all sharing a valley about as high up as Denver.

Traffic is insane. The primary requirement to get a license seems to be a functional torso; what people's eyes, hands, and feet decide to do is completely secondary. Most drivers seem convinced that their horns are actually hyperspace buttons, and the only reason they haven't blipped a hundred meters ahead is because they're not honking hard enough. Air pollution is roughly four times worse than in Los Angeles.

The brown haze of Kathmandu isn't just caused by the cars. Ritual burning of corpses is still a thing, and if you visit the holiest Hindu shrine in the city, Pashupatinath, check the wind direction carefully before approaching the nearby riverbank where cremations take place. Otherwise, like me, you might get an inadvertent lungful of dearly departed.

Below this holiest shrine, there is a dry riverbed heaping with trash and worse things. Children play soccer in it. If you visit during the Hindu spring festival of Holi, as I did, giggling kids might target you for a ritual splashing of the filthy water, drenching your body in questionable fluids as part of this joyous holiday. A real feast for the senses, this place. A potential tourist slogan crosses my mind: *It's Ne-palling!*

The poverty strikes harder than fetid water ever can. Nepal is one of the very poorest countries on earth, behind even Rwanda, ahead only of post-earthquake Haiti, warring Afghanistan, and a handful of other countries. Even Iraq has a per capita income three times higher.*

Things became seriously unstable more than a decade ago thanks to a Romeo-and-Juliet story between the two most powerful families. In 2001, the heir apparent to the Shah family throne, a drunk lad known as Dippy—Dipendra was his full name, but the former was more accurate—fell in love with a daughter of the rival Rana clan. The Shahs disapproved of the match, so Dippy disapproved of them with an M16 rifle, wiping out nearly the entire ruling family.

Into the leadership vacuum charged a long-standing Maoist rebellion that had previously spent years attacking soft-drink factories and looking up to Peru's brutal Shining Path. A civil war and thirteen thousand dead later, wrecking the tourist trade, the Maoists took over—but only years after China had decided that the whole communism thing was *so* twentieth century, rendering the rebels' ideology about as influential as MySpace. So now Maoists preside over a shifting mess of alliances as everyone tries to find a way forward.

Until they do, capital is rare in the capital. Even outside the former royal palace, the renovation of the sidewalk is undertaken not by machines, but by petite women, squatting and chipping away with hand tools.

I meet Urmila Shrestha, founder and chief of BPW Patan, over coffee in the basement of a former Rana palace, now turned into

---

* CIA World Factbook at www.cia.gov/library/publications/the-world-factbook /rankorder/2004rank.html?countryName=Nepal&countryCode=np&region Code=sas&rank=205#np.

one of the few dozen hotels in the city with a generator cranking out twenty-four-hour electricity. Urmila is proud to say that despite the high expense of dealing with clients in such hard conditions, they never charge more than 17 percent annually. This isn't easy, and early on, when the group ran low on funds, Urmila financed it with her own savings. I can't help but contrast this with the bankers who helped cause so much grief in India through their own motivations for profit. Fortunately, BPW Patan now has the support of Kiva and the Bank of Nepal, plus Rotary International, the global service organization, many of whose members have begun actively supporting microlending all over the world.*

Urmila has brought along a successful client named Kamala, a metalworker who now exports her decorative crafts and singing bowls to four European countries. Given what I've seen outside, this seems nothing short of miraculous. We talk about some of Urmila's other successful clients, and the conversation soon turns to her dream of being able to assist even Nepal's most remote villages.

It's a lovely thought. But this is a country so poor that school buses often carry children dangerously on *top*, even while climbing rutted roads on steep hills, simply because there aren't enough buses to go around. The idea of loan officers being able to reach small villages regularly seems almost impossible. I hold my tongue, however. Perhaps M-PESA-style mobile money might work here. Unlikely things happen all the time.

Also at the table are two Americans, Claudine Emeott, a Kiva Fellow helping BPW computerize its records, and her adventurous husband Brian.† The pair have given up conventional white-collar

---

*The website of the Rotarian Action Group for Microcredit is ragm.rotary global.net/p/home.asp.

†Brian and Claudine remained in Nepal for a year before returning to the U.S., chronicling their travels in a blog of tremendous enthusiasm and fun. The page

jobs back home so that Claudine can do this volunteer work, which this morning involves a small translation job: Claudine understands Urmila's accent way better than I can, so she translates English into English while I nod and feel silly. Urmila proceeds to share the stories of several women who have gone from bare-dirt-nothing subsistence to generating small but consistent incomes. I think sadly of the tiny women chipping pavement in front of the old royal palace. I wish them a similar change.

If any country on earth demonstrates why microfinance, no matter how sorely needed, might sometimes serve best as part of a larger series of poverty alleviation measures, Nepal may be it. These people don't only need financial opportunity. They need electricity, clean water, education, medicine, and a government maybe a teensy less Maoist. Microlending and its larger relatives can help bring clinics, sanitation, and solar power here, no question. But the wonder we need to imagine isn't just a business like Kamala's. It needs to be a million of them.

Sometimes I think overwhelm is as important to fight as any other aspect of poverty.

The line is slow at the Kathmandu airport, so Ganesh and I have been talking—and gesturing, drawing little pictures, miming, grunting, and laughing, since his English is limited and my Nepali is nonexistent—for nearly half an hour now.

Ganesh has told me about his wife and three kids, introduced me to men nearby going on the same voyage that he is about to

---

is at www.kathmanduo.com and highly recommended. Claudine was later hired by Kiva, where she now works as Portfolio Manager for their Strategic Initiatives Group. This means she spends her days facilitating funding for education, clean water and sanitation, renewable energy, and other large-scale high-impact stuff—exactly the sort of projects that might do the most good in Nepal.

begin, and asked me about my own family back in America, hoping that I am in a "love marriage"—a term that shocks me into remembering how many unions here are arranged.

Then I make the mistake of asking where Ganesh is going. His eyes sadden immediately.

Ganesh is going to Doha, the capital of Qatar. There, he hopes to become a laborer, live in a camp in the desert, and send money home to his family here.

Ganesh will live in conditions very much like the ones I witnessed in Dubai when this story began. Full circle.*

He will do this because he loves his family. And this is their best hope.

I had no idea in Dubai of the degree to which—exploited as they were—some of the workers there were actually doing okay, if compared to the situations they had come from. When you come from a village where one dollar a day is normal, six dollars a day is wealth.

---

* A 2012 Human Rights Watch report notes that employment practices in Qatar are in some ways even worse than in Dubai. Workers are literally trapped, unable even to leave the country without an exit permit. See Sources.

Meanwhile, CNN reported in May 2012 that about 1,300 Nepalis like Ganesh here go abroad to seek work every day, and every day "two or three coffins are coming back," according to a member of a Nepali government task force on overseas labor. Whether these deaths of Nepali workers in Gulf countries are from exposure, work accidents, or violence is unclear. Heat exhaustion is the most likely explanation. Before being hired at Kiva, Jonny Price, the project manager of Kiva Zip (described in the following chapter) worked in Qatar, and grim stories of increased shipments of human remains back to Nepal during the hottest months were not rare. In any case, the deaths are rarely if ever investigated. See Sara Sidner, "Nepalese Dying to Work," in Sources.

Other Nepalis are simply defrauded by the agents, arriving at their destination with neither a job nor a visa. See "Nepali Slaves in the Middle East," a video by Pete Pattison, in Sources. My conversation with Ganesh took place just inside the airport, within sight of the opening and closing scenes of this video, a few weeks later.

Ganesh will be in Doha for at least two years. He will not see his wife and children in that time. Not even once.

Today is the day he is leaving. Ganesh points at his heart. He is suddenly speechless. Stricken. His eyes search mine. I nod.

But—cheering himself up, he mimes with his wallet and an index finger, tracing a line from the wallet into the air—*money will travel*. "With luck," he says, they will save enough that in two years he will be able to come home.

With luck, Ganesh will miss only two years of his children's lives. *With luck.*

Between us, yes. I am the happy one.

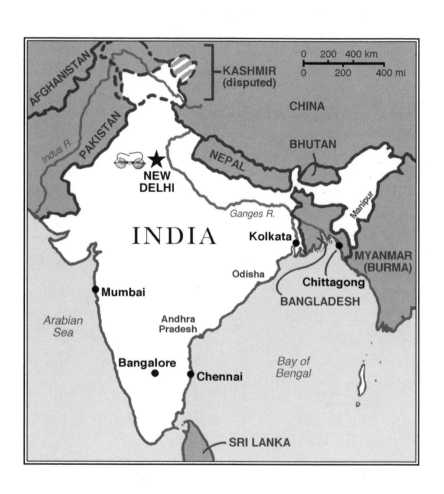

CHAPTER TWELVE

INDIA

THE WORK IS what keeps us sane," Ramakrishna says.
Ram laughs self-deprecatingly as he says this. But I'm sure he's not joking.

To begin to grasp India's immense diversity and challenges, it might be easier for a Westerner to first imagine a big circle drawn all the way around Europe: starting clockwise from Iceland in the North Atlantic, loop north and east around the top of Norway and Finland, then continue south through Russia, taking in all of Eastern Europe as far south as Turkey. From Istanbul, now loop west below the Mediterranean, hugging the northern edge of Africa all the way west to the far end of Portugal. Finally, turn north and return to Iceland. Now add 50 percent more people speaking a 50 percent wider variety of languages.*

---

* India's linguistic diversity surprises many Westerners, but there are nearly thirty languages in India with at least a million native speakers. There are more native speakers of Tamil on our planet than of Italian. Likewise, more people speak Punjabi than German, Marathi than French, and Bengali than Russian. There are more Telugu speakers than Czech, Dutch, Danish, Finnish, Greek,

Finally, cram all of this into an area just one-third the size of Europe.

In purely numerical terms, at least—leaving aside its various religions, a landscape that varies from Himalayan peaks to the beaches of Goa, and multiple cultures enriched by thousands of years of tradition—that's India.

India currently boasts one of the fastest-growing middle classes on earth, but intense poverty exists here, too—often in the shadow of immense wealth. The extremes between rich and poor here can make Dubai seem almost egalitarian. Fly into Mumbai, and your window-seat view may include glittering skyscrapers in the very same glance as sprawling slums where people get by on just a couple of dollars a day. Catch a taxi downtown, and you're likely to pass Dharavi, where at least half a million people live in less than one square mile—all a short drive from South Mumbai, India's financial center, the wealthiest part of the country.

In 2012, *Forbes* figured that India's forty-eight billionaires owned nearly $200 billion in net worth.* Meanwhile, just the eight poorest Indian states have more than 420 million people in poverty, a total one third greater than the entire population of the United States. More people live in poverty in India, in fact, than in the twenty-six poorest African countries combined.†

Worldwide, our differences in birth lottery placements, top to bottom, can be literally a million to one—a disparity ten thousand times greater than in, for example, a small Ohio suburb.‡

Slovak, and Swedish speakers *combined*. Data from *Ethnologue*, edited by M. Paul Lewis. See Sources.

* See the *Forbes* "World's Billionaires" list in Sources. The word *billionaire* here is measured in the equivalent of U.S. dollars, roughly 50 billion rupees at this writing.

† See "8 Indian States Have More Poor than the 26 Poorest African Nations" in the *Times of India* in Sources.

‡ The full calculation of this estimate is at www.bobharris.com/bank-of-bob

India can present both unimaginable extremes in nearly the same glance—challenging mere comprehension, not to mention any rational response. This may be part of why Western culture still fetishizes India as a mother lode of exotic wisdom and occult knowledge, despite examining virtually no details of its major religions, and nothing of its actual size and variety.* Perhaps emotional and intellectual overwhelm compel a retreat into mysticism, Noble Savage imagery, or even crude racism just to protect our sense of the world.

But the obvious truth is that India, for all its super-rich, accelerating middle class, and great numbers of poor, is no more inherently magical than anyplace else, and often profoundly mundane: government bureaucracy is to paper as an exploding volcano is to lava; traffic between cities may be what NASCAR would look like if it included mules, bicycles, fruit carts, cows, autorickshaws, mass pilgrim crossings, drivers who honk their horns at passing molecules, and the occasional steamroller marked with a giant *om*; and as for air travel, it's sufficient to note that Kingfisher is both an airline and a kind of beer. To imbue this automatically with holiness or wisdom is to profane both ideas.

/range-of-incomes. The short version: in the small Ohio suburb where I was born, U.S. Census data place the median annual income at almost precisely the U.S. average. Census and other data place my birthplace's range of real annual incomes at about $5,000 to $500,000, a factor of about 100. Globally, however, a family in a rough part of the Democratic Republic of the Congo might have just a tenth of the low end in my hometown—at most—while the children of the planet's ninety-two families worth more than $10 billion will grow up in a household with an annual household income up to a thousand times greater than my hometown's high end. The global range of incomes, therefore, is approximately ten thousand times greater than one might experience growing up in middle America.

*Recent Hollywood films employing India as a backdrop for attempted Caucasian enlightenment: *The Best Exotic Marigold Hotel* (2012), *Eat, Pray, Love* (2010), *The Darjeeling Limited* (2007).

In the end, to see anything clearly here is simply to see where you are, look the people around you in the eye, and realize that you risk being changed by the result. Exactly like anywhere else.

As a child, Kiva president Premal Shah was influenced by what he saw in India, as he described in a 2012 phone interview:

"I grew up in Minnesota, but my parents are from India originally. And when I was a little boy, maybe five years old, they took me back there to visit. And I'll always remember—one day we were walking through a village, and it was a poor enough area that the roads weren't paved, and it had been raining, so the road was basically just mud. So I'm walking with my mother along this muddy road, and on one side I'm holding her hand, and in the other hand I've got a coin, an Indian coin. It couldn't have been worth much, but I was just a kid, and I just really liked this coin, and so I was just walking along really happy with this coin in one hand and my mother's hand in the other.*

"I'm not sure how it happened, but the coin slipped out of my hand and fell into the mud. Well, I'm a kid, so of course I was kind of upset. But my mom was very calm and reassuring, she told me not to worry, let it go, it's all muddy now, it's not worth that much, we can get you lots more of those, it's okay.

---

* Thirty years later, Premal wasn't certain about the exact denomination of the coin, so I checked. In 1980 or 1981, when this event must have occurred, the largest Indian coin in circulation was worth 1 rupee. (Coins worth 2 rupees had a brief trial in 1982, but full circulation was not until 1990.) The rupee's typical value hovered at around one-eighth of a U.S. dollar, so the maximum worth of the coin Premal dropped, and for which the Indian woman was so grateful, was about 13 cents. Many smaller coins were also in circulation at the time, ranging all the way down to 1 paisa, worth roughly one-eighth of a U.S. penny.

"But as we were walking away, and I was sad about leaving my coin behind in the mud, I looked back over my shoulder—and this woman from the village had seen me drop the coin, and watched us walk away—and now she had run out into the street to pick the coin out of the mud. And then she looked up at the sky, like to the heavens, in obvious gratitude, like she was thanking her god for her good fortune at finding this coin—something that my mother and I could just leave behind without a care in the world.

"I'll always remember that," Premal concluded. "That was my first real lesson in thinking about wealth, and rich and poor, and where we all are in the world."

"The work is what keeps us sane," Ramakrishna repeats gently on my first day in India.

Ram is chatting with me in a meeting room near his office, describing his own life and career built around trying to help India's poorest. But I can't help thinking of Premal's story about what he saw as a boy, and how it affects him even now. I think of my own feelings in Dubai and after.

"The work is what keeps us sane." Ram may be describing a lot of the people in this book.

Ram and his wife Smita are the cofounders of Rang De, the non-profit lending platform through which I made four loans to Indians when I first started this project, before noticing in the fine print that the website wasn't supposed to permit non-Indians to lend.

Rang De is headquartered in Chennai, the largest city in Tamil Nadu, India's southernmost state.* There's a good chance that those

---

* Continuing the admittedly rough physical comparisons meant to help Western readers: to picture Tamil Nadu, one might imagine twice the population of California squeezed into a state with the size and climate of Louisiana.

men in the back of the truck in Singapore—the ones who gave me the stink-eye while I was sashaying around in a Bentley limousine—were Tamils who migrated from here. The workers whom I met in Dubai, when this story began, were from neighboring Kerala, just a day's drive to the west.

These travels have begun turning full circles at high speed.

Ram and Smita have welcomed me to India like a long-lost old friend, even asking me to give a talk to the entire Rang De staff. But first, Ram cranks up the air conditioner on my behalf and tells me how he and Smita came to create Rang De.

Ram's first political influence as a youth was a series of anti-child-labor columns published in the *Hindu*, one of India's oldest and best-respected newspapers. Young Ram was so moved by the linking of social and economic justice that he would clip the articles out, highlight the key points, and post them on his wall. In college, he began organizing charity events, discovering a love of team-building and the hustle of trying new ideas to attract local business support. His university was sharply divided along religious lines, but once Ram noticed that a non-partisan event for a good cause could also have a peacemaking effect, he was totally hooked. "Once I'd seen groups of people who ostensibly hate each other come together for a good cause . . . I thought, okay, so how can we do more of that?"

Ram later volunteered to help Bangalore's Chrysalis Performing Arts Theater, a group that helps handicapped children build self-esteem by presenting full-costume productions with kids of all abilities performing side-by-side. "You never saw anything so lovely," he says, enjoying the memory. But I get the idea from Ram's tone that he's thinking of Smita—and sure enough, the theater is where the couple met.

The match was instant—a "love marriage," Ganesh in Nepal would have called it. Smita has an M.A. in social work, and their first conversations were all about "walking the talk," finding innovative ways that their lives could be used to help others.

"There's a Hindu proverb," the couple would later explain over dinner—completing each other's phrases so smoothly that it's all one sentence in my notes—"about adopting a problem: you don't just see the problem, you *become* the problem, you absorb it, and then the solution will present itself." The early years of their marriage were largely about deciding which problem to become.

Soon, in a village outside Hyderabad, the groundwater became contaminated with chlorine and other solids. An NGO set up financing for a reverse-osmosis filtration system, plus a supply chain for selling the clean water. The supply chain was designed well enough that everyone involved profited from maintaining the system, so the solution had an excellent chance of succeeding long-term. Impressed, Ram and Smita briefly considered moving to a single village and devoting themselves to its well-being, implementing similar solutions for its infrastructure.

But helping a single village didn't seem like enough. How could they enable this sort of social business on an even larger scale? That's when they heard about Muhammad Yunus, Grameen, microfinance, and Kiva—and realized that Indian banking laws meant that Kiva's platform wouldn't easily extend into India. Smita and Ram have adopted—no, *become*—this problem ever since. After a round of raising seed and incubation money and cultivating partnerships with corporate partners and non-profit foundations, Rang De went online in 2008.* Ram and Smita have subsequently crisscrossed the country many times to expand relationships with local lenders, especially in India's poorest regions.

By this time in the telling of Rang De's story, it's Saturday night, almost thirty-six hours later. Ram, Smita, and I are now walking on Elliot's Beach, the Santa Monica of Chennai. We're munching on roasted corn from a street vendor, there's a full

---

* A full list of Rang De's corporate, technical, strategic, and other partners can be found by clicking the various tabs at www.rangde.org/corporate-partners .htm.

moon over the Bay of Bengal, and a hard hot breeze is making the tropical humidity almost comfortable on my snowy Ohio skin. For some reason, my brain chooses this moment to suddenly re-member to tell Ram and Smita that I once made four small loans on Rang De. They're both shocked—the site was supposed to re-ject any loan not originating in India, and to their knowledge I'm the only outlander who ever got through. *Have I caused a problem?* I ask.

"I—I really don't know," Ram replies, while Smita laughs. "We'll see if the government cares, I guess."

"Shh!" Smita adds, whispering now through a big grin. "Keep your voice down. Don't. Anybody. Tell."

We peer over our shoulders in all directions conspiratorially, sharing the joke. Soon, this leads Ram and Smita to notice something that I don't.

"Hey, where *is* everybody?" Ram asks, apparently expecting a much larger weekend crowd.

"I know," Smita agrees. "This place is usually packed on a Sat-urday."

I look around with completely different eyes. There are hun-dreds of people on the beach, possibly more than a thousand. Back home, this *is* crowded.

My mind goes back to the men from southern India working in Dubai, packed ten to a room in small desert living quarters. I hope that a different perception of personal space might make their lives there a little less grueling in the short term, even if im-proving the economic situation back in their home countries might be more of a long-term project.

As described earlier, the entire microlending industry was given a black eye in 2010 by two events in India: (a) the mass com-mercialization of loans to the poor, courtesy of SKS Microfinance and several others, and (b) the reported suicides of microfinance clients during the crisis in Andhra Pradesh state. The dark side of microfinance turned out to be black indeed.

I'm in India to ask about steps being taken to ensure that similar tragedies won't recur, hoping for clear indications that the destructive mistakes of aggressive MFIs were an aberration. I've also realized that even at its best, microfinance is just one key part of comprehensive measures to alleviate poverty, including improved infrastructure, education, and transparency, and I'd like to know more about how the whole puzzle connects. Fortunately, Ram knows the subject well: his work and travels have created partnerships in half of India's twenty-eight states—including seven of the eight poorest.

When I ask about SKS, Ram rolls his eyes and speaks with sadness and frustration, searching momentarily for words. "What happened was just so unnecessary, such a tragedy," he says. "Our partners, or anybody sincerely trying to help people—on a business loan, nobody pays more than just over 15 percent. But people were paying SKS so much more than that—and they [SKS] weren't alone. People smelled money, and started handing out loans, just like that—like candy."*

Ram assures me that Rang De's partners follow Grameen's original vision closely. Checking around, this seems clearly the case. For example, Rang De's partner in Bihar—until very recently, India's poorest state, adjacent to Nepal on the northern border—is the Centre for Development Orientation and Training (C-DOT), which has worked with about twenty-five thousand people in 550 villages over the last twelve years.† They're much like Arariwa or Urwego, providing not just banking but a whole gamut of services: paddy cultivation and other farming skills training, veterinary

---

*I later found an exact breakdown of all loans financed through Rang De on their site. Ram was exactly correct: the APR on Rang De business loans is a standard 15.33 percent. See www.rangde.org/frequently-asked-questions.htm#9.
†Their website is www.cdotbihar.org.

assistance, women's empowerment training, and more. For C-DOT and Rang De's other partners all over India, a "public offering" is something you do for others, not a get-rich-quick scheme.

Rang De also emphasizes educational loans, which are given equal place on the site with ordinary business loans, but financed at an even lower rate of 9.02 percent APR. The day I check out the site, a goat and poultry farmer from Odisha (another of India's poorest states) had just raised 8,500 rupees ($163) to pay the fees to put her son through tenth grade. She had also done this the year before, financing ninth grade the same way, so it's clear she knows what she's doing.

The amount of money needed is so small that I find it frustrating not to be able to personally chip in. But there's an obvious benefit to Indians lending to other Indians. Just as American TV is more focused on L.A. and Manhattan than on Kentucky and Idaho, India's mass media rarely bothers with images of Odisha, Bihar, and other poor states, a situation that Ram thinks has to change. "Many times, I've heard Indians living in India completely deny that it's a poor country," Ram says with some frustration.* "It's not on TV, so students in Mumbai think we're just like Europe or something. They really have no idea" about the poor rural countryside. Having Rang De's loans financed by Westerners wouldn't change that situation. In the long run, it's probably just as well for Rang De and its partners to convince India's own growing middle class to invest in their neighbors.

For Westerners seeking to finance Indian microloans, a recent alternative is Milaap.org, a Rang De– and Kiva-like lending platform

---

* This is not entirely an Indian phenomenon. When I tell young Americans that my own father grew up without electricity, they sometimes assume he couldn't have been born in America.

whose founders went through the bureaucratic process of creating a registered entity in India, set up a holding company in Singapore for routing funds, and spent a solid year successfully lobbying the Reserve Bank of India to grant their site the right to allow non-Indians to lend. Milaap's interface will feel familiar to anyone who has seen Kiva or Rang De, but a higher percentage of Milaap loans emphasize basic infrastructure like solar power—a great innovation where the national electrical grid hasn't reached—clean water, and basic sanitation.

At this writing, Milaap is still tiny, with only a few hundred listed loans. But Milaap is still fairly new, they're working with terrific partners, and their focus on infrastructure could make a hoped-for deluge of loans through Milaap particularly effective. And as Kiva has shown, a good idea can be explosively scalable.

In August of 2012, Kiva itself announced its first local MFI partnerships in India, their work focused mostly on Odisha, where at least 40 percent of the population lives below the poverty line.* The first loans were made available through People's Forum, which has provided health and basic literacy education, drought mitigation, financial literacy, business development, and microfinance services to more than 120,000 rural women, with a recent focus on disabled persons, widows, and single mothers; and the Mahashakti

---

* Odisha, also spelled Orissa (and spelled ଓଡ଼ିଶା in its own language), has a population almost as large as those of Ohio, Illinois, Michigan, and Pennsylvania combined, and a poverty rate that the World Bank placed in 2012 at between 40 and 46 percent, depending on the methodology used. In rough figures, there are about as many people living in poverty in this one Indian state as there are *people*—period—in New Mexico, West Virginia, Nebraska, Hawaii, Idaho, Maine, New Hampshire, Rhode Island, Montana, Delaware, North and South Dakota, Alaska, Vermont, and Wyoming combined.

Foundation, which has assisted more than twenty-five thousand families with health care, water and sanitation services, food programs, and microfinance services in six of Odisha's very poorest districts, where more than a third of local residents live on less than a dollar per day.*

Unlike Milaap, Kiva hasn't yet clawed its way through Indian government red tape, so all funds invested via Kiva must remain in India for at least three years. Twenty-five bucks sent off to a Kiva loan in Odisha won't be repaid until that term is over, even if the client repays perfectly in a much shorter period of time. Kiva's partners will simply hang on to the funds, continuing to use the money to back similar loans and services, albeit not posted directly on the Kiva website, before eventual repayment.

Kiva billboards the situation with a yellow-highlighted caution—"repayment will not be available for at least three years"—on every Indian loan, but so far Kiva lenders have barely blinked, responding instead with enthusiastic generosity. On the first day, of the eighty-five Indian loans posted, more than half were fully funded in less than six hours, and all eighty-five were funded by the following evening.

I happened to be at my computer when the new partnerships were announced, so I was fortunate to be among the very first Kiva lenders to India.† For my own part, I was perfectly happy to have People's Forum and Mahashakti hold some of my money for

---

* Loans were also soon posted from a third partner, WSDS-Initiate, located in Manipur, another state struggling with severe poverty. The Kiva partner pages are www.kiva.org/partners/241 for People's Forum, www.kiva.org/partners/242 for Mahashakti, and www.kiva.org/partners/238 for WSDS-Initiate. People's Forum's own site is www.peoplesforum.in/index.htm, Mahashakti's is at www.mahashaktiindia.org, and WSDS-Initiate's website is wsds-initiate.org.

† By the sort of serendipity that sometimes seems to have guided this project, I was completing the final draft of this very chapter.

a few extra years, lending it out or investing it in education, clean water, or health maintenance for some of the world's poorest people. So I pointed, clicked, and lent a few bucks to the Gruhalaxmi Group, led by a carpenter's wife who weaves dry leaves and bamboo twigs into inexpensive plates which she can sell to local food stalls, creating an extra dollar per day of income;* Lili, a widow who supports three pre-teen children with a photography business that currently brings in about $2.40 per day;† and Pandab, a fifty-seven-year-old man whose small grocery helps him take care of his wife, who suffers with the effects of leprosy, a disease not yet fully conquered in this corner of the world.‡

All of these clients have clear and practical plans for the funds. Lili hopes to augment her photography income by opening the first garment shop in her village, and the leader of the Gruhalaxmi Group plans to increase production enough to use the profits to help expand her husband's carpentry business. And among the products in Pandab's grocery, according to his profile: "there is good demand for mosquito repellents . . . as mosquito borne diseases are very widely prevalent in his village."

Malaria, dengue, and other viruses carried by mosquitoes are endemic to at least twenty Indian states. As to dengue, thousands of cases are reported annually; Odisha was hit so hard last year that

---

* The Gruhalaxmi Group is at www.kiva.org/lend/459299. *Gruhalaxmi* is a concept of how the stabilizing power of wise motherhood brings success to the family, named in part for Lakshmi, the goddess of wealth.

† Lili is at www.kiva.org/lend/458825.

‡ Pandab is at www.kiva.org/lend/458818. Leprosy is now easily treatable with a modern multi-drug therapy. The World Health Organization makes treatment available for free, and complete eradication may be possible in the next decades. Pandab's lender page does not specify whether his wife still suffers from the disease, or—perhaps more likely—suffers from the intense lifelong stigma caused by disfigurement. For more, see the WHO page on leprosy, www.who .int/lep/en.

three state-run hospitals canceled leave for all doctors, just to handle the caseload.* At least twenty-six fatalities were recorded.† I was
glad to chip in so that Pandab and his neighbors could stay healthy.

Kiva lenders instantly responded with such great faith in the Indian MFIs partly because of a new badge-based social performance rating system implemented by Kiva in 2012. Kiva now
rates each MFI with the presence (or absence) of up to seven little
green badges on its pages—not unlike the merit badges common
in Scouting—that summarize each partner's strengths and practices in a way that users can understand at a glance.

Kiva's due diligence on mainstream MFI partners—still the
site's bread and butter—has grown to include checks on each
partner's financial health, audit trail, information systems, and
personnel systems from management down to staff. There's also
an extensive analysis of risk and social performance indicators,
and a personal visit to the MFI by a Kiva analyst is usually involved. Dozens of MFIs want to partner with Kiva, but only one
or two new partners are approved each month, and existing partnerships are continuously reviewed.‡

As we've seen, this careful process works well enough that for
an MFI, becoming a Kiva partner is an increasingly recognized
form of certification. In Kenya, Juhudi Kilimo was able to attract
investment funds and grow thanks in large part to the credibility
they gained from their Kiva partnership. However, for a Kiva
lender like me, the process and findings of Kiva's due diligence

---

* See "Orissa Cancels Doctors' Leave as Dengue Spreads" in the *Deccan Herald*
in Sources.
† See "Death Toll Due to Dengue Rises to 26 in Orissa" in the *Orissa Diary* in
Sources.
‡ For more on Kiva's due diligence process, see www.kiva.org/about/risk and
www.kiva.org/about/risk/kiva-role.

have not always been easy to use. When I made my first Kiva loans, the five-star risk rating system was helpful, and data on default rates, portfolio yields, and so on were available for analysis, but it was hard to know what each MFI's particular strengths or weaknesses might be.

As Jonathon Stalls neared the end of his Kiva Walk, you recall, I found myself walking with JD, who had just become Kiva's new head of Social Performance. I asked how he could possibly quantify multiple social and economic factors in a useful way, and he half-jokingly replied that he didn't know yet, but I should check back in another year or so.

JD went on to spend the following year studying what works where, accomplishing what, and how to measure it. Almost twelve months later, I returned to San Francisco, and JD opened his laptop, displaying a simple but robust seven-badge system with pride and excitement.

After extensive review of each MFI's loan data, history, services, economic context, and more, Kiva now rates each MFI in seven key areas:

- Anti-Poverty Focus, for working to help the poorest of the poor
- Vulnerable Group Focus, for helping the most marginalized in their society; these may be ethnic and religious minorities, refugees, people with disabilities, or any locally vulnerable group
- Client Voice, for having exemplary feedback mechanisms
- Family and Community Empowerment, for strength in health care, education, domestic violence prevention, and similar outreach
- Entrepreneurial Support, for offering quality business training
- Facilitation of Savings, which can be at least as important to a client's future, while carrying very little risk

- Innovation, for bringing technology and new ideas to serving their clients

For every area in which a lender is particularly strong, an easy-to-parse green badge is now clearly visible on the page of every loan they provide, with Client Voice represented by a little talking client, Facilitation of Savings signified by a green piggy bank, and so on.*

Most MFIs are strong in only a few areas. Arariwa in Peru, for example, has received four of the seven badges, awarded for its programs that fight poverty, facilitate savings, address family educational needs, and provide entrepreneurial support. Juhudi Kilimo also receives four badges, but for its different strengths in innovating loan products for particularly vulnerable communities. Kiva makes these badges hard to earn. Many of their own partners have received only one badge or none at all. Combined with a five-star system to rate each partner's financial safety or risk, Kiva has created a system where users can understand the general characteristics of each partner in a matter of seconds.†

The badge system can also be used as a sorting device, so that Kiva lenders can now choose the kind of services they most want to support, simply by clicking on "Innovation," "Client Voice," and so on, maximizing the kind of impact they prefer.‡

I'm personally most pleased at the badge facilitating savings accounts, the form of microfinance that carries the least risk for clients. I've wished since my first trip to Peru that there were some

---

*A full explanation is at www.kiva.org/about/socialperformance.

†To see for yourself, just visit www.kiva.org/partners and scan the page. MFI data on a number of active partners here is current as of September 2012.

‡This sorting process is possible through www.kiva.org/about/socialperformance but not the main lending page as this book goes to press. By the time you read this, I would be surprised if social performance sorting were not made much more accessible.

way to support savings in addition to loans, since a client can't get in trouble by saving too much, and MFIs with assets in savings are able to retain clients without having to re-extend credit, making overlending far less likely. Unfortunately, legal and logistical hurdles have so far prevented any savings-based equivalent to the Kiva lending model. Fortunately, nearly half of Kiva's partner MFIs currently offer savings, including normal interest-bearing accounts, educational savings, and more. Lending to these organizations supports and strengthens those programs, if a bit indirectly.

Only two MFI partners—the first two to make loans available in India, as it happens—are currently rated with all seven badges, a level of excellence that none of Kiva's other 162 partners in the world have achieved. I have no objective data on how many Kiva lenders used the green badges to decide whether or not to feel confident in the new MFIs, but in my own experience, when the Indian loans came online, seeing all seven badges definitely made me far more confident than if I'd only seen one or two.

The MFIs have responded to this critical evaluation surprisingly well. "MFIs themselves really *want* these badges," JD said with obvious pride. "MFIs are actually calling me up and sending e-mails now, saying, 'I thought we were doing a great job in communicating with our clients—is there something we should do that we haven't thought of? What more should we be doing?'"

Not only are Kiva users learning more about MFIs, but to a small but very real extent, Kiva is becoming a knowledge base of best practices around the world.

Kiva and their partners are hardly alone in working toward improved client safety. Events like the crisis in Andhra Pradesh prompted the microfinance industry to adopt a set of standards called the Smart Campaign, headquartered at ACCION International's Center for Financial Inclusion in New York, and built around the universal adoption of seven core Client Protection Principles:*

- Appropriate loan product design and delivery
- Prevention of over-indebtedness
- Transparency
- Responsible pricing
- Fair and respectful treatment of clients
- Privacy of client data
- Mechanisms for complaint resolution

In less than three years, the Smart Campaign principles have been endorsed and adopted by more than 850 MFIs in more than 130 countries—including every MFI we've visited in this book—serving more than forty million clients, already representing nearly half of the current microlending client base. Hundreds of donors, investors, and industry organizations worldwide have also signed up. The principles aren't just lip service: through agreements with national and regional associations of MFIs on five continents, the campaign has already assisted in local assessment and training that has already reached more than seven hundred MFIs. All of these numbers continue to grow, and within a year or two, a global system of ratings and licensed certification should be in place.

On the funding end, large banks and investment funds make financing decisions meant to help MFIs grow. It's more difficult than it sounds, especially in a constantly changing, globally connected environment. Too little funding, and one country's MFI growth may be impeded; too much, the MFIs can be flooded with easy money, enabling a boom/bust cycle like the one in Bosnia. Fortunately, a similar set of safety guidelines is in development.

---

*The Smart Campaign goals are elaborated at www.smartcampaign.org/about -the-campaign/campaign-mission-a-goals. The Center for Financial Inclusion is at www.centerforfinancialinclusion.org.

The Council of Microfinance Equity Funds (CMEF), whose members range from FINCA International to Citigroup's microfinance division, issues governance guidelines that are increasingly adopted, and CMEF has also worked with the Center for Microfinance at the University of Zurich and several other organizations to compile a set of early warning indicators of over-indebtedness.* This is a first step toward averting market-wide problems before they even start.

That said, even a perfect system will fall short if it can't reach all of the people who might benefit.

"We want to think about what kind of world we'll create a hundred years in the future," Matt Flannery, Kiva's CEO, told me in a conference call with two other major lenders. "In particular, we're fascinated with reaching even the most remote areas of the globe . . . We want to think as broadly as we can about the ability to reach further than other organizations—or we—have ever imagined. That could mean partnerships with telecoms, peer-to-peer lending, exploring mobile payment systems, who knows what—almost half of the world doesn't have access to financial services. So far we've reached about 730,000 clients around the world . . . There has to be some way we can use our platform to do more."

In the same call, Premal Shah, Kiva's president, continued the thought. "We can keep doing what we do, and that's fine. But we feel there's so much more we can be doing in areas we haven't really explored yet. Terra incognita—that's where Kiva is at its best."

As a result, at this writing, Kiva is experimenting with radically expanding the types of loans they help finance. To address the

---

* CMEF is at www.cmef.com. For the over-indebtedness warning sign study, see Sources.

need for infrastructure to help build the foundation for growing economies, Kiva has begun lending through non-MFI partners to help finance clean water systems, sanitation, renewable energy, irrigation, and other large agricultural projects. This same category of non-MFI loans also includes funding for higher education, with repayment periods of ten or more years—or nearly twice as long as Kiva has thus far existed—plus a number of larger business loans meant to fill the transitional area between microenterprises and established large businesses. This gap, noted earlier in the Philippines, is known in the industry as the Small and Medium Enterprise (SME) space.

What this means for a Kiva lender: a user can continue to make cow loans in Kenya through Juhudi Kilimo or fund Cambodian fishermen through HKL, but that same user can just as easily choose to put $25 toward an irrigation system in Sri Lanka, a business education for a student in South Africa, or a $25,000 capital equipment purchase for an employer of fifty people in Mexico. Naturally, because these loans will be fundamentally different from conventional loans through MFIs, their different risks and repayment terms will be clearly spelled out.

Kiva hopes that visitors like you and me will see the new loans as opportunities and dive in. Will we? Hard to say. In keeping with Kiva's long-term philosophy of letting the user base decide, everyone will find out at the same time. "I don't know how people will react, how we'll get people to feel like they're really moving the needle with $25 on an SME loan," I've heard Premal say twice. But if users are willing to fund a loan of $20,000, say, to fund a school in Bali, that school would likely have more impact on a village's future than fifty loans of $400 to fund small craftspeople.

Another new Kiva option is peer-to-peer lending, currently in alpha testing as "Kiva Zip" at zip.kiva.org. At this writing, a few dozen small businesses in Kenya and California—a dried fish shop in Nairobi, a chocolatier in San Francisco, a cookstove maker in Bungoma (just thirty miles down the road from Tororo, Uganda, where Kiva began with seven entrepreneurs), and so on—are being funded directly by Kiva users all over the world, peer-to-peer, with no MFI handling the funds in between. Kiva Zip money can travel straight to Kenya nearly as fast as M-PESA.

Clients are screened for need and creditworthiness by local trustees, who themselves are screened by the Kiva Zip staff. A messaging system is in place so that lenders and clients can communicate, and clients who pay off their loans and the trustees who initially vouched for them may eventually build online track records similar to the seller ratings on eBay.*

So far, the increase in personal accountability seems to almost offset the increased risk. Lenders are engaging, clients are repaying, and delighted text messages are zipping back and forth even to borrowers in remote parts of Kenya. My $100 invested in Kiva Zip is being repaid perfectly, although the overall repayment rate, at this writing, is closer to just 90 percent.

If the system can be worked out, with transparent repayment data leading to increasingly reliable trustee relationships, no-interest money can soon fly halfway around the world, financing clients anywhere a mobile phone can reach, in a way that's scalable, reproducible, and potentially revolutionary. Since no MFI will be in the middle, the cost of funds to the client can drop greatly. Meanwhile, the people at MFIs in the poorest parts of the

---

* Kiva Zip has been inspired in part by the early success of Zidisha (a Swahili word for "grow") at www.zidisha.org. Zidisha has been doing peer-to-peer lending since 2009 with a different process involving lenders bidding on interest rates. The client ultimately pays an average 8-percent interest while the lender collects a few points, depending on how the bidding worked out. The 8-percent annual interest rate is substantially cheaper for the client than an MFI loan, and the repayment rate so far has been over 97 percent, so the model is workable. Zidisha has so far reached 580 businesses in Kenya, Senegal, Burkina Faso, and Indonesia. To everyone's credit, the founders of Zidisha and Kiva Zip's project manager, Jonny Price, are in friendly contact and cooperating to find ways to best develop ideas that will serve both platforms. See zip.kiva.org/blogs/4.

world—Urmila at BPW Patan in Kathmandu, for example—might be able to focus more on offering improved service to clients in their own physical area, reducing their own costs by not having to serve clients in remote, expensive-to-reach areas, who can now receive basic lending support by other means. Urmila's once-impossible dream of bringing services to the remote Himalayas might soon be a matter of routine.

The first time I interviewed Matt, I asked him where he wanted Kiva to reach next. I was thinking in terms of specific countries. Matt was much more ambitious: "It would be cool one day if people in the most remote areas of the world knew about Kiva, and they could do something good with that knowledge," he said. "In the far off streets of Zimbabwe or the most rural parts of Nicaragua, if people had access to it somehow, and they were able to get help from it."

That sounded impossible to me when Matt said it, just two years ago. Now that day seems to be approaching rapidly.

Innovation is changing more than just the means to deliver micro-finance. It's also expanding the ways in which microfinance fits into the broader picture of poverty alleviation.

Greg Rake walks through a small village in Odisha, a poor state in India's northeast. The local resident with whom he's walking stops at a teak tree, slaps the palm of his hand against it affection-ately, and smiles at Greg.

"This is my son's education," the man says of the tree.

Greg works for Landesa, a small non-profit that has worked in more than forty developing countries to help establish legal land title for farmers, laborers, and others whose ownership of land may be customary but not legally binding.* "It sounds about as

---

* Landesa's website is www.landesa.org.

exciting as working at the DMV," jokes Amy Low, their chief communications officer, "but what would you do without a driver's license?" Land title, in fact, is fundamental to poverty alleviation in much of the world. Without it, people can be forcibly moved, rights can be denied, and families must think of their futures in weeks instead of years. With land title, however, they can think long-term, plan ahead—and plant trees, for example, whose wood can be harvested and sold for education, retirement, or unforeseen emergencies.

"You wouldn't believe how much this means to people unless you've seen it," Greg says on a Skype call from Delhi. "Title means you're no longer rootless, you have access to credit, you can borrow against it, you've got resources, a place in the community—this one guy told me, the day he got his title, 'Today I was born.' And that had to feel pretty close to the truth for him, too." The joy in Greg's voice is palpable. And land title can make microloans easier to implement, secure, and pay off—investing in homes, power, sanitation, microbusinesses, and more. One form of poverty alleviation facilitates another.

In India, Landesa has helped more than 430,000 families gain title to their land. Given the average family size, they've helped more than two million people take this vital step out of poverty. And in China alone, Landesa has helped secure land rights for more than eighty million farming families. Their plots cover an area larger than the entire state of California.*

The Indian villager whose son is growing up near a literal Tree of Knowledge should soon be one of millions.

I first learned of Landesa in a conversation with Amy Klement, the VP of investments for the Omidyar Network, a philanthropic

---

* Data are online at www.landesa.org/where-we-work/india and www.landesa .org/where-we-work/china.

investment firm established by eBay founder Pierre Omidyar and his wife Pam. Pierre's business and high-tech savvy you can spot pretty easily, while Pam has a master's degree in molecular genetics and has worked with non-profits devoted to alleviating chronic pediatric illness and combating the modern-day slave trade. Not surprisingly, the Omidyar Network has supported Kiva from the outset while also investing in nearly two dozen other microfinance organizations.

Omidyar's approach to poverty is systemic, and for obvious reason: if the causes of poverty are widely varied, the solutions have to be, too, and often applied more than one at a time. Land title can work hand-in-hand with microfinance, but that requires government accountability and transparency. When those are present, a stable base for economic activity forms, encouraging entrepreneurship that helps microbusineses grow. Expanding information technology also facilitates that growth—and so on. Omidyar has invested heavily in all of these sectors, in for-profit and non-profit organizations alike.*

"Have you been to Bangladesh?" Amy asks brightly as we skim through Omidyar's investments. "BRAC is *everywhere* there."

BRAC, discussed briefly in the Tanzania chapter, is the largest non-governmental development organization on earth. BRAC approaches microfinance as part of a broad spectrum of services, using microfinance groups not as an end in themselves, but as a platform for education, health information and training, business development, savings, technical and marketing assistance, and other anti-poverty enterprises. Picture the educational work of Arariwa or Urwego, but spreading into neonatal health care, legal rights training, driver's education, and more, all with an eye to-

---

* A complete list of groups receiving Omidyar's support, ranging from Donors Choose to the Committee to Protect Journalists to the Wikimedia Foundation, is at www.omidyar.com/portfolio.

ward enterprise and profit for the client.* These services have now spread outward from Bangladesh to a dozen other developing countries, including truly challenging environments like Afghanistan and Haiti.

This would hardly seem the easy road to growth, but BRAC is huge—in microfinance alone, tens of thousands of staff members serve more than seven million clients—and its commercial enterprises include retail, food, and even a near-complete dairy supply chain, much like the one Juhudi Kilimo hopes to establish in Kenya.†

"They're always asking 'how can we do more, how can we do the distribution?' and then solving the problem—and so much of that comes right out of microfinance," Amy says. She has particular praise for BRAC's attempt to give the poor more than just loans, but a comprehensive ladder of support and opportunity. "You build a trust relationship with the customer, and you move the clients into a social entrepreneurship model, working with others, scaling up what works, and the number of people they've been able to help—it's just amazing."

"It was the women—their joy, and the similarity of our lives. I could see this would be a better learning experience than any Ph.D.," Susan Davis remembers, telling me how her first trip to Bangladesh changed her life.

Susan was planning a trip to Africa for her thirtieth birthday, but a job offer from the Ford Foundation took her to Dhaka instead. She wound up staying in Bangladesh for four-and-a-half

---

* For the best look, click the "What We Do" tab at BRAC's website, www.brac .net. The name originally stood for the Bangladesh Rehabilitation Assistance Committee.

† For more, see *Freedom from Want* by Ian Smillie in Sources.

years, spearheading a donor consortium between Grameen, BRAC, and an NGO called Proshika to streamline the funding of poverty alleviation programs.* Today, Susan is the president and CEO of BRAC USA, where she works to build bridges between BRAC and American organizations, sharing her own group's expertise while attracting support for BRAC's work in Asia and Africa. It was inevitable that BRAC would team up with Kiva to fund small enterprises, eventually forming partnerships in Sri Lanka, Uganda, Sierra Leone, Liberia, Tanzania, Pakistan, and South Sudan.†

The BRAC model also includes microfranchising, where the BRAC brand is used to help small businesses providing legal, agricultural, health, or other services. "We might train a woman who lives in a village where there's a need for better health information for pregnant mothers or infant care," Susan explains. In much of BRAC's working area, infant mortality is high, and simple childbirth may be a leading cause of death. "So we can train a woman to be self-employed, delivering a door-to-door message on how to prevent the top ten preventable causes of death—carrying with her a BRAC-supplied inventory, a safe birth kit, an insecticide-treated bed net, and so on. She can sell them at a markup, so she earns something, and the whole community benefits."

Susan and I go on to discuss other BRAC services ranging from vaccinations to veterinary care to commercial banking specifically designed for microenterprises that scale up and succeed. "Everywhere there's a need, there's an opportunity," she says. We both get excited just talking about it.

The idea of designing capitalist enterprises so they create

* Proshika is one of Bangladesh's largest NGOs, and carries its mission right in the name—a portmanteau of the Bangla words for "training," "education," and "action." Its website is www.proshika.org.

† The partnerships in Tanzania and Sri Lanka have closed, unfortunately, due to various regulatory issues with each country's central bank.

profit while doing public good is a simple one. But the potential is breathtaking.

Ultimately, microfinance is one tool of many, facilitating multiple approaches toward a unified goal. Kiva, BRAC, Landesa, Omidyar, and other related organizations may be working to solve a spectrum of challenges with a variety of appropriate solutions, but all share one common thread: the self-reliance and independence of the client.

In the center of India's flag, there is a wheel.

On the current flag, the wheel derives from a traditional portrayal of how a human life can find harmony with the universe. But that's hardly what the wheel was when Gandhi led India to independence. The wheel on the flag of Gandhi's Indian National Congress was much less philosophical: it was a simple spinning wheel, the kind that turns wool into thread for making cloth.

On Gandhi's *swaraj* ("self-rule" in Hindi) flag, the spinning wheel's meaning was economic and political: an important moment in the effort to convince the British to quit India was a boycott of British fabrics in favor of domestic and even homespun clothing. As part of a strategy of *Swadeshi* (Hindi for "self-sufficiency"), which became key to Gandhi's agenda, the boycott had a spiritual impact at least as large as its economic one.

The spinning wheel, with which Indian families could make their own cloth, became a symbol of self-reliance.

Naturally, given India's experience, Gandhi was skeptical of large corporations and multinational investment, which he saw as increasing the divide between rich and poor. In the context of microfinance, it's hard not to think of the experience in Andhra Pradesh as vindicating his view. Instead, Gandhi encouraged small villages toward craftsmanship, small business, and agricultural enterprise. "After all," Gandhi told an American writer, "the message of the spinning-wheel is that. It is mass production, but mass production in people's own homes."*

I'll leave it to you to decide if Gandhi would have approved of my friends Ram and Smita, the choices Premal has made since his first coin dropped, and the efforts of Landesa, Milaap, BRAC, and so on.

Shortly before I leave India, a check on the stats of the Friends of Bob Harris lending team at Kiva shows unexpected growth, reaching nearly four hundred members and almost $400,000 in loans. Since the average loan size at Kiva is just under $400, this figure is equal to a thousand loans fully funded.

I can't take credit, but it's wonderful to watch. The continuing growth has taken on a life of its own, having reached the top ten Kiva teams out of nearly twenty thousand. Any new visitor seeking to join a team and looking at the top ten is offered ideology (the Kiva Christians or the Atheist/Agnostic team), location (teams from Europe, Canada, and Australia), and a few very specific agendas (the GLBT team, Team Obama), plus—weirdly, if you ask me—the unexplained face of this one random dude from Ohio.

If I were just starting, I'd click on the face of the dude, just to see who he was and what Island of Misfit Toys he might lead. Inside, I'd find hundreds of fellow non-joiners, a motley gang of people kidding around and supporting each other's loans, united only in an urge to be nice to other similar people.

---

* Gandhi speaking to an American questioner, published in *Harijan*, his own weekly newspaper, November 2, 1934, quoted in *The Essential Writings* (see Sources). *Harijan* is Hindi for "child of God," the term Gandhi used for the lowest caste of society, as he felt no human being should be considered or called "untouchable."

I'd join, too. I can only wonder how big the team might become.

With dengue fever endemic in much of the country, I regret being unable to travel India as much as I'd like, especially the rural countryside. But I am trying at least to see what I can.

Now I'm walking on Chaupati Beach in Mumbai, and two feral children, a brother and sister perhaps six years old, have just passed in the other direction, about ten yards to my left. Judging from their thinness, rags, and grime, they seem homeless. They hold hands and recede into the distance, possibly the only loved ones either has in this world.

I saw them coming. And I wanted to help. But when I called out a greeting, the sister—older, protective—glanced my way, frowned, tugged on her brother's hand, and walked away faster. So now I am watching them go, taking a photo so I will not forget them, at least. For these two children, on this particular day, thinking of them seems to be all I can do.

It can be difficult to accept the limits on our ability to help others, and even harder to realize the limits on our wisdom, our kindness, our lives. It may be tempting just to turn away, think the worst of the world, and retreat into selfishness and fear. But when you help just one person, or let one person help you, it can be hard not to glimpse the better world so frustratingly near our grasp.

This beach is a short distance from several scenes of the political mass murders of 2008, when Islamists from Pakistan shot and bombed their way across South Mumbai. Walking here, reminders are fairly constant: there's a police station up the road with a memorial to the cops who died; further on, you can see one of the hotels that got shot up; and the lone surviving attacker was arrested at a police roadblock alongside this very beach.

The same attack also targeted a children's hospital, a café, a movie theater, a Jewish community center, and the main train station—the whole point being to randomly kill as many innocent people as possible, all in the name of a political dispute that arises out of the proper definition of the divine.*

Sadly, those attacks weren't even particularly isolated. Just since 2000, more than 1,800 innocent Indians have been killed in nearly sixty terrorist incidents all over the country, including attacks on cars, taxis, buses, trains, schools, hospitals, markets, houses of worship, at least one amusement park, judicial courts, and even the Parliament itself.

But even *that* is a matter of perspective.

India has 1.2 billion people, after all. Let's do the math. Even if there were a dozen uncaught connivers behind each of those attacks, all existing as separate cells—a wild exaggeration of the danger—and each one had a hundred dangerous supporters—yet another wild exaggeration—that would still leave more than 99.99 percent of the population reliably un-heinous. Humanity's batting average is actually pretty darn good.

In Mumbai's central train station, where armed men so recently mowed down more than one hundred people, metal detectors again sat idle. People walked right through, unsecured yet unworried. On the day I visited, thousands of people from all over the region—Hindu, Muslim, Christian, you name it—intermingled while carrying thousands of bags that could have concealed deadly weapons, and did so in complete confident calm.

Stop and watch, even here, for only one hour. You'll see thousands of people of different faiths and ethnicities all getting along just fine, sometimes even trusting total strangers to watch their

---

* If you've seen *Slumdog Millionaire*—a film whose merits and weaknesses might be worth yet another whole book—you recall the train platform that was key to the story. Two weeks after the film's release, 58 innocent people were killed and another 104 were wounded in that very station.

stuff in this throbbing crowd while they go off to pee, all so easily it's not even noticed.

But amazing things are worth noticing.

After all of these travels, I've started to notice how constantly people trust one another. Almost everywhere, almost all the time. And how that trust is almost always deserved.

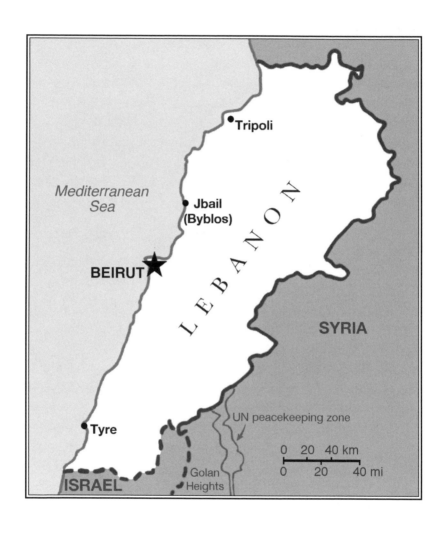

CHAPTER THIRTEEN

BEIRUT

I'M LOOKING FOR a side street—*maybe the road with the bullet-riddled wall?*—but nothing matches my folded printout from Google Maps.

I walk on, but the avenue widens, the neighborhood changes, and soon there is a tank parked on the sidewalk, blocking my way.

Hmm. There was no tank in my street directions. I'm lost.

Only a few people on earth even know that I am in Lebanon, nearly all of them total strangers whom I've only contacted by e-mail. There may be no help if I get into trouble.

And yet I cannot even force myself to worry.

I've come to trust the people at MFIs, including the local Kiva partner whose office I'm currently trying to find. I've also come to trust my instincts, and nothing here looks particularly worrisome. The bullet holes are old and chipped, and the tank is merely parked like a cop car, heading nowhere, targeting no one. There's no active conflict, and Hezbollah is currently out of the kidnapping-Westerners business. Being a wandering Ohioan here holds no more particular danger, at least for the moment, than in most other cities on earth.

So, with the blinding filters of fear, politics, identity, and conflict removed, the other people on this street—driving to work, carrying packages, grabbing a snack at a restaurant, talking on cell phones and bumping into people, walking hand-in-hand with their children, waiting for a friend—are obviously no different than anywhere else.

This should never be as hard to see as it is.

"This is our *first . . . core . . . value*," Alia says, manually chopping the air for emphasis. "The most important rule we have."

"We" here means Al Majmoua (Arabic for "the Group"), one of Kiva's local partners and the biggest MFI in Lebanon.* Alia is Al Majmoua's manager of both human resources and social performance, so she's in charge of both who works here and making sure their work matters. I've found her office not far from the bullet-riddled wall that turned out to be on the correct side street. Al Majmoua's headquarters are at the end of a long alley, marked with a large yellow logo meant to symbolize a circle of unity, although it looks more like a fried egg.

"To begin, our logo—it is not a fried egg," Alia had said with a smile as we began, before I'd even the chance to say so. Apparently I'm not the only one who has thought this.

Now Alia is telling me emphatically about Al-Majmoua's *first . . . core . . . value*:

"*No discrimination.*"

The Beirut of American media imagery is all car bombs and barracks explosions, street posters of glowering mullahs, and smoke rising from an assassination or airstrike.† But West Beirut can feel

---

* Al Majmoua's site is www.almajmoua.org.
† Then again, the America of American imagery hardly paints a full picture, either. When I turned on the hotel TV in Beirut, the very first image was an old episode of *American Gladiators*, with two beefy men in spandex pummeling each other with pugil sticks. One channel over, there was an episode of *South Park*,

downright touristy. Strolling to the waterfront on a Saturday night, I passed a store window featuring T-shirts emblazoned with Bob Marley, SpongeBob SquarePants, and the *Saturday Night Live* catchphrase "Suck It Trebek."* Along the corniche, there were almost as many skateboards and rollerblades as headscarves and beards. The Hard Rock Café showed off one of Gwen Stefani's tank tops, a Michael Jackson dress shirt, and a leather jacket worn by Billy Joel. *Time Out Beirut,* a weekly nightlife magazine, was on newsstands with a cover image of a nude European woman, eyes closed, sensually licking a white dinner plate. The headline: *Bite Me.*† On my map, I had marked the spot where the American Embassy was once blown up by a suicide van carrying nearly a solid ton of explosives. That was years ago. Now there's a Starbucks about one hundred yards away.

From West Beirut, at least—the neighborhood that most earned the city its famous nickname, "the Paris of the Middle East"—it was almost hard to imagine the decades of fighting over what Lebanon is and should be: an Islamic theocracy, perhaps, or a Western-influenced investment haven, a Mediterranean boomtown for wealthy Emiratis, a modern democracy, an appendage of Syria, or a half-dozen other visions. The answer has long depended on whom you ask, and which argument is loudest has depended on when you arrive. Since 1975, conflicts have included Lebanese Christians v. Muslims, Syrians v. Lebanese nationalists, Israel v. the PLO, Muslim infighting between Shi'a and Sunni, pan-Arab Ba'athists fighting any faction seeking independent control, and more. And nearly everybody involved—Shi'a, Sunni, Christians,

---

with Cartman's braying translated into Arabic subtitles. A few channels up, several American news networks were treating Charlie Sheen as the most important man alive. Oy.

* Yes, I did e-mail a photo of this back to my friends at *Jeopardy.*

† *Time Out Beirut,* April 2011, cover visible online at www.timeoutbeirut.com /beirut/article/5300/bite-me.html.

Jews, Alawites, Druze, you name it—claims to worship the same god of Abraham. He must be thrilled.

Most factions have had powerful patrons—the U.S., Iran, Syria, Iraq, and so on—whose strategic interests have rarely involved concessions here. Nonetheless, progress: since 1989, the government has been restructured, Israel has withdrawn, a Syrian occupation force has also withdrawn (although only after a million people took to the streets), and most militias have disbanded, save for Hezbollah, the Shi'a militia backed by Iran.

Hezbollah, which prior to 9/11 had killed more Americans than any other terror group on earth, has not only never disarmed, it now holds two cabinet positions and a dozen parliament seats, and even owns its own TV news network, Al-Manar ("the Beacon").* Two rival parties, Future and Amal, own TV networks as well.

Fortunately, Lebanon also has a small but growing non-sectarian movement. The desire for peace came up in conversation with more than half of the people I met, Christian and Muslim alike, particularly the young.

I cling to my hope in technology here. In an era of Wi-Fi, global telecoms, and affordable Internet-ready handsets, it should be increasingly difficult to convince preteens that their neighbors are so terribly different that killing them might be preferable to getting along. If discrimination and communication are indeed incompatible, non-factionalism may yet be in Lebanon's future.

It will be if Alia and Al Majmoua have anything to say about it.

---

* In Beirut, Al-Manar is seen on satellite/cable TV right next to MTV and CNN International. If you're curious, it's roughly what American cable news would look like if all the leggy blondes were replaced by old beardy guys denouncing Israel. Definitely less hot. You've probably never seen Al-Manar because the U.S. has banned it from American airwaves as a "Specially Designated Terrorist Entity." See Sources.

Alia was born in France perhaps a little more than thirty years ago (asking her age would have felt *vulgaire*) to a French mom and a Lebanese dad. I imagine she may have occasionally been on the receiving end of prejudice herself. If so, it hasn't held her back even slightly—she's a graduate of Harvard Business School and a former economic development consultant at the World Bank. Alia eventually fell in love and married a Lebanese man, they moved to Beirut, and she now works to help thousands of clients build their businesses all over the country.

There's not a trace of self-importance about her, however. We chat over coffee like old friends, Alia's story pouring forth in a lilting French accent: "I studied political science, and I was looking at a career in diplomacy, but that was not a good fit for me. I was too"—she searches here for the polite word—"*transparent* a person for diplomacy." But Alia's phrasing here is in fact supremely diplomatic—owning and defending her own basic honesty, but also spinning it as a possible shortcoming, lest any insult be taken. This seems intuitive, not premeditated. Alia is a peacemaker at heart. Who moved to Beirut. For love. I feel only respect and affection.

"In 1999, I applied to Al Majmoua," Alia continues, "and I haven't been bored a single minute." *'Boring' isn't a word I was worried about here*, I reply, and we talk for a bit about the "unstable political situation" (as Alia air-quotes this phrase with her fingers) and how it has affected Al Majmoua and its clients. The challenge has been enormous.

"In 2006"—the year of Hezbollah's most recent conflict with Israel—"we were up to nine thousand clients. Twenty-five hundred of them were directly affected, mostly in the south Bekaa valley and the south suburbs. First we had to verify that our own staff were okay. Then we had our staff work with humanitarian agencies and make sure that our clients were okay. By September"—two months after the war—"we could verify the situation of every client. Every last one." Alia is quietly proud as she says this. She should be.

"In some cases, their businesses and homes were destroyed. Sometimes just the business, sometimes just the home. Some were okay. There were some with injuries, disabilities from the war. And we had eleven deaths. But"—and here, Alia's face flashes to the determination she must have shown at the time—"we have to find solutions. So. We wrote off $750,000 in loans, and activated all of our contacts with other organizations to start the recovery. We put together a tool kit—something for barbers, plumbers, service people—to get them started, since that helps the community. We got involved with farms, bringing seeds, animal feed . . . We were able to have a real impact on the borrowers and create a lot of goodwill."

In the years since, Al Majmoua has nearly tripled in size— twenty-five thousand clients and growing—with virtually all of its promotion coming simply from word-of-mouth, neighbor to neighbor.

I ask if the lack of discrimination at Al Majmoua means that some group loans might cross religious lines, with perhaps Sunni and Christian neighbors joining in business. "It is too early," Alia says simply. "But we do exhibitions, fairs, demonstrations of our non-financial services—training and so on—right at the intersections, the borders between communities, so we can attract people of all backgrounds."

This sounds like an act of faith—a non-denominational one, granted, but an act of faith nonetheless. Alia agrees.

For my first client visit, I've given Al Majmoua a long list of my Kiva clients, hoping one or two might be nearby and available for a chat. I'm in luck, it turns out—a barber named Huseyn has a salon not far from the office.

I do need a shave.

I've sat on Sead and Munira's furniture in Bosnia and bought a Masaai-themed Christmas ornament from Lizbeth in Tanzania. So it seems only right and fair to ask this Arab Muslim in Beirut to place a razor to my throat. This will be no different from anything else in these travels, of course. I am certain that Huseyn with his barbershop in Beirut will be no different from Jinifer with her sari-sari in Cebu or Yvonne with her small grocery in Kigali. *Surely this will be no worse than the charcoal yogurt*, I think, almost laughing at the memory.

Still, if someone had told me a few years ago that I'd feel perfectly safe doing this, I'd have thought they knew nothing about me. Now, if someone told me the opposite, I'd be sure they hadn't seen enough of the world.

Huseyn is a soft-spoken man of about forty with a salt-and-pepper beard and a professorial demeanor.* We shake hands, exchange a few greetings in Arabic and English, and he ushers me in through the glass door of his salon. In about ten seconds, I am in a chair, facing a mirror, covered in a big shiny barber's cape.

Huseyn is married with a large family to support, so when he apologizes for being busy with another client, I understand. The small shop is humming with activity. Behind me, in the mirror, two more customers, a loud weightlifter and a shy student, are already waiting their turn. I'm glad for Huseyn's success.

My beard will be attended by his associate Abed, a skinny, graceful young man in a tight Dolce & Gabbana T-shirt and with a vibe as much Donna Karan as the Holy Qu'ran. Thumping Europop plays as Abed covers my cheeks with white foamy lather. I suddenly

---

* "Huseyn" and all names of people I meet from this point forward in Beirut are pseudonyms. Because it's Beirut. I actually doubt using their names here would cause any trouble, but I have to err on the side of their safety.

feel less like an American skulking around Beirut than a straight guy hanging out in the Castro.

This is my first proper shave from a real barber in years, and it feels downright luxurious. Abed's razor rakes cleanly and quickly, *zip, thwip, schwip,* and five minutes later, my face feels fantastic.

Huseyn and I step out to the sidewalk to chat. He smokes, we sip tiny cups of strong coffee, and Ali, a loan officer from Al Majmoua, kindly acts as interpreter. We run through the basic facts: Huseyn has been in business for almost ten years, and this is his third loan cycle with Al Majmoua. He's using this round of funding to invest in routine supplies, his microloans functioning like any typical line of credit.

The conversation warms, and I learn that Huseyn is a Sunni, which surprises me, since the name "Huseyn" is often Shi'a. *Does sectarianism affect his business?* No, not at all, not in this neighborhood. Huseyn's customers are Sunni, Shi'a, Christian, you name it. Sometimes he also gets foreigners—tourists from the Arabian Gulf states of Kuwait, Bahrain, Qatar, and the Emirates come in fairly frequently. Even an American here and there, he adds with a grin.

Al Majmoua was kind enough to facilitate other client visits, and I vouch for everyone I met as welcoming and thoughtful and friendly and eager for peace. But the driver on the second trip, a loan officer named Ahmad, said the one most memorable thing I heard in Lebanon.

Ahmad didn't always work for Al Majmoua, although he enjoys it there very much—"it is good, everyone equal, like family, Christian, Muslim, everybody love the same, you know?" he asks.

The Three Tenors sing on the radio as Mahmoud relates his story, clear and moving even through his imperfect English. "I ask God to bless my family. I am rich man. Beautiful wife." He also has two young daughters, and for sixteen years, he had a large and popular restaurant. He stayed out of politics. Like a lot of people everywhere, he just tried to make a good living. Ahmad's restaurant flourished, welcoming clients of all faiths. "Shi'a, Sunni—all same. Television splits us. Politics. People love God, love each other, all same," he says.

But in July 2006, Hezbollah unilaterally launched rocket strikes against Israel and kidnapped Israeli soldiers near the border. This touched off an escalating conflict that eventually led to Israeli air attacks on Beirut itself. In one of those strikes, Ahmad's restaurant was destroyed. Through no fault of his own, his entire livelihood was gone.

So now Ahmad works as a loan officer at Al Majmoua, rebuilding his own life while trying to help others do the same. And to put his daughters through school, he also works weekends—but now in someone else's restaurant. It is a major step down.

I ask Ahmad if he is bitter—if going from being the owner of a restaurant to just being the hired help has made him angry at the Israelis, or Hezbollah, or his god, or anyone.

"No, no, no. Everything is clear for me. When my god is with me, I don't care about something like that. No."

Ahmad didn't pause here while speaking, but in my memory, he did. I've thought a lot about the next five words that came out of his mouth.

"You love more, you win. You don't stop, thanks for God."

He added again, for emphasis:

"You love *more*, you win."

We drove in silence for a while, Ahmad's '70s-era Chevy somehow holding itself in one piece as we rumbled along. The radio played American stadium rock of the 1980s, and I silently mused at the apparent cultural exchange: Lebanon, after all, was the ancient home of the Phoenicians, who had popularized the alphabet; of Tyre, site of one of Shakespeare's plays; and of Byblos, the city whose name became the source of our words for paper, papyrus, and the Bible itself. In return: REO Speedwagon. This hardly seemed fair. Moments later, "Eye of the Tiger" came on, *bomp-bidda-bomp-bidda-bomp-bidda-bomp*, its testosterone level high enough to drive our conversation almost instantly to the exceptional beauty of Lebanese women. This was a respectful chat, not locker-room stuff, nothing Ahmad's wife would have minded.

Then I decided to ask about the giant billboards that dotted the road, each one with another forty- or fifty-foot face smiling down at us. *This one, Ahmad,* I asked innocently—*I see his face a lot. Who is he?*

"Oh, yes, he was a very good man. He loved this country. Then . . . he was blown up."

Oh.

I asked about another one. *How about this guy, with the mustache—is he still in power?* "Oh, him. He was very good. Worked very hard. Very famous, powerful. Then . . . he was blown up." This continued a third time: "This one, I did not agree with him, but he was very important, yes. Then . . . he was blown up."

I stopped asking.

In the silence that followed, I debated asking for the specific names of the men on the billboards, but Ahmad's sad eyes told me he was already feeling grief at their memories. I changed the subject instead, assuming that I would later discover the spelling of the names of the bombing victims, and the exact circumstances of their ends, by looking them up online. After all, car bombs are an unusual and sloppy means of assassination—there couldn't be so many that I wouldn't be sure whom we'd discussed.

I was wrong. Nearly twenty Lebanese assassinations have been carried out by car bombs since 2004. On Wikipedia, it's an entire category.*

---

* en.wikipedia.org/wiki/Category:Deaths_by_car_bomb_in_Lebanon

In the center of town, still close enough to the Mediterranean that the breeze sometimes carries the smell of salt in the air, there is a large open area called Martyrs Square. In its center is a statue memorializing Lebanese nationalists who were executed by Ottoman rulers at the outset of independence a century ago. During the civil war, the infamous Green Line dividing the city ran directly through this square, so today, the statue is a repository of bullet holes from every direction. The memorial to those who died so that Lebanon could be free has been shot to bits by the very Lebanese for whom they died.

Just steps away, the body of the late prime minister Rafik Hariri lies in state. Hariri's life was an amazing rags-to-riches tale: a boy from a poor town in southern Lebanon who grew up to become a billionaire construction magnate, thanks to a string of massive deals with the Saudis. Once in political power, Hariri shuttled frantically between all parties, striving to bring peace and investment and stability to postwar Beirut. Then . . . he was blown up.

Hariri's death unified hundreds of thousands of Lebanese to protest Syria's occupation, and Hariri's life and work helped make possible the massive rebuilding of Beirut's shattered core. Downtown, new hotels and high-rises are opening almost as fast as you can say "Abu Dhabi," with Emirati and Saudi money flowing in. As this book nears release, a $300 million super-mall is being readied to open, and the same Dubai company is spending $2 billion rehabbing a particularly scenic bit of suburbia just up the coast.

In alleys in every direction, on both sides of the former Green Line, young people have scrawled graffiti: "All You Need Is Love," "End Sectarianism," and, at least twice, the GLBT-friendly word "LEBSIANS" in all caps.*

---

* "LEBSIANS" is the only way I ever saw the word spelled in graffiti, usually in all caps. Perhaps one poor speller went on a city-wide spray-paint bender, or it's

There is reason for hope. Hundreds of thousands of ordinary Lebanese of every stripe gathered not that long ago in the Cedar Revolution, driving Syrian troops out of the country with peaceful street protest. It was an unprecedented interfaith outpouring of a desire for peace, and its anniversary has been celebrated ever since. The generation now reaching adulthood has grown up with this example, and with better communications than their parents ever imagined.

There is also reason for despair. Syria still doesn't buy the whole "Lebanon" thing, Hezbollah still doesn't buy the whole "Israel" thing, and extremists on all sides still don't buy the whole "killing is bad" thing. And at this writing, the conflict in neighboring Syria threatens to spread, already causing a fresh wave of kidnappings and shootings in Lebanon.

All of this makes Mahmoud's five words seem all the more meaningful. They came not from the bosom of a comfortable middle-class life in the West—they came from *here*, from *Beirut*. from a man who has seen his life shattered by factionalism, nationalism, religionism, and tribalism. And yet still, with all his heart, he could still summon these words and live by them:

"You love *more*, you win."

Yes, and.

I never imagined it would happen this way, much less planned it, but in these travels we've now seen almost the exact same ap-

---

a portmanteau of "Lebanese lesbians," or, I dunno, maybe it's a band name. But there's enough other gay-friendly graffiti that I'm figuring it's a persistent typo. Incidentally, Lebanese law bans anything except married hetero happytime, but enforcement is selective and varies by locale, and pro-gay activism is tolerated but frowned upon by most of the population. Picture North Carolina around 1985 and you've got the idea. This makes Lebanon one of the more gay-friendly parts of the Arab world.

proach to life's adversities—the answer to the sometimes-explicit question *how are you not insane?*—expressed by Buddhists (in Cambodia), Hindus (in India), Protestants (in Kenya and Rwanda), Muslims (in Bosnia and here in Lebanon), Catholics (in Peru and the Philippines), and non-believers (scattered throughout).

Before this project began, I might have hoped that something like "you love more, you win" might be practiced by good people all over the world. Now I will never doubt it again. I have seen it firsthand.

This is wealth I will be honored to carry home.

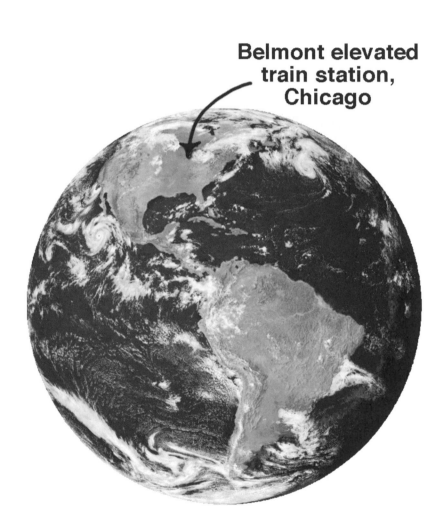

Belmont elevated train station, Chicago

CHAPTER FOURTEEN

HOME

I'M SITTING IN a small holding area in JFK airport. U.S. immigration has detained me on arrival.

About ten days earlier, I'd been on Air Arabia, the Southwest Airlines of the Middle East.* Moments after plunking down in an aisle seat, I'd suddenly found myself with a baby in my arms.

A young Lebanese mom, caring for this tiny infant and an excitable two-year-old, had needed urgently to focus on the older child, who had suddenly decided to deplane, squealing like a happy madman. With barely a second thought and not one spoken word, the mom had simply looked in my eyes and placed her youngest child in my hands. She had needed no more than two seconds of eye

---

* Air Arabia turned out to be one of my favorite airlines on earth. I've flown them in four countries now, and every flight has been clean, comfortable, on time, and a bargain. They blast loud echoey recorded prayers to Allah just before every takeoff, but they've also never had a single passenger injury in nearly ten years of operations, so hey, whatever works. At 37,000 feet, I'm not picky about deities. And as to in-flight entertainment, the Sharjah–Nairobi route was probably the only opportunity I will have on earth to enjoy episodes of *Pinky and the Brain* over Somali airspace. Their site is www.airarabia.com.

contact to assess whether I, a random strange American, could be trusted to care for one of the loves of her life.

The baby, for her part, seemed delighted with the sudden change of plans. As was I.

There are moments when languages and religions and birthplaces all fall away. In these rare holy instants, all you are is a human.

I don't know why I'm being detained. No one will tell me. I also don't know how long I'll be stuck here. No one will tell me that, either.

The clock on the wall ticks. Burly border cops eye me like I'm a perp who needs eyeing. The clock on the wall ticks.

"We're gonna need you to walk to the back for further screening," the guard in the immigration booth had said. Then, off my surprised look: "you can either just walk right back there now, or"—with a hint of comfortable intimidation—"we can make this a thing."

Welcome home.

In the course of this book and the Forbes Traveler writing that led to it, I've crossed international borders nearly forty times on six continents without much more than a glance. But it's here, back home, that I'm stuck in the cooler. All I can figure is that my passport now has an unusual number of visas and entry and exit stamps in non-Western scripts.

I hope that can't be the reason. It can't be that merely visiting a country that writes in Arabic might be a clue that I'm some sort of threat.* Then again, if I'd had a Cuban stamp in my passport, I'd

---

* Consider that the NYPD's own court testimony revealed in 2012 that its massive and once-secret decade-long spying program against NYC-area Muslims, created in part by the CIA, not only did not detect a single plot, nor make a single arrest—it did not so much as generate a single lead worth investigating.

have definitely been stopped, because Cuba is contagious and must be quarantined. Fifty years of keeping Americans from visiting Cuba did such an excellent job of weakening Castro, who remained in power more than twenty years longer than any other leader in the Western Hemisphere.*

I look around at the other people being detained: two middle-aged Hispanic guys in satin jackets, an Indian family gathered around a frail elderly woman with a cane—clearly a dangerous terrorist—a small Asian man whom I take to be Filipino, and a couple of Arab guys who look like they work at the Gap. Maybe it's coincidence, but I'm the only one here who looks like his parents might have named him for a Confederate general.†

If one defines American-ness by a certain skin tone and dress, the overwhelming majority of people on earth are visibly Other, never mind the large and peaceful Hispanic, Indian, Filipino, and Arab immigrant populations right here in New York City. And now apparently I, too, might carry the virus of Otherness. I feel like throwing up in my brain.

Finally, my name is called, and a man with remarkable biceps returns my passport, granting me entry to my own country. I don't want to make assumptions, so I ask: *Can I ask why I had to come back here . . . ?*

"We just needed to check a few things," comes the non-reply.

See "NYPD Secret Police Spying on Muslims Led to No Terrorism Leads or Cases" by Adam Goldman and Matt Appuzzo of the Associated Press in Sources.
* The embargo began in 1962. Other than Castro, who ceded power to his brother Raul in 2008, and the ceremonial status of Elizabeth II over England's former colonies, the 1962 Western Hemisphere leader who retained power longest was Alfredo Stroessner of Paraguay, who only lasted to 1989. Worldwide, only one—a Samoan chieftain who died in 2007—came remotely close to retaining power as long as Castro. Yet nearly the entire mainstream of U.S. punditry continues to believe that the embargo somehow *weakens* the Castro government. One wonders what contrary evidence would be required.
† Which they did: Robert E. Lee.

The clock on the wall ticks.

Then, adding a tiny but perceptible note of menace—*don't make trouble*—"You're free to go."

And with that, I re-enter the United States.

Fear of the Other has been a key lever in American politics since long before 9/11—long before, in fact, our grandparents were even born. Anarchists, the Palmer raids. Japanese internment. The Red Scare, blacklisting, McCarthy, Nicaragua as a harbinger of Soviet invasion. Fear of women as a political force. Fear of blacks, gays, whites, Hollywood, Mexicans, liberals, conservatives, rock and roll. Yet nowhere in human history should a people be more able to see their own deep connections to the rest of the world. For more than a century, America has been easily the most diverse nation of immigrants ever to live in relative peace.

Walk down the street of almost any major American city. (Seriously—I don't mean this rhetorically, I'm suggesting you really do this, consciously, possibly with a notepad.) Just look at the faces around you. Even in smaller cities, how long does it take to see virtually every corner of our planet represented? If there's a decent amount of bustle, it usually takes less than five minutes, and in a major downtown, as little as thirty seconds. And here's the cool part: we don't even notice. It's *normal*.

Anyone who wonders if world peace is possible is missing the obvious: yes—*of course* people from all over the world can get along. We do. Every day. Save for the descendants of Native Americans, the United States is comprised of nothing *but* the rest of the world.

An underappreciated peace is expanding all over the rest of the planet, too: this same placid mingling takes place in capitals from Santiago to Singapore, more with each passing year. The process may seem slow if measured in our own lifetimes, but against the long millennia of history, it is a lightning strike.*

As noted in Beijing—where mobile phone pics of the Forbidden City were being Facebooked around the globe—in this one wondrous way, today's fifteen-year-olds in Kansas and Kuala Lumpur are part of the first generation in history to grow up with a lifelong expectation of interconnection. They've never *not* known a world where they could instantly trade ideas and photos and dumb jokes and daydreams. As communications improve, the fear of the Other, the notion that our fellow humans are fundamentally unlike us, is receding into the past nearly everywhere. In thirty or forty years, when these young people have political and economic power, the world may be run very differently than it ever has been before.

I believe we can see it already happening in the rise of social entrepreneurship on a global scale. This may be far easier to realize while holding a mobile phone in rural Kenya than it is while watching American evening news.

In 2009, Kiva began to partner with two MFIs in the United States, Kiva's forty-fifth country served, allowing users worldwide to finance loans to Americans for the first time. This arguably completed a circle of generosity: Americans had created a website to help small enterprises in the rest of the world grow, and now prosperous Chileans, Ukrainians, and South Africans could invest in struggling American businesses, too.

Surprisingly, thousands of established Kiva lenders were

---

*Steven Pinker, one of the world's leading cognitive psychologists, has presented a great deal of data showing that modern communications, literacy, trade, and other factors are changing human behavior on personal and national scales. See Pinker, *The Better Angels of Our Nature*, in Sources.

immediately unhappy about Kiva's ever-increasing ability to reach more clients. Some were flat-out furious—so much so that a new team, Pissed Off Kiva Lenders, was formed. Why the sudden outrage? As the team page explained:

> We are really, really angry that Kiva is now making loans to US borrowers . . . It has undermined the very core of what made it so unique and special; impactful contributions to impoverished people in developing countries . . . Now the truly impoverished are being asked to COMPETE for funds with borrowers in the US . . . To even consider lending to the US is a shameful, disgraceful decision.*

Behind what looks like compassion, you'll find a bizarre yet common assumption: *America is different.* And Americans do not suffer from poverty.

The facts argue otherwise, and shockingly so. At this writing, the once-prosperous city of Detroit, after decades of decline, now has an infant mortality rate substantially worse than Botswana.†

Nonetheless, belief in American exceptionalism is so deeply ingrained—even among Kiva lenders, as internationally focused a group as you're likely to find—that the Pissed Off Kiva Lenders

---

* The team later disbanded, so their page is no longer online. However, an archive taken immediately after its founding, complete with massive rant, remains available. See Sources.

† Using the most recent numbers available: the per capita income of the city of Detroit (not to be confused with the metropolitan area), which once was the highest in the U.S., has fallen to an average, 2006–10, of just $15,062. Botswana, despite its high HIV rate and other challenges, has been one of southern Africa's success stories, cutting its estimated infant mortality rate to just 10.49 per 1,000 live births. Detroit's has risen to 14.8 per 1,000. A child apparently has a better chance of surviving infancy in a country with actual tigers than in a city where they only play baseball. See Sources.

team rapidly grew to account for as much as 1 dollar in every 14 lent by Americans on the site.

Revealingly, the Pissed Off Kiva Lenders' stress level was raised by a few early loans in which the borrowers were photographed clearly with bright smiles in good light, seeking thousands of dollars for their home businesses—funds therefore not going to people in urgent need. But as we've seen—think of Symon the coffee grower, Nermina the glassblower, Jinifer whose sari-sari store was growing enough that she could employ three people and hope to hire more soon—developing-world clients are often doing pretty well, too. The issue was not one of need, but of perception: many of the first U.S. clients simply didn't *look* like typical Kiva borrowers, but more like the lenders themselves, a thought admitted frequently on discussion boards.

Kiva's management responded with an open letter inviting continued feedback and advocating a wait-and-see approach—after all, nobody was holding a gun to people's heads and forcing them to lend to Americans. If the loans weren't filled, or if the American loans siphoned off dollars that could have helped more struggling businesses abroad, then that would rapidly become clear. In any case, the results would be determined by the free choices of hundreds of thousands of lenders, dictated neither by Kiva nor a small angry group of borrowers.*

Ultimately, Kiva's global lender base made no particular distinction between U.S. and other borrowers. Among the very first clients posted by American MFIs: a salon owner in Queens named Elizabeth, who received funding from lenders in eight countries, including Cambodia and Armenia; a scrap metal recycler named Hardyal, also in New York, who got financing from thirteen countries, including Singapore, Indonesia, and China; and a San Francisco daycare provider named Maria, who was

---

*The discussion at the time is at kivanews.blogspot.com/2009/06/letter-from -kiva-about-pilot.html.

funded from sixteen countries, including Thailand, Slovenia, and Oman.*

None of these borrowers was remotely as poor as, say, a Zambian phone card vendor. But they needed the credit, Kiva helped them grow their small businesses, and people from all over the world could appreciate the benefit.

But did Elizabeth, Hardyal, and Maria being funded mean that Zambian phone card dealers were not? Does funding a loan in San Antonio, Texas, mean *not* getting one funded in San Antonio, Chile—or worse, that ten Chilean loans go unfunded, since American loans tend to be larger?

Happily, no. That worry is based on another false assumption: that generosity has a maximum, that Kiva is a zero-sum game despite its spectacular growth. In reality, loans to the rest of the world continued to be filled at the same rate. As Premal explained at a March 2012 conference in San Francisco: "It turned out that there are lots of people who will *only* loan in their backyard. So lending to the U.S. actually expanded the pie, rather than dividing it."

In less than a year, the controversy faded. The Pissed Off Kiva Lenders changed their name to the merely Unhappy Kiva Lenders, and eventually the team was disbanded. Now it's perfectly normal in the Kiva community for Americans to receive loan funding from Turkey, South Africa, or Korea. America turned out not to be so different after all.

Kiva's American partner MFIs now include:

- ACCION USA, ACCION Texas, and ACCION San Diego, independent affiliates of ACCION International, the pioneers of microlending in Latin America. The ACCION

---

*These three client pages are at www.kiva.org/lend/114235, www.kiva.org/lend/113643, and www.kiva.org/lend/114118.

U.S. network also includes ACCION Chicago (see below) and more, covering a total of forty-six states.

- Opportunity Fund, California's largest non-profit micro-lender, located in Kiva's San Francisco backyard.

- ASI Federal Credit Union, a New Orleans lender that has helped more than one hundred thousand low-wealth and otherwise disadvantaged borrowers.

- Valley Economic Development Center, a Southern California microlender based in Los Angeles.

- Grameen America, the American outpost of the Grameen Bank founded by Muhammad Yunus, and with whom he shared the Nobel Peace Prize.

Muhammad Yunus, of course, was the speaker who inspired the creation of Kiva in the first place. Now his operations have come to America, and yet another full circle has been turned.

Mary Fran Riley works for ACCION Chicago. They haven't financed any loans through Kiva yet, but we met on a bus once in Oakland, I told her about this project, and she invited me to stop by the office sometime.

ACCION's headquarters are on the Near West Side near Union Park, an area that wasn't exactly enticing when I was twenty-three, studying improv in Chicago with Del Close and living in the Lincoln-Belmont YMCA. As I descend from the nearby elevated train station, I'm reminded of how much the city has changed since I lived here a quarter-century ago, a young man first learning to "yes, and" his way through life. Much of the West Side was in rough shape back when I first passed through this city, but its history played a vital role in determining my own—and, if you enjoy laughter, your history, too.

A century ago, this area was a patchwork of sweatshops, factories, and lumber yards populated by small, separate enclaves of working-class immigrants—Italians here, Poles around the corner, Germans over that way, and so on. Thousands of these immigrant families were aided in settlement by Jane Addams's Hull House, where volunteers offered free clubs, concerts, and classes in art, literature, and history, all open to people of any class or ethnicity.

Hull House had been established in 1889 as a place anyone could go to learn, to be encouraged, to express themselves artistically, to grow—and to become part of something bigger than just their own neighborhood. Frank Lloyd Wright, Susan B. Anthony, and Clarence Darrow were early supporters, Upton Sinclair and Eleanor Roosevelt joined Hull House residents for meals and conversation, and when Benny Goodman turned eleven years old, he took clarinet lessons here and played in the boys' band, leading to a lifetime of brilliance. For many young immigrants, the connections developed at Hull House created their sense of American patriotism. When Jane Addams won the Nobel Peace Prize, it was richly deserved.

In the 1920s, a Hull House employee named Neva Boyd founded a new project to help integrate the community by teaching young people sports, dancing, and artistic exercises. The program was a great success, and one of Boyd's apprentices, Viola Spolin, went on to run a similar Depression-era Works Progress Administration project meant to help various immigrant groups better connect. Spolin took Boyd's earlier ideas and focused them on theatrical performance games, hoping that group storytelling could be used to cross ethnic and cultural barriers, helping immigrant children and adults from completely different backgrounds to connect and find common ground.

Spolin later shared these "Theater Games," as she called them, with an improvisational theater company called the Compass

Players. One of its members was Del Close, who taught me. My "yes, and" grows *directly* out of games played at Hull House to teach people from different cultures how to work and play together. I studied the games when I was young and sought a performing career, but this project fits with improvisation's original purpose as much as any of the pure comedy that followed.

And pure comedy did follow. Several of the Compass Players went on to found The Second City, the world's most famous improv troupe, who still base much of their work on Spolin's games and principles. The Second City, in turn, would go on to influence many of the funniest minds in America ever since.*

Unfortunately for Chicago's West Side, after World War II, an influx of southern blacks was followed by white flight. Riots after the murder of Martin Luther King led to a full generation of disinvestment. Whole neighborhoods were run into the ground by ethnic tension.

In recent years, however, a nearby university has expanded, a new sports arena is attracting developers with ambitious plans, and white-collar Loop workers and latte-sipping "creatives" have begun edging in. It's not yet clear whether this will result in integrated growth or mere gentrification that simply pushes struggling residents to other areas, but at least the West Side is starting to grow again. And ACCION Chicago is a democratizing force, making opportunity and financing possible for anyone with a good idea, a

---

* Notable Second City alumni include dozens of cast members of *Saturday Night Live*, *SCTV*, *Kids in the Hall*, and numerous major comedy films, plus influential stand-up comedians like Robert Klein and David Steinberg, actors and directors like Alan Arkin and Ivan Reitman, and comedic talents as diverse as Tina Fey, Amy Sedaris, Stephen Colbert, and even Dan Castellaneta, the voice of Homer Simpson. A partial list is at en.wikipedia.org/wiki/List_of_alumni_of _the_Second_City. Moreover, many other great non–Second City–alumni of the last few decades, including former members of the Groundlings like Jimmy Fallon, Kristen Wiig, Conan O'Brien, and Will Farrell, were trained or directed by actors who were influenced by Viola Spolin's work.

strong work ethic, and some business sense. It was no surprise to learn that ACCION Chicago had historically shared some resources and clients with Hull House. This was entirely fitting.

Mary Fran's desk and shelves are bursting with books, reports, and souvenirs from decades of working full-time and volunteering with non-profits in housing, family services, and working with the homeless, all while raising two now-grown children. Her specialty is marketing and communications, so now that she's ACCION Chicago's VP of resource development, she can easily rattle off data about their clients' success and how it's measured.

So what's ACCION's batting average? "More than 90 percent of our clients are still in business two years later," she replies. The national average for all businesses, while not a perfect comparison because of size differences, is just 70 percent, she adds proudly.

Soon, the executive director of ACCION Chicago, Jonathan Brereton, plunks down next to me in jeans, a green T-shirt, and a gray hoodie. It's not conventional banker-wear, but Jonathan is hardly a conventional banker. He got the bug after hearing about microfinance in a college economics class and spending a summer volunteering in Haiti. After his senior year, he then worked in Liberia and Côte d'Ivoire, making him a veteran of three of the most challenging environments this planet offers.

Despite how much ACCION has accomplished, Jonathan is more focused on how much more he wants it to do: "So far, we've been able to help more than fifteen hundred clients, and we're growing at something like 30 percent a year. But here's the thing— by our estimates, there are at least thirty thousand potential clients out there we'd like to be serving. For all of our success, we still have to leave so much on the table . . . for the economy to grow, it needs small business to innovate and create new products and solutions. And it needs organizations like ours to stimulate and finance all that."

Mary Fran and I hop in a car to meet some of ACCION Chicago's clients. Our first stop is a small family taco shop on Chicago Avenue. I order the *pollo en mole*, sit down, and find myself shaking hands with Francisco, the owner, before the food even comes out. When he was just five years old, Francisco's mom moved from Mexico to the U.S., looking for work so she could give her family a better life—exactly the same reasons my parents moved to Cleveland. Now she works for her son, cooking and helping around the kitchen four or five days a week, while Francisco's wife works the front. Their daughter is readying herself for medical school, so every dollar counts.

How important has ACCION been to this family? Without the loans to smooth out leasing and other expenses, the business might have had to close entirely.

I later realize Francisco would be eyed with suspicion by a large portion of my fellow Americans, simply for where the birth lottery put him. But he is living the American Dream *exactly*—working hard to build a business, paying his bills and taxes, providing for his family, and getting ready to put his daughter through college, so she can have an even better life.

This is as American as we get.

Spencer stops by the ACCION office to meet me on his way up to Evanston. He has a small home repair and remodeling company called Creative Construction, and there are a hundred properties that need work up there. Winning the bidding on just five of them would easily fill his summer.

Spencer is in paint-daubed overalls and a spattered Angels baseball cap that he found on the corner of 35th and State. His beard is gray, and his fingers are thick and rough from labor, but his brain and his iPhone seem permanently in motion. He zips me through photos of his projects, his wife ("my chief operating officer," he fondly calls her, since she handles the contracts and receipts), and the check from his first $2,500 loan, which he used to buy tools, nails, ladders, and other basic essentials to start his business.

Spencer started with ACCION Chicago a year ago, following ten weeks of classes in entrepreneurship and business skills. "Everything they've given me for the class, I've applied to my business," he says, proudly. Now, after a year of sixteen-hour days, he's building up his credit score, expanding his skills, and sometimes even hiring people to help him on projects.

Asked how important his loan and training was to his business, Spencer responds with one word. It comes equipped with a long pause, a slow head turn, and extended eye contact for emphasis: *"Huge,"* he says.

This, too, is an American story, yet much like others we've heard all over the world. But once again, I think sadly about how many of our fellow Americans would regard Spencer unfairly. He's an ex-con—"formerly incarcerated" is the gentler term—and a recent graduate of the MERIT program that ACCION Chicago runs with the Jane Addams Hull House Association. MERIT was designed to help people who have paid their debt to society while they rebuild their lives with successful businesses—thus helping the entire community as well.

The language of rehabilitation is rarely spoken anymore in American media and political circles. Many of America's jails are now operated to deliver punishment, profit for contractors, and little other real purpose. Spencer, ACCION Chicago, and this particular American dream should give us hope for a better way.*

---

* Sadly, shortly before I finished this chapter, the Jane Addams Hull House Association, which had worked to build community on Chicago's West Side for more than a century, helping sixty thousand families as of 2012 with foster care, job training, and counseling, closed its doors. Hull House survived the Great

"I refuse to allow anyone to dictate my dreams for me," Kathleen says. There's no trace of bitterness in her voice, just dignity and grace.

"What she really suffers from is Eternal Optimist Disease," her grown son Keon chimes in, teasing Kathleen affectionately. The laughter they share is gentle, but you can also hear the hard times that prompted the need for eternal optimism.

Kathleen is the proprietor of KC's Academy, a private early childhood educational center on Chicago's North Side.* The school's curriculum includes programs for toddlers and preschoolers at any stage of social and emotional development, all individually planned to get kids the best start Kathleen can humanly give them. (One girl, for example, knew all of the alphabet at age three, so Kathleen immediately started a plan to move her into reading—and before long, she was years ahead of a "normal" school schedule.) "So often, the children are really waiting on the adults," Kathleen says. "It's my job to make sure they're not waiting—the *adults* are often the ones who need to keep up," she insists.

To keep things moving, children in her care are grouped by developmental readiness, not age, so they can learn from each other as well as the adults. Lessons are designed to include visual, auditory, and tactile cues, so that all forms of learning are stimulated. After a few proud stories of kids rapidly developing music and math skills, I ask how many students Kathleen is able to take on, hoping it's a large number. "Sixty-two," Kathleen replies. "But I'd love to find some way to share these programs with the government, get funding, find some way to scale it up."

None if it might be happening without her loans. "I don't know

---

Depression, riots, and two world wars. It could not, however, survive the current economic and political climate.

* The school's website is www.kcsacademy.com.

what I would have done without ACCION," she tells me, and Keon nods. Keon's loving expression toward his mother has a protective streak. I get the strong impression the struggle to stay afloat was a hard one. "ACCION gave me hope," Kathleen adds. "I'd approach banks, and they wouldn't work with us. But ACCION, they didn't make us feel like a failure—they'd just say, 'okay, this is what you *can* do.' So now we can, and we do," Kathleen adds with a smile.

We step into the main learning area for the kids, and suddenly I'm a giant stomping through the Land of the Tiny. Every single thing—the chairs, the tables, the posters on the walls, everything—has been scaled down and lowered to the eye level of a two-year old. The effect is magical. This is *their* world. And Kathleen's instructors always try to stimulate learning not by pushing a syllabus, but by following, reinforcing, and then expanding the kids' interests.

"Yes, and," Kathleen's teachers are saying, in other words.

Suddenly, as this dawns on me, I realize what neighborhood I'm in. It has changed in the last quarter-century, and I didn't recognize it because we approached from an unfamiliar direction, but the theater we passed up the street, and the train tracks right over there—*hey, wait a second.*

How did I not notice?

I'm only about a hundred yards from where CrossCurrents used to be. This is where I took classes with Del. This is where I used to go to a dank crappy bar and try to learn to "yes, and." This is right where my own story began.

I return the next day and look around. The spot where Cross-Currents once stood, and where my adult life found its first footing, is just now a vacant lot, mere gravel and parking behind the Belmont train station. Traffic grumbles by, and a departing train rattles the tracks in the distance. But as I peer through a chain-link fence, I can still hear the echoes of Del's booming baritone bouncing off walls that once stood here.

I feel my whole life spinning hard.

"Yes, and," created originally to help people from all over the world learn to connect, has now taken me from this Chicago neighborhood—at a time when I was scrambling for work, sleeping in the YMCA, and wondering if I would even have a life worth living at all—to nearly every corner of our planet and back again, eventually in an effort to help other people connect, too.

Del always taught that if you just trust and agree, eventually everything turns out to be interconnected, and in ways you would never expect.

Thank you, Del.

My own journey has completed its own full circle. But the final act of this story has yet to take place.

In most conventional Western tales, third acts tend to climax with a final, epic battle: the Rebel Alliance attacks the Death Star. The Avengers unite and fight off the bad guys. The forces of good, whoever they are, assemble to confront injustice despite overwhelming odds. Perhaps they band together at the foot of a fearsome castle, charge as one in a final great battle, brave great danger and doubt, and ultimately triumph. The nemesis—the dark, selfish mirror of their own heroic nature—is defeated.

This book cannot end with such a victory.

There is hunger. There is ignorance. One billion of our family lack even clean water to drink. Despite the unprecedented growth of connection in our world, hatred, greed, and fear remain abundant, even at home.

It can all appear massive and frightening. The odds seem against us. Only a fool would think of taking it all on alone.

But we're never alone.

In my own tiny lifetime, the unimaginable has happened all over the world, and with a frequency that seems almost reliable, if we stand back and look.

The Berlin Wall has fallen. The Cold War has ended. Apartheid has disintegrated, the Troubles are over, and dictatorships are disappearing, Europe and South America are now Unions, and peace treaties now govern nuclear tests, land mines, and chemical weapons.

None of this was remotely plausible when I was growing up in Ohio. Little of it could even be imagined until a few years before it happened, and sometimes not before the moment itself. All of it now seems almost inevitable.

In the developing world, life expectancy has risen by 40 percent. Infant mortality has been cut in half. So has illiteracy. Social enterprise is exploding, and inexpensive handsets and mobile banking will soon make it possible to communicate and trade with almost anyone, anywhere.

In the next twenty years, as humanity's first interconnected generation gradually comes into power, is it really naive to believe—no, expect—the world's interest in peace, health, and opportunity to reach a new high?

When that time arrives, it will surely sneak up, appear unexpectedly, and then seem to have been completely inevitable.

Picture it. Just for a moment.

On both sides of the road, almost to the horizon, on and on, in fields larger than we've ever imagined:

Hope.

The good guys are assembling, fighting every nemesis that we face. Join in.

If any issue you've seen here is pulling hard at your heart, I ask you to say "yes, and," even if you don't have any idea how to begin. Nelson Mandela didn't ask for permission. Nobody hired Gandhi to lead. You start when you start, where you start, with whatever you have. If poverty alleviation feels urgent to you, then it's urgent to you. Or take up political transparency, labor rights, hunger prevention, literacy and education, women's rights, press freedom, or whatever makes you feel most excited and passionate. Read, learn, engage.

Your love and your efforts should soon find a way to connect.

Whatever you choose, letting love guide your work really may be the best way to happiness. The work of Hungarian psychologist Mihaly Csikszentmihalyi (best not pronounced out loud, lest you risk cutting your tongue, but if you want to try, it's wonderfully close to "Me, Hi! Cheeks Sent Me, Hi") indicates that we feel happiest when we're fully involved in tasks we care deeply about, and most of all when the difficulty of the work and our deep emotional investment require us to become completely focused as our efforts and our passion intertwine. Our senses of time, place, and even self tend to disappear, and we develop a sense of well-being and connectedness.

Cheeks Sent Me, Hi calls this state "flow." Musicians, artists, surgeons, scientists, athletes, and anyone who has lost ten pleasant hours doing anything they love already know what he means, no words necessary. You might recognize this immediately. Some of your own best moments in life may feel exactly the same.

I've had that feeling myself many times during this project. I hope you've had it a few times while reading about it.

Helping others to build better lives really is the ultimate challenge. But if Me, Hi! Cheeks Sent Me, Hi is correct, we *need* bigger mountains to climb, better solutions to find, new worlds to explore, simply to be happy at all.

We win just by starting.

This world has great problems to solve.

This world has great opportunity for happiness.

In the meantime, while you're storming the fortress, changing the world, and giving your life greater meaning—or if you're not sure where your part really is yet, and you just feel like making some new friends—I'm sure you'd be welcome to pop over to Kiva and start your own International Bank of Emily, Kevin, Maria, or José. Or knock on the door over at Friends of Bob Harris, where hundreds of sweet, kind, funny people have now lent and re-lent more than $2.8 million, a figure likely to pass $3 million shortly after this book reaches print.* I'm honestly not sure how a number like that is even possible.

Then again, impossible things happen all the time.

As to choosing our specific paths, Mohandas Gandhi, the *mahatama* (Hindi for "great soul")—who has influenced seekers of freedom and equality from Martin Luther King to Cesar Chavez to Lech Wałęsa to the Dalai Lama to Aung San Suu Kyi—had some pretty good thoughts on that.

He wrote one in his diary shortly before his death. It's a seven-sentence talisman meant to be kept and remembered long after his departure.

In August 1947, as India gained independence from Britain, it was hardly a joyous moment for many. India's future was in some

---

*Just a reminder—you don't have to join any teams at all to make your first loan. Just go to the site and poke around until you're comfortable, same as I did. Read some of the profiles and see if you don't instantly start feeling connected to some faraway person's goals in life. Sit with it. Let it percolate. And when you finally decide to front somebody $25, I bet you'll just love it.

ways less certain than ever. The power struggle between Muslims and Hindus had become horrifically violent, and in the Noakhali district of East Bengal, Muslim massacres of Hindus had approached the level of genocide, with more than 5,000 deaths in the fall of 1946.

Gandhi had responded to the bloodshed by going to Noakhali and walking barefoot from village to village for nearly four months, sleeping in ordinary homes and huts, organizing prayer meetings, and appealing for peace literally door-to-door. Gandhi's presence calmed things considerably, but even he could not fully end the violence.

When full independence came on August 15, 1947, Delhi's political elite celebrated with fireworks and finery, but Gandhi was already on his way back to East Bengal, trying to save lives once again. Gandhi knew that his efforts were likely to fail, and that he might even soon be murdered—as, in the event, he was, just five months later, by a Hindu extremist.* But he was determined to try nonetheless.

Aware that his words would probably survive him, Gandhi now spoke directly in his diary to those with relative wealth in a world full of want—people much like you and me.

This, then, is Mohandas K. Gandhi's enduring advice on how to judge our choices in life, composed as he was nearing the end of his own:

I will give you a talisman. Whenever you are in doubt, or when the self becomes too much with you, apply the following test.

Recall the face of the poorest and the most helpless man whom you may have seen and ask yourself if the step you contemplate is going to be of any use to him.

---

* The site of Gandhi's murder was a large New Delhi home where he was a guest. (He was shot while addressing a large group on the grounds.) It's now a museum devoted to his life. The glasses through which Gandhi saw the world are still in his room. It is an interesting exercise to imagine seeing the world through them.

Will he be able to gain anything by it? Will it restore him to a control over his own life and destiny? In other words, will it lead to swaraj ["self-rule" or empowerment] *for the hungry and also spiritually starved millions of our countrymen?*

Then you will find your doubts and your self melt away.

Known as "Gandhi's Talisman," this suggestion is now literally etched in stone, six feet high and in multiple languages, at the entrance to his memorial and cremation site near the Yamuna River in Delhi.

From all of his lifetime of writings and wisdom, Gandhi's Talisman is the sole quote at the entrance.

The town where Gandhi wrote his talisman now lies in the Chittagong division of the nation of Bangladesh. Thirty years later, the division capital, the city of Chittagong, was where Muhammad Yunus was teaching when he first lent $27 to a group of bamboo-furniture makers in a nearby village.

Small world.

POSTSCRIPT

I N THE FINAL weeks before this book entered production, I sent a flurry of e-mails around the planet, hoping to provide the most recent updates possible on the lives of the people who have filled these travels, especially the clients. I have not heard back from everyone, so this is only a partial list, but I hope you will share my joy at learning that most of our new friends are doing well.

- Mohammed's motorcycle- and bike-repair shop in Rabat is humming along as always. There is no report on the ongoing popularity of fist-bumping, but I like to imagine it continues.

- In Bosnia, the Dinos are fine, and Tiro's sports bar is still in business. Tiro's favorite soccer team, Žejlo, is currently ranked 245th in the world, but they could still probably beat the Cleveland Browns. Ajla and Mirza are happily married, and she has become a dear friend. Zagorka is no longer buying and selling pigs, but the home renovation that the business helped to finance is complete, and she lives happily with her husband, son, and daughter-in-law. Admira is out of the clothing business, but Hajida is still raising and trading poultry, and I gather that the whole family is well, including Strawberry Shortcake. Nela now works for the United Nations Development Programme (UNDP), which helps Bosnians with everything from poverty reduction to infrastructure-creation to HIV prevention. UNDP recently melted down nearly two thousand weapons; the metal will be used to build railways.

- Sead's and Munira's furniture business now seems to have a Facebook page. Photos of their work are at www.facebook .com/samst.tapaciraninamjestaj/photos_stream. If shipping can be worked out, I bet you'll be tempted to buy some.

- In Kenya, Nat, Fred, Nathan, and Mosbei are all still with Juhudi Kilimo. Asset financing of livestock continues to be a successful model. Mosbei now works in Juhudi's new Kericho office, near the tea fields. The baby Nelly was carrying is now a beautiful two-year-old girl.

- The Bureti Self-Help Group for the Deaf was able to raise enough savings to begin to finance their own small businesses. Fred recently told me via Facebook that "some are even on second loans and doing great."

- Mercy's business has struggled with cash flow, but the family has other income and is doing fine. She no longer makes charcoal yogurt.

- JD, my (actually not-so-) wizened mentor, has moved to Washington, D.C., where he is now the Director of the Seal of Excellence in Poverty Outreach and Transformation (often called just the "Seal of Excellence"), a global initiative to recognize MFIs that are doing the most to help families lift themselves out of poverty. Any MFI displaying the Seal will have been certified by both the Smart Campaign and the Social Performance Task Force (see Additional Resources) as living up to their standards for client protection, outreach, and results.

- In India, Ram and Smita have moved Rang De's headquarters to Bangalore, India's answer to Silicon Valley. Rang De now has partners in fourteen Indian states, and they soon hope to be able to accept loan funds from anywhere on the planet.

- In Chicago, Francisco's restaurant is thriving, Spencer has expanded his home contracting business to include pest control, and Kathleen's early childhood learning center has grown to include a second location.

- In Beirut, Huseyn's salon now has write-ups on Beirut .com and the local equivalent of Yelp.

- When UN photographer Devra Berkowitz repeated my travels around the Philippines and Cambodia a year after my visits, all of the clients she met were still in business and doing well. Bo, the elderly morning-glory-cutter, still has a photo of the two of us together. Devra sent me a photo of Bo posed with our photo. This is one of my most cherished souvenirs.

- I gave Ganesh my e-mail address in the Kathmandu airport, but that was the last contact we had. I do not know what happened to him once he left Nepal. I hope someday to receive good news.

ACKNOWLEDGMENTS

On the morning of my forty-seventh birthday, I awoke in Kigali, Rwanda, with a sudden fever that I feared might be a sign of malaria. I spent most of that day at the hospital, feeling far from home but surprisingly comforted by thoughts of the sheer number of people whose goodwill had conspired to enable this project. Gratitude overwhelmed everything else. The fever turned out to be an ordinary flu, and I returned to my hotel having had a surprisingly lovely day, despite feeling physically like a bag of steamed rubbish. I've been eager to write this section ever since.

Jane Espenson, my best friend for more than a decade, has been a steady supply of optimism, laughter, and support.

Jennifer L. Pozner introduced me to Jeff Koyen, my *Forbes Traveler* editor, and later invited me to the convention where I first heard Premal Shah speak. Jenn has also been a constant source of encouragement and general upkeeping of chin.

The number of Kiva staff, interns, and volunteers who patiently shared time with me is impressive. The following list can't possibly be in the right order, it doesn't begin to express the affection I have grown to feel for nearly everyone here, and it surely leaves somebody out, with my horrified apologies in advance: thanks go to Matt Flannery, Premal Shah, Chelsa Bocci, JD Bergeron, Lisa Hogen, Bennett Grassano, Erin Geiger, Beth Kuenstler, Camille

Ricketts, Ali Price, Giovanna Masci, Maika Hemphill, Betsy Mc-Cormick, Claudine Emeott, Kathy Guis, Naomi Baer, Liz Nagle, Julie Ross, Sam Mankiewicz, Sam Birney, Noah Balmer, Amit Pansare, Austin Choi, Jonny Price, Paul Ericksen, Cissy Deluca, Mazen Khalife, Michelle Kreger, Noah Balmer, Rachael Caine, Devon Fisher, Fiona Ramsey, Kate Heryford, Katherine Woo, Martin Butt, Kevin O'Brien, Marc Dantona, Lisa Shah, Mollie Casper, Ben Elberger, Akash Trivedi, Jackie Bernstein, Neda Amidi, Ashley Heltne, Andy Kalinowitsch, J. J. Casas, Kelsey Dunn, Rachel Bigby, Sabrina Bozek, Jason Riggs, Brandon Smith, and Stacey Vice.

Numerous Kiva Fellows also generously shared their experiences, most notably including Sheethal Shobowale, Rachel Brooks, Peter Tashjian, Kimia Rafaat, Kevin Henderson, and Rebecca Corey.

As described, Jessica Jackley was the first microfinance person to express any confidence in my ability to pursue this project. Special thanks to Jess, of course.

The amazing management and staff at MFIs all over the world can never be thanked enough. My best wishes and appreciation to Driss Ezziani, Narimane El Maqri, and the kind folks of Al Amana in Rabat; Seida Saric, Nela Sinanović, Jasminka Malkić, and the welcoming staff at Žene Za Žene in Sarajevo and Tuzla; Nat Robinson, Albert Onchiri, Nelly Njoki, Fred Koskei, Nathan Ngetich, Mosbei Kipkosgei, Jacky Kosgei, Leah Chepkirui, Merylyn Ngeny, Caroline Cherono, and the gang at Juhudi Kilimo in Nairobi, Murang'a, and Litein; Jeffrey Lee and Daniel Ryumugabe at Urwego Opportunity Bank in Kigali; Victoria Kisyombe and Anganile Godfrey of SELFINA in Dar es Salaam; Corazon Henares, Suzette Gaston, Raymond Serios, Presy Alba, and the entire staff at the Negros Women for Tomorrow Foundation in Cebu, Mactan, and Compostela; Hout Ieng Tong, Toch Chaochek, Ou Kimthon, and Duch Bopha of Hatta Kaksekar Limited in Phnom Penh and Siem Reap; Urmila Shrestha of Business and Professional Women in Patan; Ramakrishna N. K., Smita Ram, Suresh, Arvind, Srihari, and the wonderful people at Rang De in Chennai; Alia Farhat and Nadine Mahdi of Al Majmoua in Beirut; Dalia Ouaidat, Mirna Nader, and Bassam Jardaly of Ameen, also in Beirut, whose hospitality I could not take advantage of, to this book's detriment; and Jonathan Brereton, Mary Fran Riley, Kyama Kitavi, and everyone at ACCION Chicago.

Not included in the book but much appreciated was an extensive visit with Marcos Antonio Hernandez of Fundación León 2000 in León, Nicaragua, who received me and a video crew graciously in February 2012 for a related project.

Translators not already thanked include Bouchra Mounib, Samuel Abdias, Amra Gadžo, Ajla Silajdzic-Dautbegovic, Christopher Muteti, Top Meng Nguon, and Saratt Prim. *Shukran, gracias, hvala, asante,* and *aw koohn.*

Interviewees who shared their time and insights include Paul Kagame, President of the Republic of Rwanda; Gina Harman, President and CEO of ACCION USA; Amy Klement, Vice President in charge of the Access to Capital Initiative of the Omidyar Foundation; Paul Polak, founder of International Development Enterprises; Susan Davis, President and CEO of BRAC USA; Matt Lonner, Manager of Global Partnerships and Programs for Chevron; Bill Abrams, President of TrickleUp.org; Amy Low, Chief Communications Officer at Landesa; Gregory Rake, Country Director of Landesa in India; David Roodman, Senior Fellow at the Center for Global Development; Robert Annibale, Global Director of Microfinance for Citi; Dean Baker, Co-Director of the Center for Economic Policy Research; Daryl Collins, Senior Associate at Bankable Frontier Associates; Ricardo Teran, Cofounder and Managing Director for Central America for Agora Partnerships; and Asad Mahmood, Managing Director of the Global Social Investment Funds at Deutsche Bank. Nearly everyone listed has a plate just as full as the busiest client in these pages, and I am grateful for their willingness to have their brains picked by a goofy newcomer.

Grzegorz Galusek of the Microfinance Centre in Warsaw kindly opened his doors, and Justyna Pytkowska offered all manner of assistance in research and data. I regret never having time to take full advantage of their resources. I would have loved to attend that conference in Uzbekistan.

Other friends and acquaintances who made introductions or other contributions include Michael Arnovitz, Esha Chhabra, Julie Lacouture, Zora O'Neill, Scott Jordan, Thom O'Leary, Ilan Arboleda, Tom Donahue, and Jason Perlman. Ongoing support and kindness have also been extended by Len Wein, Chris Valada, David Berman, Dan Perkins (aka Tom Tomorrow), Marie Javins, Mary Folley, Mike Gerber, Tal Vigderson, and Chris Angel. My sanity under stress, to the extent it exists, is due in large part to the devoted assistance of Deborah K. A key storytelling suggestion came from Joss Whedon, who needed ten seconds to solve a structural conundrum I'd been mulling over for weeks. Joss is a promising young talent.

A special thanks to Jono, my Australian brother, who has regularly facilitated my visits to Kiva in San Francisco by lending me his couch. To sleep on, not to carry around.

Fellow Kiva lenders who have encouraged, amused, consoled, and inspired me range at least into the hundreds, not even including more than a thousand self-described Friends of Bob Harris. Many, many names will be missing here, but Jonathon Stalls, J. B. Carioca, Good Dogg, Mambo Kitty, Christina, Katie, Birgit, Robyn, Philip, Amy, Julia, Valbona, Betty, Ed, Steven, Howard, the Jacobson Family—aw, geez, all of you, especially Aaron, who pushed me into having a team in the first place—thank you. Incidentally, at least twenty-two current members of Friends of Bob Harris are former *Jeopardy!* contestants. We should start a pub trivia team.

Others who have provided help, encouragement, networking, or just great company along the way include Dino Jusic, Amila Borealis, the other Dino, Josh Richards, Stacey Stevens, Brian

Emeott, Mark Winton, Patricia Hall, Alex Marqusee, Kirsty Henderson, Marc Epstein, Tom Allen, Dale Dawson, Milena Arciszewski, Sloane Davidson, Roshni Parikh, Lynn Molina, and Greg and Josette Blackman.

I only met Jessica (and eventually Kiva) thanks to my former TV agent Rick Ryba. Speaking of representatives, my literary agent Marly Rusoff and her partner Michael Radulescu are a treasure to know. Scott Wolfman works a phone the way Jimi Hendrix played guitar. (On his knees and not in his right mind.)

As you've read, much of my creative life has been influenced by Del Close and his longtime creative partner Charna Halpern, the godmother of the ImprovOlympic. To Charna and the CrossCurrents class of '86, my enduring appreciation.

Devra Berkowitz, UN photographer extraordinaire, traveled on her own dime to Cambodia and the Philippines to follow my tracks and photograph some of the clients I visited. A tiny sliver of her work appears here. I hope someday that it may all be displayed in a gallery. Her work is moving, often surprisingly joyful, and always humane.

While writing the manuscript, friends who were trusted early readers of various drafts include Cindy Sivak, Jon Schwarz, Sonia Borg, Bob Skir, Chase Masterson, and Lisa Klink. All were incredibly helpful. Cindy talked me out of opening the book with kopi luwak. For that alone, you owe her one, too.

Just as this project became full-time work, a total stranger named Teresa Jusino tweeted me out of the blue to ask if I needed an assistant. *Yes, and.* Teresa is the geek girl world champion and should be treated accordingly. Prior to Teresa, Donna Wilczek provided great assistance in the first months of the project.

My editor, George Gibson, has been unrelentingly patient, insightful, patient some more, and two helpings of great. He's also my publisher, so that all goes double. George's terrific team includes Laura Keefe, Marie Coolman, and Laura Gianino, the sharp marketing poobahs; Lea Beresford, a hardworking editor over at

Bloomsbury; production editor Nikki Baldauf, whose calm hand steadies the tiller; and in a wonderful coincidence, copyeditor India Cooper, whom I met ten years ago in the green room of the *Jeopardy!* "Million Dollar Masters" tournament at Radio City Music Hall. We've been friends ever since, but had gradually lost touch— until I saw her name on the comments in the copyedited draft. Small, amazing world.

My family cannot be thanked sufficiently, so I will scarcely even bother an attempt here. Tara, Joe, Jim, Vicky, other Jim (you two can fight over billing), Haley, Mom, and of course Dad wherever you are, you have my thanks every day of my life. You'll all get hugged like crazy soon enough. Including, I hope, Dad.

In all, more than two hundred people in twenty-one countries have cooperated with or made material contributions to this project.

My thanks and love to you all. I hope it is enough.

Abbreviations and Other Terms

AP	Andhra Pradesh, India (to avoid ambiguity, I do not abbreviate "Associated Press")
APR	Annual Percentage Rate
BBC	British Broadcasting System
BPW	Business and Professional Women
BRAC	No longer an acronym; it formerly stood for the Bangladesh Rehabilitation Assistance Committee
CARE	Cooperative for Assistance and Relief Everywhere (originally the UN International Children's Emergency Fund)
CDC	Centers for Disease Control
C-DOT	Centre for Development and Training
CEO	Chief Executive Officer
CIA	Central Intelligence Agency
CMEF	Council of Microfinance Equity Funds
CNBC	No longer an acronym; it formerly stood for the Consumer News and Business Channel
COO	Chief Operating Officer
DFI	Development Finance Institution
DHF	Dengue Hemorrhagic Fever
DMV	Department of Motor Vehicles
DRC	The Democratic Republic of the Congo (also commonly abbreviated DR Congo, and to be distinguished from its neighbor, the Republic of the Congo)
FAA	Federal Aviation Administration
FDIC	Federal Deposit Insurance Corporation
FBI	Federal Bureau of Investigation

FINCA	Foundation for International Community Assistance
FoBH	Friends of Bob Harris
FT	Forbes Traveler
GDP	Gross Domestic Product
GLBT	Gay, Lesbian, Bisexual, and Transgender
GM	General Motors
HKL	Hattha Kaksekar Limited ("Helping Hand for Farmers" in Khmer)
HP	Hewlett Packard
IMF	International Monetary Fund
IPO	Initial Public Offering
MBA	Masters of Business Administration
MDA	Muscular Dystrophy Association
MFI	MicroFinance Institution
MIT	Massachusetts Institute of Technology
M-PESA	Mobile Money (*pesa* is Swahili for "money")
M-KESHO	Mobile Tomorrow (*kesho* is Swahili for "tomorrow")
NGO	Non-Governmental Organization
NWTF	Negros Women for Tomorrow Foundation
NYPD	New York Police Department
PPP	Purchasing Power Parity
RCT	Randomized Controlled Trial
RPF	Rwandan Patriotic Front
RS	Republika Srpska (Republic of Serbia)
SELFINA	Sero Lease and Finance Limited
SIM	Subscriber Identity Module
SKS	Swayam Krishi Sangam (Hindi for "self-cultivation society") in the name of SKS Microfinance. The longer form is virtually never used.
SME	Small and Medium Enterprise
TBD	To Be Determined
UAE	United Arab Emirates
UK	United Kingdom
UN	United Nations
UNDP	United Nations Development Programme
UN-HABITAT	United Nations Human Settlements Programme
UNICEF	United Nations Children's Fund
US	United States
USB	Universal Serial Bus
USC	University of Southern California
USD	U.S. Dollar
WHO	World Health Organization
YMCA	Young Men's Christian Association

Sources, Recommended Reading, and Additional Resources

AUTHOR'S NOTES

Page xi

Charity Navigator's rating page for Kiva is at www.charitynavigator.org
/index.cfm?bay=search.summary&orgid=12978.

As this book goes to press, Charity Navigator puts Kiva in the 96th per-
centile in its size category (79th out of 2,025 medium-sized charities, mean-
ing those with annual overall expenses between $3.5 and $13.5 million).
Disregarding size, Kiva has a higher overall rating than the American Cancer
Society, the American Red Cross, CARE, Doctors Without Borders USA,
the National Resources Defense Council, the Nature Conservancy, Oxfam
America, Save the Children, the Smithsonian Institution, the U.S. Fund for
UNICEF, Volunteers for America, World Vision, and the World Wildlife
Fund.

CHAPTER ONE — THE FRENCH RIVIERA, DUBAI, AND THE WORLD

Page 11

"London's 10 Best Hotels" and "Italy's 25 Best Hotels," examples of my
Forbes Traveler pieces syndicated elsewhere, are at ehotelier.com/hospitality
-news/item.php?id=A14809_0_11_0_M and www.usatoday.com/travel/hotels
/2008-11-10-best-italian-hotels-forbes_N.htm.

Page 12

Two of the three pieces from that day survive online at web.archive.org /web/20081025050326/http://www.forbestraveler.com/hotel-review/europe /hotel-de-la-cite.html and web.archive.org/web/20081018181253/http://www .forbestraveler.com/hotel-review/europe/hotel-hermitage.html. The third hotel was the Hôtel d'Europe. There are no bylines, since the editors preferred the FT400 to emanate from a sort of editorial omniscience, but the credits are at web.archive.org/web/20081230085407/http://www.forbes traveler.com/forbes400/methodology. You can recognize my hand in the specific articles from compulsive overuse of dashes and parentheses—as if I'm incapable of breaking thoughts into simpler units (much like this very sentence)—and an average sentence length of twenty-four words.

Page 14

For economic data, see www.cia.gov/library/publications/the-world-fact book/rankorder/2004rank.html. This is current despite the confusing URL; "2004" is a page number, not a year.

Page 21

"Dubai Sinking—No, for Real" by Tiernan Ray, *Barron's* online, December 9, 2009, blogs.barrons.com/stockstowatchtoday/2009/12/09/dubai-sinking -no-for-real. Dubai authorities dispute the claim, pointing out that if the island is really sinking, then pipes, masonry, and windows should start to crack and fail. This may not have been the most reassuring argument.

"The World Is Sinking: Dubai Islands 'Falling into the Sea'" by Richard Spencer, *Telegraph*, January 10, 2011, www.telegraph.co.uk/news/worldnews /middleeast/dubai/8271643/The-World-is-sinking-Dubai-islands-falling-into -the-sea.html.

Page 22

A look at the expense and impact of bed nets in the fight against malaria:

My back-of-the-envelope estimate underestimated mortality and the price of bed nets, while overestimating bed net effectiveness, errors that roughly balanced each other, resulting in what turned out to be a conservative estimate.

The latest math, as of fall 2012: a middle estimate of Africa's annual malaria toll, compromising between figures offered by the British medical journal *The Lancet* and the WHO, is about 835,000. Bed nets lower mortality by 20 percent, yielding perhaps 167,000 African lives saved annually. In the five and a half years since The World was announced, any $14 billion might have saved between nine hundred thousand and one million lives. More than half of the toll would have been younger than five years old.

Cost of bed nets: my estimate of cost was high. Nothing But Nets (www .nothingbutnets.net), for example, asks for $10, but this includes delivery. Bed Nets for Children (www.cdcfoundation.org/bednets) asks for only $5.

Current mortality figures come from "Global Malaria Mortality Between 1980 and 2010: A Systematic Analysis" by Prof. Christopher J. L. Murray et al., The Lancet, February 4, 2012, online at www.thelancet.com/journals/lancet /article/PIIS0140-6736%2812%2960034-8/fulltext. This study places the 2010 African toll from malaria at between 848,000 and 1.59 million. This is essentially twice WHO estimates that place the annual African malarial death toll at between 483,000 and 816,000. Conventional estimates probably under-count the total due to a lack of reporting in rural areas that are hit hardest. The WHO report is at www.who.int/features/factfiles/malaria/en/index.html.

For more on the history of malaria's massive human cost, see The Fever: How Malaria Has Ruled Humankind for 500,000 Years by Sonia Shah (New York: Farrar, Straus & Giroux, 2012) and Shah's specific op-ed "In Africa, Anti-Malaria Mosquito Nets Go Unused by Recipients," published in the Los Angeles Times, May 2, 2010, at articles.latimes.com/2010/may/02/opinion/la-oe-shah-20100502. She has also done a densely informative Q&A at www.freako nomics.com/2010/09/02/the-malaria-wars-sonia-shah-answers-your-malaria -questions.

Finally, a caveat: this was just a thought exercise, an illustration of how much Dubai's three hundred piles of sand cost, nothing more. In the real world, throwing around a billion free bed nets could make them seem valueless, diminishing their adoption and effectiveness. Human economic behavior is not impossible to predict, but it is resistant to being modeled purely with techniques from physics and other sciences that study uncon-scious objects with no ability to change their definition of self-advantage.

Page 24

United States Department of State Bureau of Democracy, Human Rights, and Labor, 2007 Country Report on Human Rights Practices, United Arab Emirates. Accessible online at www.state.gov/g/drl/rls/hrrpt/2007/100608 .htm.

The 2012 version of the analogous report can be found at www.state .gov/j/tip/rls/tiprpt/2012/192368.htm. (Scroll down; the page covers mul-tiple countries in alphabetical order.) Sadly, the report still finds that "the

United Arab Emirates (UAE) is a destination, and to a lesser extent tran-
sit, transit country for men and women, predominantly from South and
Southeast Asia, who are subjected to forced labor and forced prostitution.
Migrant workers, who comprise more than 90 percent of the UAE's private
sector workforce, are recruited from India, Pakistan, Bangladesh, Nepal, Sri
Lanka, Indonesia, Ethiopia, Eritrea, China, Thailand, Korea, Afghanistan,
Iran, and the Philippines . . . Men from India, Sri Lanka, Bangladesh, Paki-
stan, and Nepal are drawn to the UAE for work in the construction sector;
some are subjected to conditions of forced labor, including debt bondage as
they struggle to pay off debts for recruitment fees . . . Some women from
Eastern Europe, Central Asia, Southeast Asia, the Far East, East Africa, Iraq,
Iran, and Morocco are subjected to forced prostitution in the UAE."

See also "The United Arab Emirates: Selling Immigrants into Sex Slavery" by Raid Rafei, *Los Angeles Times*, March 10, 2008, latimesblogs.latimes
.com/babylonbeyond/2008/03/united-arab-e-1.html.

"The Countertraffickers" by William Finnegan, *New Yorker*, May 5, 2008,
www.newyorker.com/reporting/2008/05/05/080505fa_fact_finnegan.

"Trafficking Tough to Tame in Rich Gulf States" by Lin Noueihed, Reuters, February 23, 2008, www.reuters.com/article/2008/02/24/us-dubai
-women-trafficking-idUSL2090616420080224.

Page 29

The November 2006 Human Rights Watch report *Building Towers, Cheat-
ing Workers: Exploitation of Migrant Construction Workers in the United Arab
Emirates*, complete with extensive photographs, is at www.hrw.org/reports
/2006/uae1106/uae1106web.pdf.

See also "The Dark Side of Dubai" by Johann Hari, *Independent*, April 7,
2009, online at www.independent.co.uk/voices/commentators/johann-hari
/the-dark-side-of-dubai-1664368.html.

Recommended further reading
Guns, Germs, and Steel: The Fates of Human Societies by Jared Diamond. New
York: W. W. Norton, 1997.

A Pulitzer Prize–winning look at how geography, climate, and other environmental factors influenced the growth of whole human civilizations,
favoring the peoples of Eurasian temperate zones while condemning many
others to centuries of struggle. The birth lottery, in my understanding at
least, has affected the rise and fall of entire civilizations.

CHAPTER TWO — SINGAPORE, BALI, AND BEIJING

Page 33

For Qatar's immigrant population, see "The Plight of Qatar's Migrant Workers," Al Jazeera report of June 14, 2012, at www.aljazeera.com/pro grammes/insidestory/2012/06/201261472812737158.html.

Page 34

Sexiest flight attendants: see www.businesstravelshow.com/en/press /pressreleases/11-02-07/VIRGIN_ATLANTIC_RED_HOTTIES_VOTED _BEST_LOOKING_CABIN_CREW.aspx. Those ALL CAPS look pretty creepy to me, too.

Page 35

See the 2011 Mercer Quality of Living Survey, for example, complied by a major human resources consultancy, at www.mercer.com/press-releases /quality-of-living-report-2011#City-Rankings. Singapore comes in twenty-fifth, four notches ahead of Honolulu, the top-rated American city. Los Angeles, where I'm writing this, doesn't make the top fifty. Hmph. If you're rich, you might prefer the Citi Private Bank Wealth Report at www .thewealthreport.net/The-Wealth-Report-2012.pdf, where Singapore comes in 2nd place worldwide in quality of life for billionaires (see p. 63 of the report), just behind London and ahead of New York.

Page 41

"The Myth of Asia's Economic Miracle" by Paul Krugman, *Foreign Affairs*, November/December 1994, www.foreignaffairs.com/articles/50550/paul -krugman/the-myth-of-asias-miracle.

Krugman argued that the "Asian Tigers" had grown via increases in basic inputs that have natural limits (e.g., you can't increase literacy past 100 percent). A bit controversial at the time but clearly correct in retrospect.

Page 43

My last *Forbes Traveler* review in Beijing: web.archive.org/web/200810210437 25/http://www.forbestraveler.com/hotel-review/asia/st-regis-hotel-beijing.html.

Page 44

"Tiananmen Killings: Were the Media Right?" by James Miles, BBC website, news.bbc.co.uk/2/hi/8057762.stm, June 2, 2009.

Miles, the BBC's reporter on the scene in 1989, discusses the implications and circumstances of the erroneous original reporting. The report stops short of a full mea culpa, and to my mind rightly so—he and other international reporters in Beijing at the time displayed great courage just by being there and trying to report the truth.

See also "Wikileaks: No Bloodshed Inside Tiananmen Square, Cables Claim" by Malcolm Moore, *Telegraph* (UK), June 4, 2011, www.telegraph.co .uk/news/worldnews/wikileaks/8555142/Wikileaks-no-bloodshed-inside -Tiananmen-Square-cables-claim.html.

Page 50

Why development projects fail: www.ictworks.org/news/2011/01/05/top -7-reasons-why-most-ict4d-projects-fail.

Recommended further reading
The Bottom Billion: Why the Poorest Countries Are Falling Behind and What Can Be Done About It by Paul Collier. New York: Oxford University Press, 2007. The author identifies four key traps for developing countries—one of which, to the great difficulty of Rwanda (see Chapter Eight), is being landlocked with unstable neighbors.

CHAPTER THREE — CHICAGO, FIJI, AND BROADWAY

Page 55

The "10 Indicators" are at www.grameen-info.org/index.php?option=com _content&task=view&id=23&Itemid=126. The "16 Decisions" are at www .grameen-info.org/index.php?option=com_content&task=view&id=22 &Itemid=109. The book described in this passage is *Creating a World Without Poverty: Social Business and the Future of Capitalism* by Muhammad Yunus. New York: PublicAffairs, 2007. Yunus's other books include *Banker to the Poor: Micro-Lending and the Battle Against World Poverty* (1999) and *Building Social Business: The New Kind of Capitalism that Serves Humanity's Most Pressing Needs* (2010), both published in New York by PublicAffairs.

Page 56

The 2003 working paper *Does Micro-credit Empower Women: Evidence from Bangladesh* by Mark M. Pitt, Shahidur R. Khandker, and Jennifer Cartwright is online at go.worldbank.org/0LC0QB6TD0.

The math on Kiva v. the S&P 500: when Kiva launched in October 2005, the S&P 500 was at 1248. When I did this calculation in July 2008, 33 months later, it had fallen to 1166. Given Kiva's then-current figures—an average loan duration of 10 months and a repayment rate of 99.73 percent—computed over those 33 months, if the S&P 500 index had the same return as Kiva loans, it would have only fallen to 1237. Calculating overall return, the difference is about six percentage points. Even using Grameen's reported 98 percent repayment rate, the result would have been 1167, beating the S&P by a hair. This should be a highly unusual circumstance, occurring as it did in a time period just before the crisis of late 2008. Presented here for entertainment value only.

Page 57

Translations vary; this one is from www.myjewishlearning.com/practices /Ethics/Tzedakah_Charity/Requirements/Preventing_Dependency.shtml.

Page 58

The Funniest One in the Room: The Lives and Legends of Del Close by Kim Howard Johnson. Chicago: Chicago Review Press, 2008.

Howard and I have been friends since 1985, when he was a member of the "house" team in Del's improv shows. I was even his lifeline on *Who Wants to Be a Millionaire* once, which you can find on YouTube if you're curious. Howard came to know Del very well and has written easily the best portrait of the man in print.

Page 59

See www.imdb.com/title/tt1032838. Working in Mexico City was fun— all fistfights, gunfire, sexy people, car chases—and the show was pretty cool, too. Useful phrases if you work on a *telenovela*: *tus ropas deben ser más apretadas* ("your clothing should be tighter"), *mira en la distancia media en silencio mientras la música se hace más fuerte* ("look silently into the middle distance while the music gets louder"), and *faneca, como si tus labios se han picados por diez mil abejas* ("pout, as if your lips have been stung by ten thousand bees"). Incidentally, I couldn't speak any Spanish at all at first, and I still don't speak it well, but that was surely no reason to say no. I like to think Del would be proud.

Page 60

MDA's support of research and care is supremely praiseworthy, but they also relied heavily on the "poster child" as a fundraising tool for more than forty years, 1952–93. As the disability rights movement grew in the 1990s, many MD patients, including several former poster children themselves, sharply criticized Jerry Lewis, the telethon, and MDA for spreading a false perception of people with disabilities as infantilized, helpless, and less than whole. For examples, see reunifygally.wordpress.com/2009/01/11/people-with-muscular-dystrophy-protesting-pity.

Page 61

For a contrarian view of Live Aid, see *Famine and Foreigners: Ethiopia Since Live Aid* by Peter Gill. Oxford: Oxford University Press, 2010. See also "Did Live Aid Do More Harm Than Good?" by David Rieff, *Guardian*, June 23, 2005, www.guardian.co.uk/world/2005/jun/24/g8.debtrelief.

More generally, for a notable critique of simple aid as an inherent good, one may consider *Dead Aid: Why Aid Is Not Working and How There Is a Better Way for Africa* by Dambisa Moyo. New York: Farrar, Straus & Giroux, 2009.

Page 64

The Great Escapade ticket, which I've done twice now and highly recommend: www.thegreatescapade.com.

Page 66

"Dengue Sparks Paraguay Emergency," BBC News report, March 2, 2007, news.bbc.co.uk/2/hi/americas/6407287.stm.

The CDC website on dengue is www.cdc.gov/dengue. The Dengue Map at www.healthmap.org/dengue/index.php tracks all global outbreaks as they happen.

For more on the climate-change-driven spread of tropical diseases into America, see www.nytimes.com/gwire/2010/06/28/28greenwire-dengue-re-emerges-in-us-spurring-race-for-vacc-14067.html and www.nytimes.com/2012/08/19/opinion/sunday/tropical-diseases-the-new-plague-of-poverty.html. It is sadly possible that this book's description of dengue will one day no longer be necessary for many Americans.

Page 68

For the 2009 version of Kiva's statement on pre-disbursals, see web.archive.org/web/20090212173926/http://kiva.org/app.php?page=help&action=entrepreneurSummary#DisbursalDate.

Roodman's blog post on pre-disbursals, where you can also find Flannery's response, is at blogs.cgdev.org/open_book/2009/10/kiva-is-not-quite-what-it-seems.php. The post was not nearly as scathing as its headline, admitting that "the way Kiva works is hidden in plain sight" and "what Kiva does behind the scenes is what it *should* do" [emphasis Roodman's]. Kiva

CEO Matt Flannery's response agreed to change an oversimplified diagram on the Kiva site, and noted that Roodman had incorrectly claimed that Kiva charged MFIs 2 percent interest, when in fact Kiva charges no interest at all. Roodman corrected his screw-up, too, and all was square—except for anyone who may have only seen the overstated headline condemning Kiva *itself*, as a whole, on the basis of one issue, lacking any evidence of ill intent or action. I am certain that Roodman had no ill intent, either—it's abundantly clear from his body of work that his primary concern is the well-being of clients—but the headline was so general that *any* kind of corruption or wrongdoing could be assumed. Had the headline been less sensational, perhaps *Many Kiva Users Don't Realize the Loans Are Pre-Disbursed*, or even the more aggressive *Kiva Users' Relationship with Clients Not Quite What It Seems*, the issue might have been addressed with less fooferah.

Two years later, the issue was resurrected by Hugh Sinclair, a former employee of Triple Jump (a major microfinance investment firm), in *Confessions of a Microfinance Heretic: How Microlending Lost Its Way and Betrayed the Poor* (San Francisco: Bennett-Koehler, 2012). The author principally indicts the reluctance of several major players in the microfinance industry to acknowledge when actual frauds have occurred, notably regarding LAPO in Nigeria (see the notes for Page 245, below, on pages 382–83). Much of the LAPO-related critique seems worthwhile to my eyes. However, referring to one notorious MFI on forty-five pages of a 249-page book might imply a narrow argument if one seeks—in the title no less—to indict an entire industry serving more than one hundred million people.

As to pre-disbursals, the author admits that it's the only practical way Kiva can work: "The alternative would be that [a client] would be knocking on the door of the MFI each day asking if the Kivans had raised the money yet." (This is on page 170.) The author nonetheless includes this in what seems to be an attempted whistle-blowing on Kiva that gets many basic facts wrong—misidentifying the CEO, for example—and sometimes draws poor conclusions from its own errors. For example, it overstates the typical delay between a loan's pre-disbursal and appearance online as "months" (the real figure is rarely more than a few weeks). It then reasons that loans may often default before posting, a near-impossibility given repayment terms of at least four months. (They could conceivably become delinquent; this is no minor difference.) It also proposes that Kiva is knee-deep in cash hidden from the lender base, despite the fact that it's a non-profit, its numbers are public (that's how the writer could attempt his calculations), and the relatively modest compensation of the entire senior

staff is completely disclosed, so even if there were some huge hidden surplus, nobody's getting rich. Jessica Jackley, one of Kiva's prime movers, visible enough to have appeared on *Oprah* and Best Buy television ads, is even
called "Jessica Jackson" in both the text and the index. This speaks for itself.

Page 73
    Matt Flannery's recounting of Kiva's origin is in "Kiva and the Birth of
Person-to-Person Microfinance" in *Innovations*, Winter/Spring 2007, online
at media.kiva.org/INNOV0201_flannery_kiva.pdf.

Page 75
    Matt's follow-up article, "Kiva at Four" appeared in *Innovations*, special
Skoll World Forum issue of 2009, online at media.kiva.org/INNOV
-SKOLL-2009_flannery.pdf.

CHAPTER FOUR — THE MISSION

Recommended further reading
For more on the Kiva Fellows, a fascinating place to start is at fellowsblog
.kiva.org, a group blog recounting many of their experiences in the field—
good and bad—as they happen.

CHAPTER FIVE — THE SACRED VALLEY OF THE INCAS

Page 105
    A good place to start is *The Shining Path of Peru*, edited by David Scott
Palmer. New York: St. Martin's Press, 1994. A readable collection of academic
articles on the circumstances, tactics, and philosophy (if it deserves the
term) of an influential revolutionary movement. A few of the essays express
enough compassion for Shining Path's impoverished recruits to be mistaken
for support, but this would be like accusing Vincent Bugliosi of supporting
Charles Manson just for trying to comprehend his actions.

Recommended further viewing
The Fall of Fujimori, documentary film produced and directed by Ellen Perry.
Los Angeles: Stardust Pictures, 2005. A brilliant look at the decade of rule
by President Alberto Fujimori, the autocratic author of the auto-coup, a

man who defeated two national rebellions and then himself. The archival footage is fascinating.

CHAPTER SIX — WELCOME TO SARAJEVO

Page 138

The data on Bosnian borrowers comes from the Warsaw-based Microfinance Centre: www.mfc.org.pl/en/programs/overindebtedness-microfinance-clients.

Bosnia's boom and bust are examined in *Due Diligence: An Impertinent Inquiry into Microfinance* by David Roodman. Washington, DC: Center for Global Development, 2011. This summary of the microfinance world was created in an admirably open way: Roodman shared drafts of each chapter on his blog (blogs.cgdev.org/open_book) as they were being written throughout 2011.

The headline chosen in questioning Kiva's pre-disbursal policy should be seen as only a minor glitch in what looks to my eyes like an extremely valuable body of work.

Page 139

Bosnia's Microfinance Meltdown by Milford Bateman, Dean Sinković, and Marinko Škare. Paper presented to the American Economics Association Annual Conference, Chicago, 2012, available at www.microfinancegateway.org/gm/document-1.9.56293/Bosnia_Meltdown.pdf.

The authors argue that the managers of some Bosnian MFIs reached the level of "control fraud"—consciously using the architecture of banking to swindle the poor. Their case is compelling, illustrating criminal behavior that well-crafted best practices and regulation must circumvent. No conclusion should be drawn, however, that this behavior is symptomatic of microlending in general. Western bankers and stock manipulators have also committed fraud, but no one would find it logical to condemn all mortgages or stock trading per se. I suggest that properly viewed, this paper provides a strong defense of ethical lenders: yes, Bosnia had a microlending crisis—*as the result of criminal behavior*—not solely due to any inherent flaw in microlending itself.

Growth and Vulnerabilities in Microfinance, a February 2010 report of the Consultative Group to Assist the Poor by Greg Chen, Stephen Rasmussen, and Xavier Reille is at www.cgap.org/p/site/c/template.rc/1.9.42393.

Page 142

Of the horrors committed in Bosnia, one example of far too many is the conviction of military policeman Dragan Zelenović, summarized at www .icty.org/x/cases/zelenovic/cis/en/cis_zelenovic_en.pdf. A full list of cases, with bad guys on all sides, is at www.icty.org/action/cases/4.

Recommended further reading
Bosnia: A Short History by Noel Malcolm. London: Macmillan, 1994.

CHAPTER SEVEN — THE GREAT RIFT VALLEY AND NAIROBI

Page 157

To sort for Rose Hill's census data, see www.factfinder2.census.gov and poke around under "Geographies."

Page 161

Crime in Nairobi: Results of a Citywide Victim Survey, a report of UN-HABITAT, September 2002, online in pdf form at www.unhabitat.org /pmss/getElectronicVersion.asp?nr=1693&alt=1+Crime+in+Nairobi:+Results +of+a+Citywide+Victim+Survey.

The then-current advice of the UN Office at Nairobi is archived at web .archive.org/web/20100906012355/http://www.unon.org/unoncomplex /security_advice.php.

Transparency International's 2011 Corruption Perceptions Index is at cpi.transparency.org/cpi2011/results.

Page 170

"Drained of Life" by Ochieng Ogodo and John Vidal, *Guardian*, February 13, 2007, www.guardian.co.uk/society/2007/feb/14/kenya.conservation.

Lake Naivasha, 2008 report of Food and Water Watch, online at www .canadians.org/water/documents/NaivashaReport08.pdf.

Page 171

See *Out of Africa* by Isak Dinesen (pseudonym of Baroness Karen Blixen). New York: Modern Library, 1992. Originally published in 1937.

More than beautifully written, it's also a valuable historical document, illuminating (among much else) the way that even well-meaning colonists struggled to conceive that Africa might rightly belong to Africans.

For more on Leopold II, see *King Leopold's Ghost* by Adam Hochschild. Boston: Houghton Mifflin Harcourt, 1998. The cited statistic—millions of dead Africans—in the wake of Leopold's rule over central Africa doesn't begin to communicate the inhumanity of its methods.

Page 175

"Nowhere People" by Becky Palstrom, *Brink* magazine online, May 8, 2011, brinkmag.org/?p=134.

Page 176

For more, you might start with *The Economics of M-PESA* by William Jack and Tavneet Suri, joint paper published August 2010, available at www .mit.edu/~tavneet/M-PESA.pdf. See also *The Performance and Impact of M-PESA*, a PowerPoint presentation by the same authors, at technology.cgap.org /technologyblog/wp-content/uploads/2009/10/fsd_june2009_caroline_pulver .pdf.

Also see "M-PESA: Transforming Millions of Lives" by Mohit Agrawal, January 19, 2010, online at www.telecomcircle.com/2010/01/m-pesa. See also "Socio-Economic Benefits of Mobile Money Transfer" by the same author, January 27, 2010, at www.telecomcircle.com/2010/01/benefits-of-mobile -money-transfer.

Page 177

Information and Communications for Development 2012—Maximizing Mobile, World Bank report, July 2012, downloadable at go.worldbank. org/oJ2CTQTYP0.

Page 179

"Mobile Banking Closes Poverty Gap" by Jane Wakefield, BBC News: Technology, May 28, 2010, online at www.bbc.co.uk/news/10156667.

On inflation, see the alarmingly titled "How M-PESA Disrupts Entire Economies" by Will Mutua, March 6, 2012, citing Africa Development Bank research, at memeburn.com/2012/03/how-m-pesa-disrupts-entire-economies. This side effect seems worth considerable note.

CHAPTER EIGHT — RWANDA

Page 188
English-Kinyarwanda Phrasebook for Tourists by Geoffrey Rugege. Kampala:
Fountain Publishers, 2010.

Page 190
For more on the case of Laurent Bucyibaruta, see The Hague Justice Por-
tal page at www.haguejusticeportal.net/index.php?id=10676.

Page 193
The 2010 figures for annual per capita GDP adjusted for PPP for Rwanda
are at web.archive.org/web/20110629165416/https://www.cia.gov/library
/publications/the-world-factbook/rankorder/2004rank.html. Since my visit,
Rwanda's estimate has slightly improved, passing Burma in the most current
rankings.

Page 200
Yunus has written that the maximum allowable interest rate should be no
more than 15 percent above the cost of the money to the bank, and advocates
for the number to be lower when possible. See "Sacrificing Microcredit for
Megaprofits" by Muhammad Yunus in the *New York Times*, January 14, 2011.

Recommended further reading
*We Wish to Inform You That Tomorrow We Will Be Killed with Our Families:
Stories from Rwanda* by Philip Gourevitch. New York: Picador, 1998.
   Shake Hands with the Devil: The Failure of Humanity in Rwanda by Lt. Gen.
Roméo Dallaire. New York: Avalon, 2003.
   Collapse: How Societies Choose to Fail or Succeed by Jared Diamond. New York:
Viking Penguin, revised edition, 2005. Chapter 10 focuses entirely on Rwanda.
   Machete Season: The Killers in Rwanda Speak by Jean Hatzfeld. New York:
Picador, 2005.
   Life Laid Bare: The Survivors in Rwanda Speak by Jean Hatzfeld. New York:
Other Press, 2007.
   A Thousand Hills: Rwanda's Rebirth and the Man Who Dreamed It by Stephen
Kinzer. New York: John Wiley & Sons, 2008.
   The Antelope's Strategy: Living in Rwanda After the Genocide by Jean Hatzfeld.
New York: Picador, 2009.
   God Sleeps in Rwanda: A Journey of Transformation by Joseph Sebaranzi.

New York: Atria Books, 2009. The memoir of a former president of Parliament who fled in fear of imprisonment or worse.

CHAPTER NINE — DAR ES SALAAM, ANDHRA PRADESH, AND A WALK TO THE SEA

Page 220

U.S. banking figures 2008–10 are from the FDIC: www.fdic.gov/bank /historical/bank/2008, www.fdic.gov/bank/historical/bank/2009, and www .fdic.gov/bank/historical/bank/2010.

"Bank Closings Tilt Toward Poor Areas" by Nelson D. Schwartz, *New York Times*, February 22, 2011, online at www.nytimes.com/2011/02/23/busi ness/23banks.html.

Page 223

"Is There a Microfinance Bubble in South India?" by Daniel Rozas, *Microfinance Focus*, November 17, 2009, online at www.microfinancefocus .com/news/2009/11/17/opinion-microfinance-bubble-south-india.

Page 224

"Lender's Own Probe Links It to Suicides" by Erika Kinetz, Associated Press, February 24, 2012, online at finance.yahoo.com/news/ap-impact -lenders-own-probe-080122405.html.

"Lunch with BS: Vikram Akula, SKS Microfinance" by Kanika Datta, *Business Standard*, October 12, 2010, online at www.business-standard.com /india/news/lunchbs-vikram-akula-sks-microfinance/411108.

Page 225

See "Banks Making Big Profits from Tiny Loans" by Neil MacFarquhar, *New York Times*, April 13, 2011, at www.nytimes.com/2010/04/14/world/14mi crofinance.html; "Compartamos: From Non-profit to Profit," *Bloomberg Businessweek*, December 12, 2007, at www.businessweek.com/stories/2007-12-12 /compartamos-from-nonprofit-to-profit; and "Yunus Blasts Compartamos," *Business Week*, December 12, 2007, at www.businessweek.com/stories/2007 -12-12/online-extra-yunus-blasts-compartamos.

For Yunus decrying "loan sharks" in print, see "Sacrificing Microcredit for Megaprofits" by Muhammad Yunus in the *New York Times*, January 14, 2011, www.nytimes.com/2011/01/15/opinion/15yunus.html. Speaking in public, see

"Profit-Focused MFIs Are Loan Sharks: Yunus," staff reporting with no byline in the *Times of India*, February 11, 2011, online at articles.timesofindia.india-times.com/2011-02-21/india-business/28618681_1_mfi-sector-vikram-akula-muhammad-yunus.

For a spirited confrontation between Yunus and Akula at the 2010 Clinton Global Initiative, see www.clintonglobalinitiative.org/ourmeetings/2010/meeting_annual_multimedia_player.asp?id=83&Section=Our Meetings&PageTitle=Multimedia.

Page 226

On farmer suicides as an ongoing tragedy in Andhra Pradesh both before and after the crisis, see all of the following:

"Seeds of Suicide," PBS *Frontline* report of July 26, 2005, www.pbs.org/frontlineworld/rough/2005/07/seeds_of_suicid.html.

"Farm Suicides Worse After 2001—Study" by P. Sainath in the *Hindu*, November 13, 2007, www.hindu.com/2007/11/13/stories/2007111352250900.htm.

"17,060 Farm Suicides in One Year" by P. Sainath in the *Hindu*, January 31, 2008, reporting 2607 farmer suicides in AP in 2006, years before the scandal, www.hindu.com/2008/01/31/stories/2008013150240100.htm.

Every Thirty Minutes: Farmer Suicides, Human Rights, and the Agrarian Crisis in India, report of New York University's Center for Human Rights and Progress, 2011, www.chrgj.org/publications/docs/every30min.pdf.

Page 228

"'Yunus Was Right,' SKS Microfinance Founder Says" by Neha Thirani, *New York Times Global Edition*, "India Ink" online blog, February 27, 2012. india.blogs.nytimes.com/2012/02/27/yunus-was-right-sks-microfinance-founder-says.

Transparency International's "Corruption Perceptions Index" as of 2006: archive.transparency.org/policy_research/surveys_indices/cpi/2006.

The World Bank ranks Bangladesh near the bottom of lawful governance worldwide: info.worldbank.org/governance/wgi/mc_chart.asp.

Page 229

The Friends of Grameen summary of the ongoing assualt on Yunus and Grameen is at www.friendsofgrameen.com/dl/2011/02/GrameenBankFact Sheet-August20121.pdf.

To give you a sense of how shoddy some of the charges against Yunus have been, a Norwegian documentary once got big headlines by alleging that Yunus's first client not only had *not* been helped by the loans, but had died in poverty, a tale attributed to her surviving daughter. Filmmaker Gayle Ferraro later retraced the Norwegians' steps and discovered that they had not even found the right woman. Ferraro then found the actual client herself—perfectly recognizable from *60 Minutes* television footage shot in 1989—still alive, healthy, prospering, and very happy for her experience. See www.youtube.com/watch?v=1JGBQnrC-cw.

Ferraro has also made a fine documentary on Yunus, Grameen, and microfinance called *To Catch a Dollar*. For more, see www.tocatchadollar.com.

Page 230

On studies of microfinance:

Chapter 6 of Roodman, *Due Diligence*, cited above, includes an overview of the shortcomings and lack of rigor in research to that point, including things like the World Bank study trumpeted early in this book where Grameen was first mentioned, plus an explanation of why randomized controlled trials (RCTs), which are marvelous in hard science like medicine, are less so in economics, and should be viewed with some care in studies of the poor. It's a good starting point for thinking about the challenges of even coming up with useful, reproducible data.

For another look at the limitations of RCTs, see "Control Freaks" in the *Economist,* June 12, 2008, online at www.economist.com/node/11535592 ?story_id=11535592, and for an exhaustive review, see *What Is the Evidence of the Impact of Microfinance on the Well-Being of Poor People* by Maren Duvendack, Richard Palmer-Jones, James G. Copestake, Lee Hopper, Yoon Loke, and Nitya Rao, published in August 2011 by the EPPI-Centre and available online at www.dfid.gov.uk/r4d/PDF/Outputs/SystematicReviews/Microfi nance2011Duvendackreport.pdf.

By the end of 2009, the picture regarding early studies was already so muddled that *New York Times* columnist Nicholas Kristof, coauthor with Sheryl WuDunn of *Half the Sky: Turning Oppression Into Opportunity for Women Worldwide* (published in New York in 2009 by Alfred A. Knopf) and certainly no enemy of microlending, lent his column to a review of the current situation by MIT economists Abhijit Banerjee and Esther Duflo and Dean Karlan of Yale. (See kristof.blogs.nytimes.com/2009/12/28/the-role-of-microfinance.) Their summary agreed that there was "little rigorous evidence," pro or con, on microlending's impact to that point. However, they also summarized two new studies, one in India, one in the Philippines, this way: "The effect on businesses is not dramatic but some clearly benefit . . . However, there is no evidence that microcredit has any effect on health, education, or women's empowerment, at least right now, eighteen months after they got the loans."

This points to one major issue precisely: "eighteen months." Long-term changes, if and where they exist, by definition do not lend themselves well to eighteen-month and similarly short windows undertaken by many widely cited studies.

Another problem is that economists, attempting to model human behavior with the same sorts of controls that a physicist might use to measure the bounce of a billiard ball, need a large volume of data in order to eliminate statistical noise and even begin drawing conclusions. This has led some to frame the question as whether microfinance raises living standards for a community *on average*.

I would suggest this might have only limited value. Clients are individual human beings, not water molecules in a pot that move faster if you apply more heat. Credit—even at its very best—simply creates opportunity. Individuals can exploit this with hard work and creativity to the degree their talents, culture, and circumstances allow. To consider average measurements only may also neglect a fairly clear historical pattern. Outstanding individuals—the ones who invent, innovate, create new businesses successful enough to employ others, generate economic activity, and so on—will be outliers by definition. Even optimally, sometimes there will be no net effect, especially in a brief eighteen-month window. Longer studies that somehow account for often non-linear nature of innovation and growth might be more telling, pro or con.

Thomas Edison was not average. If he'd received early financing in 1870s New Jersey, his Menlo Park lab might have opened even before he sold the quadruplex telegraph to Western Union. The benefits to the economy would ripple to this day. Steve Wozniak was not average. His development of the Apple computer was delayed in its early stages because he could not afford the microprocessor he wanted. In these and numerous other cases of progress one could name, community-wide effects of better financing might never have appeared in an eighteen-month study.

What current microlending studies already *do* frequently show, as cited in the Kristof column and elsewhere, and seemingly verified by my own anecdotal (and therefore academically meaningless if remarkably consistent) experience virtually everywhere I have visited, is that client spending, saving, and planning habits usually demonstrate a shift toward durable and capital expenditures and long-term planning, with results that if present almost by definition would appear outside the short-term window of many studies.

Drawing firm conclusions from gross effects in general populations over limited time windows frankly seems to me like trying to decide if automobiles provide transport by measuring the average velocity of all Californians on Tuesday. What researchers would probably find is that most people aren't driving on that day, some know how to drive but don't go far, some drive badly and crash, and a very few go really fast and leave the state, resulting in their possible exclusion from the data as outliers. Net effect, on statistical analysis: zero.

Roodman himself, in a *Washington Post* column not nearly as negative toward the industry as its headline ("Microcredit Doesn't End Poverty, Despite All the Hype," March 10, 2012, online at www.washingtonpost.com /opinions/microcredit-doesnt-end-poverty-despite-all-the-hype/2012/01/20 /gIQAtrfqzR_story.html)—a headline that an editor, not Roodman, would have chosen, in his defense—cites what appears to be the same study in India mentioned in the Kristof piece, concluding that "over the 12 to 18 months the researchers tracked, the data revealed no change in bottom-line indicators of poverty, such as household spending and whether children were attending school," albeit conceding that "small loans caused more families to start micro-businesses" and "existing businesses saw higher profits."

However, two of the Kristof guest columnists, Banerjee and Duflo, drew a conclusion that was substantially more positive: "As we see it, microcredit seems to have delivered exactly what a successful new financial product is supposed to deliver—allowing people to make large purchases that they would not have been able to otherwise. The fact that some people expected much more from it (and perhaps they are right, maybe it will just take longer), is perhaps inevitable given how eager the world is to find that one magic bullet," decrying precisely the same "hype" that Roodman also denounces. There's more agreement here than the headlines imply. And I want to reiterate that everyone involved is pursuing a massively complex question with extremely important answers.

(The India study to which Roodman refers, and the Kristof column seems to—no link is given—is *The Miracle of Microfinance? Evidence from a Randomized Evaluation* by Abhijit Banerjee, Esther Duflo, Rachel Glennerster, and Cynthia Kinnan, viewable online at www.poverty-action.org/sites/default/files /44-_june_2010-_miracle_of_microfinance.pdf.)

This is in no way a disparagement of researchers devoted to solving vital, challenging questions—after all, gaining an improving understanding of what

works and what doesn't may radically improve the ability of everyone involved to raise living standards around the world, the most noble of goals.

What I take issue with are those who take the difficulty of study as a
reason to continue to ask a fairly silly, much simpler question: *Does* microfinance have value? The fact that tens of millions of people like you and me
(a) are not idiots and (b) eagerly seek microcredit virtually anywhere it is
introduced, tells us that it rather obviously does. Until academic studies
definitively state otherwise, and fellow economists can concur and reproduce the methods and analyses across multiple contexts—and that's still
possible—we are left with a mountain of data in the obvious choices of clients themselves.

With mobile phones and internet access reaching the hands and minds
of millions of clever people every year, it seems absurd to suggest that new
opportunities enabled by microfinance may not exist simply because Americans haven't yet figured out how to quantify them.

In short, if Mongolians think the sky is blue in Mongolia, we can probably
take them at their word, even while dedicated researchers are still working
out exactly which shade of blue, how to see it best, where it doesn't look very
blue at all, and how to make it even bluer for everybody.

Page 240

The more than 20,000 lending teams can be searched and sorted by size,
loan volume, purpose, and more at www.kiva.org/community.

Page 245

In a July 2008 blog post (online at www.socialedge.org/blogs/kiva-chron-
icles/archive/2008/07/16/farewell-mr-capstick), Matt called out the following early MFI partners that "closed in bad faith." To each, I've added brief
details gleaned from the Kiva pages listed here:

The Women's Economic Empowerment Consort (WEEC) in Kenya,
   at www.kiva.org/partners/6, which became insolvent after the
   death of its founder, whose successors appropriated funds to pay
   WEEC's debts.
The Women's Initiative to Eradicate Poverty (WITEP) in Uganda, at
   www.kiva.org/partners/11, the founder of which was found to be
   diverting some of the funds into other investments. Sadly, this was
   Moses Onyango, the pastor who administered the first seven Kiva
   loans, and whom Matt personally still regards as one of the

cofounders of Kiva. (For more, see "Kiva at Four" in *Innovations*, cited above.)

Supporting Enterprises for Economic Development (SEED) in Kenya, at www.kiva.org/partners/32, which inflated the size of its requested loans, lending smaller amounts to the actual clients.

The Rural Agency for Economic Development (RAFODE) in Kenya, at www.kiva.org/partners/33, which inflated the size of its requested loans, lending smaller amounts to the actual clients.

Afrique Emergence & Investissements (AE&I) of Côte d'Ivoire, at www .kiva.org/partners/53, which Kiva found to be under-reporting their interest rate and requesting more funds than were actually lent to the clients.

Matt referred to all five of the above (while only naming WITEP) in his 2009 Innovations article (cited above), adding a reference to an Ecuadorean partner, MIFEX (whose Kiva page viewable at www.kiva.org/partners/7), which inflated the size of its requested loans, using the difference to defray operating costs.

To this list, one might also add the Lift Above Poverty Organization (LAPO) of Nigeria, at www.kiva.org/partners/20, which attracted millions from Citigroup, Deutsche Bank, the Grameen Foundation, and numerous other major players until they got caught by their funders in cooking their books, charging exorbitant rates, and so on. Kiva terminated the partnership, albeit not with the speed that some critics point out would have been wiser in retrospect.

Note that Kiva has closed many partnerships simply for changing degrees of need, regulatory changes, or other reasons wholly unrelated to any bad behavior. Picking a few closed partnerships at random from www.kiva .org/partners to use as examples: BRAC Sri Lanka at www.kiva.org/part ners/155 and BRAC Tanzania at www.kiva.org/partners/102 ran into difficulties in getting their national central banks approving transfers to and from Kiva. AMK in Cambodia at www.kiva.org/partners/109 received government approval to receive deposits, lessening their need for Kiva funds, and Iraqi Al-Aman of Kirkuk at www.kiva.org/partners/50 got a major grant that meant it no longer needed Kiva funds. You can poke around the list yourself if you're curious.

Recommended further reading

A Fistful of Rice: My Unexpected Quest to End Poverty Through Profitability by Vikram Akula. Boston: Harvard Business Review Press, 2010. The memoir of SKS's founder and chairperson. Akula was scheduled to do a major U.S. book tour at the time of the book's launch, but had to cancel when he was called back to India to testify about the crisis. My assistant's repeated attempts to arrange an interview for this book went for naught.

Microfinance for Bankers and Investors: Understanding the Opportunities and Challenges of the Market at the Bottom of the Pyramid by Elizabeth Rhyne. New York: McGraw Hill, 2009. Rhyne is the managing director of the Center for Financial Inclusion at ACCION International, one of the pioneers of microfinance from the very beginning. A thorough look at how the profit motive really *can* be used responsibly to help the very poor.

"Who's to Blame for the Crisis in Andhra Pradesh?" also by Elizabeth Rhyne, *Huffington Post*, November 2, 2010, online at www.huffingtonpost.com /elisabeth-rhyne/on-microfinance-whos-to-b_b_777911.html. Rhyne notes a number of regulatory and other problems that exacerbated the crisis, providing a level of history and detail missing from most commentary on the crisis.

"The Lessons of Andhra Pradesh" by Felix Salmon, Reuters, November 18, 2010, online at blogs.reuters.com/felix-salmon/2010/11/18/the-lessons-of-andhra-pradesh. Salmon surveys the reportage on the crisis and points out that the "debtors strike" was actually led by a governor who stood to profit from a competing microcredit scheme.

"Microfinance: What's Wrong with It" by M. Rajshekhar, *Economic Times*, November 11, 2010, online at articles.economictimes.indiatimes.com/2010 -11-11/news/27577103_1_sks-microfinance-mfis-shgs. A look at the AP crisis from India's leading financial daily.

CHAPTER TEN — MAGELLAN'S CROSS, HANOI, AND CAMBODIA

Page 250

The *dugo-dugo* recipe is at readingeagle.com/recipedetail.aspx?id=1015.

Page 263

Crafts villages in trouble: "In Vietnam, Symbols of Capitalism Falter" by Seth Mydans, *New York Times*, September 27, 2009, online at www.nytimes .com/2009/09/28/world/asia/28iht-viet.html.

Recommended further reading

For an early but still relevant overview of Vietnam's recent economic situation: "America Lost, Capitalism Won," *Economist*, April 28, 2005, www .economist.com/node/3914886.

"Vietnam's Mix of Marxism and Capitalism Brings Economic Progress" by Florence Beaugé, *Guardian Weekly*, June 29, 2010, www.guardian.co.uk /world/2010/jun/29/vietnam-economy-growth-finance-success.

"Vietnam Communists' New Challenge: Managing Capitalism" by Sion Montlake, *Christian Science Monitor*, January 11, 2011, www.csmonitor.com /World/Asia-South-Central/2011/0111/Vietnam-Communists-new-challenge -managing-capitalism.

Page 267

"Map Reveals Ancient Urban Sprawl," BBC News, August 14, 2007, news.bbc.co.uk/2/hi/science/nature/6945574.stm.

CHAPTER ELEVEN — KATHMANDU

Page 280

The June 2012 Human Rights Watch report *Qatar: Migrant Construction Workers Face Abuse* is summarized at www.hrw.org/news/2012/06/12/qatar -migrant-construction-workers-face-abuse, with the full report available as a download.

See also *Building a Better World Cup: Protecting Migrant Workers in Qatar Ahead of World Cup 2012* by Human Rights Watch (New York: June 2012). The full report is online at www.hrw.org/reports/2012/06/12/building -better-world-cup.

"Nepalese Dying to Work" by Sara Sidner, a CNN report of May 5, 2013, is online at thecnnfreedomproject.blogs.cnn.com/2012/05/13/nepalese -dying-to-work.

"Nepali Slaves in the Middle East" April 12, 2011, a video report by Pete Pattison, is at www.guardian.co.uk/world/video/2011/apr/12/nepali-slaves -united-arab-emirates-video. The opening scene, focused on a wooden coffin containing the body of a dead worker returning home to Nepal, was filmed outside the Kathmandu airport. While viewing, consider that men like Ganesh still enter that airport every day, flying into similar circumstances.

CHAPTER TWELVE — INDIA

Page 283

Linguistic data from www.ethnologue.com, the Web edition of *Ethnologue: Languages of the World*, edited by M. Paul Lewis. Dallas, SIL International, 2009.

Page 284

"The World's Billionaires" are at www.forbes.com/billionaires/list. Sort for "India" and you'll get the current list.

On the India/Africa comparison, see "8 Indian States Have More Poor than the 26 Poorest African Nations" in the *Times of India*, July 12, 2010, at articles.timesofindia.indiatimes.com/2010-07-12/india/28276383_1_ measure-ophi-multidimensional-poverty-index. This article references the Multidimensional Poverty Index, a Web project of the Oxford Poverty and Human Development Initiative, which you can explore online at www.ophi .org.uk/policy/multidimensional-poverty-index/mapping-the-mpi.

Page 296

"Orissa Cancels Doctors' Leave as Dengue Spreads" in the *Deccan Herald* of August 13, 2011, online at www.deccanherald.com/content/183459/orissa -cancels-doctors-leave-dengue.html.

"Death Toll Due to Dengue Rises to 26 in Orissa" in the *Orissa Diary* of September 6, 2011, online at orissadiary.com/CurrentNews.asp?id=28968.

Page 300

For the Smart Campaign's timeline of development and a thorough FAQ, see www.smartcampaign.org/about-the-campaign/2011-11-21-16-36-33/client -protection-certification-faq.

Several other major social performance initiatives are also promoting transparency, fair pricing, and other best practices throughout the industry. Perhaps most notable is the Social Performance Task Force, a group of more than a thousand microfinance professionals from every sector of the microfinance world. Their website is www.sptf.info, and their FAQ on social performance is at www.sptf.info/what-is-social-performance.

Other major industry organizations are listed under "Additional Resources," beginning on page 390.

Page 301

See *Overindebtedness and Microfinance: Constructing an Early Warning Index*, a study by the Center for Microfinance at the University of Zurich in cooperation with CMEF, Triodos Investment Management, and ResponsAbility Social Investments, at www.accion.org/Document.Doc?id=899.

Page 307

Freedom from Want: The Remarkable Success Story of BRAC, the Global Grassroots Organization That's Winning the Fight Against Poverty by Ian Smillie. I have the Bangladesh edition published in Dhaka in 2009 by the University Press. The U.S. edition was published the same year in Sterling, Virginia, by Kumarian Press.

Page 310

The Essential Writings by Mahatma Gandhi, edited by Judith M. Brown. Oxford: Oxford University Press, 2008.

Recommended further reading
Portfolios of the Poor: How the World's Poor Live on $2 a Day by Daryl Collins, Jonathan Morduch, Stuart Rutherford, and Orlanda Ruthven. Princeton, New Jersey: Princeton University Press, 2009. A remarkable work: the authors chronicle the lives and choices of people in challenged parts of India, Bangladesh, and South Africa in an original fashion—by asking hundreds of participants to carefully journal their economic activity. It turns out that the economic lives of people living in poverty are often at least as varied and sophisticated as those in wealthier nations. They may have to be, just to survive. Also see www.portfoliosofthepoor.com.

Out of Poverty: What Works When Traditional Approaches Fail by Paul Polak. San Francisco: Berrett-Koehler, 2008. Paul Polak is the founder of International Development Enterprises, a non-profit that pioneered the creation of "ruthlessly affordable" irrigation equipment that has been bought by more than 1.5 million Bangladeshi farmers, paying for itself in one season and then increasing their crop yields and incomes substantially. Polak is now an evangelist of reaching the "other 90 percent" through carefully designed for-profit enterprise. I have vast, huge, brightly colored respect for Paul, a self-described "troublemaker" who seriously intends to bring clean water, solar energy, and more to at least one hundred million people by similar means. There's some overlap with microfinance because many farmers obviously need to use it to finance their equipment, but there's also some contradiction, as Polak sees Yunus's strictures on profit as ultimately preventing good projects from reaching maximum scale. I considered but decided against including a long section on Paul's work here, mostly because it's off-topic from microfinance. But it's also extremely valuable. Please see Paul's website and blog at www.paulpolak.com.

The Fortune at the Bottom of the Pyramid: Eradicating Poverty Through Profits by C. K. Prahalad. Upper Saddle River, New Jersey: Wharton School Publishing, 2005. A good companion to Paul's book. A more academic text on development as driven by for-profit enterprise, addressing the needs of the poor almost like any consumer market analysis, with thoughtful analyses of successes and lessons learned. Relevant to microfinance, there's an entire chapter on the ICICI Bank of Mumbai, the first of India's Big Four banks to focus on India's four hundred million poor.

CHAPTER THIRTEEN — BEIRUT

Page 318

Al-Manar's designation as a terrorist entity is described in the U.S. Treasury Department release of March 23, 2006, online at www.treasury.gov /press-center/press-releases/Pages/js4134.aspx.

Recommended further reading

Killing Mr. Lebanon: The Assassination of Rafik Hariri and Its Impact on the Middle East by Nicholas Blanford. New York: I. B. Tauris, 2009. The best overview I've found on the last decade in Lebanese politics, even though it focuses largely on the events of 2005–06. The history leading to Hariri's death remains behind many current headlines.

Pity the Nation: The Abduction of Lebanon by Robert Fisk. New York: Thunder's Mouth Press, paperback edition, 2002. Exhaustive account spanning the period from the origins of the Israeli-Palestinian conflict through the collapse of the Oslo Accords, focusing primarily on Lebanon's civil war, written by a British journalist who has worked and lived primarily in Beirut since 1976.

CHAPTER FOURTEEN — HOME

Page 331

See "NYPD Secret Police Spying on Muslims Led to No Terrorism Leads or Cases" by Adam Goldman and Matt Appuzzo of the Associated Press,

Guardian, August 23, 2012, online at www.guardian.co.uk/world/2012/aug /23/nypd-surveillance-anti-terrorism-muslims.

Page 333

The Better Angels of Our Nature: Why Violence Has Declined by Steven Pinker. New York: Viking, 2011.

Harvard cognitive scientist Pinker documents and examines the world's remarkable if invisible-on-TV-news decline in violence on scales large and small, concluding that our world is becoming more peaceful.

Page 334

The snapshot of the Pissed Off Kiva Lenders page is at web.archive.org /web/20090621053654/http://www.kiva.org/team/pissed_off_kiva_lenders. I've edited the rant with ellipses for clarity in the text, but it remains viewable in full online.

The source for Detroit's average per capita income from 2006 to 2010 is U.S. Census Bureau data at quickfacts.census.gov/qfd/states/26/2622000. html. For Botswana's infant mortality rate, see www.cia.gov/library/publications/the-world-factbook/rankorder/2091rank.html, and for Detroit's infant mortality rate, see Michigan state government statistics at www.mdch .state.mi.us/pha/osr/InDxMain/Tab4.asp. Some sources give higher figures for Botswana's falling infant mortality rate, especially when numbers are averaged over time. The 2011 World Bank estimate is 20 (data.worldbank.org /indicator/SP.DYN.IMRT.IN). The Detroit number in any case compares with many developing countries, and nationwide, black infant mortality tragically exceeds twice that of non-Hispanic whites. See the CDC's 2012 report at www.cdc.gov/nchs/data/nvsr/nvsr60/nvsr60_05.pdf.

Page 338

Twenty Years at Hull House by Jane Addams. New York: Signet Classics reprint edition, 1999.

Page 347

Flow: The Psychology of Optimal Experience by Me, Hi! Cheeks Sent Me, Hi. New York: Harper and Row, 1990.

Recommended further reading

The Essential Gandhi: An Anthology of His Writings on His Life, Work, and Ideals by Mohandas K. Gandhi, edited by Louis Fischer. New York: Vintage,

2002. Skillfully edited to unify diverse writings by subject. I don't recall seeing the Talisman in here, but it's an excellent short primer, arranged by subject, on the thinking of the Mahatma.

ADDITIONAL RESOURCES

Social performance initiatives, industry organizations, development research-ers, MFI ratings agencies, and other centralized sources of information (by no means a complete list—this is just meant as a starter kit if you want to dive in deeper):

Center for Financial Inclusion
www.centerforfinancialinclusion.org
The Center for Financial Inclusion (CFI) at ACCION was launched in 2008 to help bring about the conditions to achieve full financial inclusion around the world.

The Smart Campaign, promoter of client protection principles
www.smartcampaign.org

The Social Performance Task Force, a group of more than a thousand microfinance professionals from every sector of the microfinance world
www.sptf.info

SPTF's FAQ on social performance
www.sptf.info/what-is-social-performance

The Microfinance Information eXchange (MIX)
www.themix.org

MicroFinance Transparency
www.mftransparency.org

Planet Rating, now partnered with MicroFinance Transparency
www.planetrating.com/EN/index.php

Micro-Credit Ratings International
www.m-cril.com

Microfinanza Rating
www.microfinanzarating.com

Microrate
www.microrate.com

The Microcredit Summit
www.microcreditsummit.org

Center for Global Development
www.cgdev.org

The Consultative Group to Assist the Poor
www.cgap.org

The Financial Access Initiative at NYU
financialaccess.org

Index

About the Author

Bob Harris has had a diverse career as a TV writer (*Bones*; *CSI: Crime Scene Investigation*), a TV and radio personality, and (briefly) a luxury travel writer, among much else. He has appeared on *Jeopardy!* thirteen times, and his playful memoir of the experience, *Prisoner of Trebekistan*, was widely praised, as was his next book, *Who Hates Whom*, a pocket summary of many of the world's major conflict zones. In an effort to address the poverty he has witnessed while traveling, Bob has made more than five thousand microloans via Kiva.org. He holds an honors degree in electrical engineering and applied physics from Case Western Reserve University. His website is www.bobharris.com.

About Microfinance and Kiva.org

Microfinance is the practice of making the financial tools of credit, savings, and insurance available to the working poor and others not served by conventional banking. Pioneered in its modern form by FINCA in Bolivia, ACCION in Brazil, and the Grameen Bank in Bangladesh, microfinance can be an important tool in poverty alleviation. The Grameen Bank and its founder, Muhammad Yunus, shared the 2006 Nobel Peace Prize.

Kiva.org, headquartered in San Francisco, is a non-profit charity and the world's leading online platform for individual financing of microloans. Since 2005, Kiva has partnered with more than 160 microfinance institutions in more than 65 countries to facilitate loans, some as small as $25, from more than 800,000 lenders to nearly a million recipients, 80 percent of whom are women. At press time, the repayment rate is precisely 99.00 percent.

James M. Duncan Library
2501 Commonwealth Avenue
Alexandria, VA 22301

RECEIVED APR 2 9 2013